C000156765

A COMPLETE GRAMMAR
OF ESPERANTO

LECTOR HOUSE PUBLIC DOMAIN WORKS

This book is a result of an effort made by Lector House towards making a contribution to the preservation and repair of original classic literature. The original text is in the public domain in the United States of America, and possibly other countries depending upon their specific copyright laws.

In an attempt to preserve, improve and recreate the original content, certain conventional norms with regard to typographical mistakes, hyphenations, punctuations and/or other related subject matters, have been corrected upon our consideration. However, few such imperfections might not have been rectified as they were inherited and preserved from the original content to maintain the authenticity and construct, relevant to the work. We believe that this work holds historical, cultural and/or intellectual importance in the literary works community, therefore despite the oddities, we accounted the work for print as a part of our continuing effort towards preservation of literary work and our contribution towards the development of the society as a whole, driven by our beliefs.

We are grateful to our readers for putting their faith in us and accepting our imperfections with regard to preservation of the historical content. We shall strive hard to meet up to the expectations to improve further to provide an enriching reading experience.

Though, we conduct extensive research in ascertaining the status of copyright before redeveloping a version of the content, in rare cases, a classic work might be incorrectly marked as not-in-copyright. In such cases, if you are the copyright holder, then kindly contact us or write to us, and we shall get back to you with an immediate course of action.

HAPPY READING!

A COMPLETE GRAMMAR OF ESPERANTO

IVY KELLERMAN REED

ISBN: 978-93-5342-016-1

First Published: -

© LECTOR HOUSE LLP

LECTOR HOUSE LLP
E-MAIL: lectorpublishing@gmail.com

A COMPLETE
GRAMMAR OF ESPERANTO

THE INTERNATIONAL LANGUAGE

WITH
GRADED EXERCISES FOR READING AND TRANSLATION
TOGETHER WITH FULL VOCABULARIES

BY

IVY KELLERMAN, A.M., PH.D.

MEMBER OF THE EXECUTIVE COMMITTEE
AND CHAIRMAN OF EXAMINATIONS
FOR THE ESPERANTO ASSOCIATION
OF NORTH AMERICA,
MEMBER OF THE
INTERNATIONAL LINGVA KOMITATO

TO
DR. L. L. ZAMENHOF

THE AUTHOR OF
ESPERANTO

PREFACE.

This volume has been prepared to meet a twofold need. An adequate presentation of the International Language has become an imperative necessity. Such presentation, including full and accurate grammatical explanations, suitably graded reading lessons, and similarly graded material for translation from English, has not heretofore been accessible within the compass of a single volume, or in fact within the compass of any two or three volumes.

The combination of grammar and reader here offered is therefore unique. It is to furnish not merely an introduction to Esperanto, or a superficial acquaintance with it, but a genuine understanding of the language and mastery of its use without recourse to additional textbooks, readers, etc. In other words, this one volume affords as complete a knowledge of Esperanto as several years' study of a grammar and various readers will accomplish for any national language. Inflection, word-formation and syntax are presented clearly and concisely, yet with a degree of completeness and in a systematic order that constitute a new feature. Other points worthy of note are the following:

The *reasons* for syntactical usages are given, instead of mere statements that such usages exist. For example, clauses of purpose and of result are really explained, instead of being dismissed with the unsatisfactory remark that "the imperative follows *por ke*," or the "use of *tiel ... ke* and *tia ... ke* must be distinguished from that of *tiel ... kiel* and *tia ... kia*," etc., with but little intimation of when and why *por ke*, *tiel ... ke* and *tia ... ke* are likely to occur.

Affixes are not mentioned until some familiarity with the general character of the language is assured, as well as the possession of a fair vocabulary. They are introduced gradually, with adequate explanation and illustration. Of importance in connection with word-formation is an element distinctly new — the explanation and classification of compound words. Such words, like affixes, are withheld until the use of *simple* words is familiar.

Another new feature is the gradual introduction of correlative words in their logical order, and in their proper grammatical categories, before they are called "correlatives," or tabulated. The tabulation finally presented is a real classification, with regard to the meaning and grammatical character of the words, not merely an arbitrary alphabetical arrangement. The use of primary adverbs precedes the explanation of adverb derivation; prepositions, especially *de*, *da*, *je*, etc., receive careful attention, also the verb system, and the differentiation of words whose English equivalents are ambiguous.

A general characteristic of obvious advantage is that almost without exception new forms and constructions are illustrated by means of words or roots already familiar. Likewise, the new words or roots of each lesson recur at least once in the next lesson, and usually in some lesson thereafter as well. Each reading exercise gives not only a thorough application of the grammatical principles of the lesson, but a review of those in the preceding lesson, and no use is made of words or constructions not yet explained. The comparative ease of the language, and the lack of necessity for reciting paradigms, permit the reading exercises to be long enough for the student to feel that he has really mastered something. These exercises are further unique, in that each after the fifth is a coherent narrative, and nearly every one is a story of genuine interest in itself. These stories, if bound separately, would alone constitute a reader equivalent to those used in first and second year work in national languages. (For list of titles, see Table of Contents.)

The second element of the twofold need which this volume meets is the necessity for a presentation of Esperanto, not as a thing apart, but in that form which will make it most serviceable as an introduction to national tongues. A stepping-stone to both ancient and modern languages, Esperanto may render invaluable aid, and pave the way for surmounting the many difficulties confronting both student and teacher. Through Esperanto, the labor in the acquirement of these languages may be reduced in the same proportion in which the pleasure and thoroughness of such acquirement are increased. For this reason, the grammatical constructions of Esperanto are here explained as consistently as possible in accordance with the usage of national languages, especially those in the school curriculum, and precise names are assigned to them. Such matters as *contrary to fact conditions, indirect quotations, clauses of purpose* and *of result, accusatives of time* and *measure, expressions of separation, reference,* etc., thus become familiar to the student, long before he meets them in the more difficult garb of a national tongue, whose exceptions seem to outnumber its rules, and whose idioms prove more puzzling than its exceptions, unless approached by the smooth and gradual ascent of the International Language, Esperanto.

IVY KELLERMAN.

Washington, D. C.,
August 3, 1910.

CONTENTS

CONTENTS

A COMPLETE GRAMMAR OF ESPERANTO.

LESSON I.

ALPHABET.—VOWELS.—CONSONANTS.—NAMES OF
THE LETTERS.—DIPHTHONGS.—COMBINATIONS OF
CONSONANTS.—SYLLABLES.—ACCENT.

ALPHABET.

1. The Esperanto alphabet contains the following letters: **a, b, c, ĉ, d, e, f, g, ĝ, h, ĥ, i, j, ĵ, k, l, m, n, o, p, r, s, ŝ, t, u, ŭ, v, z.**

VOWELS.

2. The vowels of the alphabet are pronounced as follows:

a as in *far*.
e as in *fiancé*, like *a* in *fate*.[1]
i as in *machine*.
o as in *toll*, *for*.
u as in *rude*, *rural*.

CONSONANTS.

3. The consonants **b, d, f, h, k, l, m, n, p, t, v, z,** are pronounced as in English, and the remaining eleven as follows:

c like *ts* in *hats*, *tsetse*.
ĉ like *ch* in *chin*, *much*.
g like *g* in *go*, *big*.
ĝ like *g* in *gem*, *j* in *jar*.
ĥ is produced by expelling the breath forcibly, with the throat only partially open.[2]
j like *y* in *yes*, *beyond*.

[1] This "long a" sound in English frequently ends with a vanish,—a brief terminal sound of *ĭ*, which makes the vowel slightly diphthongal, as in *day*, *aye*. Such a vanish must not be given to any of the Esperanto vowels.

[2] As in pronouncing German and Scotch *ch*, Spanish *j*, Irish *gh*, Russian *x*, Classical Greek χ etc. There are only a few words containing this consonant.

ĵ like z in *azure*, s in *visual*.
r is slightly trilled or rolled.
s like s in *see*, *basis*.
ŝ like *sh* in *shine*, *rash*, *ch* in *machine*.
ŭ like *w* or consonantal *u*. See Diphthongs, 5.

NAMES OF THE LETTERS.

4. The vowels are named by their sounds, as given in **2.** The names of the consonants are **bo, co, ĉo, do, fo, go, ĝo, ho, ĥo, jo, ĵo, ko, lo, mo, no, po, ro, so, ŝo, to, ŭo, vo, zo.** These are used in speaking of the letters, in pronouncing them in abbreviations, as **ko to po** for **k. t. p.** (= etc.), and in spelling words, as **bo, i, ro, do, o, birdo.**

DIPHTHONGS.

5. Diphthongs are combinations of two vowels uttered as a single sound, by one breath-impulse. The diphthongs in Esperanto contain an i or u sound as the second element, but in order to avoid confusion with combinations of vowels not forming diphthongs (as in **naiva**, like English *naïve*, etc.), they are written with **j** and **ŭ** instead. Their pronunciation is as follows:

aj like *ai* in *aisle*.
ej like *ei* in *vein*, *ey* in *they*.
oj like *oi* in *coin*, *oy* in *boy*.
uj like *ui* in *ruin*, *u(e)y* in *gluey*.
eŭ like *ayw* in *wayward*, or like *é(h)oo* pronounced together.
aŭ like *ou* in *out*, *ow* in *owl*.

COMBINATIONS OF CONSONANTS.

6. Each consonant, in a combination of two or more consonants, is pronounced with its full value, whether within a word or at its beginning. There are no silent letters.

a. Thus, both consonants are clearly sounded in the groups **kn, kv, gv, sv,** in such words as **knabo, kvin, gvidi, sviso.**

b. The combination **kz,** as in **ekzisti, ekzameno,** must not be modified to the *gs* or *ks* represented by *x* in *exist, execute*.

c. The combination **sc,** as in **escepte, scias,** is equivalent to the combination *sts* in *last said, first song,* pronounced together rapidly. The **s** in a word beginning with **sc** may be sounded with the end of the preceding word, if that word ends in a vowel, as **mis-cias** for **mi scias.**

d. The **n** and **g** are pronounced separately in the combination **ng,** in such words as **lingvo, angulo,** producing the sound of *ng* heard in *linger*, not that in *singer*.

e. Each of two similar letters is clearly sounded, as **interrilato, ellasi,** like *inter-relate, well-laid*.

SYLLABLES.

7. Each word contains as many syllables as it has vowels and diphthongs. The division of syllables within a word is as follows:

a. A single consonant goes with the following vowel, as **pa-no**, **be-la**, **a-e-ro**.

b. A consonant followed by l or r (which are liquids) goes with the l or r, as in **ta-blo**, **a-kra**, **a-gra-bla**.

c. Otherwise, the syllable division is made before the last consonant of the group, as **sus-pek-ti**, **sank-ta**, **deks-tra**.

d. Prefixes are separated from the words to which they are attached, as **dis-me-ti**, **mal-akra**, and compound words are divided into their component parts, as **ĉef-urbo**, **sun-ombrelo**.

ACCENT.

8. Words of more than one syllable are accented upon the syllable before the last, as **tá-blo**, **a-grá-bla**, **sus-pék-ti**.

WORDS FOR PRACTICE.

9. (To be pronounced aloud, and correctly accented) Afero, trairi, najbaro, aero, hodiaŭ, pacienco, centono, ĉielo, eĉ, samideano, treege, obei, obeu, Eŭropo, gvidi, ĝojo, ĉiujn, justa, ĝuste, juĝi, ĵaŭdo, lingvo, knabo, larĝa, pagi, kvieteco, ekzemplo, ellerni, fojo, krajono, forrajdi, kuirejo, ĉevalejo, sankteco, scio, nescio, edzo, meze, duobla, ŝipo, ŝarĝi, poŝo, svingi, sklavo, palaj, ŝafaĵo, atmosfero, monaĥo, geometrio, laŭdi, vasta, eksplodi, senĉesa, sensencaĵo, malluma, arbaranoj, manĝo, freŝa, aŭskulti, daŭri.

LESSON II.

NOUNS.

10. Words which are the names of persons or things are called nouns. The ending, or final letter, of nouns in Esperanto is **o**:

knabo, *boy*. **pomo**, *apple*.
ĉevalo, *horse*. **tablo**, *table*.

THE ARTICLE.

11. The definite article is **la**, *the*, as **la knabo**, *the boy*, **la ĉevalo**, *the horse*, **la tablo**, *the table*, **la pomo**, *the apple*. In English there is an indefinite article "a, an" for the singular, but none for the plural. Esperanto has no indefinite article for either singular or plural. Therefore **knabo** may mean *boy*, or *a boy*, **pomo** may mean *apple* or *an apple*.

ADJECTIVES

12. A word used with a noun (expressed or understood) to express a quality or characteristic is called an adjective. The ending of adjectives in Esperanto is **a**:

bela, *beautiful*. **granda**, *large*.
flava, *yellow*. **forta**, *strong*.

ATTRIBUTIVE ADJECTIVES.

13. An adjective is said to modify a noun whose quality it expresses. When directly preceding or following its noun, it is called an attributive adjective:

la granda ĉevalo, the large horse.
bela birdo, a beautiful bird.
floro flava, a yellow flower.
forta knabo, a strong boy.

PRESENT TENSE OF THE VERB.

14. Words which express action or condition are called verbs. When representing an act or condition as a fact, and dealing with the present time, they are said to be in the present tense. The ending of all Esperanto verbs in the present tense is **-as**:

kuras, *runs, is running*.   **brilas**, *shines, is shining*.
flugas, *flies, is flying*.   **dormas**, *sleeps, is sleeping*.

15. The person or thing whose action or condition the verb expresses is called the subject of the verb:

La suno brilas, *the sun shines (is shining)*, subject: **suno**.
Knabo kuras, *a boy runs (is running)*, subject: **knabo**.

VOCABULARY.
(To be memorized in this and in all following lessons.)

bela, *beautiful*.
birdo, *bird*.
blanka, *white*.
bona, *good*.
brilas, *shines, is shining*.
ĉevalo, *horse*.
dormas, *sleeps, is sleeping*.
flava, *yellow*.
floro, *flower*.
flugas, *flies, is flying*.
forta, *strong*,
granda, *large*.

kaj, *and*.
kantas, *sings, is singing*.
knabo, *boy*.
kuras, *runs, is running*.
la, *the*.
luno, *moon*.
marŝas, *walks, is walking*.
pomo, *apple*.
suno, *sun*.
tablo, *table*.
violo, *violet*.
viro, *man*.

READING LESSON.

1. Bona viro. 2. La granda tablo. 3. Blanka floro. 4. Flava birdo. 5. La bela birdo kantas. 6. Forta knabo kuras. 7. La bona viro marŝas. 8. La bela ĉevalo kuras. 9. La suno brilas. 10. Birdo flugas kaj knabo kuras. 11. Ĉevalo blanka marŝas. 12. La bela luno brilas. 13. La knabo kantas kaj la viro dormas. 14. Bela granda pomo. 15. La bona knabo kantas. 16. La granda ĉevalo dormas. 17. La suno brilas kaj la luno brilas. 18. Granda forta tablo. 19. Violo flava. 20. La bona flava pomo.

SENTENCES FOR TRANSLATION.

1. A beautiful flower. 2. A good large table. 3. A yellow violet and a white violet. 4. The moon is-shining (shines). 5. The good boy is-walking (walks). 6. The beautiful yellow bird is-flying (flies). 7. The strong man is-sleeping (sleeps). 8. The white bird is-singing (sings). 9. A strong horse runs, and a man walks. 10. The sun shines, and the boy is-singing (sings). 11. The large yellow apple. 12. An apple large and good.

LESSON III.

THE PLURAL NUMBER.

16. The plural number of nouns, that is, the form which indicates more than one person or thing, is made by adding **-j**[3] to the noun, as **viroj**, *men*, from **viro**, *man*; **tabloj**, *tables*, from **tablo**, *table*.

17. An adjective modifying a plural noun agrees with it in number, being given the plural form by the addition of the ending -j.[4] An adjective modifying two or more nouns used together is of course given the plural form:

bonaj viroj, *good men.*
grandaj ĉevaloj, *large horses.*
belaj birdo kaj floro (bela birdo kaj bela floro), *beautiful bird and (beautiful) flower.*

18. The article is *invariable*, that is, does not change in form when used with plural nouns, as **la viro**, *the man*, **la viroj**, *the men*. The verb is also invariable in form:

La viroj marŝas, *the men walk, the men are walking.*
La suno kaj la luno brilas, *the sun and the moon are shining.*
La viro estas, *the man is.*
La viroj estas, *the men are.*

PREDICATE ADJECTIVE AND NOUN.

19. When the adjective is a part of that which is told or predicated of the subject of the verb, as when used with the verbs "to be," "to seem," etc., it is called a *predicate adjective*:

La birdo estas bela, *the bird is beautiful.*
La knabo ŝajnas bona, *the boy seems good.*
La viroj estas fortaj, *the men are strong.*

20. A noun may also be used as part of the predicate, and is then called a *predicate noun*:

Violoj estas floroj, *violets are flowers.*

[3] **-oj** is pronounced like *oy* in *boy*. See 5.
[4] **-aj** is pronounced like *ai* in *aisle*. See 5.

La kolombo estas birdo, *the dove is a bird.*

21. Predicate nouns and adjectives agree in number with the word or words with which they are in predicate relation:

Rozoj estas belaj, *roses are beautiful.*
La knabo kaj la viro ŝajnas fortaj, *the boy and the man seem strong.*

VOCABULARY.

alta, *high, tall.*	**kolombo**, *dove.*
arbo, *tree.*	**kuŝas**, *lies, is lying, lie.*
ĉambro, *room.*	**longa**, *long.*
domo, *house.*	**rozo**, *rose.*
en, *in.*	**ruĝa**, *red.*
estas, *is, are.*	**seĝo**, *chair.*
folio, *leaf.*	**sidas**, *sits, sit, is sitting.*
freŝa, *fresh.*	**sur**, *on.*
ĝardeno, *garden.*	**ŝajnas**, *seems, seem.*
kampo, *field.*	**verda**, *green.*

READING LESSON.

1. La alta viro estas en la ĝardeno. 2. Blanka ĉevalo estas en la kampo. 3. Belaj birdoj sidas sur la verda arbo. 4. La bonaj knaboj estas en la domo. 5. La ĉambroj en la bela domo estas grandaj. 6. Freŝaj floroj kuŝas sur la tablo. 7. La violoj en la kampo estas belaj. 8. La luno kaj la suno ŝajnas grandaj. 9. La kolomboj estas belaj birdoj. 10. La knaboj ŝajnas fortaj. 11. Ruĝaj pomoj estas sur la tablo en la ĉambro. 12. La fortaj viroj sidas sur seĝoj en la longa ĉambro. 13. La arboj estas altaj kaj verdaj. 14. La kolomboj sur la arboj kantas. 15. Fortaj ĉevaloj marŝas kaj kuras en la verdaj kampoj. 16. La knaboj dormas en la granda domo. 17. Ruĝaj, flavaj, kaj verdaj folioj estas en la ĝardeno. 18. Longa tablo estas en la domo. 19. Belaj birdoj flugas kaj kantas en la kampo. 20. Freŝaj rozoj ŝajnas belaj. 21. La folioj estas verdaj kaj ruĝaj.

SENTENCES FOR TRANSLATION.

1. The trees in the garden are tall and green. 2. The rooms in the house are long. 3. The flowers on the table are red, yellow and white. 4. The leaves are long and green. 5. The men are-sitting (sit) on chairs in the garden. 6. In the garden are yellow roses. 7. The birds in the field are doves. 8. The boys in the room in the house seem tall. 9. Fresh violets are beautiful flowers. 10. The horses in the green fields seem strong. 11. Doves are-singing (sing) in the garden. 12. The men in the large house sleep. 13. The house is long and high, and the rooms in the house are large. 14. Red and yellow apples lie on the big table. 15. Green leaves are on the trees in the large garden.

LESSON IV.

TRANSITIVE VERBS.—THE ACCUSATIVE CASE.—THE CONJUNCTION KAJ.—THE NEGATIVE NE.

TRANSITIVE VERBS.

22. The verbs so far given have been *intransitive verbs*, expressing a state or an action limited to the subject, and not immediately affecting any other person or thing, as **la knabo kuras**, *the boy runs*. On the other hand a *transitive verb* expresses an act of the subject upon some person or thing; as, **la knabo trovas — —**, *the boy finds — —*.

THE ACCUSATIVE CASE.

23. The person or thing acted upon is called the *direct object* of a transitive verb, and is given the ending **-n**. This is called the accusative ending; and the word to which it is attached is said to be in the *accusative case:*[5]

> **La viro havas seĝon**, *the man has a chair.*
> **La knabo trovas florojn**, *the boy finds flowers.*

24. An attributive adjective modifying a noun in the accusative case is made to agree in case, by addition of the same accusative ending **-n**. This prevents any doubt as to which of two or more nouns in a sentence is modified by the adjective, and permits of variation in the order of the words:

> **La knabo trovas belan floron**, *the boy finds a beautiful flower.*
> **Florojn belajn la viro havas**, *the man has beautiful flowers.*
> **La viro havas grandan s The Plural Number.—Predicate Adjective and Noun eĝon**, *the man has a large chair.*
> **Ruĝan rozon la knabo havas**, *the boy has a red rose.*

25. A predicate adjective or noun (19) is never in the accusative case, nor is the accusative ending ever attached to the article, which is invariable as stated in 18.

THE CONJUNCTION KAJ.

26. In the expression *both ... and ...*, the conjunction **kaj** is used for both words, being merely repeated:

> **La viro kaj marŝas kaj kuras**, *the man both walks and runs.*

---

[5] The ending **-n** follows the ending **-j**, if the word to be put in the accusative case is in the plural number.

La ĉevalo estas kaj granda kaj forta, *the horse is both large and strong.*
La knabo havas kaj rozojn kaj violojn, *the boy has both roses and violets.*
Kaj la knabo kaj la viro estas altaj, *both the boy and the man are tall.*

THE NEGATIVE NE.

27. The negative word meaning "not" when forming part of a sentence, and "no" when used as an answer to a question, is **ne**. When used as a sentence-negative, it usually immediately precedes the verb. For emphatic negation of some other word than the verb, **ne** may precede that word:

Violoj ne estas ruĝaj, *violets are not red.*
La viroj ne sidas sur seĝoj, *the men are-not-sitting on chairs.*
La kolombo kantas, ne flugas, *the dove is-singing, not flying.*
La domo estas blanka, ne verda, *the house is white, not green.*

VOCABULARY.

apud, *near, in the vicinity of.*
benko, *bench.*
branĉo, *branch.*
diversa, *various.*
feliĉa, *happy.*
frukto, *fruit.*
havas, *have, has.*
herbo, *grass.*
ili, *they.*
kolektas, *gather, collect.*

koloro, *color.*
larĝa, *wide, broad.*
manĝas, *eat, eats.*
mola, *soft.*
nigra, *black.*
ne, *not, no.*
rompas, *break, breaks.*
sed, *but.*
trovas, *find, finds.*
vidas, *see, sees.*

READING LESSON.

1. La knaboj ne estas en la ĉambro en la blanka domo. 2. Ili estas en la granda ĝardeno. 3. La ĝardeno ŝajnas kaj longa kaj larĝa. 4. La feliĉaj knaboj vidas la belan ĝardenon. 5. Ili vidas florojn apud alta arbo. 6. La floroj havas diversajn kolorojn. 7. La knaboj kolektas kaj ruĝajn kaj flavajn florojn. 8. Sed ili ne trovas fruktojn en la ĝardeno. 9. Florojn blankajn ili ne vidas. 10. La alta arbo havas verdajn foliojn sur la branĉoj. 11. La knaboj rompas branĉon, kaj kolektas la fruktojn. 12. Ili vidas florojn sur la branĉoj, sed la florojn ili ne kolektas. 13. La knaboj ne sidas sur benkoj en la ĝardeno, sed kuŝas sur la mola herbo. 14. La kolomboj sidas sur la arboj, kaj ili estas feliĉaj. 15. La knaboj vidas la belajn birdojn. 16. Fortaj nigraj ĉevaloj manĝas la herbon en la kampo. 17. La knaboj vidas la ĉevalojn, sed la ĉevaloj ne vidas la knabojn. 18. La ĉevaloj ne dormas, ili manĝas. 19. La freŝa herbo estas verda kaj mola. 20. Feliĉaj estas kaj la knaboj kaj la ĉevaloj. 21. La pomo estas bona frukto.

SENTENCES FOR TRANSLATION.

1. Green leaves are on the trees. 2. The boys break branches and gather the apples. 3. They are near the tall tree in the garden. 4. They find leaves on the tree, but they do not see the fruit. 5. The house is long, broad and high. 6. The rooms in the

house are both long and wide. 7. The men have strong black horses. 8. The horses eat the fresh green grass in the field. 9. The men sit on benches in the garden. 10. The boys do not sleep, but they lie on the soft grass. 11. They see both the birds and the flowers, and they seem happy. 12. The flowers have various colors, but the grass is green. 13. The doves are not sitting on the tree, they are flying near the trees. 14. Beautiful red roses are lying on the table in the house. 15. The large red apples are near the yellow roses.

LESSON V.

THE COMPLEMENTARY INFINITIVE.—INTERROGA-
TION.—THE CONJUNCTION NEK.

THE COMPLEMENTARY INFINITIVE.

28. The infinitive is a form of the verb which expresses merely the general idea of the action or condition indicated, and has some of the characteristics of a noun. The ending of the infinitive is **-i**, as **kuri**, *to run*, **esti**, *to be*, **havi**, *to have*.

29. An infinitive used to complete the meaning of another verb, serving as a direct object to a transitive verb, is called a *complementary infinitive*. If the complementary infinitive is from a transitive verb, it may itself have a direct object:

La knabo volas kuri, *the boy wishes to run.*
Birdoj ŝatas kanti, *birds like to sing.*
La knabo volas havi ĉevalon, *the boy wishes to have a horse.*
Ili volas trovi florojn, *they wish to find flowers.*

INTERROGATION.

30. An interrogative sentence is one which asks a question. Unless some directly interrogative word (as "who," "when," "why," etc.) is used, the sentence is rendered interrogative by use of the word **ĉu**. This interrogative particle is placed at the beginning of a sentence, the words of which are left in the same order as for a statement. Since there is no inversion of order, there is no necessity for a word like English "do" or "does," to introduce the verb:

Ĉu la knabo estas bona? *Is the boy good?*
Ĉu ili havas florojn? *Have they flowers?*
Ĉu la kolomboj kantas? *Do the doves sing? (Are the doves singing?)*

THE CONJUNCTION NEK.

31. In the expression *neither ... nor ...*, the conjunction **nek** is used for both words. Since an adjective modifier of two or more words connected by **nek** must necessarily modify them separately, the adjective remains in the singular number:

Ili nek marŝas nek kuras, *they neither walk nor run.*
La viro havas nek domon nek ĝardenon, *the man has neither a house nor a garden.*
Nek la rozo nek la violo estas verda, *neither the rose nor the violet is green.*

Vocabulary.

(Verbs will hereafter be quoted in the infinitive form.)

bruna, *brown.*
ĉerizo, *cherry.*
ĉu, (30).
dolĉa, *sweet.*
gusto, *taste.*
ĝi, *it.*
Gertrude, *Gertrude.*
knabino, *girl.*

matura, *ripe.*
Mario, *Mary.*
nek, *neither, nor.*
persiko, *peach.*
jes, *yes.*
preferi, *to prefer.*
ŝati, *to like.*
voli, *to wish.*

READING LESSON.

1. Ĉu persiko estas ruĝa? 2. Jes, ĝi estas kaj ruĝa kaj dolĉa. 3. Ĉu ĉerizoj estas brunaj? 4. Ne, ili estas nek brunaj nek nigraj, sed flavaj. 5. Ĉu la pomo estas frukto? Jes, ĝi estas bona frukto. 6. Ĉu la viro kaj la knabo havas pomojn? 7. Ne, ili havas nek pomojn nek persikojn. 8. Ĉu Mario havas la maturan frukton? 9. Mario kaj Gertrudo havas la frukton. 10. Ili estas en la domo, kaj manĝas la maturan frukton. 11. La persikoj havas dolĉan guston. 12. La knabinoj volas havi florojn, sed la knaboj preferas kolekti diversajn fruktojn. 13. Ili volas trovi maturajn ĉerizojn kaj flavajn persikojn. 14. La ĉerizoj havas belan ruĝan koloron. 15. La persikoj ŝajnas molaj kaj bonaj. 16. Mario rompas branĉon, kaj vidas ĉerizojn sur la branĉoj. 17. Gertrudo estas feliĉa, kaj volas havi la belan frukton. 18. Gertrudo estas alta, bela knabino. 19. Mario ŝatas ĉerizojn. 20. La knaboj kaj knabinoj sidas sur la verda herbo, kaj manĝas la ĉerizojn. 21. Ili ne volas manĝi pomojn, ili preferas la dolĉajn ĉerizojn. 22. La folioj apud la ĉerizoj estas nek larĝaj nek longaj.

SENTENCES FOR TRANSLATION.

1. Have the girls beautiful flowers? 2. No, they have fresh fruit. 3. The boys do not wish to gather flowers. 4. They prefer to break the branches, and find the sweet cherries. 5. Gertrude wishes to eat apples, but Mary has neither apples nor peaches. 6. Do the girls like to sit in the house and eat fruit? 7. Yes, they like to sit in the house, but they prefer to walk in the field. 8. Are ripe peaches brown? 9. No, they are red and yellow. 10. Has the peach a sweet taste? 11. Do the girls see the beautiful black horses in the fields? 12. Yes, they see the horses, but the horses seem not to see the girls. 13. Mary sits on the soft green grass, and eats ripe fruit.

LESSON VI.

PERSONAL PRONOUNS.

32. Words which stand in the place of nouns, as "you," "he," "who," "which," are called *pronouns*. Pronouns referring to the person speaking (*I, we*), the person addressed (*you, thou*), or the person or thing spoken of (*he, she, it, they*), are called *personal pronouns*. They are considered singular or plural, according to whether they refer to one or more persons. Since the meaning of such pronouns indicates the number, no plural ending is ever attached to them. The personal pronouns are:

	Singular.	Plural.
First person:	**mi**, I (*me*).	**ni**, we (*us*).
Second person:	**vi**, you.[*]	**vi**, you.
Third person:	**li**, he (*him*).	
	ŝi, she (*her*).	**ili**, they (*them*).
	ĝi, it.	

AGREEMENT WITH PRONOUNS.

33. Nouns in predicate relation with pronouns, or adjectives modifying such pronouns, are made to agree with them in number:

Ni estas bonaj kaj feliĉaj, *we are good and happy.*
Rozoj estas floroj, ili ne estas fruktoj, *roses are flowers, they are not fruits.*
Gertrudo, vi estas bona, *Gertrude, you are good.*
Knabinoj, ĉu vi estas feliĉaj? *Girls, are you happy?*

CONJUGATION OF THE VERB.

34. Any pronoun may serve as the subject of a verb. The combination of the verb with each of the personal pronouns in succession for its subject, is called the *conjugation* of the verb. Following is the conjugation of the present tense of **esti**, and of **vidi**:

mi estas, *I am.*
vi estas, *you are.*
li (ŝi, ĝi) estas, *he (she, it) is.*
ni estas, *we are.*
vi estas, *you (plural) are.*
ili estas, *they are.*

mi vidas, *I see.*
vi vidas, *you see.*
li (ŝi, ĝi) vidas, *he (she, it) sees.*
ni vidas, *we see.*
vi vidas, *you (plural) see.*
ili vidas, *they see.*

VOCABULARY.

al, *to, toward.*
Arturo, *Arthur.*
aŭ, *or* (aŭ.. aŭ.., *either.. or..*)
ĉar, *because.*
doni, *to give.*
fali, *to fall.*
fenestro, *window.*

hodiaŭ, *today.*
kudri, *to sew.*
Roberto, *Robert.*
skui, *to shake.*
stari, *to stand.*
sub, *under, beneath.*
virino, *woman.*

READING LESSON.

1. Knaboj, ĉu vi volas sidi en la domo, aŭ en la ĝardeno? 2. Ni preferas sidi hodiaŭ en la ĝardeno, sub la granda arbo. 3. Ĉu vi havas pomojn, aŭ ĉerizojn? 4. Ni havas nek pomojn nek ĉerizojn, sed ni havas dolĉajn persikojn. 5. Arturo donas al vi la maturajn persikojn, ĉar li ŝatas kolekti frukton. 6. Arturo, ĉu vi rompas la branĉojn? 7. Ne, sed mi skuas branĉon, kaj la persikoj falas. 8. Mi staras sub la arbo, kaj kolektas la dolĉan frukton. 9. La frukton mi donas al Mario kaj Gertrudo. 10. Mi volas doni persikon al Heleno, sed hodiaŭ ŝi estas en la domo. 11. Ŝi sidas apud la fenestro kaj kudras. 12. Ŝi preferas kudri, kaj volas nek marŝi nek sidi en la ĝardeno. 13. Kaj ŝi kaj la virino apud ŝi volas kudri hodiaŭ. 14. Ili estas feliĉaj, ĉar ili vidas la birdojn en la arbo apud la fenestro. 15. La birdoj estas kolomboj, kaj sidas sur la arbo. 16. Sub la arboj en la kampo staras ĉevaloj, kaj ili manĝas la verdan molan herbon. 17. Ni donas pomojn al ili, ĉar ili ŝatas pomojn. 18. Ni estas feliĉaj, ĉar ni havas belajn persikojn maturajn kaj bonajn. 19. Roberto, vi estas alta, sed vi, knabinoj, ne estas altaj.

SENTENCES FOR TRANSLATION.

1. Does Arthur break the branch and gather the apples? 2. No, he shakes the branch, and the apples fall. 3. They are ripe and sweet. 4. Robert, do you wish to stand beneath the tree? 5. No, I do not wish to stand under it, but near it. 6. I wish to give both the peaches and the apples to the woman. 7. She is sitting in the house, near the window. 8. Mary is sitting in (on) a chair near her. 9. Both Mary and the woman are sewing. 10. They prefer to sew, and do not wish to walk in the garden to-day. 11. They are happy because they like to sew. 12. They do not wish to gather flowers, or walk, or see the birds. 13. They have neither apples nor peaches, but they do not wish to eat. 14. They give the fruit to the boys and girls.

LESSON VII.

THE PAST TENSE.—PREPOSITIONS.—ACCUSATIVE CASE OF PERSONAL PRONOUNS.

THE PAST TENSE.

35. The past tense of the verb expresses an action which took place in past time, or a condition which existed in past time. The ending of this tense is **-is**, as **kuris**, ran, **flugis**, flew, **brilis**, shone. The conjugation of **esti** and also of **vidi** in the past tense is as follows:

mi estis, *I was.*
vi estis, *you were.*
li (ŝi, ĝi) estis, *he (she, it) was.*
ni estis, *we were.*
vi estis, *you (plural) were.*
ili estis, *they were.*

mi vidis, *I saw.*
vi vidis, *you saw.*
li (ŝi, ĝi) vidis, *he (she, it) saw.*
ni vidis, *we saw.*
vi vidis, *you (plural) saw.*
ili vidis, *they saw.*

PREPOSITIONS.

36. A preposition is a word like "in," "on," placed before a noun or pronoun to indicate some relation between this and another word. The preposition is said to *govern* the noun or pronoun, which is called its *complement*. In English, the complement of a preposition seems to be put in the accusative case if it is a pronoun, but to remain unchanged in form if it is a noun. In Esperanto the preposition does not affect the form of the word governed, which remains in the nominative case:

La arbo estas en la ĝardeno, *the tree is in the garden.*
Bonaj pomoj estas sur ĝi, *good apples are on it.*
Mi donis ĉerizojn al li, *I gave cherries to him.*
La knabo estas apud mi, *the boy is near me.*
Sub la arbo staris ĉevalo, *under the tree stood a horse.*

ACCUSATIVE CASE OF PERSONAL PRONOUNS.

37. For use as the object of a verb, any pronoun may be put in the accusative case by addition of the accusative ending **-n** (23):

La viro vidis vin kaj min, *the man saw you and me.*
Li vidis ilin kaj nin, *he saw them and us.*
Mi vidis nek lin nek ŝin, *I saw neither him nor her.*
Ni volas havi ĝin, *we wish to have it.*

VOCABULARY.

agrabla, *pleasant, agreeable.*
bildo, *picture.*
blua, *blue.*
danki, *to thank.*
de, *from.*
diri, *to say.*
infano, *child.*
interesa, *interesting.*

luma, *light (not dark).*
muro, *wall.*
nun, *now.*
planko, *floor.*
pordo, *door.*
rigardi, *to look (at).*
tapiŝo, *carpet.*
tra, *through.*

READING LESSON.

1. Hodiaŭ la knaboj kaj knabinoj estas en la granda domo. 2. Ili staras apud la tablo, en agrabla luma ĉambro. 3. Ĝi havas altajn larĝajn fenestrojn. 4. Sub la tablo kaj seĝoj, mola tapiŝo kuŝas sur la planko. 5. La tapiŝo havas belajn kolorojn, ruĝan, bluan, flavan, kaj verdan. 6. Virino marŝis tra la pordo, kaj staris apud la tablo. 7. Ŝi havis interesajn bildojn, kaj donis ilin al la knaboj kaj la knabinoj. 8. Ŝi diris "Ĉu vi volas rigardi la bildojn?" 9. "Jes, ni dankas vin," diris la infanoj, kaj ŝi donis al ili la bildojn. 10. Granda bildo falis de la tablo, sed Arturo nun havas ĝin. 11. Li donas ĝin al Mario, ŝi dankas lin, kaj donas ĝin al Roberto. 12. Ili volis doni ĝin al Gertrudo, sed ŝi diris "Ne, mi dankas vin, mi ne ŝatas rigardi bildojn." 13. Ŝi marŝis de la tablo al la fenestro kaj diris "Mi preferas kudri." 14. Ŝi volis sidi en granda seĝo apud la fenestro. 15. La virino rigardis ŝin kaj diris "Mi donis la bildojn al vi, knaboj kaj knabinoj," ĉar ili estas interesaj bildoj. 16. Gertrudo diris "Vi estas bona al ni, sed mi volas sidi apud la pordo aŭ la fenestro. 17. Mi kolektis dolĉajn violojn en la ĝardeno, kaj nun mi volas rigardi la dolĉajn florojn, kaj kudri."

SENTENCES FOR TRANSLATION.

1. Do the boys and girls wish to be good? 2. They gathered fresh flowers and gave them to the woman. 3. The happy children were in the garden, but now they are in the house. 4. The rooms in the house are light, because they have large wide windows. 5. The doors in the room are wide and high. 6. The carpets on the floor seem soft, and have various beautiful colors. 7. A large strong table stands near the door. 8. We can sit near the table and look through the windows. 9. Gertrude is-looking-at the various pictures. 10. She looks-at them, and seems to be happy. 11. She gave a picture to me and I thanked her. 12. Helen walked near the table and shook it. 13. Arthur did not see the pictures because they were lying on the floor. 14. He looked-at the pictures on the wall, but they are neither interesting nor beautiful. 15. Robert looked through the window, and saw us in the pleasant garden.

LESSON VIII.

REFLEXIVE PRONOUNS.—REFLEXIVE VERBS.

REFLEXIVE PRONOUNS.

38. A pronoun which refers to the same person or thing as the subject of the verb in the sentence, but is used in some other relation than subject of that verb, is said to be used *reflexively*, or to be a *reflexive pronoun*.

39. The first and second personal pronouns, **mi**, **ni**, and **vi**, (**ci**) are used for the reflexive pronouns of the first and second persons. There can be no ambiguity, since words such as "me, myself, us, ourselves," can refer to no one else than the person or persons speaking; while words such as "you, yourself, yourselves (thee, thyself)," can refer to no one else than the person or persons addressed:

Mi vidas min, *I see myself.*
Mi diris al mi, *I said to myself.*
Ni havas tapiŝon sub ni, *we have a carpet under us.*
Ni amuzis nin, *we amused ourselves.*
(Ci trovas domon apud ci, *thou findest a house near thee.*)
Vi diras al vi, *you say to yourself (yourselves).*
Vi amuzas vin, *you amuse yourself (yourselves).*

40. When the verb is in the third person, a pronoun of the third person, used otherwise than as the subject, might or might not refer to the subject of that verb. For example, "He sees a bird near him," may mean that the subject sees a bird near himself, or near another person. If such a pronoun of the third person is intended to refer to the subject of the verb, Esperanto uses a special reflexive pronoun **si** (accusative **sin**), which means *him(self)*, *her(self)*, *it(self)*, *them(selves)*, according to the gender and number of the verb:[6]

Li amuzas sin, *he amuses himself.*
Arturo vidis birdon apud si, *Arthur saw a bird near him(self).*
Ŝi trovas floron apud si, *she finds a flower near her(self).*
Mario trovis sin sur blua tapiŝo, *Mary found herself on a blue carpet.*
La tapiŝo havas diversajn kolorojn en si, *the carpet has various colors in it(self).*
La birdo kaŝas sin sub la folioj, *the bird hides itself under the leaves.*
Ili amuzas sin, *they amuse themselves.*
La viroj havas seĝojn apud si, *the men have chairs near them(selves).*

---

[6] From the very fact that **si** always *refers to* the subject of the verb, it is evident that **si** can never itself be used as subject or part of the subject of the verb.

La virinoj trovas florojn apud si, *the women find flowers near them(selves).*
La arboj havas ĉerizojn sur si, *the trees have cherries on them(selves).*
Sub si la infanoj trovis molan tapiŝon, *under them(selves) the children found a soft carpet.*

REFLEXIVE VERBS.

41. A verb having a reflexive pronoun for its direct object is sometimes called a *reflexive verb*, from the fact that some languages have had or still have a special reflexive or middle form of the verb, to express an act of the subject on or for itself, or they have certain verbs whose use is chiefly or exclusively reflexive.[7] The conjugation of a verb reflexively is therefore as follows:

mi amuzas min (mi min amuzas), *I amuse myself.*
vi amuzas vin (vi vin amuzas), *you amuse yourself.*
li (ŝi, ĝi) amuzas sin (sin amuzas), *he (she, it) amuses him (her, it)self.*
ni amuzas nin (ni nin amuzas), *we amuse ourselves.*
vi amuzas vin (vi vin amuzas), *you amuse yourselves.*
ili amuzas sin (ili sin amuzas), *they amuse themselves.*

VOCABULARY.

Alfredo, *Alfred.*
amuzi, *to amuse.*
antaŭ, *before, in front of.*
aparteni, *to belong.*
griza, *gray.*
iri, *to go.*
Johano, *John.*
kaŝi, *to hide, to conceal.*
komenci, *to begin.*
laŭdi, *to praise.*
legi, *to read.*
libro, *book.*
perdi, *to lose.*
skatolo, *small box or case.*
strato, *street.*
si, *himself, etc. (40).*

READING LESSON.

1. Johano kaj Alfredo amuzis sin en la ĝardeno. 2. Johano kaŝis sin, kaj Alfredo trovis Johanon. 3. Alfredo sin kaŝis en alta arbo, kaj Johano trovis Alberton. 4. Mario kaj Gertrudo sin kaŝis apud la floroj, kaj la knaboj trovis la knabinojn. 5. La knabinoj ne volas perdi sin en la agrabla kampo. 6. Johano komencis amuzi sin en luma ĉambro en la domo. 7. La muro havas interesajn bildojn sur si. 8. Tra la fenestro antaŭ si Johano rigardas la virojn kaj la virinojn sur la strato. 9. Li havas molan grizan tapiŝon sub si, kaj ne volas seĝon. 10. Li kaj Alfredo volis iri al la strato kaj amuzi sin. 11. Ili marŝis al la pordo, kaj trovis ruĝan skatolon antaŭ si. 12. En la skatolo estis libro, kaj Johano diris al si "La libro ne apartenas al mi." 13. Li diris al Alfredo "Ĉar ni trovis ĝin, mi volas legi la libron." 14. Virino antaŭ pordo komencis rigardi la knabojn, kaj ili diris al ŝi "Ĉu la libro apartenas al vi? Ni trovis ĝin en skatolo." 15. La virino diris "Jes, ni perdis ĝin, kaj mi dankas vin, ĉar vi donas <u>al mi la skatolon</u> kaj la libron." 16. Ŝi iris al la strato, kaj la knaboj iris al la domo.

[7] As Greek ετράποντο, *they turned themselves;* Latin *exerceor,* I exercise myself, *vescor,* I eat (I feed myself); German *ich hüte mich,* I beware (I guard myself); Spanish *me alegro,* or *alégrome,* I rejoice (I gladden myself); French *il s'arrête,* he halts (he stops himself).

SENTENCES FOR TRANSLATION.

1. The book in the gray box does not belong to me. 2. I found it in front of me, near the door. 3. You began to praise yourselves, but I do not praise myself. 4. They hid themselves, and I stood near them. 5. The birds sit on the tree, because it has ripe cherries on it. 6. Alfred amused himself on the street, but we like to amuse ourselves in the house. 7. The trees have good fruit on them. 8. She found herself in a beautiful light room. 9. The carpet on the floor had various colors in it, and the high wall had pictures on it. 10. The pictures had boys and girls in them. 11. The book belongs to her, but it fell from the box. 12. The table has red and blue and yellow flowers on it. 13. Did you see the doves near the flowers in front of (before) you? 14. The birds saw the fruit on the tree in front of them, and flew to the branches. 15. I sat on the bench in the garden, and began to read an interesting book. 16. They hid themselves in the leaves and began to sing. 17. The child is in a pleasant room.

LESSON IX.

LIMITATION OF THE THIRD PERSONAL PRONOUN.—
POSSESSIVE ADJECTIVES.—PRONOMINAL USE OF
POSSESSIVE ADJECTIVES.—LA KATO KAJ LA PASE-
RO.

LIMITATION OF THE THIRD PERSONAL PRONOUN.

42. Since there is a special reflexive pronoun of the third person, the third personal pronouns, **li, ŝi, ĝi, ili**, when used otherwise than as subjects, never refer to the subject of the verb, but always to some other person or thing:

La knabo laŭdas lin, *the boy praises him* (another person).
Ŝi donas pomojn al ŝi, *she gives apples to her* (to another person).
La birdo vidis ĝin, *the bird saw it* (something else than the bird).
La knaboj kaŝis ilin, *the boys hid them* (other persons or things).
Ili trovis ilin apud si, *they found them* (other persons or things) *near them(-selves)*.
La birdoj flugis al ili, *the birds flew to them*.

POSSESSIVE ADJECTIVES.

43. Words like "my," "his," "your," which indicate ownership or some possessive relation, are called *possessive adjectives*.[8] Possessive adjectives are formed from the personal pronouns by adding the adjective ending **-a**, as **mia**, *my*, **via**, *your* (**cia**, *thy*), **lia**, *his*, **ŝia**, *her*, **ĝia**, *its*, **nia**, *our*, **via**, *your (plural)*, **ilia**, *their*. The limitation in the use of the third personal pronouns (**42**) is also true of the adjectives derived from them:

Mia domo kaj miaj ĝardenoj estas grandaj, *my house and my gardens are large*.
Johano sidas sur via seĝo, *John is sitting in your chair*.
Li havas lian ĉevalon, *he has his* (another person's) *horse*.
Ĉu vi legis ŝiajn librojn? *Did you read her books?*

44. Reflexive possessive adjectives, like the reflexive pronoun, refer to the subject of the verb in the sentence. For the first and second persons, they are the same as the personal possessive adjectives. The reflexive possessive adjective of the third person is **sia**, *his, her, its, their*, formed by adding the ending **-a** to the reflexive pronoun **si**:

---

[8] Sometimes these words are called possessive pronouns, although really they are not pronouns at all, but pronominal adjectives with a possessive meaning.

Mi havas miajn librojn sur mia tablo, *I have my books on my table.*
Johano perdis siajn librojn, *John lost his (John's) books.*
Mario estas en sia ĉambro, *Mary is in her room.*
La birdoj flugis al sia arbo, *the birds flew to their tree.*

PRONOMINAL USE OF POSSESSIVE ADJECTIVES.

45. Possessive adjectives may be used predicatively, as "the book is mine," or may modify some word or words not expressed, as "mine are large." Instead of having special forms, like English *mine, yours, hers,* etc., Esperanto uses the regular possessive adjectives preceded by the article:

La granda libro estas la mia, *the large book is mine.*
La via estas granda, la miaj estas belaj, *yours is large, mine are beautiful.*
Ili havas la sian, sed ne la lian, *they have theirs, but not his.*
La iliaj ŝajnas esti bonaj, *theirs seem to be good.*

VOCABULARY.

diro, *saying, remark.*	**manĝo,** *meal.*
ĝis, *as far as, up to, down to.*	**nesto,** *nest.*
hieraŭ, *yesterday.*	**pasero,** *sparrow.*
juna, *young.*	**patro,** *father.*
kapti, *to catch, to seize.*	**post,** *after, behind.*
kato, *cat.*	**surprizi,** *to surprise.*
kolera, *angry.*	**teni,** *to hold, to keep.*
lavi, *to wash.*	**vizaĝo,** *face.*

READING LESSON.

1. Hieraŭ mi perdis mian grizan katon. 2. Ilia kato kaptis nian birdon. 3. Via kolera diro surprizis mian patron. 4. Ĉu la granda kampo apartenas al ŝia patro? 5. Ne, ĝi ne estas la lia. 6. La lia estas bela, sed mi preferas la mian. 7. Ĉu vi ŝatas vian libron aŭ la ilian? 8. Li havas nek siajn ĉevalojn nek la iliajn. 9. La knabinoj ŝajnas esti koleraj. 10. Ili komencis legi siajn librojn. 11. La viro kaptis kaj tenis siajn ĉevalojn, sed li ne trovis iliajn ĉevalojn. 12. Ŝia libro kuŝas sur la planko, post ŝia seĝo. 13. Ŝi ne trovis ilian libron, sed la junaj infanoj trovis la nian.

LA KATO KAJ LA PASERO.

Griza kato iris de la domo ĝis la strato. Ĝi vidis paseron antaŭ si, kaj volis manĝi ĝin. La kato staris post granda arbo, kaj kaptis la paseron. La pasero diris "Bona kato lavas sin antaŭ sia manĝo, sed vi ne lavis vian vizaĝon." La interesa diro surprizis la katon. La kato ne tenis la paseron, sed komencis lavi sian vizaĝon. La pasero flugis de la kato ĝis la arbo. La kolera kato diris "Mi perdis mian manĝon, ĉar mi komencis lavi min antaŭ la manĝo!" Nun la katoj ne lavas sin antaŭ la manĝoj. Ili havas siajn manĝojn, kaj post la manĝoj ili lavas la vizaĝojn. La paseroj ne surprizas ilin nun, sed ili tenas la paserojn. La katoj estas feliĉaj, sed la paseroj ne estas feliĉaj. La junaj paseroj volas flugi al la nestoj en la arboj.

SENTENCES FOR TRANSLATION.

1. The boys are not in their (own) house, but they are in his. 2 Is the large beautiful house yours? 3. The woman walked through the door of their house, as far as her room. 4. The room has interesting pictures on its walls. 5. We praised their flowers yesterday, and they gave them to us. 6. Their books are in their (the books') box. 7. They are on their (the boys') table. 8. The gray cat was angry because it did not hold the bird. 9. The sparrow surprised it, and it commenced to wash its face. 10. The sparrow wished to fly as far as the tall tree, but the cat held it. 11. The sparrow said "A good cat washes its face, but you are not a good cat." 12. The sparrow was angry because the cat seized it and held it. 13. The bird did not lose its meal, but the angry cat lost its meal. 14. Do you see his cat or hers? 15. I see both his and hers, but ours is not in our garden. 16. My father is a tall strong man. 17. I like to look at him. 18. The children saw the young birds in the nest.

LESSON X.

THE ACCUSATIVE OF DIRECTION.—THE ARTICLE FOR THE POSSESSIVE ADJECTIVE.— APPOSITION.—LA ARABO KAJ LA KAMELO.

THE ACCUSATIVE OF DIRECTION.

46. When the verb in a sentence expresses motion, the word indicating the place, person or thing toward which the motion is directed is given the accusative ending. This is also true if the word is the complement of any preposition which does not itself sufficiently indicate motion in a certain direction. (The prepositions **al**, *to, toward,* **ĝis**, *as far as,* **tra**, *through,* express motion in the direction of their complements, and could not well be used except in a sentence whose verb expresses motion. Consequently the accusative is not used after any of these three):

Li iris ĝardenon, *he went to the garden ("gardenward").*

La viro iros Bostonon, *the man will go to Boston ("Bostonward").*[9]

Li estis en la ĝardeno, kaj kuris en la domon, *he was in the garden and ran into the house.*

Ĝi ne estas sur la tablo, ĝi falis sur la plankon, *it is not on the table, it fell upon the floor.*

Ili falis sub la tablon ĝis la planko, *they fell under the table as far as the floor* (direction expressed by whole prepositional phrase).

Mi iris tra la domo en mian ĉambron, *I went through the house into my room.*

THE ARTICLE FOR THE POSSESSIVE ADJECTIVE.

47. In many sentences where the possessor is already sufficiently indicated, English nevertheless uses a possessive adjective, as in "I wash my face," "he shakes his head," but on the other hand omits it entirely with certain words indicating relationship, as in "Brother gave it to me," etc. In both cases Esperanto uses the article instead of the possessive adjective, unless the fact of possession is to be emphasized:

Mi lavas la vizaĝon, *I wash my face.*

Li skuas la kapon, *he shakes his head.*

La patro estas alta, *Father is tall.*

Mi donis ĝin al la patro, *I gave it to Father.*

---

[9] *Cf.* English "he went home," "he went homeward," etc.

APPOSITION.

48. English often uses the preposition "of" between two words where no idea of possession really exists, as "the city of Boston." Since nouns used in apposition refer to the same thing, and are in the same grammatical construction, Esperanto does not use a preposition:

La urbo Bostono estas granda, *the city* (of) *Boston is large.*
Mia amiko Johano estas alta, *my friend John is tall.*
Ĉu vi ne konas min, vian amikon? *do you not know me, your friend?*

Vocabulary.

arabo, *arab.*	**meti,** *to put, to place.*
baldaŭ, *soon.*	**nazo,** *nose.*
Bostono, *Boston.*	**nur,** *only, merely.*
frato, *brother.*	**puŝi,** *to push.*
kamelo, *camel.*	**trans,** *across.*
kapo, *head.*	**tuta,** *whole, entire, all.*
kolo, *neck.*	**urbo,** *city.*
korpo, *body.*	**varma,** *warm.*

LA ARABO KAJ LA KAMELO.

Arabo sidis en sia domo en la urbo. Apud domo trans la strato li vidis kamel-on. La kamelo iris trans la straton ĝis la pordo, kaj diris al la arabo, "Frato, mi ne estas varma, mi volas meti nur la nazon en vian varman domon." La arabo skuis la kapon, sed la kamelo metis la nazon tra la pordo en la ĉambron. La kamelo komencis puŝi sian tutan vizaĝon en la domon. Baldaŭ li havis la kapon ĝis la kolo en la domo. Post la kapo iris la kolo en ĝin, kaj baldaŭ la tuta korpo estis en la domo. La arabo estis kolera, ĉar li ne volis havi tutan kamelon en sia domo. Li kuris al la kamelo, kaptis lin, tenis lin, kaj diris, "Frato, vi volas meti nur la nazon en mian domon. La ĉambro ne estas granda sed ĝi estas la mia, kaj mi preferas sidi en ĝi." "Via diro estas bona," diris la kamelo, "via domo ne estas granda, sed ĝi estas varma, kaj mi ŝatas stari en ĝi. Mi preferas stari kaj kuŝi en ĝi, kaj mi donos al vi mian arbon trans la strato. Ĉu vi ne volas iri sub la arbon?" Kaj la kamelo puŝis la arabon de lia domo en la straton de la urbo. La kamelo nun trovis sin en varma ĉambro, sed la juna arabo staris trans la strato kaj ne estis varma.

SENTENCES FOR TRANSLATION.

1. The cat ran across the street. 2. Across the street it found a sparrow. 3. It caught the bird, but began to wash its face, and the sparrow flew to the nest. 4. I went into the garden as far as the large tree. 5. I did not hold my book, and it fell upon the floor. 6. It began to fall under the table, but I seized it. 7. My brother pushed the books into their box, and put it on the table. 8. We went to the city of Boston yesterday and into a beautiful house. 9. The arab shook his head and said, "No." 10. But the camel commenced to go through the door. 11. His remark did not seem to surprise the camel. 12. The camel pushed its head and neck, and soon

its whole body into the warm house. 13. It wished to put merely its nose into it. 14. The arab was angry, because it pushed itself into his house. 15. He said, "Brother, the house is mine, and I do not wish to have you in it." 16. But soon after the remark, the whole camel was in the house. 17. He pushed the young arab into the street. 18. He went across the street and stood upon the grass under a tree.

LESSON XI.

POSSESSIVE CASE OF NOUNS.—IMPERSONAL VERBS.—
VERBS PRECEDING THEIR SUBJECTS.—COORDINAT-
ING CONJUNCTIONS.—LA ARABO EN LA DEZERTO.

POSSESSIVE CASE OF NOUNS.

49. The preposition **de** is used to express possession or connection:

La muroj de la domo, *the walls of the house.*
La koloroj de la floroj, *the colors of the flowers.*
La libro de la knabo, *the book of the boy (the boy's book).*
Branĉo de la arbo, *a branch of the tree.*
La ĝardeno de la viroj, *the garden of the men (the men's garden).*

IMPERSONAL VERBS.

50. Verbs with an impersonal or indeterminate subject, as "it rains," "it is snowing," are called impersonal, because there is no actual subject, the word "it" serving merely as an introductory particle. No such particle is used with impersonal verbs in Esperanto:

Pluvas, *it rains, it is raining.*
Neĝis hieraŭ, *it snowed yesterday.*

VERBS PRECEDING THEIR SUBJECTS.

51. When the verb in a sentence precedes its subject, English often uses an introductory particle, such as "there," "it." In Esperanto no such particles are needed:

Estas floroj sur la tablo, *there are flowers on the table.*
Estis Johano, ne Alfredo, en la ĝardeno, *it was John, not Alfred, in the garden.*
Estas domo en la kampo, *there is a house in the field.*
Estis mi, *it was I.*

COORDINATING CONJUNCTIONS.

52. Words like **aŭ, kaj, nek, sed,** which join words, word-groups, or sentences together are conjunctions. All the conjunctions given so far connect words, phrases, or sentences of similar rank or kind. These are called coordinating conjunctions, and the words, phrases,[10] or sentences connected by them are said to be

[10] A phrase is a word-group forming an expression, but not containing a verb, as

coordinate[11]:

Ĉu vi marŝas aŭ kuras?
(**Aŭ** connects the verbs.)

Ŝi iris, kaj ni estis feliĉaj.
(**Kaj** connects the sentences.)

Nek vi nek mi vidis ĝin.
(The second **nek** connects the pronouns, the first being introductory and adverbial.)

Aŭ li aŭ ŝi perdis la libron.
(The second **aŭ** connects the pronouns, the first being introductory and adverbial.)

Ĝi falis sur la seĝon, sed ne sur la plankon.
(**Sed** connects the phrases.)

Li ne ŝatis ĝin. Tamen li tenis ĝin.
(**Tamen** connects the sentences.)

VOCABULARY.

akvo, *water*.	**porti**, *to carry*.
amiko, *friend*.	**riĉa**, *rich, wealthy*.
ankaŭ, *also*.	**sablo**, *sand*.
bezoni, *to need*.	**sako**, *sack, bag*.
dezerto, *desert*.	**seka**, *dry*.
fidela, *faithful*.	**tamen**, *nevertheless*.
mono, *money*.	**trinki**, *to drink*.
neĝi, *to snow*.	**veni**, *to come*.
pluvi, *to rain*.	**vojo**, *road, way*.

LA ARABO EN LA DEZERTO.

Arabo iris trans grandan sekan dezerton. Kamelo, lia fidela amiko, portis lin. La kamelo ankaŭ portis belajn tapiŝojn, ĉar la arabo estis riĉa viro. La arabo havis ne nur tapiŝojn, sed ankaŭ sakojn. En la sakoj estis akvo, ĉar en la dezerto nek pluvas nek neĝas. La viro trinkis akvon, kaj ankaŭ donis akvon al sia kamelo.

"through the house," "of the man," "before me," etc.

[11] Coordinating conjunctions may be further classified according to their meaning:

Aŭ is disjunctive, connecting alternates, and expressing separation.
Kaj is copulative, expressing union.
Nek is disjunctive, expressing separation and also negation.
Sed is adversative, expressing opposition, contrast, or modification of a previous statement.
Tamen is adversative, affirming something in spite of a previous objection or concession.
Do, *so, then, consequently,* is argumentative, expressing a logical inference or result in a somewhat conversational manner.

La kamelo marŝis kaj marŝis, sed ne venis al la domo de la arabo, ĉar ili perdis la vojon. La suno brilis, kaj la sablo de la dezerto ŝajnis varma. La arabo ne trovis la vojon, kaj baldaŭ li ne havis akvon. Tamen la kamelo marŝis kaj marŝis, kaj baldaŭ la arabo vidis sakon antaŭ si, sur la seka sablo. Li estis feliĉa kaj diris al si "Ĉu estas akvo en ĝi? Mi volas trinki, kaj volas doni akvon al mia fidela kamelo." Li ankaŭ volis lavi la tutan vizaĝon en la akvo, ĉar li estis varma. Post sia diro li kaptis la sakon, kaj komencis rigardi en ĝin. Li metis la nazon en ĝin, sed ne trovis akvon en la sako. Nek li nek lia fidela kamelo havis akvon, ĉar estis nur mono en la sako. La arabo estis kolera, ĉar li ne volis monon, li bezonis akvon. Li havis monon en sia domo en la urbo, kaj volis trovi akvon. Ĉu li tamen metis la sakon trans la kolon de sia kamelo? Ne, li ne volis meti ĝin sur sian kamelon, ĉar li estis kolera. Li ne tenis la sakon, sed ĝi falis sur la sablon, kaj kuŝis apud li. La sako nun kuŝas sur la sablo de la granda dezerto, kaj la mono estas en ĝi.

SENTENCES FOR TRANSLATION.

1. Today it is raining, but yesterday it was snowing. 2. Did your friend John carry his chair into the house? 3. I saw your good friends on the way to the city. 4. Is the large sack behind the door theirs? 5. Neither she nor her brother saw the whole city. 6. They went to the city of Boston and lost their way. 7. There are interesting houses across the street. 8. The body of a camel is large, and its neck is long. 9. The camel pushed its head into the house of the arab, and he was angry. 10. On the sand in the desert there lies a sack. 11. In the sack there is money. 12. The arab was warm, and wished to drink water. 13. He also wished to give water to the faithful camel. 14. Nevertheless, he found only money in the sack. 15. He was angry, and did not keep the sack. 16. Yesterday he wished to find money, but today he prefers water. 17. Nevertheless there is only sand in the desert. 18. He wished to come from the dry desert to the house of a faithful friend. 19. Both he and his friends are rich. 20. They went to his house yesterday, and came to theirs today. 21. They do not need money.

LESSON XII.

INDIRECT STATEMENTS.—THE INDEFINITE PERSONAL PRONOUN ONI.—THE FUTURE TENSE. —LA VENTO-FLAGO.

INDIRECT STATEMENTS.

53. A statement made indirectly by means of a clause[12] dependent upon a verb meaning "say," "think," "know," "believe," or a similar expression, as in "I know that he came," "I hear that he is good," is called an *indirect statement*. (The *direct* statement is "he came," "he is good.") An indirect statement is joined to the main verb or sentence by the subordinating conjunction **ke,** *that.*[13]

Mi diras ke li estas bona, *I say that he is good.*
Johano diras ke vi venis hieraŭ, *John says that you came yesterday.*
Ŝi opinias ke estas mono en la sako, *she thinks that there is money in the bag.*
Ni vidas ke neĝas, *we see that it is snowing.*

THE INDEFINITE PERSONAL PRONOUN ONI.

54. When an indefinite personal pronoun is desired, as in the expressions "one knows," "they say," "people say," "you can see," etc., the indefinite personal pronoun **oni** is used. This pronoun may also be used in translating such expressions as "it is said," "I am told," etc.:

Oni diras ke li estas riĉa, *they say (one says) that he is rich.*
Oni vidas ke ili estas amikoj, *one sees that they are friends.*
Mi opinias ke oni ŝatas lin, *I think that people like him (that he is liked).*
Oni diris al mi ke estas sablo en la dezerto, *I was told (people said to me) that there is sand in the desert.*
Oni opinias ke ŝi estas feliĉa, *it is thought (one thinks) that she is happy.*
Ĉu oni vidis nin en la ĝardeno? *Were we seen (did people see us) in the garden?*
Oni ŝatas agrablajn infanojn, *people like agreeable children (agreeable children are liked).*

---

[12] A clause is a group of words including a verb, which is dependent upon or subordinate to a main verb or sentence, as " —that he came," " —when he went," " —that he is good," etc.

[13] In English the subordinating conjunction may sometimes be omitted, either "I think that he is good," or "I think he is good," being usually permissible. But in Esperanto there is no variation, and the conjunction **ke** is never omitted.

THE FUTURE TENSE.

55. The future tense of the verb expresses an act or state as about to take place, or as one that will take place in future time. The ending of this tense is **-os,** as **kuros,** *will run,* **flugos,** *will fly,* **brilos,** *will shine.* The conjugation of **esti** and also of **vidi** in the future tense is as follows:

mi estos, *I shall be.*	**mi vidos,** *I shall see.*
vi estos, *you will be.*	**vi vidos,** *you will see.*
li (ŝi, ĝi) estos, *he (she, it) will be.*	**li (ŝi, ĝi) vidos,** *he (she, it) will see.*
ni estos, *we shall be.*	**ni vidos,** *we shall see.*
vi estos, *you (plural) will be.*	**vi vidos,** *you (plural) will see.*
ili estos, *they will be.*	**ili vidos,** *they will see.*

VOCABULARY.

aŭdi, *to hear.*	**oni,** (see **54**).
blovi, *to blow.*	**opinii,** *to think, to opine.*
greno, *grain* (wheat, corn, etc.).	**orienta,** *east, eastern.*
ke, *that* (conjunction).	**pluvo,** *rain.*
kontraŭ, *against.*	**suda,** *south, southern.*
montri, *to show, to point out.*	**velki,** *to wilt, to wither.*
norda, *north, northern.*	**vento,** *wind.*
nova, *new.*	**ventoflago,** *weathercock.*
okcidenta, *west, western.*	**vetero,** *weather.*

LA VENTOFLAGO.

Estis varma vetero, la suno brilis, kaj suda vento blovis. Tamen la nova ventoflago sur la domo diris al si, "La sudan venton mi ne ŝatas. Mi preferas orientan venton." La vento orienta aŭdis la diron kaj ĝi venis kontraŭ la ventoflagon. Pluvis kaj pluvis, kaj oni estis kolera kontraŭ la ventoflago, ĉar ĝi montras orientan venton. Ĝi diris, "Pluvas nun, sed la greno en la kampoj bezonos sekan veteron. Oni estos kolera kontraŭ mi, ĉar mi montras orientan venton." La okcidenta vento aŭdis la ventoflagon, kaj baldaŭ venis. Ĝi ne estis forta, sed ĝi estis seka kaj agrabla vento, kaj ne portis pluvon. La viroj, virinoj, kaj junaj infanoj volis trinki, sed ili ne havis akvon. La greno kaj la floroj velkis, kaj la frukto ankaŭ falis. La nova ventoflago diris, "Oni estos kolera kontraŭ mi, ĉar ne pluvas. Oni opinios ke, ĉar mi montras okcidentan venton, la frukto falas, kaj la greno kaj floroj velkas. Mi ŝatas montri nek okcidentan nek orientan venton!" Norda vento aŭdis kaj venis al la ventoflago. La vetero ne estis agrabla, kaj la virinoj kaj la junaj infanoj ne estis varmaj. Neĝis, kaj oni estis kolera. Oni diris "La greno kaj la frukto bezonas varman veteron, sed hodiaŭ neĝas. Ni preferas la sudan venton. Ni havis ĝin, antaŭ la orienta, la okcidenta, kaj la norda ventoj. La ventoflago ne estas fidela amiko al ni. Ĝi ne montras bonajn ventojn, kaj ni volas rompi ĝin!" Oni kuris al la domo, kaptis la novan ventoflagon, kaj ankaŭ rompis ĝin. Ĝi falis, kaj kuŝis sur la vojo antaŭ la domo.

SENTENCES FOR TRANSLATION.

1. One can see that the weathercock points-out the winds. 2. They say that the west wind will be a dry wind. 3. The weathercock now shows that an agreeable south wind blows. 4. People will be angry with (against) the weathercock, because it points-out a north wind. 5. A north wind is not warm, and the grain and fruit will need a warm wind. 6. It snowed, and the young children were not warm, because the north wind blew. 7. People will like a south wind, but an east wind will carry rain. 8. Can one find money in the desert? 9. Do you think (that) he is in the house? 10. He is said to be (they say that he is) on the street. 11. It is thought (people think) that the camel is a faithful friend. 12. I am told (people tell me) that the camel has a large body, and a long neck. 13. One can see that it is not beautiful. 14. People do not like to drink warm water. 15. Nevertheless we shall drink warm water in the city. 16. It was beautiful weather yesterday, but today we shall have good weather also. 17. I think that a warm wind will blow soon. 18. My friend has a beautiful new house.

LESSON XIII.

THE DEMONSTRATIVE PRONOUN TIU.—TENSES IN IN-
DIRECT QUOTATIONS.—FORMATION OF FEMININE
NOUNS.—EN LA PARKO.

THE DEMONSTRATIVE PRONOUN TIU.

56. The demonstrative pronoun **tiu**, *that,* is used to indicate a person or a definitely specified thing. The plural is **tiuj**, *those:*

Tiu estas la via, kaj mi volas tiun, *that is yours, and I wish that one.*
Tiuj estos koleraj kontraŭ vi, *those will be angry with you.*
Li aŭdis tiujn, *he heard those (persons, or things).*

57. The demonstrative pronoun **tiu** is also used as a *pronominal adjective,* in
agreement with a noun:

Tiu vento estos varma, *that wind will be warm.*
Mi vidas tiun ventoflagon, *I see that weathercock.*
Tiuj infanoj estas junaj, *those children are young.*
Mi trovos tiujn librojn, *I shall find those books.*

TENSES IN INDIRECT QUOTATIONS.

58. The verb in an indirect statement (53) or an indirect question[14] remains in
the same tense in which it would be if the statement or question were direct. (In
English this is true only if the introductory verb is present or future, since after an
introductory past tense the tense of the indirect quotation is changed, and *am, is,
are, have, will* become *was, were, had, would,* etc.)

Mi diras ke li estas bona , *I say that he is good.*
" **diris** " " " " , *I said that he was good.*
" **diros** " " " " , *I shall say that he is good.*

Li miras ĉu mi aŭdas , *he wonders whether I hear.*
" **miris** " " " , *he wondered whether I heard.*

---

[14] An indirect question is introduced by **ĉu**, whether, after verbs meaning "ask,"
"wonder," "know," etc.:

Mi miras ĉu li venis, *I wonder whether he came.*
Oni demandas ĉu li estas riĉa, *people ask whether he is rich.*

" **miros** " " "   , *he will wonder whether I hear.*

Mi opiniis ke ĝi estas bona,   *I thought that it was good* (I thought *"it is good"*).

Oni miris ĉu li venos,   *they wondered whether he would come* (they wondered *"will he come?"*).

FORMATION OF FEMININE NOUNS.

59. Feminine nouns corresponding to distinctly masculine nouns such as **frato, knabo, viro**, may be formed from these by inserting the suffix **-in-** just before the noun-ending **-o:**[15]

fratino, sister (from frato, brother).   **patrino**, mother (from patro, father).
knabino, girl (from knabo, boy).   **virino**, woman (from viro, man).

VOCABULARY.

almenaŭ, at least.   **paroli**, to talk, to speak.
ĉapelo, hat.   **parko**, park.
ĉielo, sky, heaven.   **preskaŭ**, almost.
filo, son.   **pri**, concerning, about.
konstrui, to build.   **promeni**, to take a walk.
miri, to wonder.   **super**, above.
morgaŭ, tomorrow.   **timi**, to fear, to be afraid (of).
nubo, cloud.   **tiu**, that (56).
ombrelo, umbrella.   **zorga**, careful.

EN LA PARKO.

Miaj junaj amiko kaj amikino, kaj ankaŭ ilia patrino, iris hieraŭ al la parko. La infanoj diris al la patrino ke la parko estas agrabla, kaj ke ili volas promeni en ĝi. La knabino parolis al sia frato pri la belaj floroj. Ŝi diris al li ke la floroj velkas, kaj ke la herbo en preskaŭ la tuta parko bezonas pluvon. La knabo diris hodiaŭ al mi ke hieraŭ li kaj lia fratino aŭdis la birdojn en la arboj super siaj kapoj. Li diris ke li miris pri tiuj birdoj, tamen li opinias ke la birdoj baldaŭ konstruos siajn nestojn en tiuj arboj. La infanoj promenis, kaj baldaŭ ili vidis ke grizaj nuboj venas sur la ĉielon, kaj mia juna amikino timis ke pluvos. Ŝi parolis al la patrino pri la nuboj kaj la pluvo, montris al ŝi la grizajn nubojn, kaj diris ke ŝi volas iri al la domo. Ili komencis marŝi al la strato, kaj preskaŭ kuris, ĉar ili ne havis ombrelon. Tra la fenestroj de la domoj oni rigardis ilin, kaj la knabo miris ĉu li kaj liaj patrino kaj fratino amuzas tiujn virojn kaj virinojn. Tamen la patrino diris ke ŝi ne timas ke ŝi amuzos tiujn, sed ke ŝi timas la pluvon. Ŝi kaj la filino volas esti zorgaj pri almenaŭ la novaj ĉapeloj. La filo diris al ŝi ke li ankaŭ estas zorga, sed ke li opinias ke ne pluvos. Baldaŭ

[15] *Cf.* English names similarly formed from masculine names, as *Pauline, Josephine, Ernestine, Geraldine*, etc., also German *Königin*, queen, from *König*, king; *Löwin*, lioness, from *Löwe*, lion, etc.

la patro venis al ili, kaj portis ombrelojn, ĉar li ankaŭ timis la pluvon. Li miris ĉu la infanoj kaj ilia patrino havas ombrelojn. Baldaŭ pluvis, sed ili estis sekaj, ĉar ili havis la ombrelojn. Morgaŭ ili ne promenos en la parko, sed iros al la urbo.

SENTENCES FOR TRANSLATION.

1. The east wind is dry and the south wind will be too warm. 2. A west wind blew against the weathercock, but the grain needed a south wind. 3 A north wind is blowing and I think that it will soon snow. 4. It (51) will be beautiful weather tomorrow, because a pleasant wind is now blowing. 5. The flowers will wither because those children gathered them. 6. They are talking about that park, but I do not wish to take-a-walk, because there are clouds in (on) the sky. 7. At least we shall take an umbrella, and my brother will hold it over our heads. 8. My sister said "Mother and I are-afraid that it will rain." 9. My young sister will be careful about that new umbrella. 10. I wonder whether she will take-a-walk tomorrow. 11. That park is pleasant and the grass is soft and green. 12. The birds are building their nests now, in those branches above our heads. 13. The sky above us is blue, and a west wind is beginning to blow. 14. I can see that weathercock, on that large house near the park. 15. Mother says that my sister will have a new hat tomorrow. 16. She will be careful of (about) that hat. 17. My father's friend is very careful of his son. 18. One sees that he is not a strong boy.

LESSON XIV.

THE DEMONSTRATIVE PRONOUN ĈI TIU.—POSSESSIVE
FORM OF THE DEMONSTRATIVE PRONOUN.—THE
SUFFIX -IL-.—THE EXPRESSION OF MEANS OR IN-
STRUMENTALITY.—LAMANĜO.

THE DEMONSTRATIVE PRONOUN ĈI TIU.

60. The demonstrative pronoun (and pronominal adjective) meaning "this" is formed by using with **tiu** (56) the word **ĉi**, which expresses the general idea of nearness or proximity. (Consequently the literal meaning of **ĉi tiu** is *that one near-by, that one here.*) The word **ĉi** may either precede or follow the pronoun:

Ĉi tiu estas la mia, *this is mine.*
Mi vidis ĉi tiun, *I saw this one.*
Ĉu vi volas tiujn ĉi? *Do you wish these?*
Ĉi tiu knabino estas mia fratino, *this girl is my sister.*
Mi vidis ĉi tiujn ĉapelojn, *I saw these hats.*
Ĉi tiuj amikoj promenos, *these friends will take a walk.*

61. The words **tiu** and **ĉi tiu** may be used to distinguish between persons or things *previously* mentioned and *just* mentioned:

Gertrude kaj Mario estas en la parko. Tiu rigardas la florojn, ĉi tiu kolektas ilin.
Gertrude and Mary are in the park. The former (that one) looks at the flowers, the latter (this one) gathers them.

POSSESSIVE FORM OF THE DEMONSTRATIVE PRONOUN.

62. To express possession, the demonstrative pronouns **tiu** and **ĉi tiu** have the special possessive or genitive forms **ties**, *that one's*, and **ĉi ties**, *this one's*. The use of **ties** and **ĉi ties** to mean "the former" and "the latter" is similar to the use of **tiu** and **ĉi tiu** shown in 61:

Mi iris al ties domo, *I went to that one's house.*
Ĉi ties filoj estas junaj, *this person's (this one's) sons are young.*
Mi ŝatas ties koloron, sed preferas ĉi tiun floron, *I like that one's color, but prefer this flower.*
La patro kaj lia amiko parolas pri siaj domoj. Ties estas nova, sed ĉi ties ŝajnas bela, *Father and his friend are talking about their houses. The former's is new, but the latter's seems beautiful.*

THE SUFFIX -IL-.

63. Names of instruments, tools or utensils may be formed by adding the suffix **-il-** (followed by the ending **-o**) to roots[16] whose meaning permits:

flugilo, *wing* (from **flugi**, *to fly*).
kaptilo, *snare, trap* (from **kapti**, *to catch*).
kudrilo, *needle* (from **kudri**, *to sew*).
montrilo, *indicator, (clock) hand* (from **montri**, *to point out, show*).
tenilo, *handle* (from **teni**, *to hold*).

THE EXPRESSION OF MEANS OR INSTRUMENTALITY.

64. The means or instrumentality through which an act is accomplished is expressed by use of the preposition **per**:

Oni kudras per kudrilo, *one sews by means of (with) a needle.*
La birdoj flugas per flugiloj, *the birds fly by (with) wings.*
Li amuzas sin per tiuj bildoj, *he amuses himself with (by) those pictures.*
Mi trovis ĝin per via helpo, *I found it by (through) your help.*

Vocabulary.

akra, sharp.	**najbaro**, neighbour.
buŝo, mouth.	**per**, by means of (64).
dekstra, right (not left).	**supo**, soup.
ĉi (see 60).	**telero**, plate.
forko, fork.	**terpomo**, potato.
helpo, help.	**ties**, that one's (62).
kafo, coffee.	**tranĉi**, to cut.
kulero, spoon.	**tre**, very, exceedingly.
mano, hand.	**viando**, meat.

LA MANĜO.

Hieraŭ mi miris ĉu mi havos bonan manĝon en la domo de mia amiko. Sed mi opiniis ke mi havos tre bonan manĝon, ĉar mia amiko ŝatas doni bonajn manĝojn al siaj amikoj. Oni metis tre bonan supon antaŭ mi, kaj mi manĝis tiun per granda kulero. Post la supo mi havis viandon. Ĉi tiun mi tenis per forko, kaj tranĉis per akra tranĉilo. La forko, tranĉilo kaj kulero estas manĝiloj. Mi havis ne nur viandon, sed ankaŭ novajn terpomojn. Mi tranĉis tiujn ĉi per la tranĉilo, sed mi metis ilin en la buŝon per forko. Mi tenis la forkon en la dekstra mano, kaj metis la tranĉilon trans mian teleron. Oni bezonas akran tranĉilon, sed oni ne bezonas tre akran forkon. Post la viando kaj la terpomoj, oni donis al mi freŝajn maturajn ĉerizojn. Ili kuŝis sur granda telero, kaj havis belan koloron. Ilia gusto estis ankaŭ bona. Mi preskaŭ ne diris ke mi ankaŭ havis kafon. Mi parolos morgaŭ al mia

---

[16] The root of a word is that part of it which contains the essential meaning, and to which the verb endings **-i**, **-as**, **-is**, **-os**, the noun ending **-o**, the adjective ending **-a**, etc., are attached, when no suffix intervenes. Thus, **vir-** is the root of **viro** and of **virino**; **kur-** is the root of **kuri**, etc.

amiko pri lia kafo, kaj laŭdos ĝin. Post la manĝo, najbaro de mia amiko venis en ĉi ties domon, kaj ili parolis al mi pri siaj novaj domoj. Per la helpo de sia patro, mia amiko konstruos grandan domon. Lia najbaro volas konstrui belan sed ne tre grandan domon. Ties nova domo estos bela, sed mi opinias ke mi preferos ĉi ties domon. Mia amiko volis doni almenaŭ kafon al sia najbaro, sed li diris ke li ne volas trinki kafon. Tamen li volis persikon. Li tenis tiun en la mano, kaj manĝis tiun.

SENTENCES FOR TRANSLATION.

1. The birds have very strong wings on their bodies, but they do not have hands. 2. They will build their nests, and sing about the young birds. 3. Those children were talking to me yesterday about their cat. 4. They said that it likes to catch and eat sparrows. 5. Tomorrow it will hide (itself) behind a tree, and will catch a young sparrow. 6. The children will gather peaches in that-person's garden, and will put them upon a plate. 7. They will shake the whole tree by means of a branch. 8. The sweet fruit above them will fall upon the soft green grass. 9. The children wondered whether the cherries were ripe. 10. They seem almost ripe, and tomorrow the children will pick (gather) them, with the help of their father. 11. It is said (54) that the grain in that-man's field very [much] needs rain. 12. People also think that the flowers will wither, for (because) it did not rain yesterday or today. 13. My careful young friend will carry an umbrella in his hand tomorrow, because he fears the rain. 14. He sees those gray clouds in (on) the sky. 15. He holds the umbrella by its handle. 16. The weathercock is an indicator concerning the weather. 17. One eats meat with a fork, and soup with a spoon. 18. One holds the spoon in the right hand. 19. A knife is sharp, but one does not need a sharp fork. 20. We shall have a very good meal, and also very good coffee.

LESSON XV.

THE DEMONSTRATIVE ADJECTIVE.—ADVERBS DE-
FINED AND CLASSIFIED.—FORMATION OF OPPO-
SITES.—LA RUZA JUNA VIRO.

THE DEMONSTRATIVE ADJECTIVE.

65. The demonstrative adjective related to the demonstrative pronoun **tiu** (56)
is **tia**, *that kind of, that sort of, such:*

Tia floro estas bela, *that kind of a flower is beautiful.*
Mi ŝatas tian viandon, *I like that sort of meat.*
Tiaj najbaroj estas agrablaj, *such (that kind of) neighbors are pleasant.*
Mi volas aŭdi tiajn birdojn, *I wish to hear such birds.*

ADVERBS DEFINED AND CLASSIFIED.

66. An adverb is a word which modifies the meaning of a verb, adjective, another adverb, or phrase. It may express manner, time, degree, negation, etc. Adverbs are either primary, as "now," "almost," or derived, as "glad-ly," "sweet-ly,"
The Esperanto primary adverbs given in this and in preceding lessons may be
classified as follows:

(a) Temporal Adverbs (expressing time).

baldaŭ, soon.   **morgaŭ**, tomorrow.
hieraŭ, yesterday.   **nun**, now.
hodiaŭ, today.   **tuj**, immediately.

(b) Adverbs of Degree.

almenaŭ, at least.   **preskaŭ**, almost.
nur, merely.   **tre**, very, much.

(c) Adverbs Expressing Other Ideas.

addition: **ankaŭ**, *also.*   emphasis: **eĉ**, *even.*
interrogation: **ĉu**, (**30**).   affirmation: **jes**, *yes.*
proximity: **ĉi**, (**60**).   negation: **ne**, *not, no,* (**27**).

a. An adverb usually precedes, but may also follow, the word or words which
it modifies. It must be so placed as to leave no doubt about which of two words
or word-groups it is intended to modify. Thus, **mi preskaŭ volis havi tiun** clearly means *I almost wished to have that;* but **mi volis preskaŭ havi tiun** might mean
either "I *almost wished* to have that," or more probably "I wished *almost to have*

that." An example of permissible variation in the position of adverbs is shown in questions to which an affirmative answer is expected. Such questions may be put in the form of a statement, followed by **ĉu ne** (instead of having **ĉu** introduce the sentence, with **ne** in its normal position):

Li venos, ĉu ne? *He will come, will he not?*
La vetero estas bela, ĉu ne? *The weather is beautiful, is it not?*
Vi aŭdis tiun diron, ĉu ne? *You heard that remark, did you not?*

FORMATION OF OPPOSITES.

67. If the meaning of a word is such that it can have a direct opposite, such opposite may be formed from it by use of the prefix **mal-**:[17]

malalta, *low, short* (from **alta**, *high, tall*).
malamiko, *enemy* (from **amiko**, *friend*).
maldekstra, *left* (from **dekstra**, *right*).
malhelpi, *to hinder* (from **helpi**, *to help*).
maljuna, *aged, old* (from **juna**, *young*).
malnova, *old, not new* (from **nova**, *new*).

VOCABULARY.

dum, during.	**povi**, to be able.
eĉ, even.	**preni**, to take.
gardi, to guard.	**propono**, proposal.
helpi, to help, to aid.	**respondi**, to answer.
honti, to be ashamed.	**ruza**, sly, cunning.
kara, dear.	**ŝteli**, to steal.
kontenta, satisfied.	**tia**, that kind of (65).
kuraĝa, courageous.	**tuj**, immediately.
nokto, night.	**voĉo**, voice.

LA RUZA JUNA VIRO.

Ruza juna viro kaj bona maljuna viro iris trans dezerton. Tiu havis nigran ĉevalon, ĉi tiu havis blankan ĉevalon. "Vi gardos niajn ĉevalojn dum la nokto, ĉu ne?" diris la juna viro per dolĉa voĉo al sia amiko, "Ĉar dum la nokto oni ne povos vidi mian nigran ĉevalon, sed malamikoj povos tuj vidi vian blankan ĉevalon. Oni povos ŝteli tian ĉevalon, ĉar vi estas maljuna kaj malforta, kaj ne povos malhelpi malamikojn." Tia propono ne ŝajnis agrabla al la maljuna viro. Li ne estis kontenta, tamen li ne volis perdi sian ĉevalon, ĉar li estis malriĉa. Li diris al si ke li donos sian blankan ĉevalon al la juna viro, kaj prenos ties nigran ĉevalon. Tuj li diris al ĉi tiu "Sed per via helpo mi ne perdos mian ĉevalon: mi donos la mian al vi, kaj prenos vian ĉevalon. La via estas malbela, sed ĝi estas almenaŭ nigra; vi donos ĝin al mi, ĉu ne?" "Jes," respondis la ruza juna viro, kaj li donis sian nigran ĉevalon al tiu, kaj prenis la blankan ĉevalon. "Nun," diris la maljuna viro, "Vi estas kuraĝa kaj forta, kaj vi gardos la ĉevalojn, ĉu ne? Vi povos malhelpi malamikojn per tiu granda akra

---

[17] *Cf.* English *malcontent*, "discontented," *maladroit*, "clumsy."

tranĉilo, kaj oni ne povos ŝteli vian blankan ĉevalon." La ruza juna viro ne hontis. Li respondis "Mia kara amiko, mi nun dormos, ĉar oni ne ŝtelos blankan ĉevalon. Mi povos vidi tian ĉevalon dum la nokto, kaj malhelpi malamikojn. Sed tiu ĉevalo via (*that horse of yours*) havas la koloron de la nokto, kaj eĉ nun oni povas ŝteli ĝin." La malkontenta maljuna viro diris per kolera voĉo "Ĉu vi ne hontas pri tia propono?" Tamen la ruza juna viro tuj komencis dormi, kaj la maljuna viro gardis la ĉevalojn dum la tuta nokto.

SENTENCES FOR TRANSLATION.
(Words to be formed with the prefix mal- are italicised.)

1. Does one eat potatoes and meat with a fork or a spoon? 2. One puts soup into the mouth by means of a spoon. 3. One cuts fruit with a knife, and puts the fruit upon a plate. 4. The coffee was *cold*, and I was much *dissatisfied*. 5. My knife was *dull*, nevertheless I almost immediately cut my (the) *left* hand. 6. I was ashamed, but I think that the handle of that knife was very *short*. 7. The grass is *wet* today, and I fear that we shall not be able to take a walk, even in that *small* park. 8. I *dislike* to go-walking upon the *hard* streets. 9. The courageous young man and his *aged* friend talked about their *enemies*. 10. They wished to be careful about their horses. 11. The young man was very sly, and wished to sleep during the night. 12. He said that one can steal a black horse during the *dark* night. 13. He said that either (*aŭ*) he or the *old* man would guard the horses. 14. The *old* man answered that he would give to him his [own] white horse. 15. He took that one's black horse. 16. He was ashamed, and was very angry at his *faithless* friend. 17. But he *stayed-awake*, and guarded the horses.

LESSON XVI.

THE DEMONSTRATIVE ADVERB OF PLACE.—ACCOM-
PANIMENT.—THE ADVERB FOR.—THE MEANING OF
POVI.—MALAMIKOJ EN LA DEZERTO.

THE DEMONSTRATIVE ADVERB OF PLACE.

68. The demonstrative adverbs of place related to the pronouns **tiu** and **ĉi tiu** are **tie**, *there, in (at) that place*, and **ĉi tie**, *here, in (at) this place*:

La telero estas tie, *the plate is there (in that place).*
La libroj kuŝas ĉi tie, *the books lie here (in this place).*
Mi trovis vin tie kaj lin tie ĉi, *I found you there and him here.*
Tie la vetero ŝajnas tre agrabla, *there the weather seems very pleasant.*

69. If the verb in the sentence expresses motion toward the place indicated by **tie** or **ĉi tie**, the ending **-n** is added to the adverb (46), forming **tien**, *thither, there*, and **ĉi tien**, *hither, here*:

Li iros tien, *he will go there (thither).*
Mi venis ĉi tien, *I came here (hither).*
Ni estis tie, kaj venis ĉi tien, *we were there and came here (hither).*

ACCOMPANIMENT.

70. Accompaniment or association is expressed by the preposition **kun**, *with, along with*:[18]

La viro venis kun sia amiko, *the man came with his friend.*
Mi promenos kun vi, *I shall go walking with you.*
La knabo kun tiu viro estas lia frato, *the boy with that man is his brother.*

---

[18] **Kun** must not be confused with **per** (64), which expresses instrumentality, although per may often be translated by English "with." The English preposition "with" may be said to have three rather clearly defined different meanings. In the linguistic history of this word, the original meaning was "against," still shown in *fight with, strive with, contend with, withstand*, etc. (*Cf.* German *widerstreiten*, to strive with, *widerhalten*, to resist, etc.) Gradually this word "with" usurped the meaning of the original preposition "mid," expressing association or accompaniment (*cf.* German *mit*, "with", which it crowded out of the language except in one unimportant compound). The word "by" was also encroaching upon "mid" from another direction, and so "mid's" successor "with" came to be interchangeable with "by" in expressing instrumentality. Thus, English "with" indicates opposition, accompaniment, or instrumentality, for which three senses Esperanto has the three prepositions **kontraŭ**, **kun**, and **per**, respectively.

THE ADVERB FOR.

71. The adverb **for**, *away*, may be used independently, as **Li iris for de mi**, *he went away from me*, but it is more frequently used as a prefix[19] to give a sense of departure, loss or somewhat forcible removal:

foriri, *to go away, to depart.*
forkuri, *to run away, to escape.*
forlasi, *to leave alone, to abandon, to desert.*
formanĝi, *to eat away, to eat up.*
forpreni, *to take away, to remove.*
fortrinki, *to drink away, to drink up.*

THE MEANING OF POVI.

72. The verb **povi**, to be able, is used to translate English *can*, which is defective, that is, does not occur in all of the forms a verb may have:

Mi povas paroli, *I am able to talk, I can talk.*
Mi povis paroli, *I was able to talk, I could talk.*
Mi povos paroli, *I shall be able to talk*, — — —.
Mi volas povi paroli, *I wish to be able to talk*, — — —.

VOCABULARY.

el, *out of, out.*	**peli**, *to drive, to chase.*
ĉirkaŭ, *around, roundabout.*	**poŝo**, *pocket.*
for, *away* (71).	**rajdi**, *to ride.*
frua, *early.*	**rapidi**, *to hasten.*
glavo, *sword.*	**resti**, *to remain, to stay.*
horo, *hour.*	**saĝa**, *wise.*
kun, *with* (70).	**tie**, *there* (68).
lasi, *to leave.*	**voki**, *to call.*

MALAMIKOJ EN LA DEZERTO.

Juna viro kaj lia saĝa patro volis iri trans la dezerton, kun siaj amikoj. La amikoj estis fortaj, kaj la juna viro estis tre kuraĝa. Ili restis en malgranda urbo dum la nokto, kaj forrajdis kun tiuj amikoj. La patro kaj la filo opiniis ke la amikoj kun ili povos helpi per siaj akraj glavoj. Ili opiniis ke ili povos forpeli la malamikojn. Eĉ en la dezerto oni trovas malamikojn. Tiaj malamikoj forprenas la monon de bonaj viroj. La juna viro estis kontenta, ĉar li estis kun la amikoj. La maljuna viro estis kontenta ĉar li estis kun sia filo. Baldaŭ la nokto venis. Estis tre malluma tie en la dezerto, kaj ili preskaŭ ne povis vidi. Dum la fruaj horoj de la nokto la patro aŭdis voĉojn, kaj preskaŭ tuj li vidis la malamikojn. La ruzaj malbonaj viroj rapidis tien, kaj vokis la maljunan viron. La malkuraĝaj amikoj de la patro kaj filo nek restis tie, nek helpis forpeli la malamikojn. Ili tuj forkuris. La malamikoj staris ĉirkaŭ la patro, kaj forpuŝis lin de lia ĉevalo. La filo volis malhelpi ilin, sed li ne povis. Li povis

---

[19] *Cf.* the prefix *for-* in English "forfend," *to keep away, to avert,* "forbid," *to exclude from, to command against,* "forbear," *to refrain from,* etc.

nur resti kun la patro, kaj gardi lin tie kontraŭ la glavoj de la malamikoj. Baldaŭ la malamikoj komencis forpreni la monon el la poŝoj de la saĝa maljuna viro. La kolera filo diris per maldolĉa (*bitter*) voĉo "Ĉu vi ne hontas? Ĉu vi lasos al ni nek la ĉevalojn nek nian monon?" Sed la malamikoj respondis "Ne, ni lasos al vi nek la ĉevalojn nek la monon. Ni ne estas malsaĝaj." Post tiu diro ili tuj forrapidis, kaj prenis kun si la ĉevalojn.

SENTENCES FOR TRANSLATION.

1. The foolish friends of the young man and his aged father did not stay with them. 2. They did not help them with their swords, but ran away at once (*tuj*), and were not ashamed. 3. The old man heard disagreeable voices behind him, and soon he saw the enemy. 4. The enemy called them, and hastened there (69). 5. Those sly bad men took the money out of the pockets of the courageous young man. 6. They stood around him, and also around his father. 7. The father and son could not even guard their horses. 8. The enemy did not leave (to) these their horses, but took both the horses and the money. 9. Soon the enemy rode away, during the late hours of the night. 10. The father and son were angry and dissatisfied. 11. They said "We fear and dislike such men." 12. The father said "By the help of our neighbors we can (*povos*) find those bad men, and drive them away, out of the desert." 13. The son replied, "Dear Father, such a proposal seems good, and I will help with my long sharp sword. 14. But we are now in the desert, and the road to the city is long. 15. We cannot ride thither, but we can walk thither. 16. Can you not hasten, with (*per*) my help?" 17. The wise old man answered, "Yes, my son, with such help I can walk thither."

LESSON XVII.

THE DEMONSTRATIVE TEMPORAL ADVERB.—COMPAR-
ISON OF ADJECTIVES.—MANNER AND CHARACTER-
ISTIC.—DIRI, PAROLI AND RAKONTI.—FREDERIKO
GRANDA KAJ LA JUNA SERVISTO.

THE DEMONSTRATIVE TEMPORAL ADVERB.

73. The demonstrative temporal adverb related to the demonstrative pronoun **tiu** is **tiam**, *then, at that time:*

Tiam li rajdos al la urbo, *then he will ride to the city.*
Nun ili estas saĝaj, sed tiam ili estis malsaĝaj, *now they are wise, but at that time they were foolish.*

COMPARISON OF ADJECTIVES.

74. An adjective may have three degrees, *positive, comparative* and *superlative.* English has various ways of forming the comparative and superlative degrees (as by the suffixes *-er, -est*, the adverbs *more, most*, and irregular methods as in *good, better, best,* etc.). Esperanto has only one method, using the adverbs **pli**, *more*, and **plej**, *most:*

Positive.	Comparative.	Superlative.
bela, *beautiful*	**pli bela**, *more beautiful*	**plej bela**, *most beautiful.*
bona, *good*	**pli bona**, *better*	**plej bona**, *best.*
malbona, *bad*	**pli malbona**, *worse*	**plej malbona**, *worst.*
saĝa, *wise*	**pli saĝa**, *wiser*	**plej saĝa**, *wisest.*

75. The preposition **el** is used with words expressing the group or class out of which a superlative is selected and mentioned:

Li estas la plej juna el tiuj, *he is the youngest of (out of) those.*
Vi estas la plej feliĉa el ni, *you are the happiest of us.*
Tiu estis la plej ruza el la viroj, *that one was the craftiest of the men.*

MANNER AND CHARACTERISTIC.

76. The actions or feelings which accompany an act or state, or the characteristic which permanently accompanies a person or thing, may be expressed by a substantive with the preposition **kun**:[20]

Li prenis ĝin kun la plej granda zorgo, *he took it with the greatest care.*
Mi aŭdis lin kun intereso kaj plezuro, *I heard him with interest and pleasure.*
Ŝi estas virino kun bona gusto, *she is a woman with (of) good taste.*
Mi havas ĉevalon kun forta korpo, *I have a horse with a strong body.*

DIRI, PAROLI AND RAKONTI.

77. The verbs **diri**, *to say*, **paroli**, *to talk, to speak*, and **rakonti**, *to relate*, having in common the general idea of speech or expression, must not be confused in use:

Mi diris al vi ke pluvas, *I said to (told) you that it was raining.*
Mi diris ĝin al vi, *I said it to you (I told you).*
Mi parolis al vi pri ĝi, *I talked (spoke) to you about it.*
Mi rakontis ĝin al vi, *I related (told) it to you.*

VOCABULARY.

ami, *to love.*
ekster, *outside (of).*
Frederiko, *Frederick.*
gratuli, *to congratulate.*
intereso, *interest.*
letero, *letter.*
plej, *most* (**74**).
plezuro, *pleasure.*

pli, *more* (**74**).
plumo, *pen.*
rakonti, *to relate* (**77**).
reĝo, *king.*
servisto, *servant.*
skribi, *to write.*
tiam, *then* (**73**).
zorgo, *care.*

FREDERIKO GRANDA KAJ LA JUNA SERVISTO.

Hieraŭ mi legis interesan libron pri Frederiko Granda (*the Great*). En ĝi oni rakontas ke la reĝo kun plezuro legis aŭ skribis per sia plumo, dum malfruaj horoj de la nokto. Agrabla juna knabo, la plej juna el la servistoj, tiam restis ekster la pordo. Ĉar la reĝo legis plej interesan novan libron, li ne opiniis ke la horo estas malfrua. Li vokis sian malgrandan serviston, sed la knabo, nek venis nek respondis. La reĝo iris tien, kaj trovis la knabon ekster la pordo. Li vidis ke la knabo dormas sur malalta seĝo. Tiam Frederiko Granda ne estis kolera, sed hontis ĉar li vokis la infanon. La reĝo Frederiko vidis leteron en la poŝo de la knabo. Tuj li prenis la leteron el lia poŝo, kaj rigardis ĝin. Ĝi estis letero al la servisto, de lia patrino. Ŝi ne estis riĉa virino, ŝi ŝajnis esti tre malriĉa. En ĉi tiu letero la patrino diris per la plumo ke ŝi amas la filon. Ŝi dankis lin ĉar li skribis al ŝi longan leteron. Ŝi ankaŭ dankis lin ĉar li donis al ŝi monon. La reĝo volis esti tre bona al tia filo. Kun la plej granda zorgo li metis monon el sia poŝo kun la letero kaj tiam lasis la leteron en ties poŝo. Tiam li formarŝis al sia ĉambro, kaj vokis la malgrandan serviston. La knabo tuj aŭdis, kaj rapidis tra la pordo. Li kuris trans la ĉambron, kaj staris antaŭ la reĝo.

---

[20] Sometimes the manner of an action may be expressed by the instrument of it, expressed by the preposition **per** with a substantive modified by an adjective:

Li kantis per dolĉa voĉo, *he sang with (by means of) a sweet voice.*
Vi puŝis min per forta mano, *you pushed me with a strong hand.*

"Ĉu vi dormis?" diris Frederiko Granda. "Jes, mi timas ke mi preskaŭ dormis," respondis la knabo, "kaj mi tre hontas." Tiam li metis la manon en la poŝon, kaj trovis la monon. Li ŝajnis pli malfeliĉa kaj diris kun granda timo "Malamiko metis ĉi tiun monon en mian poŝon! Oni opinios ke mi ŝtelis ĝin! Oni malamos min, kaj forpelos min!" Frederiko respondis, "Ne, mi donis ĝin al vi, ĉar mi amas bonajn knabojn. Mi gratulas vian patrinon, ĉar ŝi havas tian filon."

SENTENCES FOR TRANSLATION.

1. An interesting story is related (54) about Frederick the Great. 2. His youngest servant stayed outside of the door. 3. The king called him, and he hastened thither and stood before him. 4. Yesterday he did not hear the king. 5. The king called him, but he did not answer. 6. The king thought that the boy had gone away with the older servants, and he was angry. 7. He left his book on the table, and went to the door. 8. Then he saw that the little boy was sleeping there. 9. He looked at him with greater interest, and saw a letter in his pocket. 10. The letter was from the boy's mother. 11. He had written a letter to her, with his pen, and had given (to) her money, because she was poor. 12. He wrote longer letters with pleasure, because he was a most faithful son. 13. The king congratulated the mother of the boy, concerning such a son. 14. (The) king Frederick wished to be kinder (*pli bona*) to the boy. 15. He placed his book upon the table, near his sword, and talked to the little servant. 16. Then the older servants came, and stood around the king. 17. They walked with great care, and the younger servant did not hear them. 18. They loved the little boy, and wished to help him.

LESSON XVIII.

THE DEMONSTRATIVE ADVERB OF MOTIVE OR REA-
SON.—DERIVATION OF ADVERBS.— COMPARISON
OF WORDS EXPRESSING QUANTITY.—COMPARI-
SONS CONTAINING OL.— CAUSAL CLAUSES.—PRI
LA SEZONOJ.

THE DEMONSTRATIVE ADVERB OF MOTIVE OR REASON.

78. The demonstrative adverb of motive or reason, related to the demonstrative pronoun **tiu**, is **tial**, *therefore, for that reason, so*:

Tial la servisto foriris, *therefore the servant went away.*
Tial mi gratulis lin, *for that reason I congratulated him.*
Tial oni forpelis lin, *so they drove him away.*

DERIVATION OF ADVERBS.

79. Adverbs may be derived from roots whose meaning permits, by addition of the adverb-ending **-e**, as **feliĉe**, *happily*, **kolere**, *angrily*. The comparison of adverbs is similar to that of adjectives:

Positive.	Comparative.	Superlative.
saĝe, *wisely*	**pli saĝe**, *more wisely*	**plej saĝe**, *most wisely*
bone, *well*	**pli bone**, *better*	**plej bone**, *best*
malbone, *badly*	**pli malbone**, *worse*	**plej malbone**, *worst*
ruze, *slyly*	**pli ruze**, *more slyly*	**plej ruze**, *most slyly*

MALPLI AND MALPLEJ.

80. The opposites (67) of **pli** and **plej** are **malpli**, *less*, and **malplej**, *least*. Their use is similar to that of **pli** and **plej**. (These adverbs may also modify verbs):

Li estas malpli kuraĝa, *he is less courageous.*
Tiuj estis malplej akraj, *those were least sharp.*
La vento blovis malpli forte, *the wind blew less strongly.*
Li skribis malplej zorge, *he wrote least carefully.*
Mi malpli timas ilin, *I fear them less.*
Vi malplej bezonos helpon, *you will need help least.*

COMPARISON OF WORDS EXPRESSING QUANTITY.

81. Since in their precise sense the words **pli, malpli, plej, malplej**, express *degree*, a *quantitative* meaning is given by **multe**, *much*, in the desired degree of comparison:

multe, much	**pli multe**, more (in amount)	**plej multe**, most
	malpli multe, less "	**malplej multe**, least
malmulte, little	**pli malmulte**, less "	**plej malmulte**, least

COMPARISONS CONTAINING OL.

82. In a comparison made by the use of **pli** or **malpli**, the case used after **ol**, *than*, must indicate clearly the sense intended:

Mi amas ilin pli multe ol ŝin, *I love them more than* (I love) *her.*
Mi amas ilin pli multe ol ŝi, *I love them more than she* (loves them).
Vi helpis la viron malpli multe ol la knabo, *you helped the man less than the boy* (helped him).
Vi helpis la viron malpli multe ol la knabon, *you helped the man less than* (you helped) *the boy.*

CAUSAL CLAUSES.

83. A clause giving a cause or reason is introduced by **ĉar**, *because, for*, or by the combination **tial ke**, *for this reason that, because, for*:

Mi venis frue, ĉar mi volis vidi vin, *I came early, for I wished to see you.*
La floroj velkis tial, ke ne pluvis, *the flowers wilted for this reason, that it did not rain.*

VOCABULARY.

anstataŭ, *instead of.*	**multa**, *much* (**multaj**, *many*).
aprilo, *April.*	**ofta**, *frequent* (**ofte**, *often*).
aŭgusto, *August.*	**ol**, *than* (**82**).
jaro, *year.*	**printempo**, *spring* (season).
junio, *June.*	**tago**, *day.*
julio, *July.*	**sezono**, *season.*
majo, *May.*	**somero**, *summer.*
marto, *March.*	**tial**, *therefore* (**78**).
monato, *month.*	**vintro**, *winter.*

PRI LA SEZONOJ.

La vintro estas la malplej agrabla sezono el la tuta jaro. Neĝas tre multe, kaj tial oni nur malofte promenas, ĉar la stratoj estas tro malsekaj. Oni marŝas kun granda zorgo, kaj malrapide (*slowly*), tial ke oni ne volas fali kaj preskaŭ rompi la kolon. Oni zorge gardas sin tiam kontraŭ la malvarmaj nordaj ventoj. La manojn oni metas en la poŝojn, sed la vizaĝon oni ne povas bone gardi. Mi ne ŝatas resti ekster la domo dum tia vetero. Mi multe preferas sidi en varma luma ĉambro, kaj skribi leterojn per bona plumo. La monatoj de la printempo estas marto, aprilo kaj majo.

La bela printempo ŝajnas pli agrabla ol la vintro. Ĝiaj tagoj estas pli longaj kaj pli varmaj, ĝiaj ventoj blovas malpli forte. En ĉi tiu sezono la kampoj kaj arboj frue komencas montri plej belajn kolorojn. La birdoj konstruas siajn nestojn, kaj dolĉe kantas. Oni povas promeni sur la mola herbo, anstataŭ sur malsekaj malagrablaj stratoj. Pluvas pli multe en aprilo, tamen post la pluvo la herbo ŝajnas pli verda, kaj la nuboj baldaŭ forflugas de la blua ĉielo. Dum majo oni trovas violojn, kaj en junio oni vidas tre multajn rozojn. Sed la plej agrabla el la sezonoj estas la somero. Anstataŭ malvarmaj ventoj la somero havas la plej belan veteron, kun suda aŭ okcidenta ventoj. La longaj tagoj estas varmaj, sed la noktoj estas tute agrablaj. Tiam oni havas pli bonajn fruktojn ol dum la printempo. La monatoj de la somero estas junio, julio kaj aŭgusto. Mi plej ŝatas junion. Ĉu vi ŝatas ĝin pli multe ol mi? Ĉu vi ŝatas aŭguston pli multe ol julion?

SENTENCES FOR TRANSLATION.

1. I read a most interesting book about Frederick the Great. 2. It relates that he often stayed-awake and read with great interest during the later hours of the night. 3. His youngest servant was a small boy. 4. The king loved this boy more than [he loved] the older servants. 5. The winter is a less pleasant season than the spring, but the summer is more pleasant than that [season]. 6. During March the east winds blow most strongly, and shake the trees very much. 7. In April one needs his umbrella, for (the reason that) there are often clouds in the sky and it rains a great deal (very much). 8. The streets are very wet, but the water does not seem to wash them. 9. In May one begins to find sweet violets, and the birds in the trees above our heads sing very sweetly. 10. In June the most beautiful roses are seen (54). 11. July and August are the warmest months of the whole year. 12. The days are longer than the nights, and the weathercock shows west and south winds, instead of those disagreeable north and east winds. 13. One stays outside [of] the house then with greater pleasure, and goes walking in the parks. 14. I think that I like the summer better than you [do]. 15. Therefore I praise the summer more than you [do]. 16. However, I praise you more than [I praise] your younger brother. 17. He is less wise than you.

LESSON XIX.

JU AND DES IN COMPARISONS.—THE PREPOSITION INTER.—THE PREPOSITION PRO.— PREPOSITIONS WITH ADVERBS AND OTHER PREPOSITIONS.—LA AŬTUNO KAJ LA VINTRO.

JU AND DES IN COMPARISONS.

84. In clauses expressing a comparison between two objects, acts or states, the adverbial use of English "the ... the ..." (meaning "by how much ... by that much ...")[21] is rendered by the adverbs **ju** and **des**, respectively:

Ju pli bona li estas, des pli feliĉa li estos, *the better he is, the happier he will be.*
Ju pli ofte mi rigardas, des pli mi volas rigardi, *the oftener I look, the more I wish to look.*
Ju pli bele la luno brilas, des pli oni ŝatas la nokton, *the more beautifully the moon shines, the more one likes the night.*
Ju malpli pluvas, des pli la floroj velkas, *the less it rains, the more the flowers wither.*
Ju malpli multe vi helpas, des malpli multe mi laŭdos vin, *the less you help, the less I shall praise you.*
Ĉar vi helpis, mi des pli multe laŭdos vin, *because you helped, I shall praise you the (that much) more.*

THE PREPOSITION INTER.

85. In English, the preposition "between" is used in reference to two persons or things, and "among" in reference to three or more. As the difference in meaning is not essential, Esperanto has but the one preposition inter to express both *between* and *among:*

Li sidas inter vi kaj mi, *he is sitting between you and me.*
Li sidas inter siaj amikoj, *he is sitting among his friends.*
La monato majo estas inter aprilo kaj junio, *the month of May is between April and June.*
Inter tiuj libroj estas tre interesa libro, *among those books there is a very interesting book.*

THE PREPOSITION PRO.

----

[21] *Cf.* Shakespeare, As You Like It, V, II, 49, *By so much the more shall I tomorrow be at the height of heart-heaviness, by how much I shall think my brother happy in having what he wishes for.*

86. Cause or reason may be expressed not only by an adverb (78) or a clause (83), but also by use of the preposition **pro**, *because of, on account of, for the sake of, for.* It directs the thought away from the complement toward the action, feeling or state caused by it, or done in its interest or behalf:

La floroj velkas pro la seka vetero, *the flowers wilt because of the dry weather.*
Mi skribis la leteron pro vi, *I wrote the letter for you (for your sake).*
Pro tiuj nuboj mi timas ke pluvos, *on account of those clouds I fear that it will rain.*
Oni ŝatas ĉerizojn pro la dolĉa gusto, *people like cherries because of the sweet taste.*

PREPOSITIONS WITH ADVERBS AND OTHER PREPOSITIONS.

87. Prepositions may be used with adverbs or with prepositional phrases when the meaning permits:

La kato kuris el sub la tablo, *the cat ran out-from under the table.*
Li venos el tie, *he will come out of there.*
De nun li estos zorga, *from now he will be careful.*
Li staris dekstre de la vojo, *he stood on the right of the road.*
Mi iros for de ĉi tie, *I shall go away from here.*

VOCABULARY.

aŭtuno, *autumn, fall.*
decembro, *December.*
des, (see **84**).
februaro, *February.*
glacio, *ice.*
inter, *between, among* (**85**).
januaro, *January.*
ju, (see **84**).
kovri, *to cover.*

neĝo, *snow.*
novembro, *November.*
nuda, *bare, naked.*
oktobro, *October.*
pro, *because of* (**86**).
rikolti, *to harvest.*
rivero, *river.*
septembro, *September.*
tero, *ground, earth.*

LA AŬTUNO KAJ LA VINTRO.

La sezonoj de la jaro estas la vintro, la printempo, la somero, kaj la aŭtuno. La aŭtuno estas inter la somero kaj la vintro. Ĝiaj monatoj estas septembro, oktobro kaj novembro. En septembro oni povas kolekti maturajn fruktojn. Tiam ankaŭ oni rikoltas la flavan grenon de la kampoj. Dum ĉi tiu monato kaj dum oktobro la folioj sur la branĉoj komencas esti ruĝaj kaj flavaj, anstataŭ verdaj. La herbo velkas, kaj bruna tapiŝo ŝajnas kovri la teron. Baldaŭ la folioj falas al la tero, kaj en novembro la arboj estas tute nudaj. Pli aŭ malpli frue neĝas. La glacio ofte kovras la akvon en la riveroj, kaj restas sur la stratoj kaj la vojoj. La mola blanka neĝo kovras la teron, kaj kuŝas sur la branĉoj de la arboj. Tiam, pro la fortaj ventoj, ĝi falas de la branĉoj al la tero. La birdoj frue lasas tian veteron, kaj flugas de ĉi tie al pli sudaj kampoj kaj arboj. Ili ne povas resti, pro la malvarmaj tagoj kaj noktoj. Ili malŝatas la neĝon kaj la glacion pli multe ol ni. Ju pli multe neĝas; des pli malofte ni volas promeni.

Ni preferas resti en la domo, anstataŭ ekster ĝi. Ju pli ni rigardas la nudajn branĉojn de la arboj, des pli malagrabla ŝajnas la vintro. Tamen la junaj infanoj tre ŝatas tian veteron, kaj ju pli neĝas, kaj ju pli forte la norda vento blovas, des malpli ili estas kontentaj en la domo. Ili volas kuri sur la neĝo, ĉirkaŭ la arboj kaj inter ili, kun siaj junaj amikoj. Ili povas bone amuzi sin per la neĝo. La monatoj de la vintro estas decembro, januaro kaj februaro. Ĝi estas la plej malvarma sezono.

SENTENCES FOR TRANSLATION.

1. September, October and November are the months of autumn. 2. In these months, people harvest the yellow grain and gather various fruits. 3. The leaves on the trees around us begin to have red and yellow colors. 4. They begin to fall from the branches and lie upon the ground. 5. The more strongly the cold north wind blows through the branches, the sooner the leaves fall from there. 6. They lie under the bare trees, with the brown grass. 7. The sooner it snows, the sooner the ground will seem to have a white carpet. 8. The snow will completely (*tute*) cover the grass during the months of the winter. 9. These months are December, January and February. 10. From that time (*de tiam*) the ice and snow will cover the roads, and altogether (*tute*) hide them. 11. There will often be ice on the water of the river. 12. We like this season of the year more than March, April and May. 13. We like it even more than the summer. 14. The months of the latter (62) are June, July and August. 15. The summer is the warmest season of the entire year. 16. Therefore we often say that the summer is the pleasantest season. 17. Because of its many pleasures, the summer is dear to me. 18. It is between the spring and the autumn.

LESSON XX.

THE DEMONSTRATIVE ADVERB OF MANNER AND DEGREE.

88. The demonstrative adverb of manner and degree, related to the demonstrative pronoun **tiu**, is **tiel**, *in that (this) manner, in such a way, thus, so*. Like English "thus," "so," **tiel** may modify adjectives and other adverbs, by indicating degree:

Ĉu oni tiel helpas amikon? *Does one help a friend in that (this) way?*
Mi ĝin skribis tiel, *I wrote it thus (in such a way).*
La vetero estas tiel bela, *the weather is so beautiful.*
Tiel mallonge li parolis, *thus briefly he spoke.*
Mi trovis tiel belan floron, *I found such a beautiful flower.*
Li prenis tiel multe, *he took that much (so much).*

PREPOSITIONS EXPRESSING TIME-RELATIONS.

89. The relations which prepositions express may be of various kinds.[22] As in English, a certain number of prepositions primarily expressing place may also express time-relations. Such prepositions are **antaŭ, ĉirkaŭ, de, en, ĝis, inter, post,** and **je** (whose use in other than time-relations will be explained later):

Mi foriros ĉirkaŭ junio, *I shall depart about June.*
De tiu horo mi estis via amiko, *from that hour I was your friend.*
Li ne parolis al mi de tiu semajno, *he did not speak to me since from) that week.*
En la tuta monato ne neĝis, *it did not snow in (at any time within) the entire month.*
Mi dormis ĝis malfrua horo, *I slept until (up to) a late hour.*
Ĝis nun li ne vidis vin, *until now he did not see you.*
Inter marto kaj junio mi iros tien, *between March and June I shall go there.*
Je malfrua horo li foriris, *at a late hour he went away.*
Mi iros tien je dimanĉo, *I shall go there on Sunday.*
Je tiu horo li vokis min, *at that hour he called me.*
Ŝi ne restis tie post julio, *she did not stay there after July.*
Post ne longe mi vokos vin, *soon (after not long) I shall call you.*

[22] As already shown, **kun** expresses accompaniment, **per** expresses instrumentality, **pro** expresses cause, **kontraŭ** expresses opposition, **anstataŭ** expresses substitution, **sur, apud, sub**, etc., express place, **dum** expresses time, etc.

90. When a definite date or point in time is expressed, **antaŭ** means "before." When used with an expression of an *amount* of time, it is to be translated by "ago" following the expression (not by "before" preceding it):

Antaŭ dimanĉo mi foriros, *before Sunday I shall go away.*
Mi vidis lin antaŭ tiu horo, *I saw him before that hour.*
Li skribos ĝin antaŭ la nova jaro, *he will write it before New Year.*
Antaŭ multaj jaroj mi trovis ĝin, *many years ago I found it.*
Mi rompis ĝin antaŭ longa tempo, *I broke it a long time ago.*
Antaŭ tre longe vi legis tiun libron, *you read that book very long ago.*
Li venis antaŭ ne longe, *he came recently (not long ago).*
Antaŭ malmultaj jaroj li forkuris, *a few years ago he escaped.*

VOCABULARY.

dimanĉo, *Sunday.*	**mateno,** *morning.*
energia, *energetic.*	**promeno,** *walk, promenade.*
frosto, *frost.*	**rakonto,** *story, narrative.*
je, *at, on* (89).	**ripozi,** *to rest, to repose.*
kota, *muddy.*	**semajno,** *week.*
labori, *to work, to labor.*	**tempo,** time.
laca, *tired, weary.*	**tiel,** *thus, so* (88)
lundo, *Monday.*	**tro,** *too, too much.*
mardo, *Tuesday.*	**vespero,** *evening.*

EN SEPTEMBRO.

Antaŭ multaj jaroj ni preferis resti en nia malgranda domo trans la rivero, dum la tuta aŭtuno. Sed nun ni restas tie nur ĝis oktobro. De aŭgusto ĝis oktobro la vetero estas tre agrabla tie, sed baldaŭ post tiu monato la fortaj ventoj blovas, kaj la folioj komencas fali. La frosto kovras la teron, kaj baldaŭ neĝas tre ofte. Ju pli nudaj estas la arboj, des pli malbelaj ili ŝajnas. La vetero antaŭ novembro ne estas tro malvarma, sed post tiu monato ni opinias ke la urbo estas pli agrabla ol domo inter kampoj kaj arboj, trans larĝa rivero. La frosto, neĝo kaj glacio kovras la teron en decembro, januaro kaj februaro. Sed la monato septembro ŝajnas tre agrabla, pro siaj multaj plezuroj. La viroj laboras energie en la kampoj, de la mateno ĝis la vespero. Ili rikoltas la flavan grenon, kaj kolektas la fruktojn. Sed je dimanĉo oni ne laboras tiel energie, sed dormas ĝis malfrua horo, tial ke je tiu tago oni ripozas. Je lundo oni komencas labori tre frue, kaj je mardo oni ankaŭ laboras energie. En septembro la vojoj ne estas tro kotaj, kaj longaj promenoj estas ofte agrablaj. Ju pli ofte mi promenas kun miaj amikoj, des pli multe mi ŝatas tiajn promenojn. Sed hieraŭ mi estis tre laca post la promeno, tial mi ripozis sur granda mola seĝo. Antaŭ ne longe la patro promenis kun mi, sed ni ne estis tiel lacaj je tiu tago. Ŝajnas ke ju pli ofte ni promenas, des malpli lacaj ni estas post la promenoj. Post ne longe mi estos pli forta.

SENTENCES FOR TRANSLATION.

1. Many years ago we had a small house across the river. 2. We did not remain

there during the entire year, but only in the warmer months of the summer. 3. Often we stayed until September or even until October. 4. My younger brothers and sisters amused themselves very well there from (the) morning until (the) evening. 5. They amused themselves among the flowers and trees, or went from there into the large fields. 6. Here the men work energetically, and harvest the ripe yellow grain. 7. Only on Sunday do they rest, because on that day one does not work. 8. Between August and November the men work more than in the winter. 9. In December and after that month they rest, for (83) from that time the frost, ice and snow cover the ground. 10. Because of the snow on the ground, long walks are not pleasant in the winter. 11. Recently (90) we went walking in the park across the river, but we were so tired after that walk! 12. The longer the walk is, the sooner one wishes to rest. 13. On Monday it rained, so (78) we read stories and wrote letters, in a pleasant light room in our house. 14. Before evening, however, the sun shone, and the streets were not so muddy. 15. On Tuesday these streets were almost dry, and soon the roads near the river and between the fields will also be dry. 16. A few years ago those roads were very good.

LESSON XXI.

THE ACCUSATIVE OF TIME.—ADVERBS AND THE AC-
CUSATIVE OF TIME.—THE PREPOSITION POR.—LA
SEZONOJ KAJ LA MONDO.

THE ACCUSATIVE OF TIME.

91. Duration of time and a date or point in time may be expressed not only by use of the prepositions **dum**, *during*, and **je**, *at, on*, but also (as in English) without the use of any preposition. When no preposition is used, the word or words indicating time are put in the accusative case:

Li restis tie la tutan semajnon (dum la tuta semajno), *he stayed there the whole week (during the whole week)*.
Ŝi estis feliĉa longan tempon (dum longa tempo), *she was happy a long time (during a long time; for a long time)*.
Ni rajdos tagon kaj nokton (dum tago kaj nokto), *we shall ride a day and a night (during a day and a night; for a day and a night)*.
Mi venis dimanĉon (je dimanĉo), *I came Sunday (on Sunday)*.
Tiun horon (je tiu horo), li forkuris, *that hour (at that hour) he escaped*.

92. Although generally preferable, an accusative construction must be carefully placed, or avoided altogether, if confusion with other accusatives (expressing direction of motion, direct object, etc.) might result:

Mi volas iri Bostonon je lundo, *I wish to go to Boston on Monday*.
Mi volas iri al Bostono lundon, *I Washington, D. C.,*
August 3, 1910. wish to go to Boston Monday.
Lundon mi volas iri Bostonon, *Monday I wish to go to Boston*.

ADVERBS AND THE ACCUSATIVE OF TIME.

93. An accusative of time, as well as a temporal adverb, may further define or be defined by another expression of time:

Li venis longan tempon antaŭ tiu horo, *he came a long time before that hour*.
Jaron post jaro ili restis tie, *year after year they stayed there*.
hodiaŭ matene, *this morning*.
hodiaŭ vespere, *this evening*.
hodiaŭ nokte, *tonight*.
hieraŭ vespere, *last evening*.
hieraŭ nokte, *last night*.

dimanĉon matene, *Sunday morning.*
lundon vespere, *Monday evening.*
mardon nokte, *Tuesday night.*

94. An accusative of time does not necessarily imply that the act or state mentioned occurs oftener than the instance cited. An adverb from the same root usually gives an idea of frequency or repetition:

Li iros al ilia domo dimanĉon, *he will go to their house Sunday.*
Li iras al ilia domo dimanĉe, *he goes to their house Sundays.*
Li laboris tagon kaj nokton, *he worked a day and a night.*
Li laboras tage kaj nokte, *he works day and night (by day and by night).*

THE PREPOSITION POR.

95. The object or purpose with reference to which an act is performed or a condition exists is expressed by the preposition **por**, *for*. It directs the thought toward its complement, contrasting thus with **pro** (86):

Mi havas libron por vi, *I have a book for you.*
Mi ne havas la tempon por tiel longa promeno, *I have not the time for so long a (such a long) walk.*
Ili faris ĝin por via plezuro, *they did it for your pleasure.*

VOCABULARY.

brila, *brilliant.*	**merkredo**, *Wednesday.*
Dio, *God.*	**mezo**, *middle.*
dividi, *to divide.*	**mondo**, *world.*
fari, *to make.*	**paci**, *to be at peace.*
forgesi, *to forget.*	**por**, *for* (95).
ĝojo, *joy.*	**plori**, *to weep.*
konstanta, *constant.*	**preta**, *ready.*
kvieta, *quiet, calm.*	**ridi**, *to laugh.*
lando, *land, country.*	**riproĉi**, *to reproach.*

LA SEZONOJ KAJ LA MONDO.

Antaŭ tre longa tempo Dio faris la mondon. Li vidis ke la floroj havas belajn kolorojn, ke la arboj estas altaj kaj verdaj. Tiam li vokis la sezonojn kaj diris "Belan mondon mi faris por vi. Ĉu vi gardos ĝin tage kaj nokte, kaj estos tre zorgaj pri ĝi?" La sezonoj respondis "Jes," kaj ridis pro ĝojo. Mallongan tempon ili ŝajnis esti tre feliĉaj inter la arboj kaj floroj de la nova mondo. Sed ne multajn semajnojn ili tiel zorge gardis la mondon. Ili komencis malpaci (*quarrel*) inter si, de la mateno ĝis la vespero, kaj ofte forgesis la arbojn kaj florojn. Ju pli ili malpacis, des malpli zorge ili gardis la mondon. La malkonstanta printempo ne ŝatis la kvietan vintron, kaj ploris pri la malvarma neĝo. La varma brila somero diris ke la aŭtuno estas tro malbrila. La laca aŭtuno volis ripozi, kaj riproĉis la malkonstantan printempon pri ĉi ties kota vetero. Pli kaj pli multe ili malpacis, kaj post ne longe ili tute ne restis amikoj. Tiam la aŭtuno diris "Mi ne povas pli longan tempon labori kun vi pro la mondo. Niaj gustoj estas tro diversaj. Tial hodiaŭ matene ni dividos la mondon inter ni." La vintro respondis "Bone! Mi estas preta," kaj la somero kaj la printempo ridis pro ĝojo. Tiun tagon ili dividis la mondon inter si. La vintro konstruis sian domon en la plej nordaj kaj sudaj landoj. Tie la frosto, neĝo kaj glacio kovras la tutan landon, dum la tuta jaro. La brila energia somero prenis por si la mezon de la mondo. Tial la vetero tie estas plej varma kaj brila. La aŭtuno kaj la printempo prenis por si la landojn inter la vintro kaj la somero. Tial la vetero estas nek tro varma nek tro malvarma en ĉi tiuj landoj. Tiam la sezonoj rakontis al Dio ke ili tiel dividis la mondon inter si.

SENTENCES FOR TRANSLATION.

1. Tuesday my brother heard an interesting story, and Wednesday evening after a pleasant walk he related it to me. 2. The story is, that many years ago God made the beautiful new world, and gave it to the seasons. 3. They laughed for joy, and said that they would guard it well. 4. They were ready for pleasure, and also were willing (*volis*) to work energetically for-the-sake-of the new young world. 5. Almost a year they were happy, but these seasons were too diverse, and could not long remain friends. 6. The brilliant summer wept and reproached the tired autumn. 7. The autumn preferred to rest, and disliked the muddy weather of the inconstant spring. 8. The quiet winter concealed itself beneath the frost and soft white snow, and wished to sleep. 9. The longer they kept the world among them, the more they quarreled. 10. Soon the autumn made the proposition, "We will divide the world." 11. Immediately that morning the seasons divided the world among themselves. 12. The northern and southern lands now belong to the winter, and the middle of the world belongs to the summer. 13. The spring and autumn took for themselves those lands between the winter and summer.

LESSON XXII.

CLAUSES EXPRESSING DURATION OF TIME.—CLAUS-
ES EXPRESSING ANTICIPATION.—THE INFINITIVE
WITH ANSTATAŬ, POR, ANTAŬ OL.—THE EXPRES-
SION OF A PART OF THE WHOLE. —DIOGENO KAJ
ALEKSANDRO GRANDA.

CLAUSES EXPRESSING DURATION OF TIME.

96. The time during which an act takes place or a condition exists may be expressed not only by an adverb or accusative of time (91), or by use of the preposition **dum**, but also by a clause introduced by **dum**:

Li venis dum vi forestis, *he came while (during-the-time-that) you were away.*
Dum la sezonoj malpacis, ili forgesis pri la mondo, *while the seasons quarreled, they forgot about the world.*
Ni ridas pro ĝojo dum neĝas, *we laugh for joy while it is snowing.*

CLAUSES EXPRESSING ANTICIPATION.

97. A clause expressing an action or condition as preceding or anticipating that of the main verb is introduced by **antaŭ ol**:

Mi foriros antaŭ ol vi venos, *I shall depart before you (will) come.*
Antaŭ ol vi riproĉis lin, li ne ploris, *before you reproached him, he did not weep.*
Vi ploris antaŭ ol vi ridis, *you wept before (sooner than) you laughed.*

THE INFINITIVE WITH ANSTATAŬ, POR, ANTAŬ OL.

98. An infinitive may be substantively[23] used with **anstataŭ** to express substitution, with **por** to express purpose (*Cf.* Old English "But what went ye out *for to see*," *Matt. xi, 8*), and with **antaŭ ol** to express anticipation.[24] It is usually translated by the English infinitive in *-ing*:

Anstataŭ resti li foriris, *instead of staying he went away.*
Vi malhelpas anstataŭ helpi min, *you hinder instead of helping me.*
Ni venis por helpi vin, *we came to help (in order to help) you.*

---

[23] *Substantive* is the general name for nouns and pronouns, that is, for words which indicate persons, things, etc., and may be used as subject or object of a verb, complement of a preposition, etc.

[24] The infinitive may be used with **antaŭ ol** if its subject is the same as the subject of the main verb. Otherwise the construction explained in **97** must be used.

Mi estas preta por iri merkredon, *I am ready to go (for going) Wednesday.*
Li havos tro multe por fari, *he will have too much to do.*
Mi laboros antaŭ ol ripozi, *I shall work before resting.*
Antaŭ ol foriri, li dankis min, *before going away, he thanked me.*
Dio faris la mondon antaŭ ol doni ĝin al la sezonoj, *God made the world before giving it to the seasons.*

THE EXPRESSION OF A PART OF THE WHOLE.

99. After nouns indicating a quantity or portion of some indefinite whole, the substantive expressing that indefinite whole is preceded by the preposition **da**, *of*:

Estas skatolo da ĉerizoj tie, *there is a box of cherries there.*
Mi trovis grandan sakon da mono, *I found a large bag of money.*
Li havas teleron da viando, *he has a plate of meat.*
Post horoj da ĝojo ofte venas horoj da malĝojo, *after hours of joy there often come hours of sorrow.*

100. The preposition **da** must not be used if a quantity or portion of a *definite* or *limited* whole is expressed. If the word indicating the whole is limited by **la**, it is thereby made definite:

Telero de la maturaj pomoj, *a plate of the ripe apples.*
Sako de la bona kafo, *a sack of the good coffee.*

VOCABULARY.

Aleksandro, *Alexander.*	**koni**, *to be acquainted with.*
barelo, *barrel.*	**laŭta**, *loud.*
bruo, *noise.*	**lito**, *bed.*
da, *of* (99).	**loĝi**, *to dwell, to reside.*
demandi, *to inquire, to ask.*	**nombro**, *number (quantity).*
Diogeno, *Diogenes.*	**pura**, *clean.*
greka, *Greek.*	**sufiĉa**, *sufficient, enough.*
kelkaj, *several, some.*	**veki**, *to wake.*
kvankam, *although.*	**viziti**, *to visit.*
ĉifono, *rag.*	**vesto**, *garment, clothes.*

DIOGENO KAJ ALEKSANDRO GRANDA.

Antaŭ multaj jaroj saĝa greka viro, Diogeno, loĝis en granda urbo. Li opiniis ke ju pli malmulte oni bezonas, des pli feliĉa oni estas. Por montri al la mondo ke li ne bezonas multe, kaj ke tial li havas sufiĉe por esti feliĉa, li loĝis en granda malnova barelo, anstataŭ havi domon. Anstataŭ kuŝi nokte sur lito aŭ almenaŭ sur mola tapiŝo, li eĉ dormis en tiu barelo. Oni multe parolis pri Diogeno en la urbo, ne nur ĉar li tiel loĝis, sed ankaŭ pro liaj saĝaj diroj. Post kelke da tempo (*some time*) la reĝo Aleksandro Granda venis tien por viziti la urbon. Dum li estis tie li aŭdis pri Diogeno, kaj demandis pri li. "Ĉu li loĝas en la urbo?" Aleksandro diris. "Kvankam vi ne konas lin, mi opinias ke mi volas vidi tian viron." Oni respondis "Diogeno estas saĝa viro, sed anstataŭ loĝi en domo, li preferas sidi la tutan tempon en malnova barelo. Anstataŭ porti (*wearing*) purajn vestojn, li portas nur malpurajn ĉifonojn, ĉar li opinias ke ju pli malmulte li bezonas, des pli feliĉa li estos." Aleksandro diris "Antaŭ ol foriri de via lando mi vizitos tiun viron." Antaŭ ol li foriris de la urbo, Aleksandro iris kun nombro da amikoj por viziti Diogenon, kaj trovis lin en lia barelo. "Ĉu tiu viro volas paroli al mi?" demandis Diogeno per laŭta voĉo. Aleksandro Granda respondis "Mi estas la reĝo Aleksandro, kaj mi volas koni vin. Mi vidas ke kvankam vi estas saĝa vi estas tre malriĉa. Ĉu vi ne volas kelkajn novajn vestojn anstataŭ tiuj malpuraj ĉifonoj?" Diogeno tuj diris "Antaŭ ol vi venis kaj staris inter mi kaj la suno, ĉi tiu tre varme brilis sur min. Ĉu vi venis por fari bruon kaj por veki min?" Aleksandro ridis kaj diris "Mi vidas ke vi havas sufiĉe por esti feliĉa. Tial mi estas preta por foriri."

SENTENCES FOR TRANSLATION.

1. Diogenes was a wise man who dwelt in a Greek city, many years ago. 2. In order to show to the inconstant world that one does not need much in order to be happy, he did not have even a house or a bed. 3. He stayed day and night in a big barrel, instead of residing in a house. 4. He preferred to wear old rags, instead of good clean clothes. 5. He said "The less one needs, the happier he will be." 6. While Alexander the Great was visiting that city, people talked to him about Diogenes. 7. They asked "Are you acquainted-with that wise man?" 8. Soon the king went with a number of his friends to that-man's big barrel, in the middle of the city. 9. Diogenes was asleep, but the noise of the loud voices waked him, and he said angrily "You are standing between me and the sun! Will you not go away at once?" 10. Although several of the men laughed, Alexander said "We did not come to quarrel with you. 11. I see that you have enough to be happy, so instead of talking and making a noise we shall leave (go away from) you at once." 12. Before Diogenes could answer, Alexander had quietly walked away.

LESSON XXIII.

ADVERBS EXPRESSING A PART OF THE WHOLE.—THE
DEMONSTRATIVE ADVERB OF QUANTITY.—RESULT
CLAUSES.—EN LA BUTIKO.

ADVERBS EXPRESSING A PART OF THE WHOLE.

101. After adverbs used to indicate a quantity or portion of some indefinite whole, as well as after nouns of such meaning (99), the substantive expressing the indefinite whole is preceded by the preposition **da**:[25]

Multe da bruo, *much (a quantity of) noise.*
Tiel malmulte da tempo, *so little (such a small quantity of) time.*
Kelke da pomoj, *some (an indefinite number of) apples.*

102. Verbs may be modified by an adverb and prepositional phrase containing **da**:

Li trinkis malmulte da akvo, *he drank little (not much) water.*
Estas multe da sablo en la dezerto, *there is much sand in the desert.*
Ju pli neĝas, des pli multe da neĝo kuŝas sur la vojoj, *the more it snows, the more snow lies on the roads.*

103. It is evident from the above examples that an adverb followed by **da** has a somewhat collective sense, indicating a general sum, mass, or portion of the whole, without distinction of particulars. An *adjective* of quantitative meaning, on the other hand, usually indicates consideration of the individuals composing the sum or mass named:

En urbo oni havas multe da bruo, *in a city one has much noise.*
Ni aŭdis multajn bruojn, *we heard many (different) noises.*
Tie oni havas multe da plezuro, *there one has much pleasure.*
Oni havas multajn plezurojn tie, *people have many (different) pleasures there.*

THE DEMONSTRATIVE ADVERB OF QUANTITY.

104. The demonstrative adverb of quantity related to the demonstrative pronoun **tiu** is **tiom**, *that (this) much, that many, that quantity, so much,* etc.:—

Mi donis tiom da mono al vi, *I gave that much (that amount of) money to you.*
Mi aĉetis tiom da viando, *I bought that much meat.*

---

[25] A prepositional phrase containing **da**, whether following a noun or an adverb, is sometimes called a *partitive* construction.

Tiom de la libroj mi legis, *that many of the books I read.*

RESULT CLAUSES.

105. A clause of result (also called a consecutive clause) expresses an action or condition as due to, or resulting from, something indicated in the main sentence, as "he is so strong that he can do it," "I had so much pleasure that I laughed heartily." In Esperanto a result clause is introduced by **ke**, preceded (directly or in the main sentence) by an adverb or adjective of manner, degree, or quantity:

Diogeno estis tiel saĝa greka viro ke Aleksandro laŭdis lin, *Diogenes was such a wise Greek man that Alexander praised him.*

Mi havis tiom da plezuro ke mi tre ridis, *I had so much pleasure that I laughed very much.*

Ĝi estas tia vilaĝo ke mi ŝatas loĝi tie, *it is such (that sort of) a village that I like to live there.*

VOCABULARY.

aĉeti, *to buy.*	**kontuzo**, *bruise.*
asparago, *asparagus.*	**lakto**, *milk.*
brasiko, *cabbage.*	**legomo**, *vegetable.*
butiko, *store, shop.*	**ovo**, *egg.*
frago, *strawberry.*	**pizo**, *pea.*
funto, *pound.*	**sabato**, *Saturday.*
glaso, *glass, tumbler.*	**tiom**, *that much* (104).
ĵaŭdo, *Thursday.*	**vendredo**, *Friday.*
kremo, *cream.*	**vilaĝo**, *village.*

EN LA BUTIKO.

Hodiaŭ matene mi iris kun la patrino al la plej granda butiko en nia vilaĝo. Tie ŝi aĉetis tiom da legomoj kaj fruktoj ke ni tute ne povis porti ilin. Tial juna knabo venis kun ni, kaj portis kelke da ili por ni. La patrino ne aĉetis tiel multe je vendredo, sed hodiaŭ estas sabato, kaj ŝi volis aĉeti legomojn por dimanĉo, ĉar dimanĉe oni ne povas iri en la butikojn. Tial sabate oni kutime aĉetas sufiĉe por la manĝoj de sabato kaj dimanĉo. Meze de la butiko staras multe da bareloj. En ĉi tiuj oni trovas grandan nombron da freŝaj puraj legomoj. La patrino aĉetis tiel multe da asparago kaj novaj pizoj, kaj tiel grandan sakon da terpomoj, ke la tablo restis preskaŭ nuda. Mi vidis brasikon tie, sed tiun legomon mi malŝatas, kvankam oni diras ke ĝi estas tre bona legomo. Antaŭ ol foriri de la butiko la patrino aĉetis kelke da ovoj, kaj rigardis la fruktojn en bareloj apud la pordo. Ili ŝajnis tiel bonaj ke ŝi aĉetis kelkajn maturajn pomojn kaj skatolon da fragoj. Dum oni donis al ŝi la fruktojn, mi aĉetis kelkajn funtojn da sukero. Tiam ni estis pretaj por foriri el la butiko. Sur la vojo ni aŭdis tiel grandan bruon ke mi lasis la patrinon kaj kuris trans la straton. Mi trovis tie infanon, la filon de nia najbaro. Li faris la bruon, ĉar li falis de la arbo antaŭ sia domo, kaj tre laŭte ploris. Li diris al mi ke li havas multajn kontuzojn sur la kapo. Ĉar mi bone konas la infanon, mi demandis "Ĉu vi volas grandan ruĝan pomon? Mi havas tian pomon por vi." Li tuj kaptis la pomon, kaj mi foriris. Tiam la patrino kaj mi iris al la domo.

SENTENCES FOR TRANSLATION.

1. I shall go to the village today with my younger sister. 2. We wish to buy some eggs, vegetables and fruit for Mother. 3. Mother prefers to remain in the house, because it is raining. 4. It rained on Thursday and Friday, but today it is not raining very much. 5. The air is warm and pleasant, and we shall carry umbrellas with us. 6. We shall buy some new peas, a box of strawberries and several pounds of sugar. 7. Thus we shall have enough for the meals of Saturday and Sunday. 8. I wonder whether we shall see such asparagus and such cabbage on the tables or in the barrels. 9. Although I do not often eat such vegetables, Father and Mother are very fond of (*multe ŝatas*) both cabbage and asparagus. 10. We shall also buy enough milk for several glasses of milk, and we shall need much cream for the strawberries. 11. It seems that we shall buy such a number of vegetables that we cannot carry them. 12. While we were standing near the door, ready to go toward the village (46), we heard a loud voice. 13. A child was standing in the street, and crying. 14. He wished to go with his mother to visit some friends. 15. I suppose that a noise on the street waked him, and he did not wish to remain in his bed.

LESSON XXIV.

THE INTERROGATIVE PRONOUN.—THE PRESENT AC-
TIVE PARTICIPLE.—COMPOUND TENSES. —THE
PROGRESSIVE PRESENT TENSE.—THE SUFFIX -EJ-.—
EN NIA DOMO.

THE INTERROGATIVE PRONOUN.

106. The interrogative pronoun (and pronominal adjective) is **kiu**, *who, which*.
Since the use of this pronoun indicates a question, the sentence containing it does
not need the interrogative adverb **ĉu** (30):

Kiu vokas vin? *Who calls you?*
Kiun vi vokas? *Whom do you call?*
Kiuj el vi vokis nin? *Which (ones) of you called us?*
Kiujn li helpis? *Whom (which ones) did he help?*
Kiun tagon vi venos? *What day will you come?*
Kiujn legomojn vi preferas? *What vegetables do you prefer?*
Mi miras kiun libron vi aĉetis, *I wonder which book you bought?*

107. The interrogative pronoun **kiu** has a possessive or genitive form **kies,**
whose:

En kies domo vi loĝas? *In whose house do you reside?*
Kies amikojn vi vizitis? *Whose friends did you visit?*

THE PRESENT ACTIVE PARTICIPLE.

108. A participle is a *verbal adjective*, as in "a *crying* child." It agrees like other
adjectives with the word modified (19, 24). The participle from a transitive verb
(22) may take a direct object, and a participle expressing motion may be followed
by an accusative indicating direction of motion (46). The present active participle,
expressing what the word modified *is doing*, ends in **-anta,** as **vidanta,** *seeing*, **iran-
ta**, *going*:

La ploranta infano volas dormi, *the crying child wishes to sleep.*
Mi vidas la falantajn foliojn, *I see the falling leaves.*
Kiu estas la virino aĉetanta ovojn? *Who is the woman buying eggs?*
Mi parolis al la viroj irantaj vilaĝon, *I talked to the men (who were) going
toward the village.*

COMPOUND TENSES.

109. A participle may be used predicatively with a form of **esti**, as **Mi estas demandanta**, *I am asking*, **La viro estas aĉetanta**, *the man is buying*. Such combinations are called *compound tenses*, in contrast to the *simple* or *aoristic*[26] tenses.

Compound tenses occur less often in Esperanto than in English, and an aoristic Esperanto tense may often be translated by an English compound tense, as **La birdoj flugas**, *the birds are flying*. When used to form a compound tense, the verb **esti** is called the *auxiliary verb*. No other verb is ever used as an auxiliary (a simpler method than in English, which uses *be, have, do, will, shall, would*, etc.).

THE PROGRESSIVE PRESENT TENSE.

110. The compound tense formed by using the present active participle with the present tense of **esti** is called the *progressive present tense*. It differs from the aoristic present by expressing an action as definitely in progress, or a condition as continuously existing, at the moment of speaking. The conjugation of **vidi** in this tense is as follows:

mi estas vidanta, *I am seeing.*
vi estas vidanta, *you are seeing.*
li (ŝi, ĝi) estas vidanta, *he (she, it) is seeing.*
ni estas vidantaj, *we are seeing.*
vi estas vidantaj, *you (plural) are seeing.*
ili estas vidantaj, *they are seeing.*

THE SUFFIX -EJ-.

111. Words expressing the place where the action indicated by the root occurs, or where the object indicated by the root may be found, are formed by inserting the suffix **-ej-** before the noun-ending:[27]

ĉevalejo, *stable* (from **ĉevalo**, *horse*).
dormejo, *dormitory* (from **dormi**, *to sleep*).
herbejo, *meadow* (from **herbo**, *grass*).
loĝejo, *lodging-place, dwelling* (from **loĝi**, *to dwell, to lodge*).

VOCABULARY.

---

[26] An aoristic tense consists of but one word (ending in **-as**, **-os**, etc.) and expresses an act or state as a whole, without specifying whether it is finished, still in progress, or yet begun.

[27] Similar formations are made in English with the suffix *-y*, as *bakery, bindery, grocery*, etc. This suffix is equivalent to the *-ei* in German *Bäckerei*, bakery, *Druckerei*, printing-office, etc., and to the *-ie* in French *patisserie*, pastry-shop, *imprimerie*, printing-shop, etc.

alia, *other, another.*
baki, *to bake.*
dika, *thick.*
facila, *easy.*
familio, *family.*
kanapo, *sofa.*
kies, *whose* (107).
kiu, *who* (106).

kuiri, *to cook.*
kurteno, *curtain.*
kutimo, *custom.*
leciono, *lesson.*
lerni, *to learn.*
pano, *bread.*
persono, *person.*
salono, *parlor.*

EN NIA DOMO.

Oni ofte miras kies domo en nia vilaĝo estas plej bela, kaj kiu domo estas la plej agrabla loĝejo. Nia domo ne estas tre granda, sed ĝi estas nova kaj ni multe ŝatas ĝin. Ĝia salono estas granda, kun belaj puraj kurtenoj kovrantaj la fenestrojn, kaj mola dika tapiŝo kovranta la plankon. Ĉi tie estas kelkaj seĝoj, malgranda tablo, kaj longa kanapo. Personoj vizitantaj nin kutime sidas en ĉi tiu ĉambro, kaj dum ni estas sidantaj tie ni nur parolas, anstataŭ skribi aŭ legi. Alia ĉambro en la domo estas tre luma kaj agrabla, sed malpli granda. Ĉi tie staras tablo sufiĉe granda por nia tuta familio, kaj en tiu ĉambro oni manĝas. Ofte ni restas tie longan tempon post la manĝo, ĉar la patro rakontas interesajn rakontojn al ni, kaj ni multe ridas, kaj demandas pri tiuj rakontoj, kaj tiel bone amuzas nin ke mi preskaŭ forgesas pri miaj lecionoj. Tamen mi havas multe da lecionoj por lerni, kaj ili tute ne estas facilaj. Je tre frua horo matene mi iras al la lernejo, kun miaj fratoj kaj fratinoj. Nur sabate kaj dimanĉe ni ne iras tien. La lernejo estas malnova kaj malgranda, sed oni estas nun konstruanta novan pli grandan lernejon apud nia domo. Dum la infanoj estas lernantaj siajn lecionojn tie, la patrino kutime iras al la bakejon, por aĉeti sufiĉe da pano, por la manĝoj de la tago. Ofte ŝi iras ankaŭ al aliaj butikoj. Ĵaŭdon ŝi aĉetis kelke da novaj pizoj, kaj da asparago. Vendredon ŝi aĉetis kelkajn funtojn da sukero, skatolon da fragoj, kaj sufiĉe da kremo kaj lakto. Hodiaŭ ŝi estas aĉetanta brasikon kaj sakon da terpomoj. Ŝi volas kuiri tre bonan manĝon, tamen ŝi havas tro multe por fari en la kuirejo, ĉar ŝi ne havas servistinon.

SENTENCES FOR TRANSLATION.

1. Who is the woman sitting on the sofa in the parlor? 2. I can not easily see her, but I hear her voice. 3. I wonder whose voice that is. 4. However, I think that it is the voice of a friend of Mother's. 5. Now I can see her, although she does not see me. 6. I am well acquainted with her. 7. She is a friend of our whole family, and is visiting a neighbor of ours (*najbaron nian*) in this city. 8. My sister is sitting on the sofa in another room, and learning her lessons. 9. Soon she will go to school. 10. Whose book is she reading? 11. That thick book is mine, but the other books on the table near her are hers. 12. She prefers to sit in the sewing-room (111) to read or write (98), because the curtains in front of the windows are not too thick, and so (78) that room is very light and pleasant. 13. She also likes to look at the falling snow, and the men and women walking on the muddy streets. 14. On account of the cold weather, people are wearing thick clothes. 15. The men and boys are keeping their hands in their pockets while they walk. 16. The girls walking toward

the school are friends of my sister's. 17. In that school they learn to cook. Soon they will be able to bake bread, and even to cook a whole meal. 18. I think such a custom is very good. 19. Many persons can not cook well enough (*sufiĉe bone*).

LESSON XXV.

THE INTERROGATIVE ADJECTIVE.—THE IMPERFECT TENSE.—SALUTATIONS AND EXCLAMATIONS.—WORD FORMATION.—KONI AND SCII.—LA NEPO VIZITAS LA AVINON.

THE INTERROGATIVE ADJECTIVE.

112. The interrogative adjective related to the interrogative pronoun **kiu**, is **kia**, *what kind of, what sort of*:

Kiajn vestojn li portis? *What sort of clothes did he wear?*
Kian panon vi preferas? *What kind of bread do you prefer?*
Mi miras kia persono li estas, *I wonder what sort of a person he is.*
Kia vetero estas? *What sort of weather is it?*
Kia plezuro! *What a pleasure!*

THE IMPERFECT TENSE.

113. The compound tense formed by using the present active participle with the past tense of **esti** represents an act or condition as in progress in past time, but not perfected, and is called the *imperfect tense*. The conjugation of **vidi** in this tense is as follows:

mi estis vidanta, *I was seeing.*
vi estis vidanta, *you were seeing.*
li (ŝi, ĝi) estis vidanta, *he (she, it) was seeing.*
ni estis vidantaj, *we were seeing.*
vi estis vidantaj, *you were seeing.*
ili estis vidantaj, *they were seeing.*

THE PROGRESSIVE FUTURE TENSE.

114. The compound tense formed by using the present active participle with the future tense of **esti** represents an act or condition as in progress—or a condition as existing continuously—at a future time, and is called the *progressive future* tense. The conjugation of **vidi** in this tense is as follows:

mi estos vidanta, *I shall be seeing.*
vi estos vidanta, *you will be seeing.*
li (ŝi, ĝi) estos vidanta, *he (she, it) will be seeing.*
ni estos vidantaj, *we shall be seeing.*

vi estos vidantaj, *you will be seeing.*
ili estos vidantaj, *they will be seeing.*

SALUTATIONS AND EXCLAMATIONS.

115. When the word or words expressing a salutation or exclamation may be regarded as the direct object of a verb which is not expressed; these words are put in the accusative case:

Bonan matenon! *Good morning!* (I wish you "good morning.")
Bonan nokton! *Good night!* (I wish you a "good night.")
Multajn salutojn al via patro! (I send) *many greetings to your father!*
Dankon! *Thanks!* (I give to you "thanks.")
Ĉielon! *Heavens!* (I invoke the "heavens.")

WORD FORMATION.

116. The majority of roots have such a meaning that at least two kinds of words, and often three or four, may be formed from them by use of the general endings for verbs, nouns, adjectives and adverbs. (Each root will hereafter be quoted but once in the vocabularies, with a hyphen separating it from the ending with which it appears first in the reading lesson, or with which it is most frequently used.) Following are examples of word formation from roots already familiar:

Verb.	Noun.	Adjective.	Adverb.
brili, *to shine*	**brilo**, *shine, brilliance*	**brila**, *shining, brilliant*	**brile**, *brilliantly*
flori, *to bloom*	**floro**, *flower, blossom*	**flora**, *floral*	**flore**, *florally*
ĝoji, *to rejoice*	**ĝojo**, *joy, gladness*	**ĝoja**, *joyful, glad*	**ĝoje**, *gladly*
kontuzi, *to bruise*	**kontuzo**, *bruise, contu-sion*		
	tuto, *whole*	**tuta**, *entire, whole, all*	**tute**, *entirely*

KONI AND SCII.

117. The verb **koni**, which means "to know" in the sense of "to be acquainted with" is used in speaking of persons, languages, places, etc. **Koni** always has a direct object. It is never followed by **ke**, **ĉu**, **kiu**, or any other interrogative word. **Scii** means "to know" in the sense of "to be aware," "to have knowledge." It is not used in speaking of persons.[28]

Ĉu vi konas tiun personon? *Do you know that person?*
Mi scias ke li estas nia najbaro, *I know that he is our neighbor.*
Mi bone konas Bostonon, *I am well acquainted with Boston.*
Mi ne scias ĉu li konas ilin, *I do not know whether he knows them.*

VOCABULARY.

---

[28] **Koni** is equivalent to German *kennen*, French *connaitre*, Spanish *conocer*, while **scii** is equivalent to German *wissen*, French *savoir*, Spanish *saber*.

av-o, *grandfather.*
buked-o, *bouquet.*
ekzamen-o, *examination.*
ferm-i, *to close.*
frap-i, *to strike, to knock.*
geometri-o, *geometry.*
german-a, *German.*
hejm-o, *home.*

kia, *what kind of* (112).
lingv-o, *language.*
nep-o, *grandson.*
nu! *Well!*
paper-o, *paper.*
salut-i, *to greet.*
sci-i, *to know* (117).
stud-i, *to study.*

LA NEPO VIZITAS LA AVINON.

Hieraŭ matene mi vizitis la avinon. Ŝia hejmo estas apud la granda nova bakejo. Mi vidis ŝin tra la fenestro, ĉar la kurtenoj kovrantaj ĝin estas tre maldikaj. Ŝi estis sidanta sur la kanapo, kaj skribanta per plumo sur granda papero. Antaŭ ol frapi sur la pordo mi vokis ŝin kaj diris "Bonan matenon, kara avino!" Tuj ŝi demandis "Kiu estas tie? Kies voĉon mi aŭdas?" Mi respondis "Estas via nepo. Ĉu vi ne konas mian voĉon?" Antaŭ ol ŝi povis veni al la pordo mi estis malfermanta ĝin. Mi iris en la salonon kaj donis al la avino bukedon da floroj. "La patrino donas ĉi tiujn al vi, kun siaj plej bonaj salutoj," mi diris. La avino respondis "Nu, kia plezuro! Multan dankon al ŝi pro la bela bukedo, kaj ankaŭ al vi, ĉar vi portis ĝin ĉi tien por mi!" Dum ŝi estis metanta la florojn en glason da akvo la avino diris "Nu, kiajn lecionojn vi havis hodiaŭ en la lernejo?" Mi respondis ke mi bone konis la lecionojn, ĉar mi zorge studis ilin. "Ni estas lernantaj la germanan lingvon," mi diris, "kaj ju pli longe ni studas ĝin, des pli multe mi ĝin ŝatas, kvankam ĝi estas tre malfacila." Mi rakontis ankaŭ pri la lecionoj de geometrio, kaj aliaj lecionoj, sed diris ke la ekzamenoj estos baldaŭ komencantaj. "Je tiu tempo," mi diris, "mi estos skribanta la respondojn al la ekzamenoj, preskaŭ la tutan semajnon." La avino demandis kun intereso "Ĉu la demandoj de la ekzamenoj estos malfacilaj?" Mi respondis "Mi ne scias, sed mi timas ke ni estos tre lacaj post tiom da laboro." Post kelke da aliaj demandoj kaj respondoj, mi opiniis ke estas la horo por foriri. Dum mi estis foriranta, la avino diris "Multajn salutojn al la tuta familio!" Mi dankis ŝin, diris "Bonan tagon!" kaj tiam foriris.

SENTENCES FOR TRANSLATION.

1. What sort of noise do I hear outside the door? 2. Are some of my friends knocking? 3. We were talking yesterday about the examinations in our school, and these boys came home to study with me. 4. I shall go to the door to open it and to greet my friends. 5. Good morning! Did you come to study geometry, or the German language? 6. Which of these is usually more difficult, and in which will the examination be the longer? 7. Well, we brought our German books, because we prefer to study these. 8. We wish to know this language thoroughly. 9. We shall go into the writing-room (111), for (83) some friends of my grandmother are in the parlor. 10. We can hear their voices here, and we can not study very well while they are talking. 11. They were carrying many flowers, and gave a beautiful bouquet to my grandmother. 12. She said "Many thanks for (86) the sweet violets! In whose garden did they bloom?" 13. Her friend's granddaughter is a friend of

my youngest sister. 14. Well, shall we begin to study? Have you enough paper, and have you a good pen? 15. I shall close this other door, because they are baking bread in the kitchen, and cooking meat. 16. We shall be hearing the voices of so many persons that I know that we can not study.

LESSON XXVI.

THE INTERROGATIVE ADVERB OF PLACE.—THE PAST
ACTIVE PARTICIPLE.—ADVERB DERIVATION FROM
PREPOSITIONS.—ADVERBS EXPRESSING DIREC-
TION OF MOTION.—THE SUFFIX -EG-.—LA PLUVEGO.

THE INTERROGATIVE ADVERB OF PLACE.

118. The interrogative adverb of place, related to the interrogative pronoun
kiu is **kie**, *where, in (at) what place.* If the verb in the sentence expresses motion
toward the place indicated by **kie**, the ending **-n** is added, forming **kien**, *whither
(where)*:

Kie li estis kaj kien oni forpelis lin? *Where was he and whither did they drive
him (away)?*
Li miros kie lia nepo estas, *he will wonder where his grandson is.*
Mi ne scias kien li kuris, *I do not know where (whither) he ran.*

THE PAST ACTIVE PARTICIPLE.

119. The past active participle, (for the characteristics of a participle see 108)
expressing what the word modified *did* or *has done*, ends in **-inta**, as **vidinta**, *having
seen*, **irinta**, *gone, having gone*:

La falintaj folioj estas brunaj, *the fallen leaves are brown.*
Kiu estas la viro salutinta nin? *who is the man having greeted (who greeted) us?*
Oni forgesas la foririntajn personojn, *one forgets the departed persons (the
persons who have gone away).*

ADVERB DERIVATION FROM PREPOSITIONS.

120. Adverbs may be derived from prepositions whose sense permits, by use
of the adverb ending **-e**:

Antaŭe li studis la geometrion, *previously he studied geometry.*
Poste li studis la germanan, *afterwards he studied German.*
Li marŝis antaŭe, ne malantaŭe, *he walked in front, not behind.*
Dume la viroj staris ĉirkaŭe, *meanwhile the men stood roundabout.*
Ili venis kune kaj sidis apude, *they came together and sat near by.*

ADVERBS EXPRESSING DIRECTION OF MOTION.

121. An adverb expressing place or direction is given the ending **-n** when used with a verb expressing motion toward that place or direction (**69, 118,** etc.):

Ĉu li rajdis norden aŭ suden? *Did he ride north or south(ward)?*
Ni kuris antaŭen, ne malantaŭen, *we ran forward, not back.*
La bukedo falis eksteren kaj suben, *the bouquet fell out and underneath.*
Li estis marŝanta hejmen, *he was walking home (homeward).*[29]

THE SUFFIX -EG-.

122. The suffix **-eg-** may be added to a root to augment or intensify its meaning, thus forming an *augmentative* of the root:

barelego, *hogshead* (from **barelo,** *barrel*).
bonega, *excellent* (from **bona,** *good*).
malbonege, *wickedly, wretchedly* (from **malbone,** *badly, poorly*).
domego, *mansion* (from **domo,** *house*).
ploregi, *to sob, to wail* (from **plori,** *to weep*).
treege, *exceedingly* (from **tre,** *very*).

VOCABULARY.

aer-o, *air.*	**pez-a,** *heavy.*
danc-i, *to dance.*	**polv-o,** *dust.*
fulm-o, *lightning.*	**sekv-i,** *to follow.*
gut-o, *drop* (of water, etc.).	**serĉ-i,** *to hunt for, to search.*
kie, *where* (118).	**silent-a,** *still, silent.*
okaz-i, *to happen, to occur.*	**subit-a,** *sudden.*
okul-o, *eye.*	**tegment-o,** *roof.*
pec-o, *piece.*	**tondr-o,** *thunder.*

LA PLUVEGO.

Nu, kia pluvego okazis hieraŭ vespere! Post kvieta varmega mateno, subite multaj nuboj kovris la ĉielon. La aero ŝajnis peza, kaj estis tute silenta kelkan tempon. Tiam forte blovanta vento frapegis la arbojn, kaj komencis fortege skui la branĉojn. Multege da polvo kaj malgrandaj pecoj da papero dancis kaj flugis ĉirkaŭen en la aero, kaj ankaŭ ĉielen. Falis tiam kelkaj grandaj gutoj da pluvo, kaj ni sciis ke la pluvego estas venanta. Ni malfermis niajn ombrelojn, kaj kuris antaŭen, por iri hejmen antaŭ ol falos multe da pluvo. La fulmo tiel ofte brilis ke ni fermis la okulojn pro ĝi, kaj treege ĝin timis. Preskaŭ tuj la tondro sekvis ĝin. Tondris tiom kaj tiel laŭtege ke la bruo ŝajnis frapi kontraŭ niajn kapojn. Tiam komencis subite pluvegi, sed je tiu tempo ni estis preskaŭ sub la tegmento de nia domo. Dume la vento pli kaj pli blovegis, kaj ju pli forte ĝi blovis, des pli peze la gutoj da pluvo falis teren, kun multege da bruo. Mi opinias ke mi malofte antaŭe

[29] The adverb may precede the verb and be united with it by simple juxtaposition, if the resulting word is not too long:

Li hejmeniris, *he went home (he "home-went").*
Ni antaŭeniros, *we shall advance (go forward).*
La bukedo subenfalis, *the bouquet fell underneath.*

vidis tian pluvegon. La sekvintan tagon mi promenis tre frue, kaj vidis ke la pordego al la ĝardeno de mia avo estas kuŝanta sur la tero. Apude mi vidis ventoflagon falintan de la tegmento de tiu granda ĉevalejo. Velkintaj floroj kuŝis sur la tero ĉirkaŭ mi, kaj inter ili estis branĉoj falintaj de la arboj, ĉar la grandega forto de la vento forrompis eĉ ĉi tiujn. Sur malgranda branĉo restis nesto, sed kie estis la birdoj! Mi serĉis la junajn birdojn sed tute ne povis trovi ilin, tial mi opinias ke ili forflugis antaŭ ol la ventoj forrompis de la arbo ilian malgrandan hejmon. Mi ne scias kien ili flugis, sed mi opinias ke ili flugis suden al la arboj en tiu granda kampo trans la rivero.

SENTENCES FOR TRANSLATION.

1. While we were walking home (121) from school yesterday, it rained very suddenly. 2. What a storm it was! 3. We were talking about the lessons in geometry, and were looking at these books about the German language. 4. So we did not see the clouds in (on) the sky. 5. Well, we forgot about examinations and began to wonder where to go. 6. We did not know whether we had enough time to run even to Grandfather's house before it would rain. 7. Many papers fell out of our books, and the wind caught them. 8. The wind chased them away from us, and they seemed to dance around in the air. 9. However, we easily caught and gathered them, and then we ran forward. 10. Suddenly it thundered very loudly, and we saw the brilliant lightning in the sky. 11. We almost closed our eyes for the lightning. 12. Big drops of rain fell heavily and struck the dust violently. 13. The air was heavy and still then, and the storm immediately followed the few drops of rain. 14. We hastened across the street, and ran faster and faster. 15. We were exhausted (**122**) and our clothes were exceedingly wet before we were in the house. 16. The rain was dropping from the roof, but we ran through it, and knocked on the door. 17. We rested some time here, before going home.

LESSON XXVII.

THE INTERROGATIVE TEMPORAL ADVERB.—THE PER-
FECT TENSE.—THE PREPOSITION ĈE.— THE SUFFIX
-AR-.—TEMPO AND FOJO.—THE ORTHOGRAPHY OF
PROPER NAMES.— ROBERTO BRUCE KAJ LA ARA-
NEO.

THE INTERROGATIVE TEMPORAL ADVERB

123. The interrogative temporal adverb, related to the interrogative pronoun
kiu, is **kiam**, *when, at what time?*

Kiam li serĉos min? *When will he look for me?*
Oni miras kiam li venos, *they wonder when he is coming (will come).*
Kiam falis tiuj gutoj da pluvo? *When did those drops of rain fall?*

THE PERFECT TENSE.

124. The compound tense formed by using the past active participle with the
present tense of **esti** is called the *perfect tense*. It differs from the aoristic past tense
(**35**) and from the imperfect (**113**) by expressing an act or condition as definitely
completed or perfected. The conjugation of **vidi** in the perfect tense is as follows:

mi estas vidinta, *I have seen (I am having-seen).*
vi estas vidinta, *you have seen (you are having-seen).*
li (ŝi, ĝi) estas vidinta, *he (she, it) has seen (is having-seen).*
ni estas vidintaj, *we have seen (we are having-seen).*
vi estas vidintaj, *you have seen (you are having-seen).*
ili estas vidintaj, *they have seen (they are having-seen).*

THE PREPOSITION ĈE.

125. The general situation of a person, object or action is expressed by the use
of the preposition **ĉe**, *at, at the house of, in the region or land of, among, with,* etc.:

Li staris silente ĉe la pordego, *he stood silently at the gate.*
Li loĝas ĉe mia avo, *he lives (dwells) at my grandfather's.*
Ili estas ĉe la lernejo, *they are at the school.*
Li restos ĉe amikoj, *he will stay with (at the house of) friends.*
Li vizitos ĉe ni morgaŭ, *he will visit at-our-house tomorrow.*

THE SUFFIX -AR-.

126. Words expressing a collection, group or assemblage of similar persons or things, as *forest* (collection of trees), *army* (assemblage of soldiers), etc., may be formed by the use of the suffix **-ar-**. This suffix may itself be used as a root to form **aro**, *group, flock*, etc., **are**, *in a group, by throngs*, etc. Words formed with the suffix **-ar-** are called collectives:

arbaro, *forest* (from **arbo**, *tree*).
ĉevalaro, *herd of horses* (from **ĉevalo**, *horse*).
kamparo, *country* (from **kampo**, *field*).
libraro, *collection of books, library* (from **libro**, *book*).
amikaro, *circle of friends* (from **amiko**, *friend*).

TEMPO AND FOJO.

127. The general word for "time" in the sense of duration, or suitability (as "the proper time"), is **tempo**. The word **fojo**, *time, occasion*, refers to the performance or occurrence of an act or event, in repetition or series:

Mi ne havas multe da tempo, *I have not much time.*
Li venis multajn fojojn, kaj la lastan fojon li restis longan tempon, *he came many times, and the last time he remained a long time.*
Kelkajn fojojn laŭte tondris, *several times it thundered loudly.*
Multe da fojoj ni fermis la okulojn pro la fulmo, *many times we closed our eyes on account of the lightning.*

THE ORTHOGRAPHY OF PROPER NOUNS.

128. Proper nouns, that is, nouns which are names of persons, cities, countries, etc., are given Esperanto spelling if they are names of continents, countries, large or very well-known cities, or if they are first (Christian) names of persons, as **Azio**, *Asia*, **Skotlando**, *Scotland*, **Bostono**, *Boston*, **Johano**, *John*, **Mario**, *Mary*. Surnames and names of places which are small or not well known are more often quoted in the national spelling. The pronunciation may be indicated in parentheses, as **Mt. Vernon (Maŭnt Vernon)**, **Roberto Bruce (Brus)**, **Martinique (Martinik')**, etc.

VOCABULARY.

arane-o, *spider.*
Azi-o, *Asia.*
ĉe, *at* (125).
fin-o, *end, ending.*
foj-o, *time, instance* (127).
kiam, *when* (123).
pacienc-o, *patience.*
pied-o, *foot.*
plafon-o, *ceiling.*

ramp-i, *to crawl.*
rekt-a, *direct, straight.*
rimark-i, *to notice.*
send-i, *to send.*
Skotland-o, *Scotland.*
soldat-o, *soldier.*
sukces-i, *to succeed.*
supr-e, *above.*
venk-i, *to conquer.*

ROBERTO BRUCE KAJ LA ARANEO.

Oni rakontas la sekvantan interesan rakonton pri Roberto Bruce, reĝo antaŭ

multaj jaroj en Skotlando. Okazis ke li estis rigardanta la soldataron de siaj malamikoj, de la fenestro de granda ĉevalejo. Por povi rigardi plej facile, kaj ankaŭ
por sin kaŝi, li forsendis siajn soldatojn kaj restis la tutan tagon sub tiu tegmento.
Kvankam la ĉevalejo estis granda ĝi estis malnova, kaj li opiniis ke la malamikoj
ne serĉos lin tie. Je la fino de la tago li subite rimarkis araneon sur la muro apud si.
La araneo estis rampanta supren, sed baldaŭ ĝi falis en la polvon ĉe liaj piedoj. Tuj
la falinta araneo komencis alian fojon supren rampi. Alian fojon ĝi falis teren, sed
post ne longe ĝi komencis rampi alian fojon. "Kia pacienco!" diris la reĝo al si. "Mi
ne sciis ke la araneo havas tiel multe da pacienco! Sed kien ĝi nun estas falinta?" Li
rigardis ĉirkaŭen kaj fine (*finally*) li vidis la falintan araneon. Kun granda surprizo
li rimarkis ke ĝi estas komencanta supren rampi. Multajn fojojn ĝi supren rampis,
kaj tiom da fojoj ĝi falis malsupren. Fine, tamen, ĝi sukcese rampis ĝis la plafono.
La reĝo malfermis la buŝon pro surprizo, kaj diris al si "Kiam antaŭe mi vidis
tiom da pacienco! Mi opinias ke la fina sukceso de tiu malgranda araneo donas
al mi bonegan lecionon. Mi estas ofte malsukcesinta, sed malpli ofte ol tiu araneo
sur la muro. Mi estas perdinta multe da soldatoj, kaj la malamikoj estas venkintaj
multajn fojojn, ĉar ili havas multe pli grandan nombron da soldatoj. Tamen, mi
estos pacienca, ĉar oni ne scias kiam li fine sukcesos." La sekvintan tagon, la reĝo
Roberto Bruce komencis treege labori kontraŭ siaj malamikoj. Post mallonga tempo li bone sukcesis, kaj tute venkis la malamikoj en granda venko ĉe Bannockburn
(Banokb'rn).

SENTENCES FOR TRANSLATION.

1. Although the enemies of Robert Bruce conquered him many times, he finally conquered them in Scotland, because he was patient and very courageous. 2. He
was sitting in a large stable, to hide (himself), and also in order to (98) look directly
from its roof (at) the soldiery (126) of the enemy. 3. At the end of the day he noticed
a spider crawling up (ward) on the wall. 4. The spider fell suddenly into the dust
and lay at the king's feet, but soon began to crawl up. 5. "Where does it wish to
go?" said the king to himself. 6. "What patience it shows! It has crawled up and
fallen down a great many times." 7. Finally however the spider succeeded, and
crawled up to the ceiling. 8. The king said that he had learned a lesson from the
patient spider. 9. He said "Although the enemy have conquered many times, because they have a larger number of soldiers, I shall finally succeed against them."
10. Soon it happened that the wind blew violently, and a rainstorm occurred. 11.
The blast shook the foliage (126) on the trees, and broke away many small branches. 12. A group of soldiers ran right (*rekte*) toward the stable, and Robert Bruce was
much afraid that they would find him. 13. But they merely stole the horses there,
and rode away.

LESSON XXVIII.

THE INTERROGATIVE ADVERB OF MOTIVE OR REA-
SON.— THE INFINITIVE AS SUBJECT.— PRESENT AC-
TION WITH PAST INCEPTION.—THE SUFFIX -UL-.—
LOĜI AND VIVI.—PRI LA AVO KAJ LA AVINO.

THE INTERROGATIVE ADVERB OF MOTIVE OR REASON.

129. The interrogative adverb of motive or reason related to the interrogative
pronoun **kiu** is **kial**, *why, wherefore, for what reason*:

Kial la araneo supren rampis? *why did the spider crawl up?*
Mi demandos kial li rimarkis ĝin, *I will ask why he noticed it.*

THE INFINITIVE AS SUBJECT.

130. The infinitive may be used as the subject of a verb.[30]

Any modifier of the infinitive is necessarily adverbial. An indefinite personal
object (or pronominal complement of a preposition) after an infinitive used as subject is expressed by the reflexive pronoun **si**:

Promeni estas granda plezuro, *to go walking is a great pleasure.*
Promeni estas agrable, *to go walking is pleasant.*
Ĉu estas facile rigardi la plafonon? *Is it easy to look at the ceiling?*
Estas bone sin helpi, *it is well to help oneself.*
Paroli al si estas malsaĝe, *to talk to oneself is silly.*

PRESENT ACTION WITH PAST INCEPTION.

131. A present act or state which began in the past is expressed by the present
tense (instead of by the past as in English):[31]

Mi estas ĉi tie de lundo, *I have been (I am) here since Monday.*
De Marto mi studas tiun lingvon, *since March I have been (I am) studying that
language.*
Ili estas amikoj de tiu tago, *they have been (they are) friends from that day.*
Ni loĝas tie de antaŭ kelkaj monatoj, *we have been living (we are living) here
since some months ago.*

---

[30] *Cf.* the complementary infinitive (28), equivalent to the object of a verb, and the use
of the infinitive after the prepositions **por, anstataŭ, antaŭ ol** (98).

[31] *Cf.* German *er ist schon lange hier*, he has already been here a long time, French *je
suis ici depuis deux ans*, I have been here two years, etc.

THE SUFFIX -UL-.

132. The suffix **-ul-** is used to form nouns indicating a person characterized by or possessing the distinguishing trait, character or quality in the root:[32]

junulo, *a youth, a young man* (from **juna**, *young*).
belulino, *a beauty, a belle* (from **bela**, *beautiful*).
maljunulo, *an old man* (from **maljuna**, *old*).
saĝulo, *a sage, a wise man* (from **saga**, *wise*).
malriĉulino, *a poor woman* (from **malriĉa**, *poor*).

LOĜI AND VIVI.

133. The verb **loĝi**, *to reside, to dwell, to lodge*, must not be confused with **vivi**, which means *to live* in the sense of "to be alive:"

Li loĝas apude, *he lives near by.*
Li vivis longan tempon, *he lived a long time.*
Vivi feliĉe estas pli bone ol loĝi riĉe, *to live happily is better than to live (lodge) richly.*

VOCABULARY.

afabl-a, *amiable, affable.*
afer-o, *thing, matter, affair.*
balanc-i, *to balance, to nod.*
barb-o, *beard.*
batal-o, *battle.*
brov-o, *eyebrow.*
bukl-o, *curl* (of hair).
har-o, *hair.*

kial, *why* (129).
mejl-o, *mile.*
okulhar-o, *eyelash.*
okulvitr-oj, *spectacles.*
pens-i, *to think, to ponder.*
vang-o, *cheek.*
verand-o, *porch, veranda.*
viv-i, *to live* (133).

PRI LA AVO KAJ LA AVINO.

Mia avo estas tre afabla persono. Li estas maljunulo kun blankaj haroj kaj blanka barbo. Li havas bluajn okulojn, kaj la brovoj super ili estas eĉ pli blankaj ol liaj haroj. Kvankam li loĝas en nia vilaĝo de antaŭ kelkaj jaroj, li antaŭe loĝis en Skotlando. Antaŭ multaj jaroj li estis soldato, kaj li ofte parolas al mi pri la bataloj kaj venkoj de tiu tempo. Sidi kviete sur la verando kaj rakonti tiajn rakontojn al la nepo ŝajne donas al li multe da plezuro. Multajn fojojn je la fino de la tago li sidas tie, kaj parolas pri tiaj aferoj ĝis malfrua horo de la vespero. Sidi ĉe liaj piedoj kaj aŭdi liajn rakontojn estas tre interese al mi. Komence, dum mi estas ĉe li, mi kutime demandas "Ĉu oni sukcesis en tiu batalo?" Tuj li balancas la kapon kaj komencas pacience rakonti pri la venkoj kaj malvenkoj (*defeats*). Li malofte respondas "Mi ne scias," al miaj demandoj "Kiam," kaj "Kial." Kelkajn fojojn li diras "Mi havas tiun opinion, sed mi ne bone scias pri la tuta afero, kaj mi miras ĉu aliaj personoj scias pli bone." Ĉar li estas multe studinta kaj pensinta, liaj opinioj estas treege interesaj. Li ĝojas tial ke mi demandas pri aferoj okazintaj (*things that have*

---

[32] *Cf.* the English adjectives *quer-ul-ous, cred-ul-ous, garr-ul-ous*, etc., and the Latin nouns *fam-ul-us*, a servant, *fig-ul-us*, a potter, and *leg-ul-us*, a gatherer.

happened), ĉar tiaj demandoj montras ke mi ankaŭ pensas pri ili. Mia avino estas malgranda, kun belaj bukloj da tute blankaj haroj. Ŝi havas belajn brunajn okulojn, kun longaj nigraj okulharoj. Oni diras ke antaŭ multaj jaroj ŝi estis belulino. Eĉ nun estas plezure rigardi ŝin, kaj vidi ŝiajn ruĝajn vangojn. De antaŭ kelkaj jaroj ŝi portas okulvitrojn por legi aŭ skribi aŭ kudri, kaj ŝi bezonas ripozon post malmulte da laboro. Promeno de eĉ mejlo estas tro longa nun por la avino. Oni diras ke ŝi ne vivos tre longan tempon, kaj tia penso donas malĝojon al ni, ĉar ni treege amas la afablan paciencan avinon.

SENTENCES FOR TRANSLATION.

1. Our grandfather is an old man, and they say that he will not live much longer. 2. He is not very strong, and can not take (*fari*) long walks. 3. The mile between his house and ours now seems long to him. 4. He prefers to sit quietly in the house or on the veranda, and think, nearly all day long (the whole day). 5. He is very amiable, and can tell exceedingly interesting stories, about the victories and defeats which happened (119) many years ago. 6. Such things are wicked I think, and I am very glad that (83) such battles do not happen now. 7. Grandfather has a long white beard and much white hair. 8. It is very interesting to hear his stories, and also to look directly at him while he is telling them. 9. He tells such stories with great pleasure. 10. Although he has lived with (125) us since February (131), he does not know (117) a great many of the neighbors, or of the other persons living (133) near. 11. Grandmother has blue eyes, red cheeks, and soft white curls. 12. She speaks slowly, with a sweet voice, and is very patient. 13. Today she said to me "Good morning, my dear (132), I have lost my spectacles. Will you look-for them for me?" I nodded (the head) and soon found the spectacles.

LESSON XXIX.

THE INTERROGATIVE ADVERB OF MANNER AND DE-
GREE.—THE PLUPERFECT TENSE.— CARDINAL
NUMBERS.—THE ACCUSATIVE OF MEASURE.—NIA
FAMILIO.

THE INTERROGATIVE ADVERB OF MANNER AND DEGREE.

134. The interrogative adverb of manner or degree, related to the interrogative pronoun **kiu**, is **kiel**, *how, in what way, to what degree:*

Kiel oni vivas en tia aero? *How do people live in such air?*
Kiel afabla ŝi estas! *How amiable she is!*
Mi miras kiel la batalo okazis, *I wonder how the battle happened.*
Kiel longe li pensis pri ĝi? *How long did he think about it?*

THE PLUPERFECT TENSE.

135. The compound tense formed by combining the past active participle with the past tense of **esti** represents an act or condition as having been completed at some time in the past, and is called the *pluperfect tense.* The conjugation of **vidi** in this tense is as follows:

mi estis vidinta, *I had seen (I was having-seen).*
vi estis vidinta, *you had seen (you were having-seen).*
li (ŝi, ĝi) estis vidinta, *he (she, it) had seen (was having-seen).*
ni estis vidintaj, *we had seen (we were having-seen).*
vi estis vidintaj, *you had seen (you were having-seen).*
ili estis vidintaj, *they had seen (they were having-seen).*

CARDINAL NUMERALS.

136. Cardinals are numeral adjectives which answer the question "How many?" The cardinals from one to twelve are as follows:

unu, *one.*	**sep,** *seven.*
du, *two.*	**ok,** *eight.*
tri, *three.*	**naŭ,** *nine.*
kvar, *four.*	**dek,** *ten.*
kvin, *five.*	**dek unu,** *eleven.*
ses, *six.*	**dek du,** *twelve.*

137. With the exception of **unu**, none of the cardinals may receive the plural ending **-j** or the accusative ending **-n**. That is, they are invariable in form. **Unuj** may be used to mean *some* in contrast to **aliaj**, *others:*

Unuj marŝis, aliaj kuris, *some walked, others ran.*
Mi prenis unujn kaj lasis la aliajn, *I took some and left the others.*

138. The preposition **el** is used after numeral adjectives expressing a number *out of* some larger number or quantity:

Ses el la knaboj venis, *six of the boys came.*
Ok el tiuj libroj estas la miaj, *eight of those books are mine.*
El tiuj ĉapeloj mi ŝatas nur unu, *of those hats I like only one.*[33]

THE ACCUSATIVE OF MEASURE.

139. A substantive in the accusative case may be used, instead of a prepositional phrase or an adverb, not only to express measure (duration) of time (91), but also to express measure of weight, price, length, etc.:

Li marŝis dek unu mejlojn, *he walked eleven miles.*
La parko estas larĝa tri mejlojn, kaj longa kvar mejlojn, *the park is three miles wide and four miles long.*
La tablo pezas dek du funtojn, *the table weighs (is heavy) twelve pounds.*

NIA FAMILIO.

Mi rakontos al vi kian familion ni havas. Ni estas ses personoj kaj ni loĝas en ĉi tiu domo de antaŭ preskaŭ kvar jaroj. Antaŭ ol veni ĉi tien al la urbo, ni estis loĝintaj tri jarojn en kvieta vilaĝo en la kamparo. Mia patro estas alta, kun grizaj haroj kaj griza barbo. Kvankam li ne estas riĉulo, li tamen havas sufiĉe da mono por vivi kontente kaj feliĉe. Li ŝatas marŝi, kaj ofte li estas marŝinta kvin aŭ ses mejlojn por unu promeno. Unu fojon mi demandis "Kiel vi povas marŝi tiel multe?" Li respondis "Dum mi estis junulo mi estis soldato, kaj tiam mi estis tre multe marŝanta. Tial mi ne forgesas la plezurojn de longaj promenoj." La patrino estas malpli alta ol mi, kaj kiel bluajn okulojn ŝi havas, sub nigraj okulharoj kaj nigraj brovoj! Ŝiaj haroj estas nigraj kaj buklaj, kaj ŝiaj vangoj estas ruĝaj. Ŝi havas dolĉan voĉon, kaj estas plezuro aŭdi ŝiajn kantojn. Por legi aŭ skribi ŝi kutime portas okulvitrojn.

Mi havas du fratojn kaj unu fratinon. La fratino havas dek unu jarojn.[34] Unu el la fratoj havas ok jarojn, la alia havas dek du jarojn. Ili povas bonege kuri, rajdi, kaj fari aliajn interesajn aferojn. Ili lernis siajn lecionojn en la lernejo tiel bone ke ses fojojn en unu monato oni laŭdis ilin. Ni multe ĝojis pri tiom da laŭdo por la fratoj. La fratino estas malpli forta, tamen ŝi ofte promenas kun ni eĉ du aŭ tri mejlojn. La avino ankaŭ loĝas ĉe ni de antaŭ sep aŭ ok jaroj. Unu el ni kutime restas ĉe la hejmo kun ŝi, dum la aliaj promenas, ĉar ŝi ne estas sufiĉe forta por marŝi eĉ unu

---

[33] The cardinal **unu** must not be used in the sense of the English pronominal "one," as in *I am searching for a book, but not the one on the table*, which should be translated **Mi serĉas libron, sed ne tiun sur la tablo.**

[34] Like French and some other languages, Esperanto commonly uses the verb *to have* rather than the verb *to be*, in expressing age: **Li havas sep jarojn**, *he is seven years old (he has seven years)*. **Mi havis dek jarojn tiam**, *I was ten years old (I had ten years) then*.

mejlon. Mi ofte miras kial ŝi preferas sidi sur la verando, kaj mi demandas al ŝi "Ĉu vi estas tro laca por marŝi?" Ŝi kutime balancas la kapon kaj diras "Jes, mia nepo, mi estas tro laca."

SENTENCES FOR TRANSLATION.

1. Three and four make seven. 2. Two and six make eight. Five and six make eleven. 3. Seven and five make twelve. 4. I have been studying geometry since five months ago, and German since January. 5. I have read three German books, but I shall not be able to talk in this language until after August. 6. To learn how to speak such a language is a difficult matter. 7. Nine of the children in our school are now studying German with me. 8. Some learn it easily, others do not like it. 9. Three of the boys and two of the girls in that school are German. 10. They had resided four years in a large city, but I think (that) they live more contentedly in our quiet village. 11. They can not talk with us very well, but merely nod their heads when we talk to them. 12. I had not seen them before they came to school, although they are neighbors of ours. 13. They are amiable children, with blue eyes, red cheeks, and yellow hair. 14. They can ride very well, and often ride eight or ten miles in one day. 15. They usually ride in a park three miles wide and four miles long, where there is but little (*nur malmulte da*) dust.

LESSON XXX.

THE INTERROGATIVE ADVERB OF QUANTITY.—MOD-
IFIERS OF IMPERSONALLY USED VERBS.— FORMA-
TION OF CARDINAL NUMERALS.—THE SUFFIX -AN-
.—LECIONO PRI ARITMETIKO.

THE INTERROGATIVE ADVERB OF QUANTITY.

140. The interrogative adverb of quantity related to the interrogative pronoun
kiu is **kiom**, *how much, how many*:

Kiom da tempo vi ripozis? *How much time did you rest?*
Kiom da sukero kaj kiom da fragoj vi aĉetis? *How much sugar and how many
strawberries did you buy?*
Ni miras kiom da mono li havos, *we wonder how much money he will have.*
Kiom de la leciono vi lernis? *How much of the lesson did you learn?*

MODIFIERS OF IMPERSONALLY USED VERBS.

141. Any modifier of an impersonal verb (**50**) or of a verb used impersonally,
that is, with an infinitive or clause for its subject, or without any definitely expressed or personal subject (as in "it is cold," "it seems too early"), must necessarily be adverbial:

Estas varme en la domo, *it is warm in the house.*
Estos malvarme morgaŭ, *it will be cold tomorrow.*
Estas bone ke li venis, *it is well that he came.*
Estas amuze ke ni forgesis lin, *it is amusing that we forgot him.*
Ke vi venis estis tre saĝe, *that you came was very wise.*
Estos pli agrable en la salono, *it will be pleasanter in the parlor.*

FORMATION OF CARDINAL NUMERALS.

142. The cardinal numerals for the tens, hundreds and thousands are formed
by prefixing **du**, **tri**, **kvar**, etc., to **dek**, *ten*, **cent**, *hundred*, and **mil**, *thousand*, respectively.

Tens.

dudek, *twenty.*	**sesdek**, *sixty.*
tridek, *thirty.*	**sepdek**, *seventy.*
kvardek, *forty.*	**okdek**, *eighty.*
kvindek, *fifty.*	**naŭdek**, *ninety.*

Hundreds.	Thousands.
ducent, *two hundred.*	**trimil**, *three thousand.*
kvincent, *five hundred.*	**kvarmil**, *four thousand.*
sepcent, *seven hundred*, etc.	**sesmil**, *six thousand*, etc.

143. The cardinals between ten and twenty, twenty and thirty, etc., are formed by placing **unu, du, tri**, etc., after **dek, dudek, tridek**, etc. (*Cf.* **dek unu**, *eleven*, **dek du**, *twelve*, **136**):

dek kvar, *fourteen.*	**tridek kvin**, *thirty-five.*
dek naŭ, *nineteen.*	**sepdek ok**, *seventy-eight.*
dudek tri, *twenty-three.*	**naŭdek ses**, *ninety-six*, etc.

144. Cardinals containing more than two figures begin with the largest number and descend regularly, as in English:

cent tridek kvin, *one hundred and thirty-five.*
kvarcent naŭdek sep, *four hundred and ninety-seven.*
sescent du, *six hundred and two.*
mil okdek, *one thousand and eighty.*
mil naucent dek du, *one thousand nine hundred and twelve (nineteen hundred and twelve).*

THE SUFFIX -AN-.

145. The suffix **-an-** is used to form words indicating an inhabitant or resident of the place denoted by the root,[35] or a member or adherent of the party, organization, etc., denoted by the root. The suffix **-an-** may itself be used as a root, forming **ano**, *member*, etc.

bostonano, *Bostonian.*	**domano**, *inmate of a house.*
kamparano, *countryman, peasant.*	**vilaĝano**, *villager.*

VOCABULARY.

aritmetik-o, *arithmetic.*	**memor-i**, *to remember.*
cent, *hundred* (142).	**mil**, *thousand* (142).
erar-o, *error, mistake.*	**minut-o**, *minute.*
grad-o, *grade, degree.*	**ricev-i**, *to receive.*
kalkul-i, *to calculate, to reckon.*	**sekund-o**, *second.*
kiom, *how much* (140).	**superjar-o**, *leap-year.*

LECIONO PRI ARITMETIKO.

---

[35] *Cf.* English *urb-an, suburb-an, Rom-an, republic-an, Mohammed-an*, etc.

Estas malvarme hodiaŭ, kaj tute ne agrable ekster la domo. La urbanoj ne estas promenantaj en la parko, ĉar ili preferas resti en la domoj. Mi ankaŭ restis en la domo, kaj parolis al mia juna frato. Mi helpis lin pri la leciono en aritmetiko, tial ke li baldaŭ havos ekzamenojn, kaj li volas esti preta por skribi tre bonajn respondojn. Mi demandis al li "Kiom faras dek tri kaj dek kvar?" Li respondis ke tiuj faras dudek sep. Tiam mi demandis kiom faras dudek unu kaj tridek kvar. Li kalkulis kvin aŭ ses sekundojn, per mallaŭta voĉo, kaj diris "Ili faras kvindek kvin." Mi demandis kiom faras ducent tri kaj sepcent ok, kaj li respondis ke ili faras naŭcent dek unu. Li tute ne faris erarojn al mi, kaj fine mi diris al li ke li povas bonege kalkuli. Mi opinias ke li ricevos bonan gradon en la ekzamenoj. Post kelkaj minutoj ni komencis paroli pri aliaj aferoj. Mi demandis "Kiom da tagoj en la monato septembro?" La frato respondis "Septembro, novembro, aprilo kaj junio havas tridek tagojn. Kvankam tiuj monatoj havas tiom da tagoj, la aliaj monatoj havas tridek unu tagojn. Sed la monato februaro havas nur dudek ok tagojn." Estas interese lerni pri ĉi tiu monato februaro. Dum tri jaroj ĝi havas dudek ok tagojn, sed en la sekvanta jaro ĝi havas dudek naŭ tagojn. La jaro havanta tian februaron estas la "superjaro." Mi rakontis tiun interesan aferon al la frato, kaj li diris ke li bone memoros ĝin. Li diris ke li ne antaŭe sciis pri la superjaro. Li ne sciis ke la superjaro havas tricent sesdek ses tagojn, kvankam la aliaj jaroj havas nur tricent sesdek kvin tagojn. Li diris ke li ankaŭ memoros pri la nombro da tagoj en la superjaro, kaj ke li rakontos la aferon al la aliaj knaboj.

SENTENCES FOR TRANSLATION.

1. (To be written out in full): 14, 18, 42, 86, 79, 236, 431, 687, 788, 1240, 1885, 9872, 4500, 1912. 2. There are twelve months in a year, and in most of the months of the year there are thirty-one days. 3. There are only thirty days in the months April, June, September and November. 4. There are seven days in a week, and twenty-four hours in a day. 5. Twelve of these hours make the day, and the others make the night. 6. There are sixty minutes in one hour, and sixty seconds in one minute. 7. There are four weeks and also two or three days in one month. 8. In the year there are fifty-two weeks. 9. How many weeks are there in ten years? 10. At least one year in ten years is a leap-year. 11. In a leap-year there are three hundred and sixty-six days, instead of three hundred and sixty-five. 12. Wise men calculated about this matter, many years ago. 13. It is well for us that they liked to study arithmetic. 15. I have often received good grades in this study. 16. I remember it easily, and seldom make mistakes.

LESSON XXXI.

THE RELATIVE PRONOUN.—THE FUTURE PERFECT TENSE.—ORDINAL NUMERALS.—ALFREDO GRANDA KAJ LA LIBRO.

THE RELATIVE PRONOUN.

146. A connecting pronoun referring to something which precedes (or follows) is called a *relative pronoun*. The person or thing to which it refers is called its *antecedent*. The relative pronoun, identical in form with the interrogative pronoun (106), as in English, is **kiu**, *which, who*.[36] The relative pronoun agrees *in number* with its antecedent. Whether it is in the accusative case or not depends upon its relation to its own verb or to other words in its own clause (called the relative clause):

La junuloj, kiuj venis, estas afablaj, *the youths who came are amiable.*
La personoj, kiujn li vidos, estas amikoj miaj, *the persons (whom) he will see are friends of mine.*
Mi kalkulis la gradon, kiun li ricevos, *I calculated the grade (which) he will receive.*
Mi memoras tiun aferon, pri kiu vi parolas, *I remember that matter about which you speak.*

147. Like English "whose" the genitive form **kies** of the interrogative pronoun (107) is also used as a relative, referring to a substantive (singular or plural) for its antecedent:

Li estas la viro, kies libron vi trovis, *he is the man whose book you found.*
Mi konas la infanojn, kies patro estas amiko via, *I know the children whose father is a friend of yours.*

THE FUTURE PERFECT TENSE.

148. The compound tense formed by combining the past participle with the future tense of the auxiliary verb **esti** represents an act or condition as having been already completed or perfected at a future time, and is called the *future perfect tense*. The conjugation of **vidi** in this tense is as follows:

mi estos vidinta, *I shall have seen (I shall be having-seen).*

---

[36] Sometimes English uses "that" for a relative pronoun, as "I saw the book *that* you have." This must always be translated by **kiu**. Likewise, English sometimes omits the relative pronoun, as "I saw the book you have." The relative pronoun is never thus omitted in Esperanto.

vi **estos vidinta**, *you will have seen (you will be having-seen).*
li (**ŝi, ĝi**) **estos vidinta**, *he (she, it) will have seen (will be having-seen).*
ni **estos vidintaj**, *we shall have seen (shall be having-seen).*
vi **estos vidintaj**, *you will have seen (will be having-seen).*
ili **estos vidintaj**, *they will have seen (will be having-seen).*

ORDINAL NUMERALS.

149. Ordinal numerals are adjectives which answer the question "Which in order?" as "first", "third", etc. They are formed by adding the adjectival suffix **-a** to the cardinals. The various parts of an ordinal must be connected by hyphens, since it is to the entire cardinal, and not any part of it, that the adjective ending **-a** is attached:

unua, *first.*	**dudek-sepa**, *twenty-seventh.*
dua, *second.*	**kvardek-sesa**, *forty-sixth.*
tria, *third.*	**cent-okdek-kvina**, *hundred and eighty-fifth.*
oka, *eighth.*	**mil-okcent-kvara**, *one thousand eight*
dek-unua, *eleventh.*	*hundred and fourth.*
dek-naŭa, *nineteenth.*	**sesmil-sepa**, *six thousand and seventh.*[37]

Vocabulary.

angl-a, *English.*	**neces-a**, *necessary.*
dezir-i, *to desire.*	**paf-i**, *to shoot.*
dolar-o, *dollar.*	**pafark-o**, *bow* (for shooting).
gajn-i, *to win, to gain.*	**part-o**, *part, share.*
kost-i, *to cost.*	**pen-i**, *to strive, to try.*
last-a, *last.*	**traduk-i**, *to translate.*
latin-a, *Latin.*	**sag-o**, *arrow.*
mar-o, *sea.*	**sam-a**, *same.*

ALFREDO GRANDA KAJ LA LIBRO.

Antaŭ pli multe ol mil jaroj vivis Alfredo Granda, unu el la plej interesaj personoj pri kiuj ni estas aŭdintaj. Li estis la unua angla reĝo, kiu deziris legi librojn. Li estis ankaŭ la lasta, kiu povis legi ilin, ĝis post multaj jaroj. Unu tagon, dum li estis malgranda knabo kun flavaj buklaj haroj, lia patrino, tre saĝa reĝino, montris al li kaj al liaj fratoj belegan libron. Ŝi diris ke la libro kostis multe da mono en lando trans la maro, kaj ke ĝi nun apartenas al ŝi. Si diris "Miaj filoj, mi donos ĉi tiun libron al tiu el vi, kiu lernos legi ĝin. Kiu el vi estos la unua, kiu povos legi? Tiu ricevos la libron." Nu, Alfredo komencis studi, kaj post ne longe li gajnis la belegan libron. Liaj fratoj eĉ ne penis gajni ĝin. Tiam oni tre malmulte pensis pri libroj. La reĝoj kaj iliaj filoj nur malofte povis legi, kaj treege malofte povis skribi. Oni laŭdis nur personojn, kiuj bone rajdis kaj batalis per sagoj kaj pafarkoj. Sed oni opiniis ke tute ne estis necese scii pri la aferoj, kiujn la libroj rakontas. Tial Alfredo

[37] Ordinal numerals may be abbreviated thus: **1a**, *1st*, **2a**, *2nd*, **3a**, *3rd*, **5a**, *5th*, **1912a**, *1912th*, **233a**, *233rd*, etc. If the ordinal number is used in an accusative construction, the abbreviation is given the accusative ending, as **1an**, **2an**, **3an**, **1912an**, etc.

ne ricevis laŭdon pro sia deziro por legi. La sesan aŭ sepan jaron post sia ricevo de la libro, Alfredo volis lerni la latinan lingvon, ĉar tiam oni skribis latine (*in Latin*) la librojn, kiuj estis plej bonaj. Oni serĉis ĝis la finoj de la lando, kaj iris multajn mejlojn, sed preskaŭ ne povis trovi personon, kiu eĉ estis aŭdinta pri tia lingvo. Fine oni trovis personon por helpi Alfredon, kiu tiam lernis la latinan lingvon. Tiu sama Alfredo estis reĝo multajn jarojn, kaj estis unu el la plej bonaj reĝoj, kiujn la angla lando estas havinta. Alfredo skribis librojn en la latina lingvo, kaj ankaŭ tradukis latinajn librojn en la anglan lingvon.

SENTENCES FOR TRANSLATION.

1. (To be written out in full): 37th, 59th, 73rd, 92nd, 846th, 119th, 1274th, 1910th, 14235th. 2. Before my friend will have finished that mansion (122), it will have cost twenty thousand dollars. 3. Before coming to visit you, I shall have ridden twelve miles on my horse. 4. The grade which you will have received in arithmetic soon after the first of March will be excellent. 5. You do not make mistakes very often in the lessons. 6. I shall try after a few minutes to translate that Latin book, for (*ĉar*) it seems interesting. 7. It is necessary to study Latin, for I desire to read the stories which are in my Latin book. 8. The one thousand nine hundred and fourth year was a leap-year. 9. The fourth year after that year was also a leap-year. 10. The 1912th year will be a leap-year. There are three hundred and sixty-six days in such a year. 12. Alfred won the book which his mother had bought. 13. Such a book now costs four or five hundred dollars. 14. Alfred the Great was the last king until many years afterward (until after many years) who could read or write. 15. He was the first king in that land who even wished to be able to read books. 16. We often talk about this same King Alfred, and say that he was the father of the English language. 17. People say so (*diras tiel*) because he translated Latin books into the language of his land, and because he also wrote books in that language.

LESSON XXXII.

KIA AS A RELATIVE ADJECTIVE.—KIE AS A RELATIVE
ADVERB.—THE FUTURE ACTIVE PARTICIPLE.—THE
PERIPHRASTIC FUTURE TENSES.—THE SUFFIX -IND-
.—ALFREDO GRANDA KAJ LA KUKOJ.

KIA AS A RELATIVE ADJECTIVE.

150. The interrogative adjective **kia** (112) is also used as a relative adjective,
referring back to **tia,** or to some equivalent phrase or word indicating quality, such
as **sama**, etc. In this use it may often be translated "as", or "which":

Mi havas tian libron, kian mi volas, *I have such a (that kind of) book as (which
kind) I wish.*
Tiaj amikoj, kiajn vi havas, estas afablaj, *such friends as (of which kind) you
have are amiable.*
Li deziras tian ĉapelon, kia kostas ses dolarojn, *he desires that kind of hat
which (kind) costs six dollars.*
Mi havas la saman deziron, kian vi, *I have the same desire as you (same kind
which you have).*

KIE AS A RELATIVE ADVERB.

151. The interrogative adverb **kie, kien** (118) is also used as a relative adverb
of place with **tie, tien,** or some other expression of place for its antecedent.[38] **Kien**
is used when the verb in the relative clause expresses motion toward the place
indicated, whether or not its antecedent has this ending. Similarly, **kie** may refer
to **tie** or to **tien**:

Mi iros tien, kie vi estas, *I shall go there where you are.*
Mi estis tie, kien vi iros, *I was there (at that place) where you will go.*
Mi iros tien, kien vi iris, *I shall go to that place to which you went (I shall go
where you went).*
Mi trovis lin en la urbo, kie li loĝas, *I found him in the city where he lives.*
Ĉu vi venos ĉi tien, kie ni estas? *Are you coming here where we are?*

THE FUTURE ACTIVE PARTICIPLE.

152. The future active participle, expressing what the word modified will do

---

[38] Any interrogative adverb may also be used to introduce an indirect question, thus
serving as a subordinating conjunction (*cf.* **ĉu**).

or is about to do, ends in **-onta,** as **vidonta,** *about to see,* **ironta,** *about to go:*

> **La forironta viro vokis sian serviston,** *the man going to depart (the about-to-de-part man) called his servant.*
>
> **La virino salutonta vin estas tre afabla,** *the woman about to greet you is very affable.*
>
> **La venonta monato estas marto,** *the coming month is March.*
>
> **La venontan semajnon mi foriros,** *the coming (next) week I shall depart.*

THE PERIPHRASTIC FUTURE TENSES.

153. The compound tenses formed by combining the future active participle with each of the three aoristic tenses of **esti** represent an act or state as about to occur in the present, past, or future, respectively, and are called *periphrastic future tenses.* Except when great accuracy is desired, these tenses are not often used. A synopsis of **vidi** in the first person singular and plural of these tenses is as follows:

Present Periphrastic Future.

mi estas vidonta,   **ni estas vidontaj,**
I am about to (going to) see.   *we are about to (going to) see.*

Past Periphrastic Future.

mi estis vidonta,   **ni estis vidontaj,**
I was about to (going to) see.   *we were about to (going to) see.*

Future Periphrastic Future.

mi estos vidonta,   **ni estos vidontaj,**
I shall be about to (going to) see. *we shall be about to (going to) see.*

THE SUFFIX -IND-.

154. The suffix **-ind-** is used to form words expressing *worthy of, deserving of,* that which is indicated in the root. It may also be used as a root, to form **inda,** *worthy,* **malinda,** *unworthy,* **indo,** *worth, merit,* etc.:

dezirinda, *desirable.*   **rimarkinda,** *noteworthy, remarkable.*
laŭdinda, *praiseworthy.*   **ridinde,** *ridiculously, laughably.*
mallaŭdinda, *blameworthy.*   **tradukinda,** *worth translating.*

VOCABULARY.

ankoraŭ, *still, yet.*[†]   **flar-i,** *to smell.*
atak-i, *to attack.*   **gast-o,** *guest.*
bat-i, *to beat.*   **ho!** *Oh!*
cert-a, *sure, certain.*   **kri-i,** *to exclaim, to cry.*
defend-i, *to defend.*   **kruel-a,** *cruel.*
difekt-i, *to spoil.*   **kuk-o,** *cake.*
edz-o, *husband.*   **lign-o,** *wood.*
fajr-o, *fire.*   **suspekt-i,** *to suspect.*

ALFREDO GRANDA KAJ LA KUKOJ.

Unu fojon antaŭ pli multe ol mil jaroj, soldatoj venis de trans la maro por ataki la anglan reĝon Alfredon Grandan. Ili nek konis nek malamis lin, sed ili sciis ke li estas persono kies landon ili deziras gajni. Ĉi tiuj malamikoj estis venintaj tiel subite ke Alfredo ne estis preta por defendi sian landon kontraŭ ili. Tial li forkuris kelkajn mejlojn de la urbo, kaj sin kaŝis en granda arbaro malantaŭ vilaĝo. Anstataŭ porti reĝajn vestojn li aĉetis tiajn ĉifonojn kiajn kamparanoj kaj malriĉuloj portas. Li loĝis ĉe malriĉa sed laŭdinda kamparano, kiu ne konis la reĝon, kaj tute ne suspektis kia persono lia gasto estas. Unu memorindan tagon Alfredo estis sidanta apud la fajro, kaj estis rigardanta siajn sagojn kaj pafarkon dum li pensis malĝoje pri sia lando. La edzino de la arbarano demandis "Ĉu vi ankoraŭ sidos tie dekkvin aŭ dudek minutojn?" "Jes," respondis la reĝo. Ŝi diris "Nu, estos necese fari pli varmegan fajron por tiaj kukoj kiajn mi nun estas bakonta. Ĉu vi gardos tiujn kukojn kiuj nun estas super la fajro, dum mi kolektos pli multe da ligno?" Alfredo respondis "Certe mi gardos ilin kontraŭ la fajro." La virino serĉonta lignon foriris en alian parton de la arbaro, kie estis multe da ligno, kaj la reĝo penis zorgi pri la kukoj. Sed baldaŭ li forgesis ilin, kaj la fajro ilin difektis. Kiam la virino venis kaj flaris la kukojn ŝi kriis "ho, vi riproĉinda viro! Kvankam vi ankoraŭ sidas tie, vi ne pensas pri la kukoj, kaj la fajro estas difektinta ilin!" Ŝi estis kruele batonta la reĝon, kiam li diris al ŝi kiu li estas, kaj kial li forgesis la kukojn. Tiam ŝi tre hontis, kaj anstataŭ mallaŭdi lin ŝi volis esti ankoraŭ pli bona al li.

SENTENCES FOR TRANSLATION.

1. Alfred the Great was a praiseworthy king who lived more than a thousand years ago. 2. People still talk about him because he not only translated many Latin books into the English language, but also wrote in English. 3. He wished to help the peasants still more. 4. But enemies often attacked him, and finally they conquered his soldiers. 5. Then they hastened to where (151) Alfred was. 6. They were about to attack him, when he rode away secretly (kaŝe) into a large forest. 7. There he dwelt some time in the house of a poor forester. 8. He wore such rags as a peasant usually wears, and did not tell the forester who he was. 9. One day he was sitting near the fire and wondering, "Will the enemy have conquered my soldiers next week?" 10. The forester's wife said, "Will you sit there yet a while and take-care of those cakes? I am about to gather more wood." 11. He replied, "Certainly, I will try to help you." 12. But when after a few minutes the woman smelled the cakes, she knew that the fire had spoiled them. 13. She exclaimed "Oh, what a blame-worthy man!" 14. She commenced to beat the king cruelly, but he did not defend himself. 15. Instead (120), he told her who he was.

LESSON XXXIII.

KIAM AS A RELATIVE ADVERB.—KIEL AS A RELATIVE ADVERB.—NUMERAL NOUNS AND ADVERBS.— WORD DERIVATION FROM PREPOSITIONS.—LA INVITO.

KIAM AS A RELATIVE ADVERB.

155. The interrogative temporal adverb **kiam** (123) is also used as a relative temporal adverb, with **tiam** or an equivalent word or phrase for its antecedent. (It may not be omitted as in English "at the time he came"):

Mi suspektis lin je la tempo kiam li venis, *I suspected him at the time when he came (the time that he came).*

Li defendis sin tiam, kiam oni atakis lin, *he defended himself then, when he was attacked.*

Mi ankoraŭ sidos tie ĝis kiam vi venos, *I shall still sit there until when you come (until you come).*

Post kiam li tiel laŭte kriis, li komencis plori, *after he shouted so loudly, he began to cry.*

KIEL AS A RELATIVE ADVERB.

156. The interrogative adverb **kiel** (134) is also used as a relative adverb of manner and degree, with **tiel**, or **same**, or an equivalent adverb or phrase for its antecedent. It may often be translated "as:"

Mi defendis min tiel, kiel li defendis sin, *I defended myself in that way in which (way) he defended himself.*

Vi ne estas tiel kruela kiel li, *you are not so cruel as he (is).*

Ili batis lin same kiel vi, *they beat him in the same way as you (did).*

Ili batis lin same kiel vin, *they beat him the same as (they did) you.*

Kiel mi diris al li, mi estas feliĉa, *as I told him, I am happy* (antecedent not expressed).

Li parolis tiel mallaŭte kiel antaŭe, *he spoke as softly as before.*

Ŝi estas tiel bona kiel ŝi estas bela, *she is as good as she is fair.*

NUMERAL NOUNS AND ADVERBS.

157. Nouns may be formed from the cardinals by addition of the ending **-o.**

After such nouns the preposition **da** or **de** is used:[39]

dekduo, *a dozen.*
dudeko, *a score.*
deko, *a ten, half a score.*
cento, *a hundred.*

milo, *a thousand.*
unuo, *a unit.*
kvaro, *a four, a quartette.*
trio, *a three, a trio.*

158. Adverbs may be formed from the cardinals by addition of the ending **-e**:

unue, *firstly, at first.*
due, *secondly, in the second place.*
kvine, *fifthly, in the fifth place.*

deke, *tenthly.*
sesdeke, *sixtiethly.*
okdek-kvare, *eighty-fourthly.*

WORD DERIVATION FROM PREPOSITIONS.

159. Adjectives, verbs and nouns, as well as adverbs (**120**), may be derived from prepositions by addition of the formative endings (**116**), with sometimes a special suffix also:

anstataŭi, *to replace, to take the place of.*
anstataŭulo, *a substitute.*
antaŭa, *previous, preceding.*
apuda, *near, contiguous, adjacent.*
ĉirkaŭi, *to surround, to encircle.*
ĉirkaŭo, *a circuit, a circumference.*
kontraŭa, *adverse, opposite, contrary.*
kontraŭulo, *adversary, opponent.*
kunulo, *comrade, companion.*
superi, *to surpass, to exceed, to be above.*
superege, *surpassingly, exceedingly.*

---

[39] The prepositions **da** and **de** follow nouns (**99, 100**) or adverbs (**101**), while **el** follows adjectives in the superlative degree (**75**), cardinal numerals (**138**), and the pronouns tiu, kiu (**106**), etc.:

dekduo da ovoj, *a dozen (of) eggs.*
dekduo de la ovoj, *a dozen of the eggs.*
dek du el tiuj ovoj, *twelve of those eggs.*
kiu el la ovoj? *which one of the eggs?*
tiu el la ovoj, *that one of the eggs.*
la plej freŝa el la ovoj, *the freshest of the eggs.*

VOCABULARY.

adiaŭ, *farewell, goodbye.*
akcept-i, *to accept, to receive.*
elekt-i, *to choose, to select.*
fest-i, *to celebrate, to entertain.*
gant-o, *glove.*
ĝentil-a, *courteous.*
invit-i, *to invite.*
ĵus, *just, at the moment.*[‡]

kuz-o, *cousin.*
malgraŭ, *notwithstanding.*
par-o, *pair.*
pend-i, *to hang.*
prez-o, *price.*
renkont-i, *to meet.*
ŝu-o, *shoe.*
uz-i, *to use.*

LA INVITO.

Hieraŭ matene mia kuzo vizitis ĉe ni, kaj invitis min al malgranda festo kiu okazos morgaŭ vespere. Tiam li festos la lastan tagon de la jaro. Li diris ke la gastoj sidos ĉirkaŭ la fajrejo kaj rakontos rakontojn ĝis malfrua horo. Mi akceptis lian ĝentilan inviton, kaj diris ke mi certe venos. Mia kuzo loĝas en la sama urbo kie nia familio loĝas, sed en alia parto. Lia hejmo estas preskaŭ du mejlojn de la nia. Tamen, ni estas bonaj kunuloj, kaj ofte promenas kune. Ĵus kiam li estis elironta el la pordo hieraŭ, mi uzis la okazon (*opportunity*) por proponi mallongan promenon. Li respondis ke li ĝoje promenos kun mi, malgraŭ la neĝa vetero. Tial ni formarŝis tien, kie la stratoj estis malplej kotaj. La kuzo havas dek ok jarojn, sed mi estas preskaŭ tiel alta kiel li. Mi estas certa ke mi estas ankaŭ tiel forta kiel li. Ni parolis pri multaj interesaj aferoj, kaj bonege nin amuzis, ĝis kiam estis necese hejmen iri. La kuzo diris "adiaŭ," kaj iris rekte hejmen, sed mi iris al granda butiko. Unue, mi volis aĉeti paron da novaj gantoj, por anstataŭi la malnovajn gantojn kiujn mi ankoraŭ estis portanta, kvankam mi aĉetis ilin antaŭ tri monatoj. Due, mi bezonis paron da novaj ŝuoj. Mi iris en la butikon kie pendis tiaj gantoj, kiajn mi ŝatas, kaj oni tuj venis por renkonti min, kaj demandis "Kiajn vestojn vi volas aĉeti?" Oni montris al mi preskaŭ dudekon da paroj da gantoj. Mi elektis tre bonan paron, kaj estis ĵus aĉetonta ilin, malgraŭ la tro granda prezo, kiam mi vidis alian pli belan paron. Tial mi aĉetis ĉi tiun, kaj poste mi rigardis la ŝuojn. Mi trovis rimarkinde bonan paron, ĉar estas centoj da ŝuoj en tiu butiko. Mi tuj aĉetis tiun paron, kaj tiam hejmen iris.

SENTENCES FOR TRANSLATION.

1. My friend likes to live in the city, but his wife prefers to live in their little wooden house in the country. 2. There she can see and smell the flowers, and can take (*fari*) long walks in the adjacent fields and forest. 3. There are often hundreds of persons in a village, but there are thousands of persons in a city. 4. The larger a city is, the larger and better its stores are. 5. In the second place, one can buy better bread, vegetables and cake in the city. 6. Thirdly, one can also find better gloves, hats and shoes there, and the price is often less. 7. Therefore I make use of the opportunity when I go to the city, and usually buy a pair of new gloves. 8. I am still wearing a pair of gloves which the rain spoiled. 9. Notwithstanding their ugly color, they are still thick and good. 10. But soon I shall buy such a pair as (150) is hanging in the window of that store. 11. The price is low, and I need a new

pair now, for my cousin has invited me to a small party (*festo*) at his house. 12. I accepted his invitation courteously, and said that I would gladly be his guest. 13. We are good comrades, although he is younger than I am. 14. My (girl) cousin, his sister, is older than he is, but he is as tall as she. 15. I was just about to send a letter to him at the minute that (155) he knocked on our door. 16. His visit will take the place of (159) my letter. 17. Just as (just when) he was going away, I said goodbye to him, and said that I would meet him in the park tomorrow. 18. I think that we shall have a pleasant walk, although the weather is still remarkably cold, the same as (156) it was two or three months ago.

LESSON XXXIV.

PREPOSITIONS AS PREFIXES.—THE SUFFIX -EBL-.—EX-
PRESSION OF THE HIGHEST DEGREE POSSIBLE.—TI-
TLES AND TERMS OF ADDRESS.—ĈE LA FESTO.

PREPOSITIONS AS PREFIXES.

160. Any preposition may be used as a prefix to a verb, provided the resulting compound is intelligible. A few prepositional compounds are given below, only verbs being shown, although nouns, adjectives and adverbs may be formed from these (116):

alveni, *to arrive.*
aldoni, *to add.*
antaŭdiri, *to predict.*
ĉirkaŭpreni, *to embrace.*
ĉeesti, *to be present.*
dependi, *to hang from, to depend.*
demeti, *to lay aside.*
depreni, *to subtract.*
enhavi, *to contain.*
eliri, *to go out.*[§]

interparoli, *to converse.*
kontraŭdiri, *to contradict.*
kunlabori, *to collaborate.*
kunveni, *to assemble.*
priskribi, *to describe.*
subteni, *to support.*
surmeti, *to put on.*
traguti, *to percolate.*
travidi, *to see through*
transiri, *to cross.*

THE SUFFIX -EBL-.

161. The suffix **-ebl-** is used to form adjectives, adverbs, etc., expressing the likelihood or possibility of that which is indicated by the root.[40] It may be used as a root, to form **ebla**, *possible*, etc.

eltrovebla, *discoverable.*
legebla, *legible.*
manĝebla, *edible.*

rompebla, *breakable.*
videbla, *visible.*
travidebla, *transparent.*

EXPRESSION OF THE HIGHEST DEGREE POSSIBLE.

162. The adverb **plej**, *most* (74), modified by **kiel eble** (*as possible*), is used to express the highest degree possible:

<u>Ĝi estas kiel</u> eble plej bona, *it is the best possible.*

[40] The suffix **-ebl-** is often equivalent to the English suffixes *-able*, *-ible*, but these suffixes have other meanings also, as in "readable," *worth reading* (**leginda**), "lovable," *deserving of love* (**aminda**), etc.

Ni estos kiel eble plej saĝaj, *we shall be as wise as possible.*
Li uzis kiel eble plej malmulte, *he used the least possible.*
Mi skribis kiel eble plej legeble, *I wrote as legibly as possible.*

TITLES AND TERMS OF ADDRESS.

163. The words **sinjoro,** *gentleman,* **sinjorino,** *lady,* **fraŭlino,** *miss,* are used like English *Mr., Mrs., Miss,* before proper names, and are also used as terms of address, without being followed by the name:[41]

Adiaŭ, Sinjoro. Adiaŭ, Sinjorino, *Goodbye (Sir). Goodbye, Madam.*

Fraŭlino B— —, ĉu vi konas tiun sinjoron kun Sinjorino C— —? *Miss B— —, do you know that gentleman with Mrs. C— —?*
Mi ne konas tiun fraŭlinon, *I do not know that young lady.*
Kien vi volas iri, Fraŭlino? *Where do you wish to go (Miss)?*
Sinjoro A— — estas tre afabla, *Mr. A— — is very amiable.*

VOCABULARY.

atent-a, *attentive.*	**onkl-o,** *uncle.*
aŭskult-i, *to listen.*	**san-a,** *in good health.*
babil-i, *to chatter.*	**sent-i,** *to feel.*
doktor-o, *doctor.*	**sinjor-o,** *gentleman.*
fraŭl-o, *bachelor.*	**ŝtup-o,** *step (of stairs).*
gaj-a, *merry, gay.*	**tas-o,** *cup.*
grup-o, *group.*	**vojaĝ-o,** *voyage, journey.*

ĈE LA FESTO.

Hieraŭ vespere mi iris al la hejmo de mia kuzo, kiu estis invitinta min al malgranda festo ĉe li. Ĉar mi deziris alveni kiel eble plej frue, mi foriris de mia loĝejo kiel eble plej baldaŭ, malgraŭ la neĝa vetero. Mi estis surmetinta paron da dikaj gantoj, kaj mi portis dikajn ŝuojn. Mi ankaŭ havis mian ombrelon, kvankam pro la vento mi ne povis uzi tiun. Tuj kiam mi supreniris la ŝtuparon ĉe la hejmo de la kuzo, li aŭdis min, kaj venis por malfermi la pordon kaj akcepti min. "Bonan vesperon, kia estas via sano?" li diris. Mi respondis "Mi sanas bonege, dankon," kaj eniris la domon kun li. Ni supren iris per granda ŝtuparo al ĉambro kie mi lasis la ĉapelon, gantojn kaj ombrelon, tiam ni malsupren venis kaj eniris la salonon. Mi salutis la onklinon, kiu afable parolis al mi, kaj ankaŭ la du kuzinojn. Unu kuzino estis ĵus priskribonta interesan libron, kiun ŝi antaŭ ne longe tralegis, kiam la aliaj gastoj komencis alveni. Sinjoro B— — ĉeestis, kaj Doktoro C— —, kun sia filino Fraŭlino Mario, kaj multe da aliaj sinjoroj kaj sinjorinoj. La gastoj sidis aŭ staris en malgrandaj grupoj, kaj interparolis kun videbla plezuro. Unu rakontis pri vojaĝo, kaj tiam oni komencis priparoli la prezojn de aferoj en aliaj landoj. Mi atente aŭskultis kelkajn minutojn, kaj tiam foriris al alia grupo, kie oni gaje babilis pri es-

---

[41] *Cf.* English *Doctor, Professor, Madam,* as terms of address, and also German *Mein Herr, gnädige Frau, gnädiges Fräulein,* French *Monsieur, Mademoiselle,* Spanish, *Señor, Señora,* Italian *Signore,* etc.

tontaj (*future*) promenoj kaj festoj. Post unu aŭ du horoj, la servistinoj alportis al ni bonan malgrandan manĝon, kune kun tasoj da bonega kafo. Fine, je malfrua horo ni ĝentile dankis la familion de mia kuzo, kaj diris adiaŭ. Tiam ni foriris hejmen, kun sentoj da granda plezuro pro la agrabla festo.

SENTENCES FOR TRANSLATION.

1. There are dozens of edible fruits, but the fruits of hundreds of trees are not at all (*tute ne estas*) edible. 2. The transparent cup and plate upon the table are very breakable. 3. I predict that you will break them as soon as you seize them. 4. That letter is worth reading. 5. But it is difficult to read it, for it is not very legible. 6. It is from my uncle, who wishes to arrive at-our-house as early as possible. 7. He is still in the city, but soon he will be here, and will go up the steps (*ŝtuparon*) of our porch and knock on the door. 8. There are very few persons who contradict his opinions. 9. His opinions, however, are worthy of attention (154) and usually I listen courteously while he is talking. 10. Now, however, I prefer to listen to the group of ladies in the adjacent room. 11. They are chattering gaily, and listening to the young lady who is about to sing. 12. Madam, do you feel the wind? I notice that it is blowing the curtains which hang before that window. 13. I will close the window, because I am not very well (*sana*) today. 14. Is that gentleman across the room a bachelor? 15. Yes. He is describing a voyage and the people whom he met.

LESSON XXXV.

KIOM AS A RELATIVE ADVERB.—THE PRESENT PASSIVE
PARTICIPLE.—FRACTIONS.— DESCRIPTIVE COM-
POUNDS.—LA ĤINOJ.

KIOM AS A RELATIVE ADVERB.

164. The interrogative adverb **kiom** (140) is used as a relative adverb of quantity, with **tiom** or some equivalent word or phrase for its antecedent. In this use it is commonly translated "as":

La taso enhavis tiom da kafo, kiom mi povis trinki, *the cup contained as much coffee as I could drink.*
Mi havos tiom da tempo, kiom mi bezonos, *I shall have as much time as I shall need.*
Li sendis tiom, kiom vi volis, *he sent as much as you wished.*

THE PRESENT PASSIVE PARTICIPLE.

165. The present passive participle (for the present *active* participle see 108), expressing that which is *undergone by* the person or thing indicated by the word modified, ends in **-ata**, as **vidata,** *being seen:*[42]

La laŭdata knabo estas feliĉa, *the boy being praised is happy.*
Mi serĉos la deziratan libron, *I shall look for the desired book.*
La vestoj farataj por vi estas belaj, *the clothes being made for you are beautiful.*

FRACTIONS.

166. Fractions are formed from the cardinals by the use of the suffix **-on-** followed by the ending **-o.** Adjectives and adverbs may be derived from these by use of the endings **-a** or **-e:**

La duono de ses estas tri, *the half of six is three.*
Li estis nur duone atenta, *he was only half attentive.*
La triona parto de ses estas du, *the third part of six is two.*
Dek unu dekduonoj, *eleven twelfths.*
Mi dudekone finis la laboron, *I one-twentieth finished the work.*

---

[42] The verb **iri,** *to go,* used to illustrate the active participles (108, 119, 152), cannot be used to illustrate a *passive* participle, since passive participles can be made from *transitive* verbs (**22**) only.

DESCRIPTIVE COMPOUNDS.

167. A compound word whose first element *modifies* the second in an adjectival or adverbial relation is called a *descriptive compound*. The final **-a** or **-e** of the first element may be omitted, unless the resulting combination would be ambiguous or harsh-sounding.

a. When the first element is adverbial (an adverb or preposition), the second element may be either an adverb or adjective:

multekosta, *expensive.*
duonkolere, *half angrily.*
nevidebla, *invisible.*
nevole, *involuntarily.*
ruĝflava (ruĝeflava), *reddish yellow.*
survoje, *on the way, en route.*
antaŭhieraŭ, *day before yesterday.*
postmorgaŭ, *day after tomorrow.*

b. An *adjective* may be used for the first element, if the second is an adverb or adjective *derived from a noun-root*:

samtempa, *contemporaneous.*
unufoje, *once, one time.*
trifoje, *thrice, three times.*
unutaga, *one day's, of one day.*
unuataga, *the first day's.*
frutempe, *at an early time.*

c. A *noun* may be used for the second element, if the resulting word has not merely unity of form, but also unity of meaning with a slightly different sense from that expressed by the noun and adjective uncombined:[43]

bonveno, *a welcome* (not "bona veno", *a good coming*).
libertempo, *a vacation, leisure* (not "libera tempo", *free time*).
superjaro, *leap-year* (not "super jaro", *above a year*).
bondeziroj, *good wishes, felicitations* (not "bonaj deziroj", *good desires*).
plimulto, *a majority* (adverb and noun combined).

Vocabulary.

ĥin-o, *Chinaman.*
jam, *already.*[¶]
kler-a, *enlightened, learned.*
komerc-o, *trade, commerce.*
lanc-o, *spear, lance.*
liber-a, *free.*
metod-o, *method, way.*

naci-o, *nation.*
paĝ-o, *page.*
pres-i, *to print.*
pulv-o, *gunpowder.*
ŝanĝ-i, *to change.*
te-o, *tea.*
ted-a, *tiresome, tedious.*

[43] In national languages a change of accent often accompanies such change in meaning, as *bla'ckberry* (not *black be'rry*), *blu'ebird* (not *blue bi'rd*), *swee'theart* (not *sweet hea'rt*), German *ju'ngfrau*, *virgin* (not *jung frau'*, *young woman*), etc.

LA ĤINOJ.

Antaŭ miloj da jaroj la ĥinoj estis la plej klera nacio en la mondo. Dum aliaj nacioj ankoraŭ ne konis metodojn por presi librojn, kaj ankoraŭ faris ilin skribe, la samtempaj ĥinoj jam estis forlasintaj tiun multekostan kaj tedan metodon. Ili jam estis presantaj la paĝojn de miloj da libroj. Aliaj nacioj tiam estis batalantaj kiel eble plej kruele, per sago kaj pafarko, kaj per lanco. Sed ili ankoraŭ ne havis pafilojn, ĉar pulvo estis tute nekonata al ili. Tamen la ĥinoj jam bone konis metodojn por fari kaj por uzi pulvon, kaj faris tiajn amuzajn flavruĝajn fajrojn, kiajn ni ankoraŭ hodiaŭ aĉetas de ili, por uzi je festaj tagoj. Sed la ĥinoj ne multe ŝatis la komercon, kaj ne deziris aĉeti aŭ lerni de aliaj nacioj. Ili ankoraŭ nun havas la samajn metodojn por presi librojn kaj por fari pulvon, kiajn ili havis antaŭ mil jaroj. Ili malofte ŝanĝas siajn kutimojn. Tial la aliaj nacioj, kiuj antaŭe ne estis tiel kleraj, antaŭeniras pli rapide ol la ĥinoj. La lando de la ĥinoj enhavas tiom da personoj, kiom tri aŭ kvar aliaj nacioj. Granda parto de tiu lando estas ankoraŭ nekonata al okcidentaj nacioj, kvankam plej multe da nia teo elvenas el la ĥina lando. Oni diras ke la parolata lingvo kaj la skribata lingvo de la ĥinoj estas du tre malsamaj aferoj. La lingvo estas almenaŭ treege malfacila, kaj post kiam oni estas longe studinta ĝin, oni tamen estas nur duone lerninta ĝin. Mi ĝojas tial ke la lingvoj studataj en la lernejoj de nia lando ne estas tiel malfacilaj kiel la ĥina lingvo. La latina kaj germana lingvoj estas sufiĉe malfacilaj, kvankam ili estas tre interesaj kaj ankaŭ konataj de la kleruloj en multaj landoj. La latina lingvo jam ne estas parolata lingvo.

SENTENCES FOR TRANSLATION.

1. Why are the persons in that merry group laughing and chattering instead of listening to Mr. B— —? 2. I think that the doctor is telling stories about a bachelor who was once a good friend of his. 3. The gentleman being talked about (160, 165) will visit us this evening, possibly. 4. My aunt and cousin will come down stairs and converse with him. 5. We shall drink as many cups of tea or of coffee as we wish. 6. He will say "How is your health, Madam?" My aunt will reply half-angrily that she is seldom ill. 7. We shall sit on the veranda, for the sun is still shining, although it is already setting. 8. That young lady who came with Mrs. C— — relates the best possible stories. 9. She says that the Chinese were already an enlightened nation hundreds of years ago, while other nations were still cruelly fighting. 10. A method for printing the pages of books, instead of writing them, was a discovery of the Chinese. They printed books in their printing-shops, a thousand years ago. 12. They also were-acquainted-with gunpowder, which they made and used for such fires as we use on national days of-celebration, when we have leisure and wish to enjoy (to amuse) ourselves. 13. But the Chinese have not changed these methods. 14. Their ways of commerce, work and pleasure are the same as they were long ago. 15. Such a nation does not progress rapidly, even though its life is very long.

LESSON XXXVI.

THE PRESENT PASSIVE TENSE.—THE USE OF DE TO EX-
PRESS AGENCY.—THE GENERAL MEANING OF DE.—
WORD DERIVATION FROM PRIMARY ADVERBS.—
THE SUFFIX -IST-.— ANTIKVA RESPUBLIKO.

THE PRESENT PASSIVE TENSE.

168. The compound tense formed by combining the present passive participle with the present tense of the auxiliary verb **esti** expresses an act or condition as *being undergone* by the subject of the verb, and is called the *present passive tense*. The conjugation of **vidi** in this tense is as follows:

mi estas vidata, *I am (being) seen.*
vi estas vidata, *you are (being) seen.*
li (ŝi, ĝi) estas vidata, *he (she, it) is (being) seen.*
ni estas vidataj, *we are (being) seen.*
vi estas vidataj, *you are (being) seen.*
ili estas vidataj, *they are (being) seen.*

THE USE OF DE TO EXPRESS AGENCY.

169. The person by whom (or the thing by which) an act, indicated by a passive verb or participle, is performed is called the *agent* of the passive voice, and is expressed by a substantive preceded by **de**:

La lanco estas portata de mi, *the spear is carried by me.*
La libroj estas jam presataj de li, *the books are already being printed by him.*
La vojoj estas kovrataj de neĝo, *the roads are being covered by snow.*
Ŝi estas laŭdata de la sinjoro, *she is being praised by the gentleman.*

THE GENERAL MEANING OF DE.

170. The preposition **de** conveys the general idea of separation from a source or starting point, in space (literal or figurative), or in time (89, 131). This meaning develops into that of the source from which connection or ownership arises (49), and also into that of the agency from which an act is done or a condition caused (169). The prepositional phrase containing **de** must be so placed as to avoid ambiguity in its meaning, or must be reinforced by an adverb or other word:

La arbo estas malproksima de la domo, *the tree is far from the house.*
Ĝi estas proksima de la ĝardeno, *it is near to (from) the garden.*

Mi prenas la libron for de la knabo, *I take the book away from the boy.*
Mi prenas la libron de la knabo, *I take the book of the boy.*
La afero dependas de vi, *the matter depends upon (from) you.*

WORD DERIVATION FROM PRIMARY ADVERBS.

171. Adjectives, verbs, and nouns may be derived from primary adverbs (66), as well as from prepositions (120, 159):

La nunaj metodoj, *the present methods (methods of-now).*
Mi adiaŭis lin per adiaŭa saluto, *I bade farewell to him by a farewell salute* (see also 273).
Ni faris tujan interŝanĝon, *we made an immediate exchange.*
Ĉu li skribis jesan aŭ nean respondon? *Did he write an affirmative or a negative answer?*
Anstataŭ nei, li respondis jese, *instead of denying, he answered affirmatively.*
La morgaŭa festo estos pli agrabla ol la hieraŭa, *tomorrow's (the morrow's) celebration will be more pleasant than that of yesterday.*
La tiamaj personoj estis liaj samtempuloj, *the persons of-that-time were his contemporaries.*

THE SUFFIX -IST-.

172. The suffix -ist- is added to roots to express the profession, trade or occupation connected with the idea in the root:

floristo, *florist.*   okulisto, *oculist.*
komercisto, *trader, merchant.*   presisto, *printer.*
servisto, *servant.*   ŝtelisto, *thief.*

VOCABULARY.

administr-i, *to manage.*
antikv-a, *ancient*[**]
Eŭrop-o, *Europe.*
grav-a, *important, serious.*
ital-a, *Italian.*
kvadrat-a, *square.*

mont-o, *mountain.*
nom-o, *name.*
proksim-a, *near.*
reprezent-i, *to represent.*
respublik-o, *republic.*
tiran-o, *tyrant.*

ANTIKVA RESPUBLIKO.

La plej antikva respubliko en Eŭropo kuŝas en la norda parto de la bela itala lando, inter la maro kaj la rivero, proksime de la montoj. Ĝia nomo estas San Marino, kaj ĝi estas respubliko de antaŭ mil kvarcent jaroj. Kvankam la ĉirkaŭaj landoj kaj nacioj apartenis en antikva tempo al la tiamaj reĝoj, San Marino jam estis libera. Ĝiaj aferoj estas ankoraŭ administrataj tiel, kiel la anoj (145) volas, ne kiel unu aŭ alia reĝo aŭ tirano deziras. Dufoje en la jaro la anoj elektas personojn, kiuj administros la gravajn aferojn de la respubliko dum la sekvontaj ses monatoj. Kvardek ses el tiuj personoj reprezentas la anojn, kaj unu alia estas reĝo tiun duonon da jaro. Per tia metodo, la anoj estas bone reprezentataj, kaj la aferoj estas administrataj kiel eble plej saĝe. La tuta respubliko enhavas nur dudek du kvadratajn mejlojn da tero. En la respubliko kaj la tiea (171) urbo kiu havas la saman nomon, ne estas tiom da personoj kiom en multaj italaj urboj. Tamen ĉi tiu respubliko estas pli granda ol multaj antikvaj grekaj respublikoj. La grekaj respublikoj estis bonekonataj, kaj enhavis multe da kleruloj inter siaj anoj. Sed en la nuna tempo la grekoj havas reĝon. Oni ne trovas tre klerajn personojn en San Marino, tamen la laboristoj estas energiaj, kaj laboras kiel eble plej multe. La rikoltistoj plej ofte havas bonajn rikoltojn, kaj la plimulto da personoj estas treege kontenta kaj feliĉa. Oni ne pensas pri komerco aŭ eksterlandaj (167, a) aferoj kaj ne volas vojaĝi malproksimen de la bone amata hejmo. Oni preferas gaje amuzi sin ĉehejme (167, a), en la libertempo inter la rikoltoj, kaj la vivo tute ne ŝajnas malfacila aŭ teda.

SENTENCES FOR TRANSLATION.

1. The serious affairs of a republic are managed by persons representing the persons who live there. 2. The inhabitants are well represented, and as free as possible. 3. Enlightened persons often prefer to live in a republic. 4. Persons who have a good king are very happy, but those who have a bad king are as unhappy as possible. 5. Nowadays (*nuntempe*) there are very few tyrants. 6. The majority of the kings of Europe are praiseworthy. 7. That nation which was most enlightened a thousand years ago was the Chinese nation. 8. The Chinese of-that-time already had good printers among them. 9. It is said (54) that the Chinese drink as much tea as two or three contemporary nations. 10. The oldest republic in Europe is named San Marino. 11. It is near the mountains, in the northern part of the much praised Italian land. 12. It contains only twenty-two square miles, and is therefore one of the smallest republics in the world. 13. Fourteen hundred years ago it was already a republic, and it is still that same republic. 14. The inhabitants are energetic and patient, and have as much to eat as they need. 15. There are bakers and shopkeepers (172) and many laborers among them. 16. They do not think about commerce, or greatly (*multe*) change their customs. 17. They seldom take (*faras*) tiresome journeys, but remain peacefully (*pace*) at home.

LESSON XXXVII.

THE DISTRIBUTIVE PRONOUN.—THE PREPOSITION
PO.—DEPENDENT COMPOUNDS.—LA ĈAPELO SUR
LA STANGO.

THE DISTRIBUTIVE PRONOUN.

173. The distributive pronoun (and pronominal adjective) is **ĉiu**, *each (one)*, *every (one)*. Sometimes it is equivalent to English *any*, as in "Any one who studies can learn," etc. The plural is **ĉiuj**, *every, all*.[44] The article is never interposed between **ĉiuj** and the noun modified (as in English "all the men"), and is used only if **ĉiuj** is pronominal and followed by **el**:

Ĉiu, kiu studos, lernos, *every one who studies will learn.*
Mi vidis ĉiun el ili, kaj parolis al ĉiu knabo, *I saw each of them, and talked to every boy.*
Mi dankas vin ĉiujn, *I thank you all (I thank all of you).*
Ni ĉiuj estas reprezentataj, *we are all (all of us are) represented.*
Ĉiuj el la maristoj alvenis, *all (every one) of the sailors arrived.*

174. The distributive pronoun has a possessive or genitive form **ĉies**, *every-one's, every-body's*:

Li konas ĉies nomon, *he knows every-one's name.*
Ĉies opinio estis diversa, *every-body's opinion was different.*
Kies voĉojn mi aŭdas? Ĉies, *whose voices do I hear? Everybody's.*

THE PREPOSITION PO.

175. The preposition **po**, *at the rate of, at*, is used chiefly before cardinals and has a distributive sense:

Li marŝas po kvar mejloj ĉiutage, *he walks at the rate of four miles daily (every-day).*
Mi aĉetis kafon po malalta prezo, *I bought coffee at a low price.*
Mi aĉetis viandon po kvarono da dolaro por funto, *I bought meat at a quarter of a dollar for (per) pound.*

[44] The use of **ĉiu** and **ĉiuj** must be distinguished from that of the adjective **tuta**, which means "all" in the sense of "entire":

Ĉiuj viroj laboras la tutan tagon, *all men work all (the whole) day.*
Mi vidis ĉiun vizaĝon, sed mi ne vidis la tutan vizaĝon de ĉiu viro, *I saw every face, but I did not see all the face of each man.*

La ĉapelisto aĉetas ĉapelojn pogrande, *the hatter buys hats wholesale.*

DEPENDENT COMPOUNDS.

176. A compound word whose first element is a substantive, dependent upon the second element in some prepositional relation, is called a *dependent compound.* (If the two words were not united into one, the first element would be preceded by a preposition, or would be in the accusative case.) The ending **-o** may be omitted from the first element of a dependent compound:[45]

jarcento, *century* (cento da jaroj).
manĝoĉambro, *dining-room* (ĉambro por manĝoj).
noktomezo, *midnight* (mezo de la nokto).
paperfaristo, *papermaker* (faristo de papero).
sunbrilo, *sunshine* (brilo de la suno).
tagmezo, *noon* (mezo de la tago).
vespermanĝo, *supper* (manĝo je la vespero).
ventoflago, *weathercock* (flago por la vento).

VOCABULARY.

ĉies, *every body's* (174).
ĉiu, *every-body* (173).
decid-i, *to decide.*
dev-o, *duty.*
fleks-i, *to bend.*
genu-o, *knee.*
intenc-i, *to intend.*
juĝ-i, to *judge.*

lag-o, *lake.*
po, *at the rate of* (175).
sever-a, *severe.*
stang-o, *pole.*
svis-o, *Swiss.*
vend-i, *to sell.*
Vilhelm-o, *William.*
vort-o, *word.*

LA ĈAPELO SUR LA STANGO.

Antaŭ ol Svislando estis tiel libera kiel la nuna svisa respubliko, ĝiaj aferoj estis administrataj de personoj kiuj reprezentis aliajn naciojn. Ofte tiuj personoj estis kiel eble plej severaj juĝistoj al la svisoj. Unufoje plej kruela tirano estis administranta aferojn svisajn. Li elpensis rimarkindan metodon por montri sian povon (*power*), kaj por esti malagrabla al la svisoj. Li decidis meti sian ĉapelon sur altan stangon en la vendejo (*market-place*), en malgranda vilaĝo apud bela lago inter la altaj montoj. Li diris ke de nun tiu ĉapelo reprezentas lin, kaj portos lian nomon. Saluti la ĉapelon estos la grava devo de ĉiu persono en la vilaĝo. Estos ĉies devo ne nur saluti la ĉapelon, sed ankaŭ genufleksi (*kneel*) antaŭ la stango. La tirano diris ke li forprenos la domon, la kampojn kaj tiom da mono, kiom li povos, de ĉiu

---

[45] A personal pronoun serving as the first element of a dependent compound may keep the accusative ending, to indicate its construction:

sinlaŭdo,   *self-praise.*
sinekzameno,   *self-examination.*
sindefendo,   *self-defence.*
sinkontraŭdira,   *self-contradictory.*

vilaĝano aŭ kamparano kiu forgesos genufleksi. "Mi intencas sendi gardistojn," li diris, "kiuj rimarkos ĉu vi ĉiuj genufleksos kiam vi estas proksimaj de la stango." Je tagmezo alvenis gardistoj, por rimarki ĉu la necesaj salutoj estos farataj de ĉiuj, kaj por kapti ĉiujn svisojn kiuj ne genufleksis. Baldaŭ la kamparanoj komencis eniri la vendejon, por vendi legomojn po kiel eble altaj prezoj, kaj por aĉeti vestojn kaj aliajn aferojn po treege plej malaltaj prezoj. Ĉiu, kiu iris proksimen de la stango, zorge genufleksis antaŭ la ĉapelo de la malamata tirano, pro timo pri la hejmoj kaj la familioj. Fine, kamparano, kies nomo estis Vilhelmo Tell, eniris la vendejon, kaj staris du aŭ tri minutojn proksime de la stango, dum li diris kelkajn vortojn al amiko. Sed anstataŭ fari tujan saluton, aŭ genufleksi, li tute ne rigardis la stangon.

SENTENCES FOR TRANSLATION.

1. The day before yesterday my youngest cousin was sitting on my knee, and I told him that a rainbow (ĉielarko) is made by the sunshine and the rain. 2. My cousin goes to school every day, after he has breakfast in the dining-room. 3. A new school is being built, not far from the home of the judge. 4. It is my cousin's duty to study those books at the rate of ten pages a day. 5. My cousin and I decided last night (93) to buy new hats for ourselves. 6. We intend to go to the hatter's early tomorrow morning. 7. I think that all clothes are being sold at a low price at-the-present-time. 8. During a visit at a friend's, I read an interesting book about ancient Europe. 9. It relates that several centuries ago a severe and cruel tyrant was managing affairs in Switzerland. 10. Once he put his hat on a pole in the market-place, and said that it was the duty of-every-one to kneel before it. 11. This serious affair happened in a village one or two miles square, on (ĉe) the lake not far from the mountains through which one goes on the way (167, a) to the Italian land. 12. William Tell did not kneel or even look at the hat representing the tyrant.

LESSON XXXVIII.

THE DISTRIBUTIVE ADJECTIVE.—THE IMPERFECT PAS-
SIVE TENSE.—COMPOUND TENSES OF IMPERSONAL
VERBS.—RECIPROCAL EXPRESSIONS.—THE SUFFIX
-UJ-.—VILHELMO TELL KAJ LA POMO.

THE DISTRIBUTIVE ADJECTIVE.

177. The distributive adjective related to the distributive pronoun **ĉiu**, giving
a comprehensive idea of the quality of some person or thing, is **ĉia**, *every kind of,
every sort of*:

Oni vendas ĉiajn fruktojn tie, *they sell every sort of fruit there.*
Estas ĉiaj personoj en la mondo, *there are all sorts of persons in the world.*

THE IMPERFECT PASSIVE TENSE.

178. The compound tense formed by combining the present passive participle
with the past tense of the auxiliary verb **esti** expresses an act or condition as being
undergone by the subject of the verb *at some time in the past*. It is called the *imperfect
passive tense*. The conjugation of **vidi** in this tense is as follows:

mi estis vidata, *I was (being) seen.*
vi estis vidata, *you were (being) seen.*
li (ŝi, ĝi) estis vidata, *he (she, it) was (being) seen.*
ni estis vidataj, *we were (being) seen.*
vi estis vidataj, *you were (being) seen.*
ili estis vidataj, *they were (being) seen.*

COMPOUND TENSES OF IMPERSONAL VERBS.

179. When impersonal verbs, or other verbs used impersonally, are in compound tenses, the participial element is given the ending **-e**, like other modifiers of
impersonally used verbs (141):

Estis pluvante antaŭ unu minuto, *it was raining a minute ago.*
Estis multe neĝinte, *it had snowed a great deal.*
Estis vidate ke ĉiu ploras, *it was seen that every one wept.*

RECIPROCAL EXPRESSIONS.

180. To give a reciprocal sense, when there are two or more subjects and the
action goes from one to the other (expressed in English by "each other," "one an-

other," "mutually," "reciprocally"), the phrases **unu la alian, unu al la alia**, etc., or the adverb **reciproke**, is used:

Estas nia devo helpi unu la alian, *it is our duty to help one another.*
Ili parolas unu al la alia, *they are talking to each other.*
La viroj reciproke uzis siajn pafilojn, *the men used each other's guns.*
Ili falis unu sur la alian, *they fell upon each other.*

THE SUFFIX -UJ-.

181. The suffix **-uj-** may be used to form words indicating *that which contains, bears, or is a receptacle for*, some number or quantity of that which is expressed by the root. It may be used instead of **-lando** to form the name of a region containing any one race or tribe, and instead of **-arbo** to form the names of fruit trees:

ujo, *a receptacle.*	**patrujo (patrolando)**, *fatherland.*
monujo, *purse.*	**sukerujo**, *sugar-bowl.*
supujo, *soup-tureen.*	**pomujo (pomarbo)**, *apple-tree.*
leterujo, *letter-case.*	**sagujo**, *quiver.*

VOCABULARY.

ag-i, *to act.*	**mort-i**, *to die.*
ceter-a, *remaining.*	**pet-i**, *to plead, to request.*
ĉia, *of every kind* (177).	**prepar-i**, *to prepare.*
fier-a, *proud.*	**pun-i**, *to punish.*
imag-i, *to imagine.*	**reciprok-a**, *reciprocal, mutual.*
konduk-i, *to lead.*	**simil-a**, *like, similar.*
kor-o, *heart.*	**tuŝ-i**, *to touch.*

VILHELMO TELL KAJ LA POMO.

Tuj kiam la gardistoj rimarkis ke la ĉapelo sur la stango ne estis salutata de Vilhelmo Tell, ili kaptis lin, kaj kondukis lin al la tirano, por esti juĝata. La tirano demandis de Tell kial li ne genufleksis antaŭ la ĉapelo, simile al la aliaj vilaĝanoj. Tell respondis fiere ke li ne sciis pri la ĉiutagaj genufleksoj de la aliaj personoj. Li diris ke li tute ne intencis agi kontraŭ la deziroj de la juĝistoj. Sed la tirano malamis la altan fortan svison, tial li decidis puni lin per severa puno, kaj demandis "Kiun el viaj infanoj vi plej amas?" Vilhelmo Tell ne povis imagi kial la demando estas farata al li, kaj respondis "Mi amas ĉiujn el ili, sinjoro." La tirano diris "Nu, estas rakontate inter la vilaĝanoj ke vi estas rimarkinda arkpafisto (*archer*). Ni eltrovos kia arkpafisto vi estas. Ni vidos ĉu vi povos forpafi pomon de sur la kapo de via plej juna filo. Aldone (*in addition*), estos via devo forpafi la pomon per la unua sago, alie (*otherwise*) mi punos vin kaj vian filon per tuja morto." Tell diris ke li estas preta por ricevi ĉian alian punon, anstataŭ tia puno, sed malgraŭ ĉies petoj la tirano estis jam elektanta pomon de apuda pomarbo. Li kondukis la knabon malproksimen de la ceteraj personoj, kaj metis la pomon sur lian kapon. Tell kaj la filo reciproke rigardis sin, dum la patro diris ke li ne tuŝos haron de lia kapo. Tiam li elprenis sagon el la sagujo, faris la necesajn preparojn, kaj rapide pafis. Tuj la pomo forfalis de la kapo de la infano, kaj ĉiu havis feliĉan koron. Dum Tell ĉirkaŭ-prenis la filon, la tirano demandis "Kial vi havas tiun ceteran sagon en la mano." Tell laŭte respondis "Por mortpafi vin, tuj post la infano, ĉar mi treege timis pro la vivo de mia kara filo."

SENTENCES FOR TRANSLATION.

1. William Tell had a strong flexible (161) bow. 2. He could shoot-with-a-bow (*arkpafi*) excellently, therefore he was a well-known archer. 3. He put six or eight arrows into his quiver, and went with his sons to the village. 4. Possibly he saw the hat upon the pole, but he did not kneel before it. 5. It was being noticed already in the village that Tell hated the tyrant very much. 6. When the guards seized him for that act, and led him before the tyrant, who was also the judge, Tell said "I did not know about this new duty, and could not imagine why the hat was on the pole there." 7. The tyrant replied with (*per*) angry words, for he hated the proud Swiss whom every one else loved. 8. He said severely "It is said that you are a praise-worthy archer. 9. Therefore I was wondering whether you could shoot an apple from your son's head. 10. Now we shall see whether you can shoot off the apple, or whether you will touch the child's head." 11. Amid the pleadings of all, Tell successfully shot off the apple. 12. A similar second arrow was ready in his hand. 13. The tyrant saw the remaining arrow, and prepared to punish Tell by death. 14. But he escaped, and the Swiss congratulated each other heartily (*kore*). 15. After some time they followed him, at the rate of six miles an hour.

LESSON XXXIX.

THE DISTRIBUTIVE ADVERB OF PLACE.—THE FUTURE PASSIVE TENSE.—POSSESSIVE COMPOUNDS.—THE TIME OF DAY.—THE SUFFIX -OBL-.—EN LA STACIDO-MO.

THE DISTRIBUTIVE ADVERB OF PLACE.

182. The distributive adverb of place, related to the distributive pronoun **ĉiu**, is **ĉie**, *everywhere*. The ending **-n** may be added to **ĉie** to show direction of motion (121):

Oni trovas tiajn virojn ĉie, *such men are found everywhere.*
Li iris ĉien, kie mi estis estinta, *he went everywhere where I had been.*
Mi vidas lin ĉie, kien mi iras, *I see him everywhere I go.*

THE FUTURE PASSIVE TENSE.

183. The compound tense formed by combining the present passive participle with the future tense of **esti** indicates that an act or condition *will be undergone* by the subject of the verb. It is called the *future passive tense*. The conjugation of **vidi** in this tense is as follows:

mi estos vidata, *I shall be seen.*
vi estos vidata, *you will be seen.*
li (ŝi, ĝi) estos vidata, *he (she, it) will be seen.*
ni estos vidataj, *we shall be seen.*
vi estos vidataj, *you will be seen.*
ili estos vidataj, *they will be seen.*

POSSESSIVE COMPOUNDS.

184. Compound adjectives may be formed with an adjectival root for the first element, and a noun-root for the second element. Such adjectives have the meaning "possessed of" that which is indicated in the compound. (Similar adjectives are formed in English, with *-ed* as the final syllable):

belbrova, *beautiful-browed.*　　　**longnaza**, *long-nosed.*
bonintenca, *good-intentioned.*　　**kvarpieda**, *four-footed.*
dumana, *two-handed.*　　　　　　**ruĝhara**, *red-haired.*

THE TIME OF DAY.

185. The ordinals are used in expressing the hour of the day, with **horo** expressed or understood. The minutes are expressed by the cardinals. In questions the adjective **kioma** (from **kiom,** *how much*) is used:

Kioma horo estas? *What hour (what o'clock, what time) is it?*
Je kioma horo vi venos? *At what time (what o'clock) will you come?*
Estas la dua horo, *it is two o'clock (it is the second hour).*
Estas la tria kaj kvin minutoj, *it is five minutes past three.*
Ni iris je la sesa kaj duono, *we went at half past six.*
Estas la oka kaj kvardek kvin (*or:* **estas unu kvarono antaŭ la naŭa**), *it is eight forty-five (a quarter of nine).*

THE SUFFIX -OBL-.

186. The suffix **-obl-** is used to form multiples indicating how many fold, as "two fold," "double," "triple," etc.:

duoblo, *a double.*
duobla, *double.*
duoble, *doubly.*
kvarobla, *quadruple.*
kvindekobla, *fifty-fold.*
multobla, *manifold.*
Trioble du estas ses, *three times two is six.*

VOCABULARY.

bilet-o, *ticket.*
cend-o, *cent.*
ĉie, *everywhere* (182).
esprim-o, *expression.*
giĉet-o, *wicket, ticket-window.*
horloĝ-o, *clock.*

pag-i, *to pay.*
preter, *beyond, past.*[††]
staci-o, *station.*
telefon-i, *to telephone.*
vagon-o, *car.*
valiz-o, *valise.*

EN LA STACIDOMO.

Du bonkoraj (184) amikoj miaj loĝas en la urbo B——. Ni reciproke konas nin de antaŭ ses jaroj. Mi estis duoble ĝoja hieraŭ kiam mi ricevis leteron de ili, ĉar en tiu ili petis de mi baldaŭan viziton. Tial mi telefonis hieraŭ posttagmeze[46] al la stacidomo, por demandi je kioma horo foriros la vagonaro (*train*) al B——. Oni respondis per la telefono ke la vagonaro foriros je la tria kaj tridek kvin. Tuj poste mi enmetis kelkajn vestojn en mian jam preskaŭ eluzitan valizon, kaj faris ĉiujn preparojn por la mallonga vojaĝo. Je la dua horo, tuj post la tagmanĝo (*midday meal*), mi marŝis stacidomon. Survoje mi eniris butikon kaj aĉetis paron da novaj gantoj. Kiam mi eniris la stacidomon, mi kuris preter la aliaj personoj al la giĉeto kie biletoj estas vendataj. Mi diris al la sinjoro ĉe la giĉeto "Mi deziras bileton al B——. Kiom estos necese pagi?" La brunokula sinjoro respondis "Tia bileto kostos

---

[46] **Posttagmezo,** *afternoon,* is a descriptive compound (167, a) whose second element **tagmezo** is a dependent compound (176).

dolaron dudek cendojn." Mi puŝis tiom da mono tra la giĉeto, kaj tuj ricevis la bileton, kiun la sinjoro jam havis en la mano. Tiam mi iris proksimen de la pordego tra kiu oni estos enlasata al la vagonaro. "Kiom da tempo antaŭ la foriro de la vagonaro al B— —?" mi demandis al la gardisto. Li laŭtvoĉe respondis "Nur sep minutojn. Ĉu vi ne vidas tiun horloĝon?" Mi ne estis rimarkinta la horloĝon, tial mi almetis la montrilojn de mia poŝhorloĝo (*watch*) por montri la saman horon. Mi estis multe tuŝata de ĉiaj bonintencaj personoj kurantaj ĉien preter mi, kaj puŝantaj unu la alian. Fine oni malfermis la pordegon. Mi kaj la ceteraj personoj rapidis al la vagonaro kaj kiel eble plej baldaŭ eniris ĝin.

SENTENCES FOR TRANSLATION.

1. Because of the request of my friend whose brother died recently, I went last (*la antaŭan*) week to visit him. 2. The remaining persons of his family were not at home. 3. I telephoned to find out at what time the train would depart. 4. I was told (54) that it would leave at four twenty-seven. 5. I put enough money into my purse, and carried along (*kunportis*) a valise into which I had put some clothes. 6. When I entered the station, I hurried past the other people to the wicket, and asked for (*petis*) a ticket to B— —. 7. The ticket seller said "Two dollars and forty cents." 8. I could not imagine why it was necessary to pay so much, but I at once pushed that much money through the window, and received the ticket. 9. Then I looked at my watch and went near the gate, but the yellowhaired guard who conducts persons to the trains said "Persons who go through that gate before the train arrives will be severely punished." 10. So all of us stood near the double gate. 11. The trains are much like each other, and it is better to act as the guards request, and not express impatience.

LESSON XL.

THE DISTRIBUTIVE TEMPORAL ADVERB.—THE DIS-
TRIBUTIVE ADVERB ĈIAL.—THE PAST PASSIVE
PARTICIPLE.—THE PERFECT PASSIVE TENSE.—THE
PREPOSITION LAŬ.—THE SUFFIX -EM-.—LA PERDITA
INFANO.

THE DISTRIBUTIVE TEMPORAL ADVERB.

187. The distributive adverb of time, related to the distributive pronoun **ĉiu**, is
ĉiam, *always, at all times*:

Vi ĉiam pagas tro multe, *you always pay too much.*
Mi estas ĉiam preta por helpi vin, *I am always ready to help you.*

THE DISTRIBUTIVE ADVERB ĈIAL.

188. The distributive adverb of motive or reason, related to the pronoun **ĉiu**, is
ĉial, *for every reason, for all reasons*:

Ĉial li estas feliĉa hodiaŭ, *for every reason he is happy today.*
La mia ĉial estas la plej bona, *mine is for all reasons the best.*

THE PAST PASSIVE PARTICIPLE.

189. The past passive participle expresses an act or condition as *having been
undergone* by the person or thing indicated by the word modified. This participle
ends in **-ita**, as **vidita**, *having been seen*:

La prezo pagita de vi estis tro granda, *the price paid by you was too great.*
La punita infano ploras, *the (having-been) punished child is crying.*
Mi aĉetos bonefaritajn gantojn, *I shall buy well-made gloves.*
Li serĉis la forgesitan bileton, *he looked for the forgotten ticket.*

THE PERFECT PASSIVE TENSE.

190. The compound tense formed by combining the past passive participle
with the present tense of the verb **esti** expresses an act or condition which *has been
undergone* by the subject of the verb. It is called the *perfect passive tense.* The conjugation of the verb **vidi** in this tense is as follows:

mi estas vidita, *I have been seen* (*I am having-been-seen*).
vi estas vidita, *you have been seen.*

li (ŝi, ĝi) estas vidita, *he (she, it) has been seen.*
ni estas viditaj, *we have been seen.*
vi estas viditaj, *you have been seen.*
ili estas viditaj, *they have been seen.*

THE PREPOSITION LAŬ.

191. In expressing that *in accordance with which* something is done, takes place, moves, etc., the preposition **laŭ** is used:

Li agis laŭ sia opinio, *he acted in accordance with his own opinion.*
Mi faros ĝin laŭ bona metodo, *I shall do it according to a good method.*
Laŭ kia maniero li agis? *In what manner did he act?*
Mi marŝis laŭ la strato, *I walked down (or up) the street.*
Li iris laŭ la rivero per tiu vojo, *he went along the river by that road.*
Nuboj nigraj kuris laŭ la ĉielo, *black clouds raced along the sky.*
Ĝi kuŝas laŭlonge de la domo, *it lies lengthwise of the house.*

THE SUFFIX -EM-.

192. The suffix **-em-** indicates a *tendency* or *inclination* toward that which is expressed in the root:

agema, *active.*	**pacema,** *peaceful, pacific.*
mallaborema, *lazy.*	**pensema,** *pensive, thoughtful.*

VOCABULARY.

atend-i, *to wait (for), to expect.*	**laŭ,** *according to* (191).
ĉial, *for every reason* (188).	**manier-o,** *manner, way.*
ĉiam, *always* (187).	**mov-i,** *to move* (transitive)
gazet-o, *magazine, gazette.*	**okup-i,** *to occupy.*
ĵurnal-o, *journal, paper.*	**pal-a,** *pale.*
kompat-i, *to pity.*	**polic-o,** *police.*
larm-o, *tear.*	**trankvil-a,** *calm, tranquil.*

LA PERDITA INFANO.

Dum mi estis atendanta hieraŭ posttagmeze en la stacidomo, mi subite rimarkis palan sinjorinon kun larmoj en ŝiaj okuloj. Ŝi rigardis ĉien kun esprimo de nekaŝebla timo, kaj estis videble maltrankvila. Ŝi serĉis du aŭ tri minutojn inter la personoj ĉirkaŭ si, kaj fine ŝi vidis bluevestitan policanon, kiu estis parolanta al unu el la gardistoj. Ŝi rapide diris kelkajn vortojn al li, kaj tuj li ankaŭ komencis serĉi cie. Mi tre kompatis la ploreman sinjorinon, kaj kiam la policano preteriris, mi demandis ĉu mi ne povas helpi. Mi diris ke mi ne estos okupata (*busy*) ĝis la alveno de la vagonaro. Li respondis ke la filo de tiu virino estas perdita, kaj li donis al mi la sekvantan priskribon de la infano, laŭ la vortoj de la patrino: la knabo estas agema brunhara sesjarulo, kun bluaj okuloj, kaj li estas ruĝe vestita (*dressed in red*). Lia patrino estis ĵus aĉetinta sian bileton ĉe la giĉeto, kaj post kiam ŝi pagis la naŭdek cendojn por ĝi, subite ŝi rimarkis ke la infano ne estis kun ŝi. Kvankam ŝi jam serĉis ĉie, la filo ŝajnas ankoraŭ netrovebla. Ŝi multe timas pro li, kvankam li ĉiam estas bona knabo. Mi tuj komencis marŝi ĉien inter la personoj ĉirkaŭ mi, kaj fine eniris malgrandan ĉambron apud la horloĝo ĉe la fino de la stacidomo, kie estas vendataj tagĵurnaloj (*newspapers*), gazetoj kaj libroj. Tie antaŭ nemovebla tablo kovrita de brile koloritaj ĵurnaloj staris malgranda ruĝevestita knabo. Mi diris al li "Mia studema juna amiko, oni ne vojaĝas laŭ tiu metodo. Via patrino jam de longe atendas vin. Mi montros al vi kie ŝi estas." Li venis kun mi, kaj proksime de la pordo kie mi estis lasinta mian valizon staris la sinjorino. Ŝi estis ĉial ĝoja kiam ŝi vidis nin, kaj dankeme ĉirkaŭprenis la infanon.

SENTENCES FOR TRANSLATION.

1. The poor (to-be-pitied) lady whose little boy (son) was lost in the station yesterday afternoon was very uneasy about him for every reason. 2. She was pale and tearful (*plorema*) when I saw her, and looked in every direction in a most impatient manner. 3. There was an expression of fear upon her face and she went as quickly as possible to a nearby policeman, and said a few (*kelkajn*) words to him. 4. I heard the last words, and at once said to myself "It is now only ten minutes past two. 5. My train will leave (*foriros*) at half-past two, so I have time to help." 6. I said to the blue-garbed policeman "During the next (*sekvontajn*) twenty minutes I shall not be busy. Do you desire my help?" 7. He answered "Yes, you are very kind (*ĝentila*). The son of that lady has been lost. 8. According to her description, he is a yellow-haired blue-eyed five-year-old, and apparently (*ŝajne*) too restless (*movema*). 9. I shall find him as soon as possible, nevertheless I shall gladly accept your help. 10. The child is dressed in white and wears a red hat." 11. As (*ĉar*) I am not at all lazy (*mallaborema*), I went along the stationary (*nemoveblaj*) tables as-far-as the end of the station, and there I saw that-sort-of child, looking at the magazines and newspapers. 12. I led him to the lady, who with tears in her eyes was just going to telephone to her husband.

LESSON XLI.

THE DISTRIBUTIVE ADVERB ĈIEL.—THE DISTRIBU-
TIVE ADVERB ĈIOM.—THE PLUPERFECT PASSIVE
TENSE.—THE FUTURE PERFECT PASSIVE TENSE.—
THE EXPRESSION OF MATERIAL. —THE SUFFIX -ET-
.—LA DONACO.

THE DISTRIBUTIVE ADVERB ĈIEL.

193. The distributive adverb of manner, related to the distributive pronoun
ĉiu, is ĉiel, *in every way, in every manner*:

Li povas ĉiel prepari ĝin, *he can prepare it in every manner.*
Li estos ĉiel helpata, *he will be helped in every way.*

THE DISTRIBUTIVE ADVERB ĈIOM.

194. The distributive adverb of quantity, related to the distributive pronoun
ĉiu, is ĉiom, *every quantity, the whole, all*:

Li prenis multe da sukero, sed ne ĉiom da ĝi, *he took a great deal of sugar, but
not all of it.*
Li elprenis ĉiom de la teo el la teujo, *he took all of the tea out of the tea caddy.*

THE PLUPERFECT PASSIVE TENSE.

195. The compound tense made by combining the past passive participle with
the past tense of the verb **esti** expresses an act or condition which *had been undergone* by the subject of the verb at some point in past time. It is called the *pluperfect
passive tense*. The conjugation of **vidi** in this tense is as follows:

mi estis vidita, *I had been seen (I was having-been-seen).*
vi estis vidita, *you had been seen.*
li (ŝi, ĝi) estis vidita, *he (she, it) had been seen.*
ni estis viditaj, *we had been seen.*
vi estis viditaj, *you had been seen.*
ili estis viditaj, *they had been seen.*

THE FUTURE PERFECT PASSIVE TENSE.

196. The compound tense made by combining the past passive participle with
the future tense of the verb **esti** expresses an act or condition which *will have been
undergone* by the subject of the verb at some point in future time. It is called the

future perfect passive tense. The conjugation of **vidi** in this tense is as follows:

mi estos vidita, *I shall have been seen (shall be having-been-seen).*
vi estos vidita, *you will have been seen.*
li (ŝi, ĝi) estos vidita, *he (she, it) will have been seen.*
ni estos viditaj, *we shall have been seen.*
vi estos viditaj, *you will have been seen.*
ili estos viditaj, *they will have been seen.*

THE EXPRESSION OF MATERIAL.

197. The material *out of which* something is made or constructed is expressed by use of the preposition **el**. As in English, an adjective may be used instead of the prepositional phrase unless a verb or participle lays stress upon the fact of construction:

La tablo estas farita el ligno, *the table is made out of wood.*
La tablo estas ligna (el ligno), *the table is wooden (of wood).*
La infanoj konstruis domon el neĝo, *the children built a house of (out of) snow.*
Oni faras supon el asparago, *they make soup out of asparagus.*

THE SUFFIX -ET-.

198. The suffix **-et-** indicates diminution of degree in that which is expressed by the root. It is thus in contrast to the augmentative suffix **-eg-** (122). Sometimes an affectionate significance is given:

beleta, *pretty.*	**libreto,** *booklet.*
dormeti, *to doze.*	**monteto,** *hill.*
floreto, *floweret, floret.*	**rideti,** *to smile.*
lageto, *pond, small lake.*	**vojeto,** *path.*

Vocabulary.

best-o, *animal.*	**leon-o,** *lion.*
ĉiel, *in every way* (193).	**lud-i,** *to play.*
ĉiom, *the whole, all* (194).	**material-o,** *material.*
donac-o, *gift, present.*	**posed-i,** *to own, to possess.*
drap-o, *cloth.*	**pup-o,** *doll.*
hund-o, *dog.*	**rost-i,** *to roast.*
konsist-i, *to consist.*	**verŝ-i,** *to pour.*

LA DONACO.

Mi volas doni beletan donacon al mia plej juna fratino morgaŭ, sed ju pli mi pensas pri ĝi, des pli malfacile estas decidi pri la afero. Estas duoble malfacile, ĉar ŝi jam posedas ĉiun ludilon (*toy*) kiun oni povas imagi. Ĉiu el ŝiaj amikoj ĝoje donacas (*make presents*) al tiel afabla knabino. Tamen mi iris hieraŭ matene al ludilobutiko, kaj rigardis la ludilojn tie. Multaj konsistis el diversaj pupoj, grandaj kaj malgrandaj, kaj belege vestitaj. Sed mi estas certa ke la fratineto jam posedas sufiĉe da pupoj—tial mi ne aĉetis tian ludilon, kvankam ili estas ĉiam interesaj al knabinetoj. Sur unu tablo kuŝis ĉiaj malgrandaj bestoj, faritaj el ligno, drapo, kaj diversaj materialoj. Estis ĉevaletoj, hundetoj, katetoj, kaj flavaj leonetoj. Proksime de tiuj staris malgrandaj brile koloritaj vagonaroj, kiujn oni povis rapide movi, laŭ la maniero de grandaj vagonaroj. Etaj policanoj staris apude, kaj estis ĉial malfacile elekti la plej interesan el tiom da interesaj ludiloj. Baldaŭ mi rimarkis knabineton apud mi. Ĉiel ŝi tre similis al mia fratino, kaj tial mi decidis elekti tian ludilon, kia estos elektita plej frue de la nekonata knabineto. Mi atendis trankvile, kaj eĉ legis unu aŭ du paĝojn de miaj ĵus aĉetitaj gazetoj kaj tagĵurnaloj. Fine la beleta infano estis rigardinta preskaŭ ĉiom de la ludiloj kiuj okupis la tablojn, dum la kompatinda servistino lace ŝin sekvis. Tiam la knabineto kriis "Ho, kiel beleta pupodomo! Estas litoj en la dormoĉambroj; legomoj kaj rostita viando, faritaj el papero, kuŝas sur la tablo en la manĝo-ĉambro; kaj mi vidas tie pupon, kiu certe ĵus faris la teon, kaj estas elverŝonta ĝin en tiujn tasetojn!" Tuj mi faris decidon laŭ la plezuro de la knabineto, kaj baldaŭ la pupodomo estis aĉetita por mia fratineto.

SENTENCES FOR TRANSLATION.

1. My pale delicate (*malsanema*) little sister is always happy when she has a new toy. 2. Her dolls were made out of cloth when she was a very little girl, because otherwise she could too easily break them. 3. But yesterday my grandmother made a present of a doll (presented a doll) to her, and since that moment she has been as happy as possible. 4. I have not seen tears in her eyes, or heard a cross (*koleretan*) word. 5. This new doll is made out of cloth, and its dress consists of very pretty material. 6. My sister decided that she likes it better than her other playthings, and I think that those poor (*kompatindaj*) other dolls will soon have been forgotten. 7. The doll seems in every way more interesting than the little animals made out of cloth or wood, which are on the table with her dolls. 8. She possesses a little dog and a little cat, and a little lion, and until yesterday she had a wooden pony. 9. The pony is already broken, and has been given away to a poor (*malriĉa*) child, the daughter of our laundress (*lavistino*). 10. My sister possesses a small train of cars which she can move everywhere, and she is very fond of (*ametas*) this toy. 11. There are small sacks of sand in the cars, and usually she is happy when she is pouring the sand out of one of these into another, or putting all of the sand into a box, by means of a small spoon. 12. For every reason I am doubly glad today that she is busied in this manner (*tiamaniere*). 13. I wish to take a walk along that pleasant path toward the hill, instead of waiting for my little sister. 14. I must buy the meat to roast for supper, before I come home from my walk.

LESSON XLII.

THE FUTURE PASSIVE PARTICIPLE.—THE PASSIVE PERI-
PHRASTIC FUTURE TENSES.—THE GENERIC ARTI-
CLE.—THE SUFFIX -EC-.—SUR LA VAPORŜIPO.

THE FUTURE PASSIVE PARTICIPLE.

199. The future passive participle, expressing that which *will be or is about to be
undergone* by the person or thing indicated by the word modified, ends in **-ota**, as
vidota, about to be seen:

La punota infano mallaŭte ploretas, *the child about to be punished whimpers
softly.*
La formovota tablo estas peza, *the table about to be moved away is heavy.*
La domo konstruota de li estos bela, *the house going to be built by him will be
beautiful.*

THE PASSIVE PERIPHRASTIC FUTURE TENSES.

200. The compound tenses formed by combining the future passive participle
with each of the three aoristic tenses of **esti** represent an act or condition as *about
to be undergone* in the present, past, or future, respectively. These are called *passive
periphrastic future tenses*. Except when great accuracy is desired, these tenses, like
those of the active voice (153) are not often used. A synopsis of **vidi** in the first
person singular of these tenses is as follows:

Present Periphrastic Future.

mi estas vidota, *I am about to be (going to be) seen.*

Past Periphrastic Future.

mi estis vidota, *I was about to be (going to be) seen.*

Future Periphrastic Future.

mi estos vidota, *I shall be about to be (going to be) seen.*

THE GENERIC ARTICLE.

201. The article is placed before nouns used in a comprehensive or universal
sense, indicating a whole class, kind, substance, or abstract quality. In such use it
is called the *generic article*:[47]

[47] Cf. French *La patience est amère, mais son fruit est doux, patience is bitter, but its fruit is
sweet,* German *Das Leben ist kurz, life is short,* Italian *La speranza è il pan de miseri, hope is the*

La pacienco estas laŭdinda, *patience is praiseworthy.*
La vivo surtera estas nur parto de la vivo ĉiama, *life on earth is merely a part of the life eternal.*
La viro estas pli forta ol la virino, *man is stronger than woman.*

THE SUFFIX -EC-.

202. The suffix **-ec-** is used to form words indicating the *abstract quality* of that which is expressed in the root, or formation, to which it is attached:

amikeco, *friendship.*	**fleksebleco,** *flexibility.*
ofteco, *frequency.*	**patreco,** *fatherhood.*
indeco, *worthiness.*	**patrineco,** *motherhood.*
dankemeco, *thankfulness.*	**maltrankvileco,** *uneasiness.*

VOCABULARY.

bord-o, *bank, shore.*	**pont-o,** *bridge.*
brak-o, *arm.*	**sonor-i,** *to ring* (intrans.).
fabrik-i, *to manufacture.*	**surtut-o,** *overcoat.*
krut-a, *steep.*	**sving-i,** *to swing, to brandish.*
lan-o, *wool.*	**ŝip-o,** *ship.*
mebl-o, *piece of furniture.*	**ŝton-o,** *stone.*
pas-i, *to pass* (intrans.).	**vapor-o,** *steam.*
pitoresk-a, *picturesque.*	**vetur-i,** *to travel* (in a vehicle).

SUR LA VAPORŜIPO.

Unu el la plezuroj de la kampara vivo konsistas el la multenombraj (*numerous*) okazoj por veturi ĉien, kien oni volas iri, per kvietaj pitoreskaj vojoj. Ni havas ankoraŭ unu (*still one, yet another*) okazon por plezuro en nia vilaĝo, ĉar ni povas veturi per vaporŝipo sur la bela lago ĉe kies bordo kuŝas la vilaĝo. Hieraŭ du kuzinoj venis por viziti ĉe ni, kaj tuj post la tagmanĝo ni decidis promeni laŭ tiu pitoreska vojeto al la lago. Kiam ni alvenis al la lago, ni rimarkis ke beleta vaporŝipeto estis ĵus forironta. Tial mi aĉetis tri biletojn, kaj kiel eble plej rapide ni suriris la ŝipeton. La sonoriloj (*bells*) estis jam sonorintaj, kaj tuj post kiam ni transmarŝis la ponteton, de la tero al la planko de la ŝipeto, oni forprenis la ponteton. Kelkaj personoj kiuj estis ankoraŭ sur la tero kuris kun granda rapideco al la ponteto. Ili svingis la brakojn kaj la ombrelojn tre energie, sed la ŝipeto ne atendis eĉ unu minuton. La personoj ŝajnis tre koleraj pro sia malfrueco, kaj ankoraŭ pli koleraj pro la trankvila foriro de la ŝipeto. Ĉiu sur la ŝipeto ridetis, ĉar la koleremo (*irascibility*) estas ĉiam amuza. Tiam ĉiu komencis sin amuzi tiel, kiel li deziris. Mi estis kunportinta dikan lanan surtuton, sed pro la varmeco de la vetero mi ne bezonis ĝin, kaj lasis ĝin sur apuda seĝo. Ni atendis kun plezuro por vidi la krutajn montetojn kiuj estos videblaj tuj kiam la ŝipeto estos pasinta preter malgranda arbaro. La pitoreskeco de la belaj montetoj estas difektota, ĉar grandaj fabrikejoj estas jam konstruataj ĉe

poor man's bread, Spanish *Las riquezas son bagajes de la fortuna, riches are the baggage of fortune,* etc. In English the generic article (as in "the life eternal" above) may often be replaced by omission of both "a" and "the."

la montpiedoj. La ŝtonoj por la muroj jam kuŝas pretaj apude, kune kun grandaj stangoj kaj aliaj pecoj da ligno. Tie oni fabrikos tablojn, seĝojn, kaj aliajn meblojn el zorge elektita ligno.

SENTENCES FOR TRANSLATION.

1. It is difficult in every way to select a present for a child who already possesses enough toys. 2. In a toy-shop yesterday I examined the dolls made out of woolen cloth and other material, and also looked at the various little animals. 3. There were ponies, little dogs and little lions and camels. 4. There were also little sets of furniture (126), which consisted of tables, sofas and chairs. 5. On the tables were small plates containing vegetables, fruits and roast (189) meat, entirely made out of colored paper. 6. There were also little cups and tumblers of thin glass, into which one could pour water or milk. 7. As (ĉar) one dollar was all (194) of the money which I had in my purse, I left the shop. 8. I walked along a stony picturesque path toward the lake, swinging my overcoat on my arm, while I thought over (*pripensis*) the difficulty, and tried to decide what sort of present to choose. 9. The steamboat to B— — was just leaving, so I went across the footbridge (*ponteto*) on to the pretty little ship, while its bells were ringing, and rode an hour in the open (*libera*) air. 10. The shore which we passed is very picturesque, but its beauty is about to be spoiled, for a large furniture factory is going to be built between that steep hill and the lake. 11. Its proximity to the water is necessary, for water-power (*akvoforto*) will be used.

LESSON XLIII.

THE INDEFINITE PRONOUN.—PARTICIPIAL NOUNS.—
THE PREFIX EK-.—THE SUFFIX -ID-. —LA NESTO SUR
LA TENDO.

THE INDEFINITE PRONOUN.

203. The indefinite pronoun (and pronominal adjective) **iu**, *any one, a certain one*, presents the idea of some person or thing, without definitely characterizing it:

Mi parolas pri iu, kiun vi konas, *I am talking about a certain one whom you know.*
Mi vizitis iujn el viaj amikoj, *I visited some of your friends.*
Mi havas kelkajn pomojn, sed iuj ne estas bonaj, *I have several apples, but certain ones are not good.*
Iuj pontoj estas bone faritaj, *some bridges are well made.*

204. The indefinite pronoun **iu** has a possessive or genitive form **ies**, *somebody's, someone's, a certain one's*:

Mi tuŝis ies brakon, *I touched someone's arm.*
Ĉu ies surtuto kuŝas sur la tablo? *Is anybody's overcoat lying on the table?*
Ies ludiloj estas rompitaj, *someone's playthings are broken.*

PARTICIPIAL NOUNS.

205. Nouns may be formed from participles, by substituting the noun ending **-o** for the adjectival ending **-a**. Such participial nouns indicate persons temporarily or non-professionally performing or undergoing that which is expressed by the root:[48]

helpanto, *one who is helping, an assistant.*
elpensinto, *one who has thought out something, an inventor.*
legonto, *one who is about to read.*

[48] Participial nouns must not be confused with nouns formed by the suffix **-ist-** (172) expressing professional or permanent occupation:

rajdanto, *a rider,*
rajdisto, *jockey, horseman,*
juĝanto, *a judge* (of something),
juĝisto, *judge* (professional),
laboranto, *a person working,*
laboristo, *laborer.*

vidato, *one (being) seen.*
sendito, *one (having been) sent, an envoy.*
la juĝoto, *the one about to be judged, the accused.*

THE PREFIX EK-.

206. Sudden or momentary action, or the beginning of an action or state, is indicated by the prefix **ek-**:

ekdormi, *to fall asleep.*
ekkanti, *to burst into song.*
ekiri, *to set out, to start.*
ekridi, *to burst into a laugh*
ekrigardi, *to glance at.*

THE SUFFIX -ID-.

207. Words indicating the *young of, the child of, the descendant of,* are formed by use of the suffix **-id-**:

ĉevalido, *colt* (from **ĉevalo,** *horse*).
hundido, *puppy* (from **hundo,** *dog*).
katido, *kitten* (from **kato,** *cat*).
leonido, *a lion's whelp* (from **leono,** *lion*).
reĝidino, *a king's daughter, a princess* (from **reĝo,** *king*).

VOCABULARY.

amas-o, *heap, throng.*
daŭr-i, *to continue.*
hirund-o, *swallow.* (bird).
hom-o, *human being.*[‡‡]
humor-o, *temper, humor.*
ies, *some one's* (204).
iu, *some one* (203).

kugl-o, *bullet.*
milit-i, *to fight, to make war.*
ost-o, *bone.*
renvers-i, *to upset, to overturn.*
sign-o, *sign, mark.*
tend-o, *tent.*
tru-o, *hole.*

LA NESTO SUR LA TENDO.

Unufoje iu reĝo estis farinta militon kontraŭ la homoj de lando ĉe la bordo de pitoreska rivero. La soldatoj ne venis tien per vaporŝipoj, sed estis konstruintaj ponton trans la rivero, por la veturiloj (*vehicles*). Estis necese resti kelkan tempon apud urbo kiun la reĝo volis ekataki, kaj li havis grandan tendaron (*encampment*) antaŭ tiu urbo. Unu tagon en la daŭro (*course*) de la milito, iuj el la soldatoj pasis preter la tendo de la reĝo, laŭ la ŝtona vojeto laŭ kiu ili ĉiutage marŝis por gardi la tendaron. Unu el ĉi tiuj ekrimarkis ke hirundo estas konstruinta sian neston sur la reĝa tendo. Sur la nesto, kiu estis bone konstruita el koto, sidis trankvile la hirundo. Dum la soldatoj svingis la brakojn kaj ekridis unu post la alia, pri la kuraĝa birdo, la reĝo aŭdis ies voĉon. Li elvenis el sia tendo por eltrovi kial la parolantoj faras tiom da bruo, kaj kial ili tiel ekkriis kaj ekridis. Kiam la viroj montris al li la birdon, li diris kun bonhumora rideto, "Tiu hirundo estos mia gasto. Ĉiuj el la militistoj certe zorgos de nun pri la hirundo kaj la hirundidoj." Tial la nesto restis netuŝata en la daŭro de ĉiu batalo. Kelkaj kugloj pasis preter ĝi, sed la trankvileco de la birdo daŭris same kiel antaŭe. Fine la reĝo venkis, per kruelega batalo. Tuj la venkintoj forportis la tendojn, kune kun multaj militkaptitoj (*prisoners of war*). Nur la tendon de la reĝo oni lasis tie, ĉar la reĝo diris ke ĝi nun apartenas al la hirundo. Ĝi jam estis malnova kaj eluzita, tra kiu la pluvo eniris per multe da truoj. Sed ĝi ankoraŭ staris, ĝis iu tago somera kiam la hirundidoj povis jam bone flugi. Tiam la vento subite renversis ĝin, kaj ĝi ekfalis, kaj kuŝis, amaso da ĉifonoj, inter multe da kugloj, homaj ostoj, kaj la ceteraj malgajaj postsignoj (*traces*) de ies venko sur la batalejo.

SENTENCES FOR TRANSLATION.

1. There is a pretty story about a swallow which built its nest for its young (*idoj*) on the king's tent. 2. The soldiers who were walking along the steep path past the tent glanced at it, and caught sight of (206) the bird. 3. Some of them burst into a laugh, and gestured (*svingis la brakon*) toward the bird, to point it out to their comrades. 4. The good-humored king put on a thick woolen overcoat, and came out of his tent, to inquire why his soldiers were conversing so noisily there. 5. The tent was an expensive one, and contained handsome furniture, as well as (*kaj ankaŭ*) a bell which always rang as soon as (*tuj kiam*) one touched it. 6. The king immediately noticed the swallow's nest, and said with an amiable smile "Surely such a courageous bird is a worthy (154) guest for a king." 7. The warriors (172) cared for the swallow as much as possible during the course of the war. 8. When the victors departed, they left that tent there. 9. Finally the wind upset it, and it fell to the ground. 10. The young swallows already could fly, by (*je*) that time. 11. The battleground is covered with bullets, piles of human bones, and similar melancholy signs of war. 12. War (201) is wicked and shameful (154). 13. Why do kings and princes wish to make war upon each other (180)? 14. When their sons have gone away to (make) war, the mothers of the soldiers are very uneasy. 15. Perhaps those sons will be prisoners of war.

LESSON XLIV.

THE INDEFINITE ADJECTIVE.—THE INDEFINITE AD-
VERB OF PLACE.—PREDICATE NOMINATIVES.—LA
ĈEVALO KAJ LA SONORILO.

THE INDEFINITE ADJECTIVE.

208. The indefinite adjective, related to the indefinite pronoun **iu**, is **ia**, *of any kind, some kind of, a certain kind of*, expressing indefinitely the quality of a person or thing:

Estas ia birdo sur tiu arbo, *there is a bird of some sort on that tree.*
Mi vidis iajn ostojn sur la tero, *I saw some kind of bones on the ground.*
Estas ia homo en tiu tendo, *there is some sort of human being in that tent.*

THE INDEFINITE ADVERB OF PLACE.

209. The indefinite adverb of place, related to the indefinite pronoun **iu**, is **ie**, *anywhere, somewhere, in (at) a certain place.* If the verb in the sentence expresses motion toward the place indicated by **ie**, the ending **-n** is added (121):

Ie en tiu arbaro estas leono, *somewhere in that forest is a lion.*
Ie malantaŭ la soldatoj vi trovos amason da kugloj, *somewhere behind the soldiers you will find a heap of bullets.*
La hirundo flugis ien, *the swallow flew somewhere (in some direction).*
Mi iros ien, sed mi ankoraŭ ne scias kien, *I am going somewhere, but I do not yet know where.*

PREDICATE NOMINATIVES.

210. An adjective may stand in predicate relation to the *direct object of a transitive verb,* as well as to the subject of an intransitive verb (19). Such a predicate adjective, agreeing in number (21) with the object of the verb, *but remaining in the nominative case,* indicates the result produced by the verb upon the object, or the condition, quality or temporary state in which this object is found:[49]

---

[49] *Cf.* the difference between the examples given and sentences with the same words in an attributive (13) use:

Dio faris la mondon feliĉan, *God made the happy world.*
Mi lasis la knabon trankvilan, *I left the calm boy.*
Mi trovis la jam faritan truon, *I found the already made hole.*
Mi lasis ilin bone punitajn, *I left those who had been well punished.*

Li faris la mondon feliĉa, *he made the world happy (made-happy the world).*
Mi lasis la knabon trankvila, *I left the boy calm (undisturbed).*
Mi trovis la truon jam farita, *I found the hole already made.*
Mi lasis ilin bone punitaj, *I left them well punished.*

211. A *noun* may be used similarly in predicate relation after a transitive verb, as well as after an intransitive verb (20):[50]

Ŝi nomis sian filinon Mario, *she named her daughter Mary.*
Oni elektis tiun reprezentanto, *they elected that one representative.*
Mi vidos lin venkinto, *I shall see him a conqueror.*
Mi trovis lin ŝtelisto, *I found him a thief.*

VOCABULARY.

anonc-i, *to announce.*
ia, *some kind of* (208).
ie, *somewhere* (209).
just-a, *upright, just.*
klar-a, *distinct, clear.*
kresk-i, *to grow.*
oportun-a, *convenient.*

paŝt-i, *to feed* (flocks, etc.).
plend-i, *to complain.*
proces-o, *legal process.*
rajt-o, *right, privilege.*
ripar-i, *to mend, to repair.*
sufer-i, *to suffer.*
ŝnur-o, *string.*

LA ĈEVALO KAJ LA SONORILO.

Unufoje en malgranda urbeto (*town*) en Italujo, la reĝo, kiun oni estis nominta Johano, metis grandan sonorilon en la vendejon. Li anoncis ke ĉiu plendanto pri maljusteco havos la rajton alvoki (*to summon*) juĝiston per tiu sonorilo. Tiam la juĝisto faros proceson en la juĝejo pro tiaj plendantoj. Oni multe uzis la sonorilon, laŭ la anonco de la reĝo, kaj multe da plendantoj ricevis justecon. Sammaniere, granda nombro da maljustuloj estis punata per ĝia helpo. Kiam okazis ke iu homo montris sin maljusta al alia, ĉi tiu anoncis la aferon per la oportuna sonorilo. Kiam iu faris la edzinon malfeliĉa, la sonorilo tuj sonoris por anonci ŝiajn suferojn, kaj por alvoki la juĝiston. Fine, oni tiom uzis la sonorilon justecan, ke la ŝnurego (*rope*) estis tute eluzita, kaj ĝia lasta uzinto okaze forrompis ĝin. Sed iu preterpasinto vidis la duonon de la ŝnurego kuŝanta sur la tero, kaj riparis ĝin per kelkaj branĉetoj de apuda arbo. Li pensis en si "Iu plendonto nun trovos ĝin preta por esti uzata." Rimarkinde, la branĉetoj ne velkis, sed restis verdaj, kaj kreskis kiel antaŭe.

En la sama urbo loĝis riĉulo kiu estis forvendinta preskaŭ ĉiom de siaj domoj, ĉevaloj, ĉevaletoj, ĉevalidoj, hundoj kaj multekostaj vestoj, ĉar en sia maljuneco li amis nur la monon, kaj tiun li amegis. Li ankoraŭ posedis nur unu maljunan ĉevalon, kaj fine li forsendis eĉ tiun, por sin paŝti laŭ la vojo. En la daŭro de la tago, la ĉevalo ekrimarkis la branĉetojn kreskantajn sur la ŝnurego de la sonorilo. Tuj ĝi kaptis la branĉetojn, por manĝi ilin, kaj tuj la juĝisto aŭdis la sonorilon klare so-

---

[50] *Cf.* the examples given and the following sentences using the same words in apposition (48) or attributive relation (13):

Ŝi nomis sian filinon Marion, *she named (mentioned) her daughter Mary.*
Oni elektis tiun reprezentanton, *they elected that representative.*

noranta. Li rapidis al la vendejo, kaj laŭte ekridis kiam li vidis ies ĉevalon tie. Li decidis puni la riĉulon ĉar tiu ĉi ne donis sufiĉe por manĝi al la maljuna militĉevalo.

SENTENCES FOR TRANSLATION.

1. The horse caught sight of the twigs with which a passer-by had mended the bellrope. 2. Because it wished to eat the green leaves, it seized the rope, and the bell immediately rang loudly and clearly. 3. The horse almost upset the poles which supported (160) the roof over the bell of-justice. 4. Any one (173) had the right to use this bell, to announce any kind of injustice. 5. The judge burst into a laugh as soon as he saw that sort of plaintiff standing there. 6. More often he saw human beings as plaintiffs, instead of animals. 7. When a laborer showed himself unkind to his wife and children, they could announce their sufferings by means of the convenient bell. 8. People called it the bell of justice. 9. According to everyone's opinion, it is the duty of a just judge to punish evildoers and unjust persons. 10. He decided that he would institute proceedings (*faros proceson*) against the owner (205) of the horse. 11. The man had driven away the horse, and it was grazing (*sin paŝtanta*) along the road. 12. It was some one's duty to give some sort of home to his horse. 13. The judge said, "I will find out whose horse that poor beast is, and will put a mark opposite the name of that man. I will not leave him alone (*trankvila*), but will show myself very severe."

LESSON XLV.

THE INDEFINITE TEMPORAL ADVERB.—THE INDEFI-
NITE ADVERB IAL.—CAUSATIVE VERBS. —EMPHA-
SIS BY MEANS OF JA.—ĈE LA MALNOVA PONTO.

THE INDEFINITE TEMPORAL ADVERB.

212. The indefinite temporal adverb, related to the indefinite pronoun **iu**, is
iam, *sometime, any time, ever, once upon a time*:

Iam mi rakontos la aferon al vi, *sometime I will tell you the affair.*
Reĝo iam loĝis tie, *a king once (upon a time) dwelt there.*
Ĉu vi iam faris proceson kontraŭ li? *Did you ever go to law against him?*

THE INDEFINITE ADVERB IAL.

213. The indefinite adverb of motive or reason, related to the indefinite pronoun **iu**, is **ial**, *for any reason, for some reason, for certain reasons*:

Ial li ne riparis la tendon, *for some reason he did not repair the tent.*
Ĉu vi opinias ke ial li maljuste suferas? *Do you think that for any reason he is
suffering unjustly?*

CAUSATIVE VERBS.

214. The suffix **-ig-** is used to form verbs indicating the *causing, rendering or
bringing about* of that which is expressed in the root or formation to which it is
attached. Verbs containing the suffix **-ig-** are called *causative verbs* and are always
transitive (22).

a. Causative verbs from *adjectival* roots indicate that the quality or condition
expressed in the root is produced in the object of the verb:[51]

dolĉigi, *to sweeten, to assuage* (from **dolĉa**, *sweet*).
moligi, *to soften* (from **mola**, *soft*).
plilongigi, *to lengthen, to make longer* (from **pli longa**, *longer*).
faciligi, *to facilitate* (from **facila**, *easy*).
beligi, *to beautify* (from **bela**, *beautiful*).

b. Causative verbs from *verbal* roots indicate that the action expressed in the

---

[51] The meaning often resembles that of the predicate nominative (210), as:

Li faris la mondon ĝoja, *he made the world glad.*
Li ĝojigis la mondon, *he gladdened the world.*

root is made to take place:

dormigi, *to put to sleep* (from **dormi**, *to sleep*).
konigi, *to make acquainted with* (from **koni**, *to know*).
mirigi, *to astonish* (from **miri**, *to wonder*).
mortigi, *to kill* (from **morti**, *to die*).

c. Causative verbs may be formed from noun-roots, prepositions, adverbs, prefixes and suffixes whose meaning permits:

amasigi, *to amass, to heap up* (from **amaso**, *pile*).
kunigi, *to unite, to bring together* (from **kun**, *with*).
forigi, *to do away with* (from **for**, *away*).
ebligi, *to render possible* (**-ebl-**, 161).

EMPHASIS BY MEANS OF JA.

215. The emphatic form of the verb, expressed in English by "do", "did", as in "I do study", "I did find it", "Do tell me", and by adverbs such as "certainly", "indeed", etc., is expressed in Esperanto by placing the adverb **ja**, *indeed*, before the verb:

Vi ja mirigas min! *You do astonish me!*
Li ja estas justa juĝisto, *he is indeed an upright judge.*
Li ja havis tiun rajton, *he did have that right.*

Vocabulary.

akompan-i, *to accompany.*
danĝer-o, *danger.*
gvid-i, *to guide.*
ial, *for some reason* (213).
iam, *sometimes* (212).

indiferent-a, *indifferent.*[§§]
ja, *indeed* (215).
kred-i, *to believe.*
salt-i, *to leap, to jump.*
tir-i, *to draw, to pull.*

ĈE LA MALNOVA PONTO.

Iam loĝis en nia urbeto junulo kiu havis afablan pli junan fratinon. Unu tagon en la daŭro de la bela printempa vetero la junulo invitis la fratinon veturi ien en veturilo tirata de du ĉevaloj. La invito ĝojigis la knabinon, kaj ŝi respondis ke ŝi kun plezuro akompanos la fraton. Tuj ŝi pretigis sin por iri, kaj ili ekveturis. Ili pasis preter pitoreskaj kampoj kaj arbaretoj, kaj fine alvenis al ponto trans la rivero. Ili kredis ĝin malnova kaj ne tre forta, kaj ial la junulino estis treege timigita (*frightened*). "Ho, kara frato," ŝi ekkriis, kun eksalteto pro timo, "tiu ponto ja estas danĝera! Mi deziras marŝi trans ĝin, ĉar iam la pezeco de unu persono estos tiom tro multe por veturilo sur malforta ponto!" Sed la timemaj petoj de lia fratino ŝajne kolerigis la junulon, kaj li respondis malafable, "Nu, vi ja mirigas min! Vi montras vin tre malsaĝa, ĉar la konstruintoj de tiu ponto certe faris ĝin sufiĉe forta por tia veturilo kia la nia. Ne estos necese eksalti de ĝi, kaj piede transiri la ponton." Tiamaniere li penis trankviligi la kompatindan knabinon, sed tiaj vortoj nur silentigis ŝin, kaj ŝi komencis mallaŭte ploreti. Tamen la frato montris sin indiferenta al ŝiaj timemaj sentoj, kaj tute malatentis ŝiajn larmojn. Li gvidis la ĉevalojn rekte trans la ponton, dum la fratino atendis la bruegon de rompigita ligno, kaj imagis ke ŝi estas tuj mortigota. Tamen, la ponto estis tiel forta kiel la junulo estis klariginta, kaj tute ne estis danĝera. Sed pro la malafableco de la frato al la fratino, ili tute ne agrable pasigis la ceterajn horojn de la posttagmezo, malgraŭ la beleco de la vetero kaj de la kamparo.

SENTENCES FOR TRANSLATION.

1. Somewhere in that same town, there lived another youth, who also had an amiable sister. 2. One convenient day, she accompanied him for a ride in a vehicle drawn by a fast horse. 3. When they reached (*alvenis al*) the bridge, this girl also was frightened for some reason, the same as the girl in the other story. 4. She said "I do not intend to complain, but the carriage will certainly be too heavy while we are in it. I am afraid that that bridge is dangerous, so I will jump out and walk. I will also pick (*kolektos*) some sort of flowers, among the flowers growing there, near where someone's horses are grazing. I will not delay (*atendigi*) you long." He replied, "That bridge is entirely safe (*nedanĝera*) but instead of explaining (*making-clear*) to you about it, I will lead the horse across the bridge, while you walk across, for I am not indifferent to your fear." Then he helped his sister get out (*eliri*) of the carriage, and guided the horse across. Then he said with a pleasant smile, "It was not necessary to cross on foot." She replied, "No, but you showed yourself a courteous brother, and were very patient." Then they rode on (*antaŭen*), and talked to each other very amiably.

LESSON XLVI.

THE INDEFINITE ADVERB IEL.—THE INDEFINITE AD-
VERB IOM.—THE SUFFIX -AD-.—THE USE OF MEM.—
ARĤIMEDO KAJ LA KRONOJ.

THE INDEFINITE ADVERB IEL.

216. The indefinite adverb of manner, related to the indefinite pronoun **iu**, is **iel**, *somehow, in any way, in some (any) manner:*

Mi penis vin iel gvidi tien, *I tried somehow to guide you thither.*
Iel ni anoncos la decidon, *we shall announce the decision in some way.*

THE INDEFINITE ADVERB IOM.

217. The indefinite adverb of quantity, related to the indefinite pronoun **iu**, is **iom**, *some, any quantity, a certain amount:*

Ĉu vi havas iom da tempo? *Have you some time?*
Ŝi varmigos iom da akvo, *she will heat some water.*
Tiu metodo estas iomete danĝera, *that way is a little dangerous* (198).
La ŝnuro estas iom tro longa, *the string is somewhat too long.*

THE SUFFIX -AD-.

218. The suffix **-ad-** is used to form words indicating that the action expressed in the root is *continuous, habitual or repeated.*

a. Verbs formed with the suffix **-ad-** are called *frequentative verbs*, and may often be translated by the root meaning, preceded by "keep (on)", "used to", etc.:

frapadi, *to keep knocking, to knock repeatedly.*
rigardadi, *to keep on looking, to gaze.*
vizitadi, *to keep visiting, visit repeatedly, frequent, haunt.*
Antaŭ du jaroj ŝi tre dolĉe kantadis, *two years ago she used to sing very sweetly.*

b. Nouns formed with the suffix **-ad-** are often equivalent to English verbal nouns ending in *-ing*, and (with the generic article, 201) may replace the infinitive as subject (130) and sometimes as object (29):

kriado, *crying, shouting* (from **krio**, *cry, shout*).
movado, *motion, movement in general* (from **movo**, *a movement*).
pafado, *shooting, fusillade* (from **pafo**, *a shot*).
parolado, *a speech, address* (from **parolo**, *a word spoken*).

pensado, *thought, contemplation* (from **penso**, *a thought*).
La promenado donas plezuron, *the taking of walks gives pleasure.*
Mi preferas la legadon de tiaj libroj, *I prefer the reading of (to read) such books.*

THE USE OF MEM.

219. The invariable pronoun **mem**, *self, selves*, is intensive, and lays stress upon the substantive which immediately precedes it, or which it obviously modifies. (The combination of **mem** with personal pronouns must not be confused with reflexive pronouns, 39, 40):

Mi mem akompanos vin, *I myself shall accompany you.*
La gvidisto mem perdis la vojon, *the guide himself lost the way.*
Mi kredos al la viro mem, *I shall give credence to the man himself.*
La viroj mem defendis sin, *the men themselves defended themselves.*
Ĝi pendas sur la muro mem, *it hangs on the very wall (the wall itself).*
Ŝi venis mem por vidi vin, *she came herself to see you.*
Mi ekvidis la ŝteliston mem, *I caught a glimpse of the thief himself.*

VOCABULARY.

Arĥimed-o, *Archimedes.*
ban-i, *to bathe* (trans.).
fals-i, *to debase, to forge.*
Hieron-o, *Hiero.*
honest-a, *honest.*
ide-o, *idea.*
iel, *somehow* (216).
iom, *some* (217).

ĵet-i, *to throw, to cast.*
kompren-i, *to understand.*
kron-o, *crown.*
lev-i, *to lift, to raise.*
lok-o, *place.*
mem, *self, selves* (219).
or-o, *gold.*
Sikeli-o, *Sicily.*

ARĤIMEDO KAJ LA KRONOJ.

I am bonekonata reĝo, nomita Hierono, vivadis en granda urbo en Sikelio, kiu estas sudokcidenta de Italujo. Li suspektis ke iam la kronfaristoj, kiuj fabrikadis kronojn por li, ne uzis ĉiom de la oro donita al ili de la reĝo, sed falsadis ĝin per la uzado de iu alia materialo. Tamen, Hierono ne povis per si mem eltrovi ĉu oni falsadas la oron. Tial li venigis grekan klerulon, kies nomo estis Arĥimedo, kaj rakontis al li sian timon pri la falsita oro. Arĥimedo certigis lin ke iel li ja eltrovos pri la falsado, kaj helpos la reĝon kontraŭ la falsintoj, kiuj estis tiel indiferentaj al la honesteco. Ĉiutage li multe pensadis pri la afero, sed ju pli longe li pensadis, des malpli sukcesaj estis liaj penoj, ĝis iu tago, kiam li okaze faris interesan eltrovon. Li estis ĵus baninta sin, kaj subite ekrimarkis ke dum li mem restis en la akvo, ial ŝajnis esti iomete pli multe da akvo en la banujo ol antaŭe. Tuj li komprenis ke lia korpo estas forpuŝinta iom de la akvo el ĝia loko. Li komprenis ke tiom da akvo estas elpuŝita, kiom antaŭe estis en tiu loko kie li mem estas. Tia levado de la akvo per lia korpo donis al li saĝan ideon, kaj li prenis en la mano du aŭ tri orajn kronojn. Li ĵetis ilin unu post la alia en la banujon, kaj zorge rimarkis al kiu alteco ĉiu el ili levis la akvon. Tiam li eltiris ilin, kaj enmetis la kronon pri kiu Hierono estis plej suspektema. Li rimarkis ke ĉi tiu ne tiel alten levis la akvon, tial li estis certa ke la oro en ĝi estas multe falsita. Oni diras ke kiam li eltrovis ĉi tiun metodon por montri la falsadon de la malhonestaj kronfaristoj, li eksaltetis pro ĝojo kaj ekkriis "eŭreka," kiu estas la greka vorto por "mi estas trovinta." Tiun saman vorton oni ankoraŭ nun uzadas en la angla lingvo.

SENTENCES FOR TRANSLATION.

1. Several centuries ago, a rich and powerful (*multepova*) king, named Hiero, lived in Sicily. 2. Sometimes he was suspicious about the crown-makers who wrought (*faris*) crowns for him, out of the gold which he himself gave them. 3. He wondered whether these men were honest. 4. He suspected that perhaps (*eble*) they did not use all of the gold which was given them, but kept some of it for themselves. 5. He could not of himself (*per si mem*) discover whether they were debasing the gold in his crowns, so he summoned a wise man from (*el*) Greece. 6. To this well-informed man, whose name was Archimedes, he made clear his fears. 7. Archimedes assured the king that he would find out somehow about the matter. 8. He meditated several hours every day, and tried to discover a satisfactory (*kontentiga*) method, but for some reason he did not succeed. 9. One day, however, when he was bathing (himself), he noticed that there seemed to be a little more water in the bathtub when he himself was in it, than before. 10. The rising of the water gave him an idea. 11. He threw the crowns one after another into the water, and noticed how much water each displaced. 12. In this manner (*tiamaniere*) he understood how much each had been alloyed by the local (*lokaj*) crown-makers, whom Hiero soon threw into prison (*la malliberejon*).

LESSON XLVII.

THE NEGATIVE PRONOUN.—THE ADVERBIAL PARTICI-
PLE.—THE PREFIX RE-.—LA FILOZOFO ARĤIMEDO.

THE NEGATIVE PRONOUN.

220. The negative pronoun (and pronominal adjective) is **neniu**, *no one, nobody,
no* (formed of **ne** and **iu**, with a medial **n** inserted for the sake of euphony):

Neniu el vi komprenas min, *no one of you understands me.*
Mi trovis neniun preta por iri, *I found nobody ready to go.*
Li havis neniun honestan serviston, *he had no honest servant.*

221. The negative pronoun **neniu** has a possessive or genitive form, **nenies**,
nobody's, no one's:

Ĉies afero estas nenies afero, *everybody's affair is nobody's affair.*
Li laŭdos nenies ideojn, *he will praise no one's ideas.*

THE ADVERBIAL PARTICIPLE.

222. A participle may be equivalent not only to a clause describing or deter-
mining the substantive modified, as in **la parolanta viro,** *the man who-is-talking,* **la
sendota knabo,** *the boy who-will-be-sent,* but also to an *adverbial* clause.[52]

Such a participle has for its subject the subject of the verb in the sentence
(though not in attributive or predicate relation with it), and indicates some relation
of time, cause, manner, situation, etc., between the action of the participle and that
of the main verb in the sentence. An *adverbial participle* is given the ending **-e**:[53]

Ĝojante, mi ridis, *rejoicing, I laughed.*
Forironte, ni adiaŭis lin, *being about to depart, we bade him farewell.*
Baninte la infaneton, ŝi dormigis ĝin, *after bathing (having bathed) the baby,
she put it to sleep.*
Estante ruzaj, ili falsis la oron, *being sly, they debased the gold.*
Tiel helpate de vi, mi sukcesos, *thus helped by you, I shall succeed.*

---

[52] An adverbial clause modifies a verb, as in **dum vi atendis, li foriris,** *while you wait-
ed, he went away;* **ĉar mi ĝojis, mi ridis,** *because I was happy, I laughed.*

[53] The adverbial participle must not be used in rendering the English "nominative
absolute" construction of a participial clause referring to something else than the subject.
In such a sentence a clause must be used: *The youth being young, everyone watched him,* **ĉar
la junulo estis juna, ĉiu rigardadis lin;** *the work being finished, he went away,* **kiam la lahoro
estis finita, li foriris.**

Silentigite de li, ili ne plendis, *(having been) silenced by him, they did not complain.*
Punote, li ekkriis, *being about to be punished, he gave a cry.*
Ne parolinte, li foriris, *without speaking (not having spoken), he left.*
Li venis, ne vokite, *he came without being (came not-having-been) called.*

THE PREFIX **RE-**.

223. The prefix **re-** indicates the repetition of an action or state, or the *return* of a person or thing to its original place or state. (*Cf.* English prefix **re-**; meaning either "again" or "back.")

rekapti, *to recapture.*	**rebrili**, *to shine back, to reflect.*
renovigi, *to renew.*	**reteni**, *to hold back, to retain.*
rekoni, *to recognize.*	**reveni**, *to come back, to return.*
ĝis la revido, *au revoir.*	**reiri**, *to go back, to return.*
ree, *again, anew.*	**reĵeti**, *to throw back, to reject.*

VOCABULARY.

brul-i, *to be in flames, to burn.*	**maŝin-o**, *machine.*
cilindr-o, *cylinder.*	**nenies**, *nobody's* (221).
detru-i, *to destroy.*	**neniu**, *no one* (220).
fam-a, *famous.*	**problem-o**, *problem.*
filozof-o, *philosopher.*	**Sirakuz-o**, *Syracuse.*
fizik-o, *physics.*	**spegul-o**, *mirror.*
insul-o, *island.*	**ŝraŭb-o**, *screw.*

LA FILOZOFO ARĤIMEDO.

Eble neniu greka klerulo estis pli fama ol la filozofo Arĥimedo. Longe studadinte la problemojn de la geometrio kaj de la fiziko, li faris multe da eltrovoj. Li tiel multe komprenis pri la uzado de la levilo (*lever*) ke oni rakontas la sekvantan rakonteton pri li: Li diris al la reĝo Hierono "Kiam oni donos al mi lokon sur kiu mi povos stari, mi mem ekmovos la mondon per mia levilo!" Zorge ekzameninte la ecojn (202) de la ŝraŭbo kaj de la cilindro, li elpensis diversajn maŝinojn en kiuj ŝraŭboj kaj cilindroj estas iamaniere kunigitaj. Uzante unu el tiuj maŝinoj, oni povis facile puŝi al la akvo la ŝipojn (necese konstruitajn sur la tero); kiujn antaŭe la viroj mem enpuŝis en la akvon, kun multe da laboro, aŭ tiris tien per ĉevaloj. Uzante alian maŝinon elpensitan de tiu greko, oni povis levi akvon de unu loko al alia. Ankoraŭ nun oni nomas tian maŝinon la "ŝraŭbo de Arĥimedo." En la daŭro de granda militado kontraŭ la urbo Sirakuzo, sur la insulo Sikelio, Arĥimedo elpensis diversajn maŝinojn por helpi la Sirakuzanojn. Vidinte ke la sunlumo rebrilas de spegulo, li faris el speguloj maŝinon per kiu li ekbruligis (*set on fire*) la ŝipojn de la malamikoj. Ĉi tiuj, ne komprenante **kiamaniere**[54] la ŝipoj ekbrulis, estis multe timigitaj. Sed eĉ helpite de Arĥimedo la Sirakuzanoj ne venkis. Post

---

[54] The use of **kiamaniere**, *in what manner, how*, is preferable to that of **kiel** in indirect questions, as the latter might be confused with the use of **kiel**, meaning "as" (156).

iom da tempo, la malamikoj kaptis kaj tute detruis la urbon Sirakuzon. Nenies domo restis netuŝita, kaj centoj da personoj estis mortigataj. Oni ne scias per kia morto Arĥimedo mortis, sed eble la malamikoj, iel rekoninte la elpensinton de la spegulmaŝino, ĵetis lin en la maron aŭ alimaniere lin mortigis.

SENTENCES FOR TRANSLATION.

1. The Greek philosopher Archimedes was not only famous long ago, among his contemporaries (167, b, 132), but even today his name is well known everywhere. 2. No one's knowledge about the problems of geometry and physics was greater. 3. No one understood better the properties of the cylinder and the screw. 4. Having studied these properties a long time, and having meditated a great deal about them, he understood them a little (217) better than any one else (*iu alia*). 5. The story about the debasing of the gold crowns has already been told. 6. There is another anecdote, namely (*nome*), that he remarked to Hiero, king of Syracuse, that with a lever he would move the world, as soon as he had a place on which he himself could stand. 7. Having discovered how (*kiamaniere*) the sunlight is reflected by a mirror, and heats the wood upon which it shines, he invented a machine made out of mirrors. 8. Aided by this machine, the Syracusans were able to set on fire the wooden ships of the enemy. 9. The enemy, however, were not repulsed from the island, but at once rebuilt and repaired their ships, and sent them back to attack the city again. 10. Finally, having captured the city, they destroyed it, and killed a large number of the inhabitants (*loĝantoj*), also Archimedes himself.

LESSON XLVIII.

THE NEGATIVE ADJECTIVE.—THE NEGATIVE ADVERB
OF PLACE.—THE NEGATIVE TEMPORAL ADVERB.—
THE SUFFIX -AĴ-.—THE ADVERB JEN.—DU ART-
KONKURSOJ.

THE NEGATIVE ADJECTIVE.

224. The negative adjective, related to the negative pronoun **neniu,** is **nenia,**
no kind of, no sort of, expressing a negative idea concerning the quality of a person
or thing:

Mi havas nenian spegulon, *I have no sort of mirror.*
Nenia problemo estas tro malfacila por li, *no sort of problem is too difficult for
him.*

THE NEGATIVE ADVERB OF PLACE.

225. The negative adverb of place is **nenie,** *nowhere.* The ending **-n** may be
added, as to other adverbs (121), to indicate direction:

Nenie estas pli bona maŝino, *nowhere is there a better machine.*
Mi iros nenien morgaŭ, *I shall go nowhere tomorrow.*

THE NEGATIVE TEMPORAL ADVERB.

226. The negative adverb of time is **neniam,** *never, at no time*:

Neniam vivis pli fama filozofo, *there never lived a more famous philosopher.*
Vi neniam trovos tiajn ŝraŭbojn aŭ cilindrojn, *you will never find that kind of
screws or cylinders.*

THE SUFFIX -AĴ-.

227. The suffix **-aĵ-** is used to form *concrete* words. It is thus in contrast to the
abstract-forming suffix **-ec-** (202).

a. A word formed from a *verbal* root by means of the suffix **-aĵ-** expresses a
concrete example of *a thing which undergoes* (or, in the case of intransitives, *results
from*) the action indicated in the root:

konstruaĵo, *a building.*	**kreskaĵo,** *a plant, a growth.*
sendaĵo, *consignment, thing sent.*	**rebrilaĵo,** *a reflection.*
manĝaĵo, *food.*	**restaĵo,** *remainder.*

b. A word formed from an *adjectival* root or formation by means of the suffix -aĵ- indicates *a thing characterized by* or *possessing the quality* expressed in the root or formation to which it is attached:

belaĵo, *a thing of beauty.*   mirindaĵo, *a marvel.*
maljustaĵo, *an injustice.*   okazintaĵo, *an occurrence.*

c. A word formed from a *noun-root* by means of the suffix -aĵ- indicates *a thing made* or *derived from* that which is expressed in the root:

sukeraĵo, *a sweet, confection.*   oraĵo, *a gold object.*
ovaĵo, *an omelet.*   araneaĵo, *a spider-web.*

THE ADVERB JEN.

228. The adverb **jen**, *behold, here, there,* is used to point out or call attention to something:

Jen estas la problemo! *There is the problem!*
Jen la filozofo! *Behold the philosopher!*
Jen ŝi ludas, jen ŝi studas, *now she plays, now she studies.*
Mi faris ĝin jene, *I did it as follows.*
Mi agis laŭ la jena metodo, *I acted in the following way.*
Li diris la jenajn vortojn, *he spoke the following words.*

VOCABULARY.

aranĝ-i, *to arrange.*   neniam, *never* (226).
art-o, *art.*   nenie, *nowhere* (225).
ber-o, *berry.*   pentr-i, *to paint.*
jen, *there, behold* (228).   postul-i, *to demand.*
ĵaluz-a, *jealous.*   precip-a, *principal, chief.*
konkurs-o, *competition.*   regul-o, *rule.*
lert-a, *skilled, clever.*   tromp-i, *to deceive.*
nenia, *no kind of* (224).   vin-o, *wine.*

DU ARTKONKURSOJ.

Vivadis en Grekujo antaŭ multaj jarcentoj du lertaj famaj pentristoj. Ili estis reciproke ĵaluzaj, kaj neniam povis interparoli paceme. Ne povinte decidi la problemon, kaj eltrovi kiu el ili estas la plej lerta, ili fine aranĝis konkurson pri la pentrado. Laŭ ĝiaj reguloj, ĉiu el ili pentris pentraĵon, por montri sian lertecon. Unu pentris teleron da vinberoj (*grapes*). Ĝi estis tiel mirinde kolorigita ke eĉ la birdoj venis kaj penis ĝin manĝi, pensinte ĝin ne nur pentraĵo, sed la vinberoj mem. "Nenia pentraĵo povos superi la mian," ĝojege ekkriis la pentristo, "jen, la birdoj mem rekonas mian lertecon!" Tiam li diris al la alia artisto, "Nu, kial vi ne fortiras tiun kurtenon? Mi volas rigardi vian pentraĵon." La dua pentristo respondis kun rideto, "Jen estas mia pentraĵo. Nenie apud vi estas kurteno, sed vi vidas nur pentraĵon de kurteno antaŭ tiu konstruaĵo." Tre mirigite, la pentrinto de la vinberoj diris "Vi ja superas min en la pentrado. Mi trompis la birdojn per mia pentraĵo, sed vi trompas eĉ aliajn artistojn! Tia lerteco estas ja mirindaĵo!"

Oni rakontas similan okazintaĵon pri fama artisto kiu pentris multe da pentraĵoj por Aleksandro Granda. Malgajninte en konkurso kontraŭ iuj aliaj artistoj, li opiniis ke la juĝintoj estas maljustaj al li, precipe pro la ĵaluzeco. Li ekkriis "Ĉar niaj pentraĵoj estas bildoj de ĉevaloj, ili certe postulas ĉevalajn juĝantojn!" Tial oni enkondukis du aŭ tri ĉevalojn. La ĉevaloj, tute ne rigardinte la pentraĵojn de la aliaj artistoj, kuris rekte al tiu de la plendinta artisto, kaj klare montris sian rekonadon de la tie pentritaj ĉevaloj. Surprizite, oni diris "Jen estas justaj juĝantoj!" Tuj oni laŭdis la pentriston kaj severe punis la malhonestajn homajn juĝintojn.

SENTENCES FOR TRANSLATION

1. Syracuse was the largest city on the island of Sicily. 2. The famous philosopher and physicist Archimedes lost his life when that city was destroyed and entirely burned. 3. At least, no sort of trace of him seems to have been found after that occurrence. 4. Never, perhaps, was there a more learned man in Syracuse. 5. Greece was also famous for its skilled painters, and there are many anecdotes about them. 6. A painter who failed in a certain competition believed that none of the judges had been just to him. 7. He exclaimed "Behold this iniquity (injustice)! Nowhere can I find a human being who is not jealous. 8. Since the paintings are chiefly of horses, do they not require horses for judges?" 9. His proposal was accepted (54), and some horses were led in. 10. Without noticing (222) the other paintings, the horses walked at once to the picture of the unsuccessful artist, and showed immediate recognition of the horses painted there. 11. This act showed which competitor (*konkursinto*) was the most skilful. 12. The painter, having deceived the horses, as another artist had once deceived birds by a picture of grapes, said "Animals decide not by rules, but by feelings."

LESSON XLIX.

THE NEGATIVE ADVERBS NENIAL, NENIEL, NENIOM.—
THE SUFFIX -IĜ-.—LA KREPUSKO.

THE NEGATIVE ADVERBS NENIAL, NENIEL, NENIOM.

229. The negative adverb of motive or reason, related to the negative pronoun **neniu**, is **nenial**, *for no reason:*

Li estas nenial ĵaluza, *he is jealous for no reason.*
Nenial li trompis vin, *for no reason he deceived you.*

230. The negative adverb of manner is **neniel**, *in no way.*

Mi povos neniel aranĝi konkurson, *I can in no way arrange a competition.*
Tiu ago estas neniel laŭregula, *That act is in no way regular.*

231. The negative adverb of quantity is **neniom**, *no amount of, not any, none, no:*

Tiu pentraĵo postulas neniom da lerteco, *such a painting requires no skill.*
Estas neniom da vino en lia glaso, *there is no wine in his glass.*

THE SUFFIX -IĜ-.

232. The suffix **-iĝ-** is used to form intransitive verbs of an *inchoative* nature.

a. Inchoative verbs from the roots of *intransitive verbs* indicate the *beginning* or *coming into existence* of the act or condition expressed in the root:

sidiĝi, *to become sitting, to sit down, to take a seat.*
stariĝi, *to become standing, to stand up.*

b. Intransitive verbs may be similarly formed from the roots of *transitive* verbs, and indicate an action of the verb not immediately due to the subject's acting upon itself (as in the case of reflexive verbs, 41) and not caused by any direct agency (as in the case of the passive voice, 169):[55]

---

[55] *Cf.* the examples given and the following sentences in which the same verbal roots are used in the simple form and in the passive voice:

Ni fermas la pordon, *we close the door.*
La pordo estas fermita, *the door is (has been) closed.*
Oni movas la veturilon, *they move the vehicle.*
La veturilo estas movata, *the vehicle is being moved.*
Mi rompas la branĉon, *I break the branch.*
La branĉo estas rompita, *the branch is (has been) broken.*

La pordo fermiĝas, *the door closes (goes shut).*
La veturilo moviĝas, *the vehicle moves.*
La branĉo rompiĝas, *the branch breaks.*
Grupo da personoj kolektiĝis, *a group of persons gathered.*

c. Intransitive verbs may similarly be formed from *adjectival* roots, and indicate the acquiring of the characteristic or quality expressed in the root:

laciĝi, *to become tired, to get tired.*
varmiĝi, *to become warm, to get warm.*
maljuniĝi, *to become old, to age.*

d. Verbs may similarly be formed from noun-roots, adverbs, prepositions, prefixes and suffixes whose meaning permits:

amikiĝi, *to become a friend.*   **kuniĝi**, *to become joined.*
foriĝi, *to go away, to disappear.*   **ebliĝi**, *to become possible.*

VOCABULARY.

apenaŭ, *hardly, scarcely.*   **nenial**, *for no reason* (229).
atmosfer-o, *atmosphere.*   **neniel**, *in no way* (230).
dub-i, *to doubt.*   **neniom**, *none, no* (231).
efektiv-a, *effective, real.*   **ombr-o**, *shadow.*
hel-a, *clear, bright.*   **pejzaĝ-o**, *landscape.*
horizont-o, *horizon.*   **radi-o**, *ray.*
krepusk-o, *twilight.*   **tropik-a**, *tropical.*

LA KREPUSKO.

Estas tre agrable sidiĝi sur la herbon, kaj rigardi la plilongiĝantajn ombrojn, en la daŭro de bela somera vespero. La suno grade malleviĝas post la montetoj, la nuboj fariĝas (*become*) bele kolorigitaj, kaj la tuta pejzaĝo pli kaj pli beliĝas. Malrapide la krepusko anstataŭas la helan sunlumon, kaj fine ĉie noktiĝas. La krepusko estas la rebrilado de la sunlumo tra la atmosfero, post la malleviĝo de la suno mem, laŭ la jena maniero: la radioj suprenbriladas, en la aeron super niaj kapoj, en la okcidenta parto de la ĉielo. De tie ili rebriladas tiamaniere ke la ĉielo lumiĝas. Kiam estas iom da nuboj sur la ĉielo okcidenta, la sunradioj briladas rekte kontraŭ ilin, belege kolorigante tiujn nubojn. En tropikaj landoj la krepuskiĝo okazas tre rapide. Ĝi ne nur komenciĝas subite, sed ankaŭ daŭras tre mallongan tempon. La noktiĝo preskaŭ tuj sekvas la taglumon, kun rimarkinda subiteco. Apenaŭ komenciĝas la krepusko, kiam la subiranta suno ŝajnas fali preter la horizonto. Tute male (*quite on the contrary*), en landoj treege nordaj, krepuskiĝas tre frue en la tago, kaj la krepusko daŭras longan tempon antaŭ ol la nokto venas. Efektive (*really*), en tiuj landoj la krepusko tute anstataŭas la nokton, dum ses monatoj de la jaro. Tie oni havas krepuskon dum la unua duonjaro, kaj la taglumon dum la sekvinta duonjaro. Krepusko daŭranta tiom da tempo estas tiel rimarkinda kiel tago de tia

---

Li kolektis florojn, *he gathered flowers.*
Floroj estas kolektitaj, *flowers have been gathered.*

sama longeco. Mi dubas ĉu tia dividado de la tempo inter tago kaj malhela nokto estas agrabla, sed oni povas neniel malhelpi ĝin. Ĉiu tre norda lando havas la saman travivaĵon (*experience*), ĉiujare, kaj efektive oni apenaŭ rimarkas ĝin. Pri ĉiu plendanto oni nur diras "Li estas nenial malkontenta."

SENTENCES FOR TRANSLATION.

1. Nowhere have I read a more amusing story than that of (*pri*) the two painters who, being mutually (180) jealous, arranged a competition. 2. One painted a cluster (126) of grapes, so excellently that the birds flew to it. 3. The other deceived his rival (competitor) himself, by a painting of a curtain. 4. The most famous artists, however, often show their skill by painting (222) pictures of the sunset, chiefly, I think, because of the brilliant colors. 5. In fact (*efektive*), I doubt whether there is a more beautiful sight (227, b) than the sunset. 6. It is made by the bright rays of the sun, which shine back through the atmosphere, long after the sun itself has passed below the horizon. 7. The more moisture (*malsekaĵo*) there is in the air, the more brilliant the colors are, and the more beautiful the entire landscape becomes. 8. In tropical lands, night falls very suddenly, and there is almost no sort of twilight. 9. In fact, a twilight scarcely occurs there. 10. In the lands far north, on the contrary, the twilight lasts six months, and the remainder of the year is the day. 11. To dwell in such a land is surely a remarkable experience. 12. It can in no way be understood by persons who have never lived there. 13. Such things increase (make greater) my desire to visit those northern lands. 14. For no reason, however, do I wish to reside in the tropical countries.

LESSON L.

THE PRONOUNS ENDING IN -O.—CORRELATIVE WORDS.—THE USE OF AJN.—THE SUFFIX -ING-.—LA GORDIA LIGAĴO.

THE PRONOUNS ENDING IN -O.

233. In contrast to the pronouns ending in **-u** (**tiu, kiu, ĉiu, iu, neniu**), a similar series ending in **-o** refers to an object, fact or action not definitely specified (but never to a person), like English *what, anything, something, nothing*, etc. Because of their somewhat vague meaning, these pronouns do not occur in the plural, nor are they ever used as pronominal adjectives:

Demonstrative:	**tio**, *that (thing, fact or action).*
	ĉi tio, *this (thing, fact or action).*
Interrogative and Relative:	**kio**, *what.*
Distributive:	**ĉio**, *everything.* **ĉio ĉi**, *all this.*
Indefinite:	**io**, *anything, something.*
Negative:	**nenio**, *nothing.*

234. A pronoun (not personal) in predicate or relative relation to a pronoun ending in **-o** must itself be of the same series:

Kio estas ĉi tio, kion vi diras? *What is this, which you say?*
Ŝi vidis tion, kio ĵus okazis, *she saw that which just occurred.*
Ĉio ĉi, kion vi vidas, estas farita de ili, *everything here (all this), which you see, was done by them.*
Li havas ion por vi, sed nenion por mi, *he has something for you, but nothing for me.*

CORRELATIVE WORDS.

235. Pronouns, adjectives and adverbs, which are related to each other as corresponding demonstratives, interrogatives, relatives, etc., are called *correlatives*. In Esperanto the correlative system is more complete than in any other language, and may be summarized as follows:

Demonstrative	Interrogative and Relative	Distributive	Indefinite	Negative
tio (233) *that (thing)*	**kio (233)** *what, which*	**ĉio (233)** *everything*	**io (233)** *anything*	**nenio (233)** *nothing*
tiu (56) *that (one)*	**kiu (146)** *who, which*	**ĉiu (173)** *every, each*	**iu (203)** *any (one)*	**neniu (220)** *no (one)*
ties (62) *that one's*	**kies (147)** *whose*	**ĉies (174)** *every one's*	**ies (204)** *any one's*	**nenies (221)** *no one's*
tia (65) *that kind of*	**kia (150)** *what kind of*	**ĉia (177)** *every kind*	**ia (208)** *any kind*	**nenia (224)** *no kind of*
tie (68) *there*	**kie (151)** *where*	**ĉie (182)** *everywhere*	**ie (209)** *anywhere*	**nenie (225)** *nowhere*
tiam (73) *then*	**kiam (155)** *when*	**ĉiam (187)** *always*	**iam (212)** *any time*	**neniam (226)** *never*
tial (78) *therefore, so*	**kial (129)** *wherefore, why*	**ĉial (188)** *for every reason*	**ial (213)** *for any reason*	**nenial (229)** *for no reason*
tiel (88), (156), *thus, so*	**kiel (156)** *how, as*	**ĉiel (193)** *every way*	**iel (216)** *any way*	**neniel (230)** *in no way*
tiom (104) *that much, so much*	**kiom (164)** *how much, as*	**ĉiom (194)** *all, the whole of*	**iom (217)** *some, any amount*	**neniom (231)** *none, no quantity*

THE USE OF AJN.

236. The word **ajn** may be placed after any interrogative-relative or indefinite correlative word, to give a generalizing sense. In order to avoid confusion with the accusative plural ending, **ajn** is *never attached* to the correlative which it follows:

kio ajn, *whatever.*   **kiam ajn**, *whenever.*
kies ajn, *whosesoever.*   **kiom ajn**, *however much.*
kie ajn, *wherever.*   **ia ajn**, *any kind whatever.*

THE SUFFIX -ING-.

237. The suffix **-ing-** is used to form words indicating that which holds *one* specimen of what is expressed in the root:

glavingo, *scabbard.*   **plumingo**, *pen-holder.*
lumingo, *torch-holder.*   **ingo**, *sheath, case, socket.*

VOCABULARY.

ĉio, *everything* (233).
Gordio, *Gordius.*
io, *anything* (233).
jug-o, *yoke.*
klin-i, *to bend, incline* (trans).
kio, *what* (233).
lig-i, *to tie, to bind.*

nenio, *nothing* (233).
ofer-o, *offering.*
reg-i, *to rule, to govern.*
sankt-a, *sacred, holy.*
templ-o, *temple.*
tio, *that (thing)* (233).
util-a, *useful.*

LA GORDIA LIGAĴO.

Unufoje en antikva tempo la regatoj de iu reĝolando en Azio ne havis reĝon. Ne sciante kion fari, ili demandis de la dioj. La dioj respondis, "Kiu ajn venos unue en nian sanktan templon hodiaŭ, por fari oferojn, estos via reĝo." Okaze kamparano nomita Gordio venis al la templo, ĵus post la tagiĝo. La regatoj tuj rekonis la estontan reĝon, kvankam li veturis sur peza malbela veturilo. Salutinte la surprizitan kamparanon, oni nomis lin reĝo. Decidinte fari dankoferon al la dioj, Gordio metis en la templon la veturilon mem sur kiu li tien veturis, antaŭ ol li komencis regi kiel la nova reĝo. La jugo estis alligita (*tied fast*) per granda ligaĵo el ŝnurego. Post la morto de Gordio oni grade komencis kredi ion tre interesan pri tio. Oni diris ke tiu, kiu povos iel ajn malligi tiun ligaĵon, fariĝos reganto super ĉiuj reĝoj de Azio.

Post kelkaj jaroj Aleksandro Granda decidis fari grandan militadon kontraŭ Azio, kaj alproksimiĝis al la lando kie estis reginta Gordio. Kiam li demandis, "Kio estas ĉi tie la plej interesa vidindaĵo?" oni rakontis al li tion, kion oni diras pri la ŝnurega ligaĵo sur la veturilo de Gordio. Kompreneble (*of course*) Aleksandro deziris fari ion ajn utilan por venki Azion, tial li tuj venigis gvidiston por konduki lin al la templo. Alveninte tien, li zorge rigardadis la ligaĵon, kaj ekzamenis la ŝnuregon el kiu ĝi estis farita. Tiam, elpreninte sian glavon el la glavingo, subite kliniĝante li rekte tratranĉis la tutan ligaĵon. "Nenio estas pli facila ol tio," li diris, "kaj nun mi ne dubas ĉu mi certe regos super ĉiuj reĝoj de Azio." Pro tio, kion faris Aleksandro Granda, oni ankoraŭ nuntempe diras, kiam iu ajn superas malfacilaĵon per kia ajn subita metodo, "Li tranĉis la gordian ligaĵon."

SENTENCES FOR TRANSLATION.

1. One often hears the remark "I will cut the Gordian knot." 2. There is an interesting story about this. 3. A wagon whose yoke was tied to the pole by a large knot had been put in the middle of the temple. 4. It was a thank-offering to the sacred gods, by whose help Gordius had in olden time become king. 5. It was said that whoever would be able to untie that rope would no doubt become ruler over the whole of Asia. 6. Alexander the Great, having begun a campaign against Asia, approached the city where this temple was. 7. Having heard the story, he at once had a guide come, and went thither, guided by him. 8. He desired to do everything which was useful to the conquering of Asia. 9. Having examined the knot carefully, he bent over and tried for a few minutes to untie it. 10. Then he chose another method. 11. He seized his sword, and suddenly cut through the whole knot. 12. Having done this, he put the sword back into the scabbard. 13. This he did, instead of continuing (*daŭrigi*) his efforts to untie the knot. 14. In fact, having no patience,

he had become tired. 15. Perhaps the conquering of Asia did not in any way become possible on account of this, but at least the story is interesting, whatever actually (*efektive*) happened. 16. Nothing is impossible, whenever one tries enough. 17. In a tropical country, such as part of Asia is, the landscapes are beautiful. 18. A tropical twilight is very short, however, and the shadows have scarcely become long when the sun seems to sink suddenly below the horizon, although the last bright rays continue to shine back through the atmosphere for a few minutes.

LESSON LI.

THE PRONOUN AMBAŬ.—FORMATIONS WITH -IG- AND
-IĜ-.—FACTUAL CONDITIONS.—LA MONAĤOJ KAJ
LA AZENO.

THE PRONOUN **AMBAŬ**.

238. The pronoun (and pronominal adjective) **ambaŭ**, *both*, indicates two persons or things considered together. It is invariable in form:[56]

Ili ambaŭ venis al la templo, *they both came to the temple.*
Ambaŭ faris oferojn al la dioj, *both made offerings to the gods.*
Vidante kaj la plumon kaj la plumingon, mi prenis la ambaŭ, *seeing both the pen and the penholder, I took both.*

FORMATIONS WITH **-IG-** AND **-IĜ-**.

239. Some verbs may be used in the simple form, and also with both the suffix **-ig-** and the suffix **-iĝ-**. Thus from one verb-root three verbs of distinct meaning may be made, and the formation with **-ig-**, being transitive, may also be used in the passive:

sidi, *to sit, to be sitting.*
sidiĝi, *to become sitting, to take a seat.*
sidigi, *to cause to sit, to seat.*
esti sidigata, *to be caused to sit.*
silenti, *to be silent.*
silentiĝi, *to become silent.*
silentigi, *to cause to be silent, to silence.*
esti silentigita, *to be silenced.*
kuŝi, *to lie, to be lying.*
kuŝiĝi, *to lie down, to go to bed.*
kuŝigi, *to cause to lie, to lay.*
esti kuŝigita, *to be laid.*
stari, *to stand, to be standing.*
stariĝi, *to rise, to stand up, to become erect.*
starigi, *to raise, to cause to stand up, to erect.*
esti starigita, *to be raised, to be erected.*

---

[56] This pronoun must not be confused with the use of **kaj**, translated *both* in the combination **kaj ... kaj ...**, *both ... and ...* (26).

FACTUAL CONDITIONS.

240. A conditional sentence consists of two parts, an *assumption* and a *conclusion*. The assumption is a clause (introduced usually by the conjunction **se**, *if*) which assumes something as true or realized. The conclusion is a statement whose truth or realization depends upon the truth or realization of the assumption. *Factual conditions* (conditions of fact) may deal with the present, past or future time:

Se li vidas tion, li ploras, *if he sees that, he weeps (is weeping)*.
Se li vidis tion, li ploris, *if he saw that, he wept*.
Li ploros, se li vidos tion, *he will weep, if he sees that*.
Se li venis hieraŭ, li foriros morgaŭ, *if he came yesterday, he will go away tomorrow*.
Se li estas vidinta tion, li nun ploras, *if he has seen that, he now is weeping*.
Se tio estas vidota, li estas punota, *if that is going to be seen, he is going to be punished*.
Se li estas kaptita, li estos jam punita, *if he has been captured, he will already have been punished*.

VOCABULARY.

ambaŭ, *both* (238).
azen-o, *ass, donkey*.
ben-i, *to bless*.
dors-o, *back*.
form-o, *form*.
halt-i, *to stop* (intrans.).
monaĥ-o, *monk*.

mut-a, *dumb, mute*.
orel-o, *ear*.
petol-a, *mischievous*.
propr-a, *own, one's own*.
se, *if*.
spir-i, *to breathe*.
turment-i, *to torment*.

LA MONAĤOJ KAJ LA AZENO.

Iam du monaĥoj reiris tra la arbaro al la monaĥejo, dum grade krepuskiĝis. Ambaŭ portis pezajn sakojn da terpomoj, kaj baldaŭ laciĝis, sed ne sciis kion fari. Okaze ili ekvidis azenon ligitan al arbo, kaj unu monaĥo, haltinte, diris petole al la alia "Se vi anstataŭos la beston, mi havos portanton por miaj propraj sakoj, kaj ankaŭ por la viaj." Lia kunulo respondis "Nu, se la azeno portos miajn sakojn, mi mem ĝoje restos en ĝia loko." Ĵus dirite, tuj farite (*no sooner said than done*). Malliginte la ligaĵojn kiuj tenis la azenon, ili ĵetis la sakojn trans la dorson de la utila besto. Unu monaĥo tuj forkondukis la azenon, dum ambaŭ viroj laŭte ridis. Post tio, la dua monaĥo sin ligis per la sama ŝnurego kiu antaŭe tenis la azenon. Kiam revenis la kamparano, kies azeno estis ĵus ŝtelita, li ekhaltis, multe mirigite, vidante homon tie ligita. La monaĥo anoncis al li, "Ĉar mi estis tro manĝema, Dio faris azenon el mi, antaŭ du jaroj. Mi ĵus ricevis mian propran formon." Tuj la kredema kamparano invitis la petolan monaĥon al sia hejmo. La monaĥo restis tiun nokton ĉe la kamparano, kaj la sekvintan tagon li foriris, beninte la kamparanon, sed kaŝe ridante pri la afero. Tiam la kamparano iris vendejon, por aĉeti alian azenon. Li ekvidis sian propran azenon, kiun la unua monaĥo estis sendinta tien, post sia reveno al la monaĥejo. La malsaĝa kamparano, kliniĝinte al la besto, diris "Ho, bona monaĥo, mi vidas ke duan fojon vi jam estis tro manĝema!" La muta besto forte svingis la orelojn kaj skuis la kapon, pro la varma elspiraĵo apud sia orelo. Tio ŝajne estis respondo al la ĵus diritaj vortoj, tial la malsaĝa kamparano ree aĉetis sian propran azenon. Ĉiam poste li nek turmentis nek eĉ laborigis ĝin, kredante la azenon la sankta monaĥo mem.

SENTENCES FOR TRANSLATION.

1. If the subjects of any kingdom whatever did not have a king, in ancient times, they usually asked the sacred gods about it. 2. If the gods informed (*sciigis*) them that whatever man would come to the temple first would become their king, they immediately chose the first comer (*la unuan veninton*) king. 3. Whoever was chosen king made the blessed gods a thank-offering, which consisted of something out of his own possessions (227, a). 4. Gordius did not offer to the gods merely the yoke of his wagon, but the whole wagon. 5. A knot of rope was tied between the yoke and the pole. 6. People soon began to say, "If any one soever can untie that knot, he will become ruler of Asia." 7. If any other men tried to untie that rope, they failed. 8. Alexander, though (*tamen*), had scarcely arrived when he drew (out) his sword from the scabbard, and cut the knot. 9. If you will take-a-seat, I will tell you about the two mischievous monks, returning to the monastery. 10. Both were breathing with difficulty, and stopped to rest. 11. Having noticed a donkey near by, they untied it. 12. One led the long-eared dumb animal away, while the other tied himself in its own place. 13. The credulous (192) peasant believed everything which was told (54) him, even that the monk had formerly had the form of an ass.

LESSON LII.

THE CONDITIONAL MOOD.—COMPOUND TENSES OF THE CONDITIONAL MOOD.—LESS VIVID CONDITIONS.—INDEPENDENT USE OF THE CONDITIONAL MOOD.—THE PREFIX DIS-. —PRI LA GRAVITADO.

THE CONDITIONAL MOOD.

241. That indication of the speaker's frame of mind which is given by the form of the verb is called the *mood* of the verb. All verbs given so far have been in the *indicative mood*, which represents an act or state as a reality or fact, or in the *infinitive mood*, which expresses the verbal idea in a general way, resembling that of a substantive. The *conditional mood* does not indicate whether or not the act or state mentioned is a fact, but merely expresses the speaker's idea of its likelihood or certainty, or is used in an assumption or conclusion dealing with suppositions, not with actual facts. The ending of the conditional mood is **-us**. The conjugation of **vidi** in the aoristic tense of the conditional mood is as follows:

mi vidus, *I should see.*
vi vidus, *you would see.*
li (ŝi, ĝi) vidus, *he (she, it) would see.*
ni vidus, *we should see.*
vi vidus, *you would see.*
ili vidus, *they would see.*

COMPOUND TENSES OF THE CONDITIONAL MOOD.

242. In addition to the aoristic tense, the conditional mood has three active and three passive compound tenses, formed by combining the participles with the aoristic tense of **esti** in the conditional mood. A synopsis of **vidi** in these compound tenses is as follows:

Active Voice.

Present:	**mi estus vidanta,**	*I should be seeing.*
Past:	**mi estus vidinta,**	*I should have seen.*
Future:	**mi estus vidonta,**	*I should be about to see.*

Passive Voice.

Present:	**mi estus vidata,**	*I should be seen.*
Past:	**mi estus vidita,**	*I should have been seen.*

Future: **mi estus vidota,**   *I should be about to be seen.*

LESS VIVID CONDITIONS.

243. A conditional sentence dealing with *suppositions* concerning events in *present* or *future* time is called a *less vivid condition*[57], and the conditional mood is used in both the assumption and the conclusion:

Se li vidus tion, li plorus, *if he should see that, he would weep.*
Mi ĝoje helpus vin, se mi povus, *I would gladly help you, if I could.*
Se vi metus ilin sur la dorson de la azeno, ĝi portus ilin, *if you should put them on the donkey's back, it would carry them.*
La petola junulo turmentus la monaĥon, se li revenus, *the mischievous youth would torment the monk, if he should return.*
Se li estus kaptata, li estus punata, *if he should be caught, he would be punished.*

INDEPENDENT USE OF THE CONDITIONAL MOOD.

244. The conditional mood may be used in a conclusion whose assumption is merely *implied*, serving thus to soften or make vague the statement or question in which it is used:

Mi ĝoje helpus vin, *I would gladly help you.*
Ĉu vi bonvole dirus al mi? *Would you kindly tell me?*
Kiu volus enspiri tian aeron? *Who would wish to inhale such air?*
Estus bone reteni vian propran, *it would be well to keep your own.*
La ĉielo vin benus pro tio, *Heaven would bless you for that.*

THE PREFIX DIS-.

245. The prefix **dis-** indicates separation or movement in several different directions at once:[58]

disdoni, *to distribute.*	**disiĝi,** *to separate* (intrans.).
dispeli, *to dispel.*	**disiĝo,** *separation, schism.*
disigi, *to separate* (trans.).	**dissendi,** *to send around.*

VOCABULARY.

ĉes-i, *to cease, to leave off.*	**kaŭz-i,** *to cause.*
dens-a, *dense.*	**leĝ-o,** *law.*
difin-i, *to define.*	**natur-o,** *nature.*
ekzist-i, *to exist.*	**objekt-o,** *object.*
flu-i, *to flow.*	**plu,** *further, more.*[¶¶]
gravit-i, *to gravitate.*	**turn-i,** *to turn* (trans.).

---

[57] *Less vivid,* in contrast to factual conditions (240), which are *vivid,* because they deal with facts.

[58] *Cf.* the English prefix *dis-* in *disperse, disseminate, distribute,* etc.

PRI LA GRAVITADO.

1. Ofte oni parolas pri la pezeco de diversaj objektoj. Tia pezeco estas kaŭzata de la forto kiun oni nomas la gravitado. Pro tiu forto ne nur objektoj sur la tero, sed ankaŭ la tero mem, havas konatan pezecon, kiun la kleruloj jam antaŭ longe kalkulis. La suno kaj la luno simile havas pezecon, ĉar ili ambaŭ, same kiel la tero, moviĝas laŭ tiu sama gravitado kiu efektive regas ĉiujn el la ĉielaj korpoj. Se la gravitado ĉesus ekzisti, la riveroj ne plu fluus antaŭen en siaj fluejoj (beds). Ne fluante de altaj ĝis malaltaj lokoj, la akvo disfluus, aŭ restus tie, kie ajn ĝi okaze estus. Neniom da pluvo falus; kontraŭe, la malsekaĵo en la aero ankoraŭ restus tie, en la formo de densaj mallumaj ĉiamaj nuboj. Ĉiuj vivaj estaĵoj (beings), ĉiuj konstruaĵoj, efektive ĉio, baldaŭ disflugus de la rapide turniĝanta mondo. Ĉiuj ĉi (all these) nun devas resti sur la tero, tial ke la gravitado restigas ilin ĉi tie. Se la gravitado ne plu ekzistus, nenio restus plu sur la tero. La aero mem ne plu ĉirkaŭus nin, sed ĝi ankaŭ forlasus la mondon, tuj maldensiĝinte (having become rarefied). La fama angla filozofo Newton estis la unua, kiu studadis la kialon (reason) de la falado de objektoj. Li komencis, laŭ la rakonto, per okaza ekrigardo al falantaj pomoj en sia propra pomarbejo. Antaŭ tri jarcentoj, li eltrovis ke estas tia forto kia la gravitado, kaj difinis la naturajn leĝojn laŭ kiuj la gravitado sin montras. Ĉi tiu forto, kiu restigas ĉion sur la tero, estas tamen la kaŭzo de nia laciĝado, kiam ni marŝas aŭ kuras, ĉar ĝi faras nin pezaj, kaj tial ni ofte deziras halti kaj ripozi. Estas ankaŭ la malfacileco en la superado de tiu sama forto, kiu faras tiel malfacila la konstruadon de utilaj aerŝipoj.

SENTENCES FOR TRANSLATION.

1. Newton was an Englishman who lived three centuries ago. 2. One day he was walking in his orchard, and, noticing the falling apples, he stood still (ekhaltis) and began to wonder why they fall. 3. He studied the cause of their falling, wishing to discover whatever laws of nature he could. 4. He watched various falling objects, and tried to calculate their velocity (rapideco). 5. Finally he recognized that force which is called gravitation. 6. Of course (kompreneble) gravitation had always existed, but its laws were not noticed or clearly defined until Newton studied the matter. 7. If gravitation should not exist any more, no rain would fall, but instead of condensing, the moisture would remain above our heads in eternal clouds. 8. But gradually the moisture and the air itself, becoming rarefied, would fly away from the earth, being held no longer by the force of gravitation. 9. The water in the rivers would leave off flowing (cease to flow) on toward the sea, because now the water flows from high to low places only on account of gravitation. 10. Instead of gravitating toward the sea, in fact, the water would flow in every direction (245) out of the riverbeds, or would remain there, without moving at all (tute ne movante). 11. Nothing on earth would remain here very long, but everything would fly off the quickly moving world, and leave it entirely bare. Soon, also, the earth itself would break-into-pieces (245).

LESSON LIII.

THE CONDITIONAL MOOD.—COMPOUND TENSES OF
THE CONDITIONAL MOOD.—LESS VIVID CONDI-
TIONS.—INDEPENDENT USE OF THE CONDITIONAL
MOOD.—THE PREFIX DIS-. —PRI LA GRAVITADO.

CONDITIONS CONTRARY TO FACT.

246. A *condition contrary to fact* indicates that the opposite of what is mentioned
has really taken place or is taking place. It expresses the speaker's certainty that an
act or state would have been realized, if some other act or state were also realized.
Such conditions cannot refer to the future, but only to present or past time. The
conditional mood is used:

Se vi estus turninta vin, vi estus vidinta tion, *if you had turned, you would
have seen that.*

Se la malsekaĵo ne estus densiĝinta, ne estus pluvinte, *if the moisture had not
condensed, it would not have rained.*

Se li estus kaptita, li estus punita, *if he had been caught, he would have been
punished.*

Se li estus sidanta tie, mi vidus lin, *if he were (if he should be) sitting there, I
should see him.*

Se la gravitado ne ekzistus, tiu pluvo ne estus falanta, *if gravitation did not
(should not) exist, that rain would not be falling.*

THE VERB DEVI.

247. The verb **devi** (*cf.* devo, *duty*) is equivalent to the verb *must* (which in English has no future, past, infinitive, etc.), and to *to have to, to be obliged to*, etc., carrying the idea of *must* into all tenses and moods. In the conditional mood its meaning
is softened into a vaguer sense (of *moral* obligation), and carries the idea of *ought*:

Objektoj en la aero devas fali, *objects in the air have to fall.*

Ni devis agi laŭ la leĝoj, *we had to act according to the laws.*

Vi devos iri, *you must (will have to) go.*

Ŝi ne volas devi fari tion, *she does not wish to have to do that.*

Ili devigis min iri, *they compelled me to go.*

Vi devus iri, *you should go (you ought to go).*

Oni devus pensi antaŭ ol paroli, *one ought to think before speaking.*

Li estus devinta veni, *he ought to have come.*

Tio devus esti farita, *that ought to have been done.*

THE PREPOSITION SEN.

248. The preposition **sen**, *without*, indicates the omission, absence or exclusion of that which is expressed by its complement.[59] It may be used as a prefix (160), giving a sense of deprivation or exclusion (like that given by the English suffix *-less*):

Li difinis la vorton sen eraro, *he defined the word without an error.*
La rivero sencêse fluas, *the river flows without ceasing.*
Tio estas ne nur senutila sed eĉ malutila, *that is not only useless but even harmful.*
Li ne plu estas senmona, *he is no longer penniless.*
Li sentime alproksimiĝis al ĝi, *he fearlessly approached it.*

VOCABULARY.

akuz-i, *to accuse.*
instru-i, *to teach.*
kondamn-i, *to condemn.*
konfes-i, *to confess, to admit.*
konscienc-o, *conscience.*
kulp-o, *guilt.*
merit-i, *to deserve.*

nobl-a, *noble.*
pardon-i, *to pardon.*
pek-i, *to sin.*
prav-a, *right, correct.*
sen, *without* (248).
So-krato, *Socrates.*
venen-o, *poison.*

LA FILOZOFO SOKRATO.

Unu el la plej famaj grekaj filozofoj estis nomita Sokrato. Li estis malbela malalta persono, kun senhara kapo kaj dika korpo, sed malgraŭ tio li estis treege bona, nobla kaj saĝa. Li instruadis per interparolado kun la lernantoj. Kutime li komencis per demando pri io ajn, pri kio la aŭskultanto respondos. Fine, la lernanto grade komprenis ĉu liaj propraj opinioj pri la afero estas pravaj. Ankoraŭ nun oni nomas tiun metodon de instruado per la interparolado "la Sokrata metodo." Sokrato diradis tute sen timo ĉion, kion li pensis, eĉ pri la dioj kaj pri la nekredeblaj rakontoj pri la dioj. Se li ne estus tiel multe klariginta, eble li estus vivinta pli longan tempon. Sed multaj personoj malamis lin, precipe ĉar li donis novajn ideojn al la junuloj, kiuj sekve komencis pensi por si mem, anstataŭ fari tion kion faras ĉiu alia. Tial oni akuzis Sokraton en la juĝejo, nomante lin pekanto kaj malbonfaranto, unue, ĉar li ne disdonas oferojn al la dioj, due, ĉar li enkondukas novajn diojn (ĉar li diris ke supernatura voĉo, kiu sendube estis lia nomo por la konscienco, parolis mallaŭte ĉe lia orelo), trie, ĉar li malbonigas la junularon de la urbo. Se li estus kon-

---

[59] English phrases containing "without" as in "without reading," must be changed to phrases clearly containing verbal nouns, as "without the reading of," before translating into an Esperanto phrase with **sen**. Otherwise a participle with **ne** should replace the phrase (**222**):

Sen la legado de tio, mi ne komprenus, *without (the) reading (of) that, I should not understand.*
Ne leginte tion, mi ne komprenus, *without reading (not having read) that, I should not understand.*

fesinte la kulpon kaj petinte pardonon, tiam la juĝistoj eble estus punintaj lin per nura (*mere*) monpago (*fine*). Sed li fiere respondis ke efektive li multe plibonigas la junularon, kaj anstataŭ esti malutila, aŭ eĉ neutila, li treege utilas al la urbo. Li diris ke oni havas nenian rajton puni lin, sed ke, kaŭze de sia bonfarado al la urbo, li efektive meritas ĉiutagan manĝon senpagan. Tamen, tute ne kompreninte kiel prava Sokrato estas, la juĝistoj mortkondamnis lin. Oni devigis lin trinki la venen-on. Iom poste, en la malliberejo, li trankvile adiaŭis siajn plorantajn amikojn, kaj akceptinte la venenan trinkaĵon, sentime ĝin trinkis.

SENTENCES FOR TRANSLATION.

1. Socrates believed that if one knows about good and evil (201) he will do good, but will not do evil. 2. Therefore he wished to help mankind (*la homaron*), teaching them what the good is. 3. He also wished to discover for himself what is right and what is wrong. 4. So he asked every one whom he met (about) his opinions, and the one-talking-with [him] would also notice whether his own ideas were right or not. 5. But the fellow-citizens of Socrates were jealous, and hated him, because they did not understand him. 6. Therefore they accused him, called him a sinner, and sent around (245) false reports (*falsajn sciigojn*) about him. 7. Because he said that conscience guided him (in the form of a soft voice at his ear), they accused him of (*pri*) introducing (218, b) new gods. 8. They also said that he was corrupting the youth of the city. 9. If Socrates had pleaded guilty, and begged for a fine instead of the death-punishment, without doubt he would have been pardoned and fined (*monpunita*). 10. But he said "I have never in my life sinned in any way, and I do not deserve any sort of punishment." So the judges condemned him to death by the drinking of poison.

LESSON LIV.

SUMMARY OF CONDITIONS.—CLAUSES OF IMAGINA-
TIVE COMPARISON.—THE USE OF AL TO EXPRESS
REFERENCE.—THE SUFFIX -ESTR-.—LA OSTRACIS-
MO DE ARISTEJDO.

SUMMARY OF CONDITIONS

249. The three kinds of conditional sentences, together with the moods and tenses used in them, may be tabulated as follows:

Name	Factual	Less Vivid	Contrary to Fact
Subject Matter	facts	suppositions	opposite of facts
Time	any	(usually) future	present or past
Mood	indicative	conditional	conditional
Tense	any	(usually) aoristic	(usually) compound

CLAUSES OF IMAGINATIVE COMPARISON.

250. Clauses of imaginative comparison are introduced by the conjunction **kvazaŭ**, *as though, as if*. Sometimes the verb in the comparison may be left unexpressed or merely implied:

Li trinkas la venenon kvazaŭ ĝi estus vino, *he drinks the poison as though it were wine.*
La kondamnito marŝis kvazaŭ kun malfacileco, *the condemned man walked as if with difficulty.*
Li konfesis kvazaŭ kulpulo, *he confessed like a culprit.*

THE USE OF AL TO EXPRESS REFERENCE.

251. Personal pronouns, and less frequently nouns, may be used with the preposition **al** to express *concern* or *interest* on the part of the person indicated by the complement of this preposition:[60]

Li bruligis al si la manon, *he burned his hand.*

---

[60] The use of **al** in this sense, approaching that of **por** but less purposeful and definite, resembles the "dative of reference" and "ethical dative" of other languages, as in French *je me suis brulé la langue, I have burned my tongue*, German *ich wasche mir die Hände, I wash my hands*, Latin *sese Caesari ad pedes proicerunt, they threw themselves at the feet of Cæsar*, Greek τί σοι μαθήσομαι, *what am I to learn for you?* etc.

Hi tranĉis al li la barbon, *they cut his beard (the beard for him).*
Ŝi preparas al ni bonan manĝon, *she is preparing us a good meal.*
Ĉu vi faros servon al mi? *Will you do me a service?*

252. By an extension of its use in expressing reference, **al** may often be used in the place of **de** expressing separation (170), when the use of **de** might seem to indicate agency (169) or possession (49):[61]

La luno estas kaŝata al ni de la nuboj, *the moon is hidden from us (to us) by the clouds.*

Ĝi estas stelita al mi de li, *it has been stolen from me by him.*

THE SUFFIX -ESTR-.

253. The suffix **-estr-** is used to indicate the *chief, head,* or *one in control* of that which is expressed in the root:

lernejestro, *(school) principal.*
monaĥestro, *abbot.*
policestro, *chief of police.*

urbestro, *mayor.*
estraro, *governing body.*
ŝipestro, *ship-captain.*

VOCABULARY.

Aristejd-o, *Aristeides.*
ekzil-i, *to exile.*
enu-i, *to be wearied, bored.*
ĝust-a, *exact.*[***]
kvazaŭ, *as though, as if* (250).
ostr-o, *oyster.*
ostracism-o, *ostracism.*

popol-o, *a people.*
pot-o, *pot.*
senc-o, *meaning, sense.*
signif-i, *to signify.*
son-i, *to sound.*
strang-a, *strange.*
ŝel-o, *shell, bark, peel.*

LA OSTRACISMO DE ARISTEJDO.

La vorto ostracismo havas interesan devenon (*origin*). En ĝia komenco oni re-konas la grekan vorton kiu signifas "ŝelon de la ostro." En ĝia fino oni vidas la saman "-ismon " kiu, deveninte de la greka, ankoraŭ estas uzata kiel vortfino en multaj diversaj lingvoj. La nuna senco de la vorto, facile trovebla en anglaj vortaroj (*dictionaries*), devenas de la jena greka kutimo:

Sepdek jarojn antaŭ ol vivadis Sokrato, oni faris strangan leĝon en lia urbo. Laŭ tiu, oni povis ekzili iun ajn estron kies ideoj pri la administrado de la urbo ne ŝajnis pravaj. Ĉi tion oni povis fari, tute sen juĝado aŭ eĉ akuzado, ĉar oni havis la jenan metodon: se ĉe popola kunveno ses mil urbanoj voĉdonis (*vote*) kontraŭ iun ajn, tiu estis devigata foriri de la urbo, kaj forresti dek jarojn. Li povis neniel havigi (*get*) al si pardonon, sed devis tuj foriri kvazaŭ konfesinta kulpulo. Por voĉdonoj, oni skribis la nomon de la kondamnoto sur peco da potaĵo (*pottery*), aŭ pli ofte sur

---

[61] This use resembles the "dative of separation" of other languages, as in German *es stahl mir das Leben, it stole the life from me,* French *il me prend la vie, it takes my life,* Latin *hunc mihi timorem eripe, remove this fear from me,* Greek δέξατό οι σκῆπτρον, *he took his sceptre from him,* etc.

ostroŝelo. Ĝuste tial oni nomas la kutimon ostracismo. Unufoje, kelkaj malamikoj proponis voĉdonadon pri la ostracismo de tre bona kaj nobla viro, nomita Aristejdo, kiu tute ne meritis tian punadon.

Antaŭ ol la kunveno disiĝis, kamparano alproksimiĝis al Aristejdo (kiu mem ĉeestis), petante lian helpon, ĉar la neinstruita kamparano ne povis skribi. La saĝulo diris "Kion vi volas skribi sur la ŝelo?" La kamparano, ne sciante ke li parolas al la viro mem, respondis "Aristejdon." Skribinte ĝin, Aristejdo demandis kun trankvila konscienco "Pro ĝuste kiaj pekoj vi malamas Aristejdon?" La kamparano respondis, "Ho, mi ne kaŝos al vi ke mi eĉ ne konas lin! Sed mi deziras ekzili lin nur ĉar min enuigas la sono de lia nomo. Mi tre enuas ĉiam aŭdante lin nomata Aristejdo la justa!"

SENTENCES FOR TRANSLATION.

1. Aristeides had just arrived at the popular assembly when a peasant approached him. 2. If Aristeides had not had a pleasant countenance and musical (*belsonan*) voice, doubtless the peasant would not have asked his help. 3. Ought Aristeides to have written his own name on the oyster-shell or piece of pottery which was going to be used as a vote against him? 4. Without just (exactly) this help, the peasant could not have voted. 5. Doing him the service requested, Aristeides said, as if (**250**) he himself were not the man under-discussion (**205**), "Why do you hate Aristeides? 6. Could you tell me how he has sinned against the city?" 7. The silly-creature (**132**) replied, "Oh, I know nothing about him, but I am weary [of] always hearing him called the just." 8. Ought such persons as that ignorant peasant have-the-right to vote about important affairs? 9. The ancient law about ostracism was a strange [one]. 10. The name of the person to-be-exiled (**199**) was usually written upon an oyster-shell, and the meaning of the word signifying the custom comes from that. 11. Through (*per*) ostracism, any leader could be banished, justly or unjustly, without trial of any kind, or explanation of the reasons.

LESSON LV.

THE IMPERATIVE MOOD.—RESOLVE AND EXHORTA-
TION.—COMMANDS AND PROHIBITIONS. —LESS
PEREMPTORY USES OF THE IMPERATIVE.—THE USE
OF MOŜTO.—LA GLAVO DE DAMOKLO.

THE IMPERATIVE MOOD.

254. For expressions of command, exhortation, entreaty, etc., there is an *imperative mood*, as in English. The ending of the imperative mood is **-u**. Beside the aoristic tense, six compound tenses are formed by combining the participles with the imperative mood **estu** of the auxiliary verb, but these tenses are seldom used. The conjugation of **vidi** in the aoristic tense of this mood, together with a synopsis in the compound tenses, is as follows:

Aoristic Tense.

mi vidu!	let me see!	ni vidu!	let us see!
(vi) vidu!	(you) see!	(vi) vidu!	(you) see!
li (ŝi, ĝi) vidu!	let him (her, it) see!	ili vidu!	let them see!

Compound Tenses.

Active.		Passive.	
Present:	**mi estu vidanta,**	Present:	**mi estu vidata,**
Past:	**mi estu vidinta,**	Past:	**mi estu vidita,**
Future:	**mi estu vidonta.**	Future:	**mi estu vidota.**

RESOLVE AND EXHORTATION.

255. The *first person singular* of the imperative mood is used to express the speaker's resolve concerning his own action, or an exhortation to himself concerning such action. The *first person plural* is used to express resolve or exhortation concerning the joint action of the speaker and the person or persons addressed:[62]

Mi pensu pri tio! *Let me think about that!*
Mi ne forgesu tion! *I must not (do not let me) forget that!*
Ni ekzilu lin! *Let us exile him!*
Ni ne sidiĝu tie! *Let us not sit down there!*

---

[62] This force is usually expressed in English by "let" with an accusative and infinitive construction.

Ni estu grize vestitaj! *Let us be dressed in gray!*

COMMANDS AND PROHIBITIONS.

256. The *second and third* persons of the imperative are used to express peremptory commands and prohibitions.

a. In the *second* person the pronoun is usually omitted, as in English, unless special emphasis is placed upon it:

Estu trankvila! *Be calm!* (One person is addressed.)
Estu pretaj por akompani min! *Be ready to accompany me!* (Two or more persons are addressed.)
Parolu kvazaŭ vi komprenus! *Talk as though you understood!*
Ne fermu tiun pordon! *Do not shut that door!*
Ne estu vidata tie! *Do not be seen there!*

b. In the *third* person a circumlocution in English is necessary in translation (as *let, must, are to, is to*, etc.):

Li estu zorga! *Let him be careful (he must be careful)!*
Ŝi ne faru tion! *Do not let her do that (she is not to do that)!*
Ĉio estu pardonata! *Let everything be forgiven!*
Oni lasu min trankvila! *People are to let me alone!*
Ili neniam revenu! *Let them never (do not let them ever) return!*
La kulpuloj estu punataj! *Let the culprits be punished!*

LESS PEREMPTORY USES OF THE IMPERATIVE.

257. By an extension of its use in resolve, exhortation, command and prohibition, the imperative mood may be employed for less peremptory expressions, such as *request, wish, advice*, etc., and in *questions of deliberation or perplexity*, or *requests for instruction*:

Request: **Ĉesu tiun bruon, mi petas!** *Stop that noise, I beg!*
  Bonvolu fari tion! *Please do that!*
  Pardonu al ni niajn pekojn! *Forgive us our sins!*

Wish: **Ili estu feliĉaj!** *May they be happy!*
  Dio vin benu! *God bless you!*
  Vivu la reĝo! *(Long) live the king!*

Advice: **Pensu antaŭ ol agi!** *Think before acting!*
  Foriru, se vi ne estas kontenta! *Go away, if you are not satisfied!*

Consent: **Nu, parolu, sed mi ne aŭskultos!** *Well, talk, but I shall not listen!*
  Iru tuj, se vi volas. *Go at once, if you like.*

Question: **Ĉu mi faru tion aŭ ne?** *Am I to do that or not?*
  Ĉu ni disdonu la librojn? *Shall we distribute the books?*
  Ĉu li estu kondamnita? *Shall he be condemned?*
  Ĉu ili venu ĉi tien? *Are they to (shall they) come here?*

THE USE OF MOŜTO.

258. The word **moŝto** may be used alone, or after a title, to denote respect. When used after a title, the title becomes an adjective:

Lia reĝa moŝto, *his majesty.*
Lia juĝista moŝto, *his honor the judge.*
Ŝia reĝina moŝto, *her majesty.*
Lia urbestra moŝto, *his honor the mayor.*
Ĉu via moŝto lin aŭdis? *Did your honor (excellency, etc.) hear him?*

VOCABULARY.

Afrik-o, *Africa.*	**moŝt-o,** a title (see 258).
barbar-o, *barbarian.*	**ordon-i,** *to order, to bid.*
Damokl-o, *Damocles.*	**permes-i,** *to permit.*
flank-o, *side.*	**plaĉ-i,** *to please.*
imperi-o, *empire.*	**sklav-o,** *slave.*
konsent-i, *to consent.*	**sol-a,** *sole, only.*
konsil-i, *to advise.*	**volont-e,** *willingly.*

LA GLAVO DE DAMOKLO.

Antaŭ pli multe ol dumil jaroj vivis en Sirakuzo, sur la insulo Sikelio, tre kruela tirano. Li diris al si "Mi estu ĉiopova (*all-powerful*)!" Tial li faris multe da militadoj, kaj venkis ne nur barbarajn popolojn, sed ankaŭ multajn urbojn en Italujo kaj norda Afriko. Detruinte ĉion sen kompato, li ordonis "La loĝantoj estu vendataj por sklavoj!" Li deziris fari por si, el la venkitaj kaj sklavigitaj popoloj, unu grandan imperion. Sed la urboj ĉie, eĉ en Grekujo, ne kaŝis al li sian grandan malamon al tia tirano. Tial li ĉiam timis pri sia vivo, timante ke iu subite mortigos lin. Unufoje Damoklo, amiko de la tirano, diris al li, "Se mi estus tiel riĉa kaj pova kiel via reĝa moŝto, mi estus treege feliĉa!" La tirano respondis, "Venu al festo ĉe mi, se tio plaĉas al vi, kaj eltrovu ĉu mi devus esti feliĉa aŭ ne." "Mi venos tre volonte," ekkriis Damoklo, "kaj mi dankas vian moŝton pro tia afableco!" La tirano ĝentile respondis "Ho, estas nenio (=*you are welcome*)! Nur ne forgesu la deciditan horon!" Je la ĝusta horo Damoklo iris al la festo, kie oni donis al li seĝon flanke de la tirano mem. "Manĝu kaj trinku kiom ajn vi volas," konsilis la tirano, "kaj poste ni parolos pri la feliĉeco." Damoklo tuj konsentis al tia propono, kaj agis laŭ la permeso tiel afable donita al li. Manĝante bonegan manĝaĵon, kaj trinkante dolĉan vinon, li tute ne enuis ĉe la festo. Baldaŭ la tirano diris "Rigardu supren, kaj vidu ĝuste kian feliĉecon mi havas!" Supren rigardinte, Damoklo ekvidis akran glavon, antaŭe kaŝitan al li de kurteno. Subtenate de unu sola haro, la glavo ŝajnis kvazaŭ tuj falonta sur la kapon de Damoklo. "La dioj min helpu!" li ekkriis, forsaltinte de la tablo. Pro la ĵus dirita stranga rakonto, oni ankoraŭ nun nomas la atendadon por io timeginda, kio ŝajnas ĉiam okazonta sed efektive ne okazas, "la glavo de Damoklo."

SENTENCES FOR TRANSLATION.

1. The word ostracism comes from the Greek word signifying "oyster-shell."
2. It has its present meaning because oyster-shells or pieces of pottery were used

for the voting. 3. The story about Aristeides is interesting, but that about the sword of Damocles is also interesting. 4. His friend, the Syracusan tyrant, had permitted all sorts of injustices, against not only barbarians but even Greeks. 5. His only bidding usually was "Let every inhabitant be sold as a slave!" 6. He thought "Let me make one sole empire out of Africa, Italy and Sicily!" 7. Damocles said to him "Your royal highness ought to be very happy!" 8. The tyrant answered, "Come to a feast tomorrow, and find out. I will give you a seat (214, b) beside me." 9. Damocles willingly consented, and went thither. 10. The tyrant advised "Let us eat and drink until midnight, if that would be-pleasing to you. Then let us discuss the problem about happiness." 11. After a few hours Damocles heard a slight sound over his head, and the tyrant said to him, "Look up and you will see what kind of happiness mine is." 12. "Heaven defend me!" exclaimed Damocles, catching sight of a sharp sword hanging by a single (sole) hair.

LESSON LVI.

THE IMPERATIVE IN SUBORDINATE CLAUSES.—THE PREPOSITION JE.—THE SUFFIX -OP-. —LA MARŜADO DE LA DEKMIL GREKOJ.

THE IMPERATIVE IN SUBORDINATE CLAUSES.

259. The imperative mood is used in a subordinate clause, with a meaning similar to that in its independent use, after a main verb expressing *command, exhortation, resolve, consent, wish*, etc.,[63] or after any word or general expression of *command, intention, necessity, expedience*, etc. Such clauses are introduced by the conjunction ke:

Command and Prohibition.
Li diras ke vi iru, *he says that you are to go.*
Ŝi skribis al li ke li venu, *she wrote him to come.*
Mi malpermesas ke vi restu, *I forbid you to remain.*
Ni ordonos ke li estu punata, *we shall order that he be punished.*

Request and Wish.
Mi petas ke vi ne lasu min, *I beg that you do not leave me.*
Mi petegas ke vi estu trankvilaj, *I implore you to be calm.*
Li deziras ke ili estu sklavigitaj, *he desires that they be enslaved.*
Ni volis ke li ne forgesu tion, *we wished him not to forget that.*

Advice, Consent, Permission.
Mi konsilis al li ke li iru, *I advised him to go.*
Mi konsentis ke li restu, *I consented that he remain.*
Ili permesos ke la barbaroj forkuru, *they will permit the barbarians to escape (that the barbarians escape).*

Questions.
Li demandas ĉu ili foriru, *he inquires whether they are to go away.*
Oni demandis ĉu lia moŝto eniru, *they asked whether his honor was to enter.*
Mi miras ĉu mi faru tion, *I wonder whether I am to do that.*

Intention, Expedience, Necessity, etc.
Ni intencas ke vi estu helpata, *we intend that you shall be helped.*

---

[63] In English and some other languages an imperative idea may often be expressed by the infinitive, as "I wish you to go," but in Esperanto this must be expressed by the equivalent of "I wish *that* you go." The infinitive may not be used except when it can itself be the subject of the verb in such general statements as "it is necessary to go."

Lia propono estas ke ni ricevu la duonon, *his proposal is, that we receive the half.*

Lia lasta ordono estis, ke vi venu, *his last order was that you come.*

Estos bone ke vi ne plu nomu lin, *it will be well for you not to (that you do not) mention him any more.*

Estas dezirinde ke ni havu bonan imperiestron, *it is desirable that we have a good emperor.*

Estis necese ke ĉiu stariĝu, *it was necessary for everyone to rise.*

Plaĉos al li ke vi iru, *he will be pleased to have you go.*

THE PREPOSITION JE.

260. Since prepositional uses are not exactly alike in any two languages, it is not always possible to translate a preposition of one language by what is its equivalent in some senses in another.[64] In order to insure some means of translating correctly into Esperanto any prepositional phrase of the national languages, the preposition **je** is regarded as of rather indefinite meaning. In addition to its use in dates and allusions to time (**89, 185**), it may be employed when no other preposition gives the exact sense required, especially in protestations and exclamations, expressions of measure (see also **139**), and of indefinite connection:[65]

[64] The translation given for a preposition in any dictionary is the general one which serves in the majority of cases. The finer shades of meaning and real or apparent exceptions can merely be touched upon if mentioned at all.

[65] The preposition **je** is used to express indefinite connection after the following words (other prepositions sometimes used are given in parentheses):

ekkrii je (pro), *to cry out at.*
enui je, *to be bored with.*
fiera je (pri), *proud of.*
fidi je (al), *to rely upon.*
ĝoji je (pri), *to rejoice at.*
gratuli je (pri), *congratulate on.*
honti je (pri), *to be ashamed of.*
inda je, *worthy of.*
interesiĝi je, *to take interest in.*
kapti je, *to seize by.*
kontenta je (kun), *content with.*
kredi je, *to believe in.*
(sin) okupi je, *to busy (oneself) at.*
plena je (de), *full of.*
preni je, *to take by.*
provizi je (per), *to provide with.*
riĉigi je (per), *to enrich with.*
ridi je, *to laugh at.*
satiĝi je, *to be sated with.*
senigi je, *to deprive of.*
simila je (al), *similar to.*
sopiri je (al), *to yearn for.*

Je la nomo de ĉielo! *In the name of Heaven!*
Je mia honoro mi ja elfaros tion! *On my honor I will accomplish that!*
Ĝi estas longa je du mejloj, *it is two miles long (long by two miles).*
Ili venis je grandaj nombroj, *they came in great numbers.*
Li estas tenata de la policano, je la brako, per forta ŝnurego, *he is held by the policemen, by the arm, with (by) a strong rope.*

THE SUFFIX -OP-.

261. The suffix **-op-** is used to form *collective* numerals:

duope, *by twos, in pairs.*   **milope,** *by thousands.*
kvarope, *by fours.*   **sesopigi,** *to form into groups of six.*

VOCABULARY.

cel-i, *to aim.*   **prokrast-i,** *to delay* (trans.).
Cirus-o, *Cyrus.*   **proviz-i,** *to provide.*
fidi, *to rely.*   **rezult-i,** *to result.*
ĝu-i, *to enjoy.*   **sopir-i,** *to yearn, to sigh.*
honor-o, *honor.*   **spac-o,** *space.*
krom, *beside, save, but.*   **terur-a,** *terrible.*
plen-a, *full.*   **ver-o,** *truth.*

LA MARŜADO DE LA DEKMIL GREKOJ.

Iam Ciruso, nepo de Ciruso Granda, sopiris je la imperio de sia pli maljunafrato, kiu sekvis la patron de ambaŭ fratoj kiel reĝo, aŭ pli ĝuste imperiestro. Decidinte forigi de la reĝeco (*to dethrone*) sian fraton, Ciruso petis la grekojn ke ili partoprenu (*take part*) en kelkaj negravaj militadoj. Multaj tiamaj grekoj tre volonte sin okupis je la batalado, pro la granda pago ricevata. La venditaj sklavoj kaj la detruitaj konstruaĵoj ĉiam provizis ilin je multe da riĉaĵo, kaj krom tio la militistoj ŝajnis ĝui eĉ la militadon mem. Estis tute indiferente al ili ĉu la kaŭzo de la militado estas prava kaj justa aŭ ne. Unue Ciruso nur petis ke ili helpu liajn proprajn soldatojn kontraŭ iuj najbaroj. Li kaŝis al ili sian veran celon, ĉar se la grekoj estus suspektintaj tion, kion li intencis fari, ili neniam estus akompanintaj lin tiel malproksimen de sia patrolando. Grade li kondukis ilin trans tutan Azion, kaj fine la dekmil grekoj komprenis ĉion, kaj treege koleriĝis. Paroladante al ili, Ciruso tuj diris "Mi ne permesas ke vi reiru, kaj mi petegas ke vi antaŭen marŝadu kun mi, sen plua (*further*) prokrasto! Se mi sukcesos kontraŭ mia frato, mi certigas vin je mia honoro ke ĉiu el vi revenos havante sakojn plenajn je riĉaĵo! Estas nur necese ke vi fidu je mi, kaj ĉio estos bona!" Tiam la soldatoj hontis je sia antaŭa timo, kaj kuraĝe antaŭen marŝadis. Fine, apud granda urbo, la frato de Ciruso elvenis havante okcentmil soldatojn, por batali kontraŭ la centmil de Ciruso. Per la helpo de siaj grekoj, Ciruso estis preskaŭ venkinta en terura batalo, kiam subite li ekvidis sian fraton, je malgranda interspaco. Ekkriante "Mi vidas la viron!" li rajdis rekte al la

---

ŝarĝi je, *to load with.*
teni je, *to hold by.*

reĝo, ĵetante sian pezan lancon al li. La sola rezulto estis la morto de Ciruso mem, ĉar la amikoj de la reĝo, kvinope kaj sesope atakinte Ciruson, lin tuj mortigis.

SENTENCES FOR TRANSLATION.

1. Cyrus did not desire that his brother should remain king. 2. He decided, "Let me myself become (*fariĝi*) king! I should much enjoy that!" 3. So he asked the Greeks to help him in some battles against nearby enemies. 4. Gradually an army (126) of a hundred thousand men, ten thousand of whom were Greeks, gathered (232, b) around him. 5. He led them farther and farther, into the middle of Asia, until finally the Greeks suspected his true aim. 6. They said to each other in terror, "He did not at first propose that we fight against the Great King. Let us return home without delay!" 7. Cyrus addressed (218) them as follows: "Must I permit you to go back? I implore you to be courageous, and I do advise you not to forget your longing for (260) honor! 8. Only be worthy of your leader, and rely upon me! Do you not wish to return home provided with wealth, beside the money which I shall pay to you?" 9. Immediately the soldiers were ashamed of their fear, and advanced by hundreds, full of courage. 10. Soon the brother of Cyrus approached, with (*havante*) eight hundred thousand men. 11. By the aid of the Greeks, Cyrus won the battle, but he himself lost his life. 12. So neither he nor the Greeks could enjoy the result of their efforts.

LESSON LVII.

CLAUSES EXPRESSING PURPOSE.—FURTHER USES OF THE ACCUSATIVE.—SYNOPSIS OF THE CONJUGATION OF THE VERB.—THE SUFFIX -UM-.—LA REIRADO DE LA DEKMILO.

CLAUSES EXPRESSING PURPOSE.

262. *Purpose* may be expressed by a subordinate imperative clause, introduced by **por ke**:[66]

Mi faras ĝin por ke li helpu vin, *I do it in order that he may help you.*
Mi ekkriis por ke vi aŭdu, *I cried out in order that you should hear.*
Li venos por ke ni estu feliĉaj, *he will come that we may be happy.*
Mi studas por ke mi lernu, *I study that I may learn.*
Ili restu por ke ni punu ilin, *let them stay for us to punish them.*

FURTHER USES OF THE ACCUSATIVE.[67]

263. The accusative of direction of motion is used after *nouns* from roots expressing motion:

Lia eniro en la urbon estis subita, *his entrance into the city was sudden.*
La irado tien estos plezuro, *(the) going thither will be a pleasure.*
Ĝia falado teren timigis min, *its falling earthward terrified me.*

264. a. An intransitive verb may be followed by a noun in the accusative case, if the meaning of the noun is related to that of the verb:

Li vivas agrablan vivon, *he lives an agreeable life.*
Ŝi dancis belan dancon, *she danced a beautiful dance.*
Ili ploris maldolĉajn larmojn, *they wept bitter tears.*

b. Verbs of motion (**iri, veni, pasi, marŝi, veturi,** etc.) compounded with prepositions or adverbs (**121**) indicating direction, also compounds of such verbs as **esti** and **stari** with prepositions expressing situation, may be followed by the accusative, instead of by a prepositional phrase in which the preposition is repeated:

---

[66] *Cf.* the expression of purpose by the *infinitive* with **por** (**98**), which however cannot be used except when the subject of the main verb is the subject of the subordinate verb, or when the object of the main verb is the subject of the subordinate verb.

[67] *Cf.* the accusative of direct object (**23**), direction of motion (**46, 121**), time (**91**), and measure (**139**).

La viro preterpasis la domon, *the man passed (by) the house.*
Lin antaŭvenis du sklavoj, *there preceded (came before) him two slaves.*
Ni supreniru la ŝtuparon, *let us go up the stairs.*
Mi ĉeestis la feston, *I attended (was present at) the entertainment.*
Mi kontraŭstaras vian opinion, *I oppose (withstand) your opinion.*

c. The slight change in meaning given by **pri** used as a prefix may render intransitive verbs transitive.[68] The same is true of **el** prefixed to intransitive verbs not expressing motion:

Ŝi priploris la mortintan birdon, *she mourned the dead bird.*
Mi pripensos la aferon, *I shall consider (think over) the matter.*
Ni ĝin priparolos, *we shall talk it over.*
Li klare elparolas la vortojn, *he pronounces the words clearly.*

265. The accusative may be used after verbs of such meaning that either a prepositional phrase or an accusative would seem correct:

Mi pardonas lin (al li), *I pardon (grant pardon to) him.*[69]
Mi helpis lin (al li), *I helped (gave aid to) him.*
Ĝi plaĉas min (al mi), *it pleases (is pleasing to) me.*
Li obeis nin (al ni), *he obeyed (was obedient to) us.*
Ŝi ridis mian timon (je mia timo), *she ridiculed (laughed at) my fear.*

266. The accusative may be used after certain adverbs which are normally followed by a prepositional phrase:

Rilate tion (rilate al tio), *in regard to that.*
Escepte tion (escepte de tio), *with the exception of that.*
Koncerne la aferon (koncerne je la afero), *concerning the affair.*
Kompare la alian (kompare kun la alia), *in comparison with the other.*
Konforme la leĝon (konforme al la leĝo), *in conformity to the law.*

SYNOPSIS OF THE CONJUGATION OF THE VERB.

267.   **vidi,** to see.

ACTIVE.   PASSIVE.

INDICATIVE.

Present.

(*Aoristic*) **mi vidas**   **mi estas vidata**
(*Progressive*) **mi estas vidanta**

Past.

(*Aoristic*) **mi vidis**   **mi estis vidata**
(*Imperfect*) **mi estis vidanta**

---

[68] In this use **pri** resembles the English and German inseparable prefix *be-*, as in English *bemoan, bewail, bethink, bespeak,* German *beklagen, besprechen, sich* , etc.

[69] When ambiguity would be caused, as by the presence of another accusative, this construction may not be employed. One may say **pardonu nin**, but must say **pardonu al ni niajn pekojn.**

Future.

(*Aoristic*) **mi vidos**   **mi estos vidata**
(*Progressive*) **mi estos vidanta**

Perfect.

mi estas vidinta   **mi estas vidita**

Pluperfect.

mi estis vidinta   **mi estis vidita**

Future Perfect.

mi estos vidinta   **mi estos vidita**

Periphrastic Futures.

(Present).

mi estas vidonta   **mi estas vidota**

(Past).

mi estis vidonta   **mi estis vidota**

(Future).

mi estos vidonta   **mi estos vidota**

CONDITIONAL.

Present.

(*Aoristic*) **mi vidus**   **mi estus vidata**
(*Progressive*) **mi estus vidanta**

Past.

mi estus vidinta   **mi estus vidita**

Future.

mi estus vidonta   **mi estus vidota**

IMPERATIVE.

Present.

(*Aoristic*) **mi vidu**   **mi estu vidata**
(*Progressive*) **mi estu vidanta**

Past.

mi estu vidinta   **mi estu vidita**

Future.

mi estu vidonta   **mi estu vidota**

INFINITIVE.

Present.

(*Aoristic*) **vidi**   **esti vidata**
(*Progressive*) **esti vidanta**

Perfect.

esti vidinta   **esti vidita**

Future.

esti vidonta   **esti vidota**

THE SUFFIX -UM-.

268. The indefinite suffix **-um-** serves the same general purpose in word formation which **je** serves as an indefinite preposition (260):

aerumi, *to air*.   **kolumo**, *collar*.
buŝumo, *muzzle*.   **plenumi**, *to fulfil*.
gustumi, *to taste*.   **proksimume**, *approximately*.

VOCABULARY.

eben-a, *level, even*.   **nepr-e**, *inevitably, certainly*.
escept-o, *exception*.   **obe-i**, *to obey*.
esper-i, *to hope*.   **obstin-a**, *obstinate*.
fremd-a, *foreign*.   **promes-i**, *to promise*.
histori-o, *history*.   **rilat-o**, *relation*.
kompar-i, *to compare*.   **sat-a**, *satiated*.
koncern-i, *to concern*.   **sav-i**, *to save*.
konform-i, *to conform*.   **verk-i**, *to compose* (books or music).

LA REIRADO DE LA DEKMILO.

La grekaj militistoj sentis grandan teruron kiam Ciruso ne plu vivis. La celo de la longa marŝado ne povis esti plenumata, pro la morto de la obstina trokuraĝa militestro mem. Kvankam la grekoj estis venkintoj, ili estis tute solaj en fremda lando, ĉirkaŭitaj de barbaroj kiuj, per trompemaj proponoj kaj falsaj promesoj pri amikaj interrilatoj, tuj okazigis la morton de la grekaj estroj. Senigite je siaj estroj, la kompatindaj viroj tute malesperis. Sed kelkaj subestroj, rapide kunveniginte la soldatojn, diris, "Ni mem kondukos vin per kiel eble plej rekta vojo hejmen! Ni faros nian eblon (*utmost*) por ke ni ĉiuj estu savitaj!" Ĉar restis nenio alia por fari, la malfacila malgaja reirado de la grekoj komenciĝis sen prokrasto. Ili transiris varmegajn ebenaĵojn (*plains*), supreniris kaj malsupreniris krutajn neĝkovritajn montojn, meze de la vintro, kaj sen pontoj transiris larĝajn riverojn. Ĉie la malfidindaj barbaroj atakis ilin, kvazaŭ por ke neniu greko restu viva. Krom tio, la grekoj mortis dekope kaj dudekope ĉiutage, pro varmegeco, malvarmegeco, laceco kaj malsateco (*hunger*). Fine, post nekredeblaj suferoj, la restaĵo de la dekmil soldatoj alvenis sur monton, kaj ekvidis la maron. Laŭta ekkriego "La maro! La maro!" eksonis inter la lacaj viroj, el kiuj multaj ploris larmojn de ĝojo. De infaneco ili alkutimis al la vojaĝado per akvo, kaj post iom da ripozo ili sin provizis je ŝipoj, por transiri la maron al la patrujo je kiu ili estis tiel longe sopirintaj. Treege interesa historio koncerne la tutan aferon estas verkita de fama greka verkisto (*writer*), kiu estis akompaninta Ciruson por ke li povu ĝui kaj studi ĉion interesan sur la vojo. Tiu azia militado de Ciruso nepre estas unu el la plej rimarkindaj okazintaĵoj iam priskribitaj, eĉ sen escepto de la posta irado tien de Aleksandro Granda.

SENTENCES FOR TRANSLATION.

1. After the death of Cyrus, the leaders of the Greek warriors did not know what to do. 2. In the course of the following day, one of the leaders of the enemy sent a messenger (205) with deceitful promises about help. 2. He said "Assemble in our leader's tent, in order that you may all discuss the matter." 3. The Greek leaders went, although they suspected danger, because they did not know how else to save their men. 4. But they never returned, and soon the Greeks understood that the barbarians had killed them. 5. They wept tears of despair, and said "The barbarians will inevitably destroy us, for we are in a foreign land, where we know neither the languages nor the roads, and the peoples are without exception hostile to us." 6. But the leaders-of-lesser-rank said "Obey us and follow us, and we shall do our best to save you!" 7. Their return, across hot plains and snow-covered mountains, made-more-difficult by hunger and by the unceasing attacks of the barbarians, is related in the history written by a famous Greek historian. 8. One can still read this interesting narrative, in Greek or in a translation.

LESSON LVIII.

PERMISSION AND POSSIBILITY.—THE PREFIX GE-.—
THE SUFFIX -AĈ-.—INTERJECTIONS.— ALEKSANDRO
GRANDA.

PERMISSION AND POSSIBILITY.

269. Permission is usually expressed by the use of **permesi, lasi,** or the imperative mood:

Ĉu vi permesas ke mi restu? *May I (do you permit me to) stay?*
Jes, mi permesas (jes, restu), *yes, you may (yes, stay).*
Ne estas permesate eniri tien, *it is not allowed to enter there.*
Lasu lin veni, *let him come.*

270. The idea of possibility or probability is given by the use of some such adverb as **eble, kredeble, verŝajne,** etc.:

Eble li obeos al vi, *he may (perhaps he will) obey you.*
Kredeble li sukcesos, *probably he will succeed.*
Verŝajne vi estas prava, *you are probably right.*
Eble oni lin savus, *they might (possibly they would) save him.*
Ili nepre ne batis lin, *they could not have (surely did not) beat him.*
Tio estas neebla! *That can not be (that is impossible)!*

THE PREFIX GE-.

271. Words formed with the prefix **ge-** indicate the two sexes together:

gepatroj, *parents.*   **gefiloj,** *son(s) and daughter(s).*
geavoj, *grandparents.*   **gefratoj,** *brother(s) and sister(s).*
genepoj, *grandchildren.*   **geedzoj,** *husband(s) and wife (wives).*
gesinjoroj, *Mr. and Mrs., lady (ladies) and gentleman (gentlemen).*

THE SUFFIX -AĈ-.

272. The suffix **-aĉ-** has a disparaging significance:

domaĉo, *a hovel.*   **pentraĉi,** *to daub.*
hundaĉo, *a cur.*   **popolaĉo,** *rabble, mob.*
obstinaĉa, *obstinate.*   **ridaĉi,** *to guffaw.*

INTERJECTIONS.

273. Interjections are words used to express feeling or call attention.[70] Among the more common interjections are:

Adiaŭ! *Farewell!* (171).
Fi! *Fie!*[†††]
Ho! *Oh! Ho!*

Hura! *Hurrah!*
Nu! *Well!*
Ve! *Woe!* (Ho ve! *Alas!*).

VOCABULARY.

Aleksandri-o, *Alexandria.*
Amerik-o, *America.*
Aristotel-o, *Aristotle.*
Aŭstrali-o, *Australia.*
bibliotek-o, *library.*
eduk-i, *to bring up, educate.*
Egipt-o, *Egypt.*
estim-i, *to esteem.*
firm-a, *firm.*

fond-i, *to found, establish.*
hispan-o, *Spaniard.*
kapabl-a, *capable.*
komun-a, *common, mutual.*
kontinent-o, *continent.*
Krist-o, *Christ.*
milion-o, *million.*
spite, *in spite of.*
vast-a, *vast, extensive.*

ALEKSANDRO GRANDA.

Permesu ke mi diru kelkajn vortojn pri la vivo de Aleksandro Granda, kiu ne estis matura viro sed havis nur dudek jarojn kiam li fariĝis reĝo. Liaj gepatroj estis tre zorge edukintaj lin, kaj la filozofo Aristotelo, kiun li tre alte estimis, estis unu el liaj instruistoj. Aleksandro firme tenadis sian propran reĝolandon, kaj ankaŭ Grekujon, kiun lia patro estis venkinta; krom tio, li faris militadojn kontraŭ diversaj fremdaj landoj, unue en Azio, tiam en Afriko, kie li fondis urbon, kaj ĝin nomis Aleksandrio. Aleksandrio nepre estis belega riĉa urbo. Tie **troviĝis**[71] poste la fama Aleksandria biblioteko. Se ĝi ne estus detruita de fajro, en la daŭro de iuj militadoj, ni sendube konus multe pli bone la sciadon de la antikvaj grekoj, kiuj verŝajne estis la plej klera popolo iam vivinta en Eŭropo. Venkinte Egipton, Aleksandro reiris en Azion, ĝis tre orienta kaj suda partoj, venkante ĉiujn ĉie, kvazaŭ ili estus la plej malkuraĝaj popolaĉoj en la mondo. Sed spite ĉies petoj li estis obstinaĉe nezorgema pri sia sano, kaj subite, ho ve, li mortis pro febro, tricent dektri jarojn antaŭ Kristo. Se li ne estus tiel frue mortinta, kiel multe li estus eble elfarinta!

---

[70] Verbs in the imperative, and adverbs, are frequently used as interjections, as **Atentu!** *Look out!* **Aŭskultu!** *Hark!* **Bonvenu!** *Welcome!* **Antaŭen!** *Forward!* **Bone!** *Good!* **For!** *Away!* **Ja!** *Indeed!* **Jen!** *There! Behold!*

[71] The use of **troviĝi**, and also of **sin trovi**, **kuŝi**, **stari** and **sidi**, in a sense not greatly differing from that of **esti**, avoids the monotonous repetition of forms of **esti**, just as English uses *lie, sit, perch*, etc., in narration for similar reasons:

Multaj vilaĝoj troviĝas tie, *many villages are (situated) there.*
Egipto troviĝas en la nordorienta parto de Afriko, *Egypt is (found) in the northeastern part of Africa.*
Li sin trovis sola en la dezerto, *he found himself (he was) alone in the desert.*
La urbo kuŝis inter du lagoj, *the city lay between two lakes.*
Sur la montflanko sidis vilaĝeto, *on the mountainside perched a tiny village.*

Li esperis venki Hispanujon, Italujon, kaj, mallongavorte, tiom de la okcidenta mondo kiom li jam posedis de la orienta. Tiam li celis kunigi ĉion en unu vastan imperion, kvazaŭ por fari el la mondo unu grandan familion. Li intencis ke la milionoj da enloĝantoj akceptu komunajn leĝojn kaj kutimojn, eĉ komunan lingvon, — kredeble la grekan. Eble li ja havis la kapablecon por fari ĉion ĉi. Estas pro tio ke oni ofte aŭdas la diron "Aleksandro sopiris je aliaj mondoj por venki." Tamen, kiel malgranda estis tiu mondo kiun li konis! La tiamuloj konis nur malgrandan parton de Afriko, de Azio, eĉ de Eŭropo. Ili sciis nenion pri Anglujo, aŭ pri la vastaj kontinentoj Aŭstralio, norda kaj suda Amerikoj.

SENTENCES FOR TRANSLATION.

1. Alexander the Great wished to unite the whole world into one vast empire. 2. He intended that all the different peoples should conform to common laws and that their sons-and-daughters should speak one common language, and in spite of their love for their national languages, should leave-off speaking them. 3. Possibly he might have accomplished his object to some extent (217), if he had not died suddenly when he was only thirty-two years old. 4. His soldiers marched weeping past his tent, to bid farewell to their dying leader. 5. They must have esteemed him very highly! 6. It was Alexander who founded the city of Alexandria, in Egypt, where approximately three hundred years before Christ the famous Alexandrian library was located. 7. It contained an enormous collection-of-books — almost seven hundred thousand. 8. Alas, this extensive library was destroyed by fire! 9. Alexander, who "sighed for other worlds to conquer," did not even know of the existence of North and South America, Australia, or even of England and Northern Europe. 10. Beside his Asiatic empire, he knew very little of Asia, even of China, with its millions of inhabitants. 11. How small the world was in those days!

LESSON LIX.

THE POSITION OF UNEMPHATIC PRONOUNS.—SOME
INTRANSITIVE VERBS.—THE SUFFIX - ER-.—THE
PREFIXES BO- AND DUON-.—CORRESPONDENCE.—
KELKAJ LETEROJ.

THE POSITION OF UNEMPHATIC PRONOUNS.

274. An unemphatic personal, indefinite or demonstrative pronoun very frequently precedes the verb of which it is the object. This is especially true if the verb in question is an infinitive:[72]

Mi volas lin vidi, *I wish to see him.*
Li povos tion fari, *he will be able to do that.*
Vi devus ion manĝi, *you ought to eat something.*
Ĉu vi ĝin kredis? *Did you believe it?*
Se li min vidus, li min savus, *if he should see me, he would save me.*

SOME INTRANSITIVE VERBS.

275. Some intransitive verbs have English meanings which do not differ in form from the *transitive* English verbs to which they are related.[73] In Esperanto the suffix **-ig-** (214) must be used when the transitive meaning is desired. Some examples are given in the following table:

Verb.	Intransitive Use.	Transitive Use.
Boli . . .	**La akvo bolas** *The water boils*	**Li boligas la akvon** *He boils the water*
Bruli . . .	**La fajro brulas** *The fire burns*	**Li bruligis la paperon** *He burned the paper*

---

[72] *Cf.* in other languages, as in German *ich möchte ihn sehen*, French *je veux le voir*, Latin *se alunt, me defendi*, etc. That such pronouns *are* unemphatic can be seen from English *let her come* (= *let'er come*), *make him stop* (= *make'im stop*), etc., in which the unemphatic forms *er, im*, replace *him, her*, in pronunciation (*cf.* the Greek enclitic pronouns μοῦ, μοι, μέ, σου, σοι, σέ, οὖ, οι, ἑ, the Sanskrit enclitic forms mā, me, tvā, te, nas, vas, enam, enat, enām, also sīm, and the Avestan ī, īm). The same phenomenon is indicated in *prithee* (= *pray thee*), and in the spellings *gimme* (= *give me*), *lemme* (= *let me*), in dialect stories.

[73] A transitive use of such intransitive verbs would be like using the English intransitive verb "learn" for the transitive verb "teach," as in the "I'll learn you" (for "I'll teach you") of illiterate speech.

Ĉesi . . .	**La bruo ĉesas** *The noise stops*	**Li ĉesigas la bruon** *He stops the noise*
Daŭri . . .	**La bruo daŭras** *The noise continues*	**Li daŭrigas la bruon** *He continues the noise*
Degeli . . .	**La glacio degelas** *The ice thaws*	**Li ĝin degeligas per fajro** *He thaws it with fire*
Droni . . .	**La knabino dronis** *The girl drowned*	**La viro ŝin dronigis** *The man drowned her*
Eksplodi . . .	**Pulvo eksplodas** *Gunpowder explodes*	**Li ĝin eksplodigos** *He will explode it*
Halti . . .	**Li haltis timigite** *He halted in alarm*	**Li haltigis la soldatojn** *He halted the soldiers*
Lumi . . .	**La suno lumas** *The sun shines*	**Li lumigis la lampon** *He lighted the lamp*
Pasi . . .	**La tempo pasas** *Time passes*	**Tiel li pasigis la tagon** *Thus he passed the day*
Pendi . . .	**Ĝi pendas de branĉo** *It hangs on a branch*	**Li ĝin pendigis de branĉo** *He hung it on a branch*
Soni . . .	**La saluta pafo sonis** *The salute sounded*	**Oni sonigis la salutan pafon** *They sounded the salute*
Sonori . . .	**La sonorilo sonoris** *The bell rang*	**Oni sonorigis la sonorilon** *They rang the bell*

THE SUFFIX -ER-.

276. The suffix **-er-** is used to form words expressing units or component parts of that which is indicated in the root:

fajrero, *spark* (of fire). **neĝero**, *snowflake*.
monero, *coin*. **sablero**, *grain of sand*.

THE PREFIXES BO- AND DUON-.

277. The prefix **bo-** indicates relationship by marriage. To indicate half-blood relationship, or step-relationship, **duon-** (166) is used:

bopatro, *father-in-law*. **duonpatro**, *stepfather*.
bofratino, *sister-in-law*. **duonfrato**, *half-brother*.

CORRESPONDENCE.

278. a. Letters should be dated as indicated in the following:

Bostono, je la 24a de decembro, 1912a.
Nov-Jorko, la 24an decembro, 1912a.
Sirakuzo, 24/XII/1912.

b. The usual methods of address are (to strangers and in business letters):

Sinjoro, Sinjorino, Estimata Sinjoro, Karaj Sinjoroj, Tre estimata Fraŭlino, etc.; (to friends and relatives) **Kara Fraŭlino, Karaj Gefratoj, Kara Amiko, Kara Mario, Patrino mia,**[74] etc.; (to persons whose opinions on some subject are known to agree with those of the writer) **Estimata (Kara) Samideano** (*follower of the same idea*).

   c. Among the more usual forms of conclusion are (to strangers and in business letters): **Tre fidele la via, Tre vere, Kun granda estimo, Kun plej alta estimo,** etc., (to friends): **Kun amika saluto, Kun ĉiuj bondeziroj, Kun samideanaj salutoj, Frate la via,** etc.

VOCABULARY.

adres-o, *address.*
apart-a, *separate.*
bedaŭr-i, *to regret.*
ĉef-a, *chief.*[‡‡‡]
do, *so, then.*
fontan-o, *fountain.*
hotel-o, *hotel.*
ink-o, *ink.*
konven-a, *suitable.*
kovert-o, *envelope* (for letters).

krajon-o, *pencil.*
mend-i, *to order* (of stores, etc).
Nov-Jorko, *New York.*
numer-o, *number* (numeral).
ofic-o, *office, employment.*
poŝt-o, *post* (letters, etc.).
respekt-o, *respect.*
special-a, *special.*
stat-o, *state* (political body)
tram-o, *tram.*

KELKAJ LETEROJ.

Sirakuzo, la 2an de marto, 1911.

Kara Amiko,

   Sendube vin surprizos ricevi leteron skribitan de mi ĉe hotelo en ĉi tiu urbo, ne tre malproksime de via propra oficejo! Via bofrato, kiun mi okaze renkontis hieraŭ en la poŝtoficejo, donis al mi vian adreson. Ĝis nun, mi estas tiel okupata ke mi ne havis la tempon eĉ por telefoni al vi. Sed nun mi havas du aŭ tri minutojn da libera tempo, kaj mi tuj ekkaptas la okazon por skribi letereton, petante ke vi vespermanĝu kun mi hodiaŭ vespere, ĉe la hotelo kie, kiel vi vidas, mi loĝas de antaŭ unu tago. (Pardonu, mi petas, ke[75] mi finas ĉi tiun leteron per krajono, sed mi ĵus eltrovis ke restas neniom plu da inko en mia fontanplumo.) Venu je la sesa, se tiu horo estas konvena. Bedaŭrinde (*unfortunately*), mi devos forresti de la hotelo la tutan poŝttagmezon, pri komercaj aferoj, alie mi vin renkontus ĉe la tramvojo, kie haltas la tramveturiloj (*streetcars*). Estos plej bone, mi opinias, ke vi iru rekte al mia ĉambro, numero 26, kie mi senprokraste vin renkontos, se mi ne estos efektive jam vin atendanta. Ni esperu ke la ĉefkuiristo preparos al ni bonan manĝon! Mi esperas ke vi malatentos la falantajn neĝerojn, kaj nepre venos, responde al mia iomete subita invito, ĉar ni ja havos multe da komunaj travivaĵoj por priparoli. Do

---

[74] Placing the possessive adjective after the noun in this way gives an affectionate sense, as in English "Mother mine," etc.

[75] The word **tial** may be omitted from the combination **tial ke** (83), if the meaning is obvious.

ĝis la baldaŭa revido je la vespermanĝo!

Kun plej amikaj salutoj,
Roberto.

Boston, 13/VII/1911.

Wilson kaj Jones,
Nov-Jorko.
Estimataj Sinjoroj:—

Bonvolu sendi al mi per revenanta poŝto vian plej novan prezaron (*price-list*). Ni baldaŭ bezonos iujn novajn meblojn por niaj oficejoj, precipe skribtablojn, tablojn konvenajn por skribmaŝinoj (*typewriters*), kaj specialajn librujojn, farotajn laŭ niaj bezonoj. Se viaj prezoj estas konvenaj, ni sendube volos mendi de vi tian meblaron.

Kun respekto,

J. F. Smith,
ĉe Brown kaj Brown.

Nov-Jorko, 17/VII/1911.

Sinjoro J. F. Smith,
ĉe Brown kaj Brown,
Nov-Jorko.
Estimata Sinjoro:—

Ni havas la honoron sendi al vi en aparta koverto nian plej novan prezaron, al kiu ni petas ke vi donu vian atenton, precipe al paĝoj 15-29. Tie vi trovos priskribitaj niajn plej bonajn oficejajn meblarojn. Ni senpage metos ĉiujn aĉetitajn meblojn sur la vagonaron, sed komprenoble ni ne pagos la koston de la sendado.

Ni plezure fabrikos specialajn librujojn laŭ viaj bezonoj, kaj volonte ricevos viajn ordonojn pri tio. Niaj prezoj estos kiel eble plej malaltaj.

Esperante ke la meblaroj priskribitaj en nia prezaro, kune kun la tie-presitaj prezoj, estos plene kontentigaj, kaj certigante al vi ke ni zorge plenumos ĉiun mendon, ni restas,

Tre respekte la viaj,

Wilson kaj Jones.

Bostono, la 27an Majo.

Sinjoro B. F. Brown,
Sirakuzo, Nov-Jorka Ŝtato.
Kara Sinjoro:—

Vian adreson ni dankas al niaj komunaj amikoj Sinjoroj Miller kaj White, kaj per ĉi tio ni permesas al ni proponi al vi niajn servojn por la vendado de tiaj infan-ludiloj, kiajn vi fabrikas. Ni havas bonegajn montrajn fenestrojn (*show-windows*), en nia butiko, preskaŭ meze de la ĉefstrato en la urbo, kaj en nia butiko troviĝas sufiĉe da grandaj vitramebloj (*show-cases*). Tial ni povus tre oportune administri tian aferon. Ni multe ĝojos se vi respondos kiel eble plej baldaŭ, sciigante al ni kiom da procento vi donos, kaj kiajn aranĝojn vi volus fari. Ni certigas al vi ke en ĉiu okazo ni penos fari nian eblon por via plej bona intereso.

Kun alta estimo,

D. Rose.

LESSON LX.

SOME TRANSITIVE VERBS.

279. Some transitive verbs have English meanings which do not differ in form from the *intransitive* English verbs to which they are related (conversely to the use explained in 275). In Esperanto the suffix **-iĝ-** (232), or a different root, must be used when an intransitive meaning is desired. Following are the more common verbs of this character, together with examples of the intransitive use of several of them:

balanci, *to balance.*
etendi, *to extend, to expand.*
fermi, *to close, to shut.*
fini, *to end, to finish.*
fleksi, *to bend, to flex.*
hejti, *to heat.*
klini, *to incline, to bend.*
kolekti, *to gather, to collect.*
komenci, *to begin, to commence.*
mezuri, *to measure.*
montri, *to show.*
movi, *to move.*
paŝti, *to pasture, to feed.*

renversi, *to upset, to overturn.*
rompi, *to break.*
ruli, *to roll, (a wheel, ball, etc.).*
skui, *to shake.*
streĉi, *to stretch.*
svingi, *to swing.*
ŝanceli, *to cause to vacillate.*
ŝanĝi, *to change.*
ŝiri, *to tear.*
turni, *to turn.*
veki, *to wake.*
verŝi, *to pour.*
volvi, *to roll* (around something).

La laboro nun finiĝas, *the work is now coming to an end.*
La glavo fleksiĝis, *the sword bent.*
La folioj disvolviĝas, *the leaves unroll (develop).*
Ĉiu kutimo ŝanĝiĝos, *every custom will change.*
La vintro jam komenciĝas, *the winter is already beginning.*
Mi vekiĝos je la sesa, *I shall awake at six (o'clock).*
La montrilo ŝanceliĝis, *the indicator trembled (vacillated).*
Vasta ebenaĵo etendiĝis antaŭ li, *a vast plain extended before him.*

ELISION.

280. Elision is not common, and its use in writing as well as in speaking is best avoided. It occurs most frequently in poetry.

a. The **-a** of the article may be elided before a word beginning with a vowel, or after a preposition ending in a vowel:

"**L' espero, l' obstino kaj la pacienco.**"
"**De l' montoj riveretoj fluas.**"
"**Kaj kantas tra l' pura aero.**"

b. The final **-o** of a noun may be elided in poetry. The original accent of the noun remains unchanged:

"**Ho, mia kor', ne batu maltrankvile.**"
"**Sur la kampo la rozet'.**"

c. The final **-e** of an adverb is very rarely elided (except in the expression **dank' al**, which occurs in prose as well as in poetry):

"**Ke povu mi foj' je eterno ekdormi!**"
Dank' al vi, mi sukcesis, *thanks to you, I succeeded.*

THE PREFIX **EKS-**.

281. The prefix **eks-** is used to form words expressing a previous incumbent of a position, or removal from such position:

eksprezidanto, *ex-president.*
eksreĝo, *ex-king.*
eksigi, *to put out of office, to discharge.*
eksiĝi, *to withdraw from one's office, to resign.*

THE PREFIX **PRA-**.

282. The prefix **pra-** is used to form words expressing precedence in the line of descent, or general remoteness in past time:

praavo, *great grandfather.*   **prapatroj**, *forefathers, ancestors.*
pranepo, *great grandson.*   **pratempa**, *primeval.*

THE SUFFIXES **-ĈJ-** AND **-NJ-**.

283. The suffix **-ĉj-** is used to form affectionate diminutives, from the first syllable or syllables of masculine names or terms of address. The suffix **-nj-** forms similar feminine diminutives:

Joĉjo, *Johnnie, Joe.*   **Manjo**, *May, Mamie.*
Paĉjo, *Papa.*   **Panjo**, *Mamma.*

WEIGHTS AND MEASURES.

284. National systems of weights and measures translated into international form (as **mejlo**, *mile*, **funto**, *pound*) cannot convey a very definite meaning to one not familiar with the particular system used. Consequently the metric system (already used by scientists everywhere and by the general public in many countries) is adopted for the international system of weights and measures:

Length and Surface.

milimetro, *millimeter* (.0394 inch).
centimetro, *centimeter* (.3937 inch).
decimetro, *decimeter* (3.937 inches).
metro, *meter* (39.37 inches).
dekametro, *dekameter* (393.7 inches).
hektometro, *hektometer* (328 feet 1 inch).
kilometro, *kilometer* (3280 feet 10 inches; .62137 mile).
kvadrata metro, *square meter* (1550 square inches).
hektaro, *hektare* (2.471 acres).

Weight.

gramo, *gram* (15.432 grains avoirdupois).
dekagramo, *dekagram* (.3527 ounce avoirdupois).
hektogramo, *hektogram* (3.5274 ounce avoirdupois).
kilogramo, *kilogram* (2.2046 pounds avoirdupois).

Capacity.

decilitro, *deciliter* (6.1022 cubic inches; .845 gill).
litro, *liter* (.908 quart, dry measure; 1.0567 quart, liquid).
dekalitro, *dekaliter* (9.08 quart, dry measure; 2.6417 gallons).
hektolitro, *hektoliter* (2 bushels 3.35 pecks; 26.417 gallons).
kilolitro, *kiloliter* (1.308 cubic yards; 264.17 gallons).

THE INTERNATIONAL MONEY SYSTEM.

285. Names of national coins translated into international form (as **dolaro,** *dollar,* **cendo,** *cent*) cannot convey a very definite meaning to persons not familiar with these coins. Consequently the system devised for international use (not for actual coins, but for calculation and price quotations) is based upon a unit called the **speso.** The multiples of this unit are the **spesdeko** (10 **spesoj**), **spescento** (100 **spesoj**), and **spesmilo** (1000 **spesoj**). Ten *spesmiloj* have approximately the value of a five-dollar gold piece, twenty marks, twenty-five francs, one pound sterling, etc. The *spesmilo,* equivalent to about $0.4875 in the money of the United States and Canada, is the unit commonly used. (To reduce dollars to *spesmiloj*, multiply by 2.051.)

ABBREVIATIONS.

286. The following abbreviations are often used (for those of the metric system see any English dictionary):

Dro., Doktoro, *Dr.*
Fino., Fraŭlino, *Miss.*
Pro., Profesoro, *Prof.*
Sro., Sinjoro, *Mr.*
Sino., Sinjorino, *Mrs.*
Ko., K-io., Kompanio, *Co.*
No., N-ro., Numero, *No.*
&, kaj, *&.*

Sm., spesmilo(j).
Sd., spesdeko(j).
k. t. p., kaj tiel plu, *and so forth.*
k. c., kaj ceteraj, *etc.*
k. sim., kaj simila(j), *et. sim.*
t. e., tio estas, *i.e.*
e., ekzemple, *e.g.*
p.s., postskribaĵo, *P.S.*

VOCABULARY.

abon-i, *to subscribe to, take.*
aparat-o, *apparatus.*
aŭtomat-a, *automatic.*
bov-o, *ox.*
dimensi-o, *dimension.*
ekzempl-o, *example.*
fokus-o, *focus.*
fotograf-i, *to photograph.*
funkci-i, *to function, work.*
kamer-o, *camera.*

led-o, *leather.*
metal-o, *metal.*
moment-o, *moment.*
negativ-o, *negative.*
objektiv-o, *lens, objective.*
original-o, *original.*
plat-o, *plate* (photographic, etc)
prov-i, *to try.*[§§§]
reklam-i, *to advertise.*
streĉ-i, *to stretch* (trans.).

PRI LA KAMERO.

Bostono, 12/XI/1910.

Brown kaj Ko.,
Nov-Jorko.
Sinjoroj:—

Vidinte vian reklamon en gazeto al kiu mi abonas, mi skribas por peti ke vi sendu al mi priskribaĵon de via kamero nomita "La Infaneto," kiun eble mi deziros provi.

Bonvolu ankaŭ sendi dekduonon da platoj, 6 x 9 centimetrojn, por kiu mi ĉi kune[76] send as spesmilon kaj duonon.

Kun respekto,

J. C. Smith.

Nov-Jorko, 18an novembro, 1910.

Kara Sinjoro:—

Respondante al via estimata letero de la 12a, ni donas ĉi sube mallongan priskribaĵon de nia bonega fotografilo nomita "La Infaneto."

"La Infaneto" kamero havis neesperitan sukceson, kaj estas vendita po miloj

[76]   The particle **ĉi** (used with **tiu, tio, ties, ĉiu, ĉio**) may also be used with certain adverbs, as **ĉi sube**, here below, **ĉi supre**, here above, **ĉi kune**, herewith, etc.

da ekzempleroj. Ĉie oni unuvoĉe laŭdas ĝian malgrandan kaj tamen bonegan konstruon, kaj ankaŭ ĝian firman samtempe facilan funkciadon. Ĝi ne estas pli granda ol monujo, tial ĝi ne bezonas pli multe da spaco ol tiu, kaj povas esti portata kaj uzata treege konvene.

La dimensioj de la fermita kamero estas 8 x 5 x 6.5 centimetroj. La pezo, kun objektivo, tri platingoj, kaj malbrila (*ground*) vitro, estas 365 gramoj. "La Infaneto" estas konstruita tute el metalo, kaj kovrita de bonega bovledo. Kiam oni malfermas la aparaton, la objektivo samtempe enfokusiĝas, tiamaniere ke la kamero estas preta por uzado post unu sekundo, ĉar la objektivfermilo (*shutter*) estas ĉiam streĉita. Sekve: neniaj preparadoj, nenia prokrasto je la ekfotografado.

La negativoj estas klaraj ĝis la bordo, kaj tial konvenaj por pligrandigo. Cetere, oni scias ke bona pligrandigo ofte pli kontentigas ol malgranda originalo. Precipe ĉe promenoj kaj vojaĝoj oni tial volonte preferas la malgrandan "Infaneton," por poste pligrandigi la negativojn.

Por la pligrandigo ni fabrikas specialajn taglum-pligrandigajn aparatojn, kies prezoj estas malaltaj (vidu en nia prezaro).

Ni ne ŝanĝis la konstruon de "La Infaneto" de post 1909, ĉar ĝis nun ĝi estas ĉiurilate kontentiga. Sole la rapideca reguligo de la momenta (*instantaneous*) fermilo estas plibonigita, ĉar ni ĝin fabrikas kun speciala aŭtomata fermilo, kiu estas aranĝita por malfermoj daŭraj (*time exposures*), kaj momentaj, je unu sekundo ĝis unu centono da sekundo.

Esperante ke ni baldaŭ ricevos mendon de vi, kaj certigante al vi ke ni tre zorge plenumos iun ajn mendon, ni restas.

Tre respekte la viaj,
Brown & Ko.
Per C.

ESPERANTO-ENGLISH VOCABULARY.

The following vocabulary includes all roots used in the preceding Lessons, all primary words of the language, and a large number of additional roots (to facilitate original composition). No attempt has been made, however, to include all of the roots in the language, for which an Esperanto-English Dictionary should be consulted.

References are to sections, unless the page (p.) is given. For other parts of speech than those indicated under each root or primary word, see Word Formation, **116**, **120**, **159**, **171**. See also the references given under each prefix and suffix. For formation of compound words, see **160**, **167**, **176**, **184**. The following abbreviations are used: adj. = adjective; adv. = adverb; conj. = conjunction; intrans. = intransitive; prep. = preposition; trans. = transitive; — = repetition of the word.

A.

abel-o, bee.
abi-o, fir.
abiturient-o, bachelor of arts (A.B.).
abomen-a, abominable.
abon-i, to subscribe to, take (magazine, etc.).
abrikot-o, apricot.
acer-o, maple (tree).
acid-a, acid, sour.
-aĉ-, *derogatory suffix* (**272**).
aĉet-i, to buy.
-ad-, *suffix indicating duration* (**218**).
adiaŭ, (*adv. and interjection*), farewell, good-bye (**171**, **273**).
adjektiv-o, adjective.
administr-i, to administer, to manage.
admir-i, to admire.
admon-i, to exhort, admonish.
ador-i, to worship, adore.
adres-o, address (on letters, etc.).
adverb-o, adverb.
advokat-o, lawyer, barrister.
aer-o, air.
afabl-a, affable, amiable.
afer-o, affair, matter, thing, cause.
afiŝ-o, handbill, placard, poster.

afrank-i, to frank (letters), prepay; —**ite**, post-paid.
Afrik-o, Africa.
ag-i, to act, perform action.
agac-i, to set on edge (of teeth).
agent-o, agent.
agit-i, to agitate.
agl-o, eagle.
agoni-o, agony.
agrabl-a, agreeable, pleasant.
aĝ-o, age.
ajn (*adv.*), ever (**236**).
-aĵ-, *suffix forming concrete words* (**227**).
akademi-o, academy.
akcel-i (*trans.*), to accelerate, hasten.
akcent-o, accent, stress.
akcept-i, to accept, receive, welcome.
akcident-o, accident.
akir-i, to acquire.
akompan-i, to accompany.
akr-a, sharp, acute, shrill.
akrid-o, grasshopper.
aks-o, axis, axle.
akt-o, act (of a play).
aktiv-a, active (grammatical).
aktor-o, actor (player).
akurat-a, accurate, exact.
akuz-i, to accuse.
akuzativ-o, accusative.
akv-o, water.
akvarel-o, water-color painting.
akvari-o, aquarium.
al (*prep.*), to, toward (**46, 160, 251, 252**).
alaŭd-o, lark (bird).
ale-o, avenue, walk, path (of garden, park, etc.).
Aleksandri-o, Alexandria.
Aleksandr-o, Alexander.
alfabet-o, alphabet.
Alfred-o, Alfred.
algebr-o, algebra.
ali-a, other.
alk-o, elk.
alkohol-o, alcohol.
alkov-o, alcove, recess.
almanak-o, almanac.
almenaŭ, (*adv.*), at least (**66**).
almoz-o, alms; —**ulo**, beggar.

alt-a, high, tall.
altar-o, altar.
alud-i, to allude to.
alumet-o, match (for fire).
am-i, to love.
amas-o, crowd, throng, mass.
ambaŭ (*pronoun*), both (of two objects naturally in pairs, or of persons or things assumed or already known to be thus grouped) (**238**).
ambos-o, anvil.
amel-o, starch.
Amerik-o, America.
amfibi-a, amphibious.
amfiteatr-o, amphitheatre.
amik-o, friend.
amindum-i, to woo, make love.
ampleks-o, extent, dimension.
amuz-i, to amuse.
-an-, *suffix denoting membership, etc.* (**145**).
analiz-i, to analyse.
ananas-o, pineapple.
anas-o, duck.
anekdot-o, anecdote.
Angl-o, Englishman.
angul-o, angle, corner.
anĝel-o, angel.
anim-o, soul.
ankaŭ (*adv.*), also.
ankoraŭ (*adv*), still, yet.
ankr-o, anchor.
anonc-i, to announce.
ans-o, latch, door-handle.
anser-o, goose.
anstataŭ (*prep.*), instead of (**98, 159**).
antaŭ (*prep.*), before (**89, 90, 120, 159, 160**), **antaŭ ol** (*conj.*), **97, 98**.
antikv-a, ancient, antique.
antilop-o, antelope.
antipati-o, antipathy.
aparat-o, apparatus.
apart-a, separate.
apartament-o, apartment, suite (of rooms).
aparten-i, to belong.
apati-o, apathy.
apenaŭ (*adv.*), scarcely, hardly.
aper-i, to appear.
apetit-o, appetite.
aplaŭd-i, to applaud.

aplomb-o, assurance, self-command.
apog-i, to lean, to rest (upon).
apologi-o, apology, vindication.
apotek-o, pharmacy, drugstore, chemist's shop.
april-o, April.
aprob-i, to approve.
apud (*prep.*), near to, close by (**120, 159**).
-ar-, *suffix forming collectives* (**126**).
Arab-o, Arab.
arane-o, spider.
aranĝ-i, to arrange.
arb-o, tree.
arbitraci-i, to arbitrate.
ardez-o, slate (stone).
aren-o, arena.
arest-i, to arrest.
argil-o, clay.
argument-i, to argue.
arĝent-o, silver (metal).
arĥitektur-o, architecture.
Arĥimed-o, Archimedes.
ari-o, tune, air (music).
Aristejd-o, Aristeides.
aristokrat-o, aristocrat.
Aristotel-o, Aristotle.
aritmetik-o, arithmetic.
ark-o, arc.
arkad-o, arcade.
arm-i, to arm.
arme-o, army.
armoraci-o, horse-radish.
arogant-a, arrogant.
arom-o, aroma, fragrance.
art-o, art.
artik-o, joint.
artikol-o, article (grammatical or literary).
Artur-o, Arthur.
asekur-i, to insure (with a company).
asoci-o, association (organization).
asparag-o, asparagus.
aspekt-o, aspect, appearance.
astr-o, heavenly body, star.
atak-i, to attack.
atend-i, to wait, wait for, expect.
atent-a, attentive.
atest-i, to attest, give witness, certify.

ating-i, to attain, reach.
atlas-o, satin.
atlet-o, athlete.
atmosfer-o, atmosphere.
atribut-o, attribute.
aŭ (*conj.*), or, either.
aŭd-i, to hear.
aŭgust-o, August.
aŭskult-i, to listen.
Aŭstrali-o, Australia.
aŭtomat-a, automatic.
aŭtor-o, author.
aŭtun-o, autumn.
av-o, grandfather.
avar-a, avaricious, miserly.
avel-o, hazel-nut.
aven-o, oats.
avert-i, to warn, caution.
avid-a, eager.
aviz-i, to give notice.
azen-o, ass, donkey.
Azi-o, Asia.
azot-o, nitrogen.

B.

babil-i, to chatter, babble.
bagatel-o, trifle, bagatelle.
bal-o, ball (dance).
bak-i, to bake.
bala-i, to sweep (a floor, etc.).
balanc-i (*trans.*), to balance, poise; **—i la kapon**, to nod the head.
baldaŭ (*adv.*), soon.
balen-o, whale.
ban-i (*trans.*), to bathe.
banan-o, banana.
bandaĝ-i, to bandage.
bank-o, bank (financial).
bankrot-i, to become bankrupt, fail.
bant-o, bow (of ribbon).
bar-i (*trans.*), to bar, to obstruct.
barakt-i, to wrestle, struggle.
barb-o, beard.
barbar-o, barbarian.
barel-o, barrel.
bariton-o, barytone.
bas-o, bass (voice).

baston-o, stick.
bat-i, to beat.
batal-i, to fight, battle.
batat-o, sweet potato.
bedaŭr-i, to regret.
bek-o, beak, bill.
bel-a, beautiful, handsome.
belg-o, Belgian.
ben-i, to bless.
benk-o, bench.
ber-o, berry.
best-o, animal, beast.
bet-o, beet.
bezon-i, to need, want.
bibliotek-o, library.
bicikl-o, bicycle.
bien-o, land, property, estate.
bier-o, beer.
bifstek-o, beefsteak.
bild-o, picture, image.
bilet-o, ticket, note; **bank—**, bank-note, bill.
bird-o, bird.
bis (*adv.*), once more, a second time, encore.
biskvit-o, biscuit.
blank-a, white.
blek-i, to neigh, bleat, give its cry (of any animal).
blind-a, blind.
blov-i, to blow.
blu-a, blue (color).
bluz-o, blouse.
bo-, *prefix expressing relationship by marriage* (**277**).
boat-o, boat.
boj-i, to bark (of dogs).
bol-i (*intrans.*), to boil.
bombon-o, bonbon, sweet.
bon-a, good; **—veni**, to welcome.
bor-i, to bore (holes).
bord-o, shore, bank, edge (of rivers, etc.).
Boston-o, Boston.
bot-o, boot.
botel-o, bottle.
bov-o, ox; **—aĵo**, beef; **—idaĵo**, veal; **—viro**, bull.
brak-o, arm (of the body).
branĉ-o, branch, bough.
brand-o, brandy.
brasik-o, cabbage; **florbrasiko**, cauliflower.

brav-a, brave.
bret-o, shelf, bracket.
brid-o, bridle (of harness).
brik-o, brick, tile.
bril-i, to shine (**116**).
Brit-o, Briton.
brod-i, to embroider.
bronz-o, bronze.
bros-i, to brush.
broŝur-o, pamphlet, brochure.
brov-o, eyebrow.
bru-o, noise.
brul-i (*intrans.*), to burn (**275**).
brun-a, brown.
brut-o, cattle, dumb animal.
bub-o, street arab, gamin.
buĉ-i, to slaughter, butcher.
buf-o, toad.
buk-o, buckle (metal).
buked-o, bouquet.
bukl-o, curl, ringlet (of hair).
bulb-o, onion, bulb.
bulgar-o, Bulgarian.
bulk-o, roll (bread).
bulvard-o, boulevard.
burĝon-o, bud, young shoot.
buŝ-o, mouth.
buter-o, butter.
butik-o, shop, store.
buton-o, button.

C.

cel-i, to aim, have as purpose or goal.
celeri-o, celery.
cend-o, cent (coin).
cent, hundred (**142**).
centigram-o, centigram (**284**).
centilitr-o, centiliter (**284**).
centimetr-o, centimeter (**284**).
centr-o, center.
cerb-o, brain.
cert-a, certain, sure.
cerv-o, stag, deer.
ceter-a, remaining.
ci (*pronoun*), thou (**40**).
cidoni-o, quince.

cifer-o, cipher.
cigar-o, cigar.
cigared-o, cigarette.
cign-o, swan.
cilindr-o, cylinder.
cinam-o, cinnamon.
cindr-o, ashes.
cir-o, blacking (for shoes).
cirkonstanc-o, circumstance.
cirkuler-o, circular (letter).
Cirus-o, Cyrus.
cit-i, to quote.
citron-o, lemon.
civiliz-i, to civilize.
col-o, inch (measure).

Ĉ.

ĉagren-i (*trans.*), to grieve, vex, annoy.
ĉambr-o, room.
ĉap-o, cap.
ĉapel-o, hat.
ĉapitr-o, chapter (of book).
ĉar (*conj.*), because, since (**83**).
ĉarm-a, charming, delightful.
ĉarnir-o, hinge.
ĉas-i, to hunt (game or wild animals).
ĉe (*prep.*), at, in the house or presence of (**125, 160**).
ĉef-a, chief, principal, head.
ĉek-o, cheque.
ĉemiz-o, shirt, chemise.
ĉen-o, chain (for watch, etc.).
ĉeriz-o, cherry.
ĉes-i (*intrans.*), to cease, leave off (**275**).
ĉeval-o, horse; — **viro**, stallion.
ĉi (*adv.*), *expresses proximity* (**60, 66**).
ĉia, of every kind (**177**).
ĉial (*adv.*), for every reason (**188**).
ĉiam (*adv.*), always (**187**).
ĉie (*adv.*), everywhere (**182**).
ĉiel (*adv.*), in every way (**193**).
ĉiel-o, heaven, sky.
ĉies (*pronoun, possessive*), everybody's (**174**).
ĉifon-o, rag.
ĉio (*pronoun*), everything, all (**233**).
ĉiom (*adv.*), all (**194**).
ĉirkaŭ (*prep.*), around, roundabout (**89, 120, 159, 160**).

ĉiu (*pronoun and adj.*), every one, each (**173**).

-ĉj-, *suffix forming affectionate diminutives* (**283**).

ĉokolad-o, chocolate.

ĉu (*adv.*), whether (*when translated*) (**30, 66**).

D.

da (*prep.*), of (*after quantitative noun or adv.*) (**99, 101, 103**).

daktil-o, date (fruit).

Damokl-o, Damocles.

dan-o, Dane.

danc-i, to dance.

danĝer-o, danger.

dank-i, to thank.

dat-o, date (chronological).

daŭr-i (*intrans.*), to continue, last.

de (*prep.*), of, from, by (49, 89, l00, 160, 169, 170).

dec-i, to be proper, decent; **ne decas ke vi iru**, it is not proper for you to go.

decembr-o, December.

decid-i, to decide.

decigram-o, decigram (**284**).

decilitr-o, deciliter (**284**).

decimetr-o, decimeter (**284**).

defend-i, to defend.

degel-i (*intrans.*), to thaw (**275**).

deĵor-i, to be on duty (of officer, attendant, etc.).

dek (*adj.*), ten (**136**).

dekagram-o, dekagram (**284**).

dekalitr-o, dekaliter (**284**).

dekametr-o, dekameter (**284**).

deklam-i, to declaim, recite.

dekstr-a, right (not left).

deleg-i, to delegate.

delikat-a, delicate, dainty, nice.

demand-i, to ask, inquire.

dens-a, dense, thick, close.

dent-o, tooth.

depeŝ-o, a dispatch.

des (*adv.*), the more (*used with* pli, 84).

desert-o, dessert.

detal-o, detail.

detru-i, to destroy.

dev-i, to have to, must (**247**).

dezert-o, desert, waste.

dezir-i, to desire.

Di-o, God.

diamant-o, diamond.

difekt-i, to damage, spoil.
diferenc-a, different.
difin-i, to define, to destine.
dik-a, thick, corpulent.
dikt-i, to dictate (letters, etc.)
diligent-a, diligent.
dimanĉ-o, Sunday.
dimensi-o, dimension.
Diogen-o, Diogenes.
diplom-o, diploma.
diplomat-o, diplomat.
dir-i, to say (**77**).
direkt-i, to direct, guide, manage.
dis-, *prefix expressing separation* (**245**).
diskut-i, to discuss.
distanc-o, distance.
disting-i, to distinguish.
distr-i, to distract, take away the attention.
diven-i, to guess.
divers-a, varied, diverse, different.
divid-i (*trans.*), to divide.
do, consequently, then, so.
doktor-o, doctor.
dolar-o, dollar.
dolĉ-a, sweet, pleasant.
dolor-o, pain, ache.
dom-o, house.
domaĝ-o, pity, regrettable affair.
don-i, to give.
donac-i, to make a gift, present.
dorlot-i, to caress, fondle, pet.
dorm-i, to sleep.
dorn-o, thorn.
dors-o, back (of the body).
dot-i, to endow.
drap-o, cloth.
drog-o, drug.
dron-i (*intrans.*), to drown (**275**).
du (*adj.*), two (**136**)
dub-i, to doubt.
dum (*prep and conj.*), during, while (**96, 120, 159**).
dung-i (*trans.*), to hire (persons).

E.

eben-a, even, flat, level.
-ebl-, *suffix expressing possibility* (**161, 162**).

ebri-a, inebriate, intoxicated.
-ec-, *suffix forming abstracts* (**202**).
eĉ (*adv.*), even.
eduk-i, to bring up, educate.
edz-o, husband, married man.
efekt-o, effect.
efektiv-a, real, actual.
efik-i, to be efficacious, act (on), produce a result.
-eg-, *suffix forming augmentatives* (**122**).
egal-a, equal.
Egipt-o, Egypt.
eĥ-o, echo.
-ej-, *suffix forming words indicating place* (**III**).
ek-, *prefix expressing suddenness or beginning* (**206**).
eks-, *prefix expressing former incumbency* (**281**).
ekscit-i, to excite.
eksperiment-i, to experiment.
eksplod-i (*intrans.*), to explode.
ekster (*prep.*), outside of (**120, 121**).
ekzamen-i, to examine, test.
ekzempl-o, example.
ekzempler-o, copy (of book or magazine).
ekzerc-i (*trans.*), to exercise.
ekzil-i, to exile, banish
ekzist-i, to exist.
el (*prep.*), out of, of, out (75, 106, 138, 197, 264, c).
elekt-i, to choose.
elektr-a, electric.
elokvent-a, eloquent.
-em-, *suffix expressing propensity or inclination* (**192**).
eminent-a, eminent.
en (*prep.*), in (**89,160**), into (**46**).
energi-o, energy.
entrepren-i, to undertake.
entuziasm-o, enthusiasm.
enu-i, to be wearied, be bored.
envi-i, to envy.
epok-o, epoch, period, time.
-er-, *suffix expressing a component part* (**276**).
erar-i, to err, make a mistake.
escept-i, to except (**266**).
esper-i, to hope.
esplor-i, to investigate, explore.
esprim-i, to express.
est-i, to be (**109**).
establ-i, to establish.

estim-i, to esteem.
esting-i, to extinguish.
-estr-, *suffix expressing leadership or authority* (**253**).
-et-, *suffix forming diminutives* (**198**).
etaĝ-o, story (of a house); teretaĝo, ground floor; unua etaĝo, second story.
etend-i (*trans.*), to extend, lengthen, widen.
etern-a, eternal.
Eŭrop-o, Europe.
evangeli-o, gospel, evangel.
evit-i, to avoid, shun.
evoluci-o, evolution.

F.

fab-o, bean (leguminous fruit).
fabel-o, story, tale.
fabl-o, fable.
fabrik-i, to manufacture.
facil-a, easy.
faden-o, thread.
fajf-i, to whistle.
fajr-o, fire.
fak-o, department, specialty.
fakt-o, fact.
fal-i, to fall.
fald-i, to fold.
fals-i, to falsify, forge, debase.
fam-o, fame, renown, rumor.
famili-o, family.
familiar-a, familiar, accustomed.
fand-i (*trans.*), to smelt, fuse (metals, etc.).
fanfaron-i, to boast, vaunt oneself, brag.
fantom-o, phantom, ghost.
far-i, to make, do, render.
faraon-o, pharaoh (Egyptian ruler).
farm-i, to farm (as a tenant).
farmaci-o, pharmacy (knowledge of the use of drugs).
fart-i, to be in (good or bad) health.
farun-o, flour.
fask-o, bundle, bunch.
fason-o, cut, mode, fashion.
fatal-a, fatal, predestined.
faŭk-o, jaw (literal and figurative).
favor-a, favorable.
fazeol-o, bean (garden bean).
fe-o, fairy, fay; —ino, fairy.
febr-o, fever.

februar-o, February.
fel-o, skin, hide (of animals).
feliĉ-a, happy.
femur-o, thigh.
fend-i (*trans.*), to split.
fenestr-o, window.
fer-o, iron; —**vojo**, railway.
ferdek-o, deck (of ship).
ferm-i (*trans.*), to close, shut.
fervor-o, zeal, fervor.
fest-i, to celebrate.
festen-o, banquet.
fi (*interjection*), fie! (**273**).
fiakr-o, cab.
fianĉ-o, betrothed man, fiance.
fid-i, to rely upon, trust.
fidel-a, faithful, loyal.
fier-a, proud, haughty.
fil-o, son.
filozof-o, philosopher.
fin-i (*trans.*), to finish, end.
fingr-o, finger; **dika fingro**, thumb; **montra fingro**, index finger; **longa fingro**, middle finger; **ringa fingro**, ring-finger; **malgranda fingro**, little finger.
firm-a, firm, steady.
fiŝ-o, fish.
fizik-o, physics, physical science.
flag-o, flag, banner, small standard.
flank-o, side.
flar-i (*trans.*), to smell, scent.
flav-a, yellow.
fleks-i (*trans.*), to bend, flex.
flik-i, to patch.
flor-o, flower (**116**).
flu-i, to flow.
flug-i, to fly.
fluid-a, fluid, liquid.
foj-o, time, occasion (**127**).
fojn-o, hay.
fokus-o, focus.
foli-o, leaf.
fond-i, to found, establish.
font-o, spring (of water), fount.
fontan-o, fountain (artificial).
for (*adv.*), away (**71**).
forges-i, to forget.
fork-o, fork.

form-o, shape, form.
formik-o, ant.
forn-o, stove.
fort-a, strong.
fos-i, to dig.
fotograf-i, to photograph
frag-o, strawberry.
frak-o, evening dress (for men).
frakas-i, to shatter, break to pieces.
framb-o, raspberry.
franc-o, Frenchman.
frand-i, to be fond of sweets, be an epicure.
franĝ-o, fringe.
frap-i, to knock, strike.
frat-o, brother.
fraŭl-o, bachelor, unmarried man.
fraz-o, sentence, phrase.
Frederik-o, Frederick.
fremd-a, foreign.
frenez-a, crazy, mad.
freŝ-a, fresh, new.
fripon-o, rogue, rascal, knave.
frit-i (*trans.*), to fry.
fromaĝ-o, cheese.
frost-o, frost.
frot-i, to rub.
fru-a, early.
frukt-o, fruit.
frunt-o, forehead.
fulm-o, lightning.
fum-i, to smoke.
fund-o, bottom.
fundament-o, foundation, base.
funebr-o, mourning.
fung-o, mushroom.
funkci-i, to function, work.
funt-o, pound.
furioz-a, furious, raging.
fuŝ-i, to bungle.
fut-o, foot (measure).

G.

gaj-a, gay, merry.
gajn-i, to gain.
galeri-o, gallery.
galop-i, to gallop.

gant-o, glove.
gard-i, to guard, watch over.
gas-o, gas.
gast-o, guest.
gazet-o, gazette, magazine.
ge-, *prefix indicating both sexes together* (**271**).
general-o, general (military).
genu-o, knee; —**fleksi**, to kneel.
geometri-o, geometry.
german-o, German.
Gertrud-o, Gertrude.
giĉet-o, wicket, ticket-window, turnstile.
girland-o, garland, wreath.
glaci-o, ice; —**aĵo**, an ice (food).
glad-i, to iron (linen, etc.).
glas-o, tumbler, glass.
glat-a, smooth, polished, flat.
glav-o, sword.
glit-i, to glide, slide.
glob-o, globe.
glor-o, glory.
glu-o, glue.
glut-i, to swallow.
gorĝ-o, throat.
graci-a, graceful.
grad-o, grade, degree.
graf-o, count; —**lando**, county.
gram-o, gram (**284**).
gramatik-o, grammar.
grand-a, great, large, big.
gras-o, fat.
gratul-i, to congratulate.
grav-a, important, serious, grave.
gravit-i, to gravitate.
grek-o, Greek.
gren-o, grain (wheat, corn, etc.).
grimp-i, to climb up, creep up.
grinc-i, to grind, gnash.
griz-a, gray.
grup-o, group.
gurd-o, hurdy-gurdy, barrel organ.
gust-o, taste.
gut-i, to drip.
gvid-i, to guide.

Ĝ.

ĝarden-o, garden.
ĝem-i, to groan.
ĝen-i, to disturb, incommode.
ĝeneral-a, general, common.
ĝentil-a, courteous, polite.
ĝi (*pronoun*), it (**32, 37, 42, 274**).
ĝis (*prep.*), as far as, until (**46, 89**).
ĝoj-i, to rejoice, be glad (**116**).
ĝu-i, to enjoy, find pleasure in.
ĝust-a, exact, just.

H.

hajl-o, hail (frozen rain).
hak-i, to chop, hack; —ilo, axe.
halt-i (*intrans.*), to halt, stop.
har-o, a hair.
haŭt-o, skin (human).
hav-i, to have.
haven-o, harbor, port.
hazard-o, chance, hazard.
hebre-o, Hebrew.
hejm-o, home.
hejt-i (*trans.*), to heat (a place).
hektar-o, hektare (**284**).
hektogram-o, hektogram (**284**).
hektolitr-o, hektoliter (**284**).
hektometr-o, hektometer (**284**).
hel-a, bright, clear.
help-i, to help, aid, assist.
herb-o, grass, herb.
hero-o, hero.
hezit-i, to hesitate.
hieraŭ (*adv.*), yesterday (**93, 171**).
Hieron-o, Hiero.
hipokrit-i, to play the hypocrite.
hirund-o, swallow (bird).
hispan-o, Spaniard.
histori-o, history.
ho (*interjection*), ho, oh (**273**).
hodiaŭ (*adv.*), today (**93, 171**).
Holand-o, Holland.
hom-o, human being.
honest-a, honest.
honor-i, to honor.
hont-i, to be ashamed.
hor-o, hour (**185**).

horizont-o, horizon.
horizontal-a, horizontal.
horloĝ-o, clock; poŝhorloĝo, watch.
hotel-o, hotel.
humil-a, humble.
humor-o, humor, temper.
hund-o, dog.
hura! (*interjection*), hurrah!

Ĥ.

ĥemi-o, chemistry.
ĥin-o, Chinaman.
ĥor-o, choir.

I.

ia, any kind of (**208**).
ial (*adv.*), for any reason (**213**).
iam (*adv.*), ever, at any time, once (**212**).
-id-, *suffix indicating descendant or young of* (**207**).
ide-o, idea.
ideal-o, ideal.
ident-a, identical.
idiom-o, idiom.
idiot-o, idiot.
ie (*adv.*), somewhere (**209**).
iel (*adv.*), somehow (**216**).
ies (*pronoun, possessive*), somebody's (**204**).
-ig-, *suffix forming causative verbs* (**214, 239, 275**).
ignor-i, to ignore.
-iĝ-, *suffix forming inchoative and intransitive verbs* (**232, 239, 279**).
-il-, *suffix forming names of instruments* (**63**).
ili (*pronoun*), they (**32, 37, 42**).
ilustr-i, to illustrate.
iluzi-o, illusion, delusion.
imag-i, to imagine, fancy.
imit-i, to imitate.
imperi-o, empire.
implik-i, to implicate.
impost-o, tax, impost.
impres-i, to impress.
impuls-o, impulse.
-in-, *suffix forming feminines* (**59**).
incit-i, to incite, arouse, provoke.
-ind-, *suffix expressing worth or merit* (**154**).
indian-o, Indian (American).

indiferent-a, indifferent, unconcerned, unimportant.
industri-o, industry (trade, business).
infan-o, child.
infekt-i, to infect, contaminate.
influ-i, to influence.
inform-i, to give information.
-ing-, *suffix expressing a holder or container* (**237**).
inĝenier-o, engineer.
ink-o, ink.
insekt-o, insect.
insist-i, to insist.
inspir-i, to inspire.
instru-i, to instruct, teach.
insul-o, island.
insult-i, to insult.
inteligent-a, intelligent.
intend-i, to intend.
inter (*prep.*), between, among (**85, 89, 160**).
interes-i (*trans.*), to interest.
intermit-i, to be intermittent.
intern-a, internal; — **e**, inside.
interpret-i, to interpret.
intim-a, intimate.
invit-i, to invite.
io (*pronoun*), something (**233**).
iom (*adv.*), some, a certain amount; iom post iom, little by little (**217**).
ir-i, to go.
-ist-, *suffix indicating profession, etc.* (**172**).
ital-o, Italian.
iu (*pronoun*), some one, a certain (one) (**203**).

J.

ja (*adv.*), indeed, in fact (**215**).
jak-o, jacket, short coat.
jam (*adv.*), already.
januar-o, January.
jar-o, year.
je, *prep. of indefinite meaning* (**89, 185, 260**).
jen (*adv.*), there, behold (**228**).
jes (*adv.*), yes (**171**).
Jesu-o, Jesus.
Johano, John.
ju (*adv.*), the more (*used with* pli, 84).
jug-o, yoke.
juĝ-i, to judge.
juli-o, July.

jun-a, young.
jung-i, to harness.
juni-o, June.
jup-o, skirt.
jurist-o, jurist.
just-a, just, upright.
juvel-o, jewel.

Ĵ.

ĵaluz-a, jealous.
ĵaŭd-o, Thursday.
ĵet-i, to throw, cast, hurl.
ĵongl-i, to juggle.
ĵur-i, to take oath, swear.
ĵurnal-o, newspaper, journal.
ĵus (*adv.*), a moment before, just.

K.

kadavr-o, corpse.
kadr-o, frame (of pictures).
kaduk-a, decaying, in ruin.
kaf-o, coffee.
kaĝ-o, cage.
kahel-o, tile (for paving).
kaj (*conj.*), and; kaj..kaj.., both..and.. (**26**).
kajer-o, notebook.
kaldron-o, caldron.
kalendar-o, calendar.
kaleŝ-o, carriage.
kalkan-o, heel (of the foot); —**umo**, heel of a shoe.
kalkul-i, to calculate, reckon.
kamel-o, camel.
kamen-o, chimney.
kamer-o, camera.
kamp-o, field.
kanajl-o, scoundrel, rascal.
kanap-o, sofa.
kand-o, candy.
kandel-o, candle.
kanot-o, canoe.
kant-i, to sing.
kap-o, head.
kapabl-a, capable.
kapel-o, chapel (for prayer).
kapital-o, capital (money).

kapitol-o, capitol.
kapt-i, to catch, seize.
kar-a, dear, prized.
karakter-o, character.
karb-o, coal.
karcer-o, jail.
kares-i, to caress.
karn-o, flesh.
karot-o, carrot.
kart-o, card; poŝtkarto, postcard; vizitkarto, visiting card.
karton-o, pasteboard.
karusel-o, merry-go-round.
kas-o, money-box, treasury; —**isto**, cashier, treasurer.
kaskad-o, waterfall, cascade.
kastel-o, castle.
kaŝ-i, to hide, conceal (**252**).
kaŝtan-o, chestnut.
kat-o, cat.
katen-o, fetter, chain.
kaŭz-o, cause.
kav-o, cavity, hole.
kaz-o, case (grammatical).
ke (*conj.*), that (**53, 83, 105, 259, 262**).
kel-o, cellar.
kelk-a, some; —**aj**, several, more than one or two.
kelner-o, waiter (in hotel or restaurant).
kest-o, chest; tirkesto, drawer.
kia, what kind of (**112, 150**); kiamanier-e, how.
kial (*adv.*), why (**129**).
kiam (*adv.*), when (**123, 155**).
kie (*adv.*), where (**118, 151**).
kiel (*adv.*), how, in which way, as (**134, 156**).
kies (*pronoun, possessive*), whose (**107, 147**).
kilogram-o, kilogram (**284**).
kilolitr-o, kiloliter (**284**).
kilometr-o, kilometer (**284**).
kio (*pronoun*), what (**233**).
kiom (*adv.*), how much (**140, 164, 185**).
kis-i, to kiss.
kiu (*pronoun*), who (**106, 146**).
klak-i (*trans.*), to clap, clatter.
klar-a, clear, distinct.
klav-o, key (of piano, etc.).
klas-o, class.
kler-a, enlightened, well-in-formed.
klimat-o, climate.

klin-i (*trans.*), to incline, bend.

kling-o, blade (of knife, etc.).

klopod-i, to undertake initiative work, take steps toward, labor for the success or completion of something.

klub-o, club (organization)

knab-o, boy.

kobold-o, sprite, kobold, brownie.

kofr-o, trunk, chest with a lid.

kok-o, cock (domestic fowl).

koket-a, coquettish.

koks-o, hip.

kol-o, neck.

kolbas-o, sausage.

kolegi-o, college.

kolekt-i (trans.), to collect, gather.

koler-i, to be angry, lose the temper.

kolomb-o, pigeon, dove.

kolon-o, column, pillar.

kolonel-o, colonel.

kolor-o, color.

kolport-i, to peddle.

komand-i, to command (military and naval).

komb-i, to comb.

komedi-o, comedy.

komenc-i (trans.), to begin, commence.

komerc-i, to trade, engage in commerce.

komfort-o, comfort (freedom from pain, want, etc.).

komisi-i, to entrust with, put in charge of, give the agency for.

komitat-o, committee.

komiz-o, clerk, employee, assistant.

kompani-o, company (commercial organization).

kompar-i, (*trans.*) to compare, (**266**).

kompat-i, to pity, have compassion for.

komplet-o, suit (of clothes).

komplez-o, kindness, courtesy, disposition to oblige.

komplik-i, to complicate.

kompost-i, to compose, set (type); —**isto**, compositor.

kompot-o, jam, preserve,

kompren-i, to understand.

komun-a, common, mutual.

komunik-i, to communicate.

kon-i, to be acquainted with, know; —**atiĝi kun**, to become acquainted with (**117**).

koncern-i, to concern (**266**).

koncert-o, concert (musical).

kondamn-i, to condemn.

kondiĉ-o, terms specified, stipulation, condition.
konduk-i, to conduct, lead.
konduktor-o, conductor (of car, train, etc.).
kondut-i, to behave, conduct oneself.
konfes-i, to confess, admit.
konfid-i, to trust, have confidence in.
konfit-i, to preserve, pickle (fruits, etc.).
konform-i, to be in conformity with (**266**).
konfuz-i, to confuse, confound.
kongres-o, congress (assembly).
konk-o, shell (of mollusk, etc.).
konkur-i, to vie, compete.
konkurenc-o, competition (in business, etc.).
konkurs-o, prearranged trial of skill, formal competition (for prizes, etc.).
konsci-i, to be conscious.
konscienc-o, conscience.
konsent-i, to consent, agree.
konserv-i, to keep, preserve, save.
konservativ-a, conservative.
konsil-i, to advise, counsel.
konsist-i, to consist.
konsol-i, to console, comfort.
konsonant-o, consonant.
konspir-i, to conspire, plot.
konstant-a, constant.
konstat-i, to verify, ascertain the truth of, certify.
konstituci-o, constitution.
konstru-i, to build.
konsul-o, consul.
konsult-i, to seek advice of, consult.
kont-o, account (book-keeping, commercial).
kontent-a, content, satisfied.
kontinent-o, continent (geographical).
kontrakt-i, to contract, agree.
kontralt-o, contralto.
kontraŭ (*prep.*), against, opposite, opposed to (**159, 160**).
kontrol-i, to control, inspect, examine and check.
kontur-o, outline, contour.
kontuz-i, to bruise.
konven-i, to be suitable, be fitting or convenient.
konvink-i, to convince, persuade.
kopi-i, to copy.
kor-o, heart (of the body).
korb-o, basket.
korekt-i, to correct.
korespond-i, to exchange letters, correspond.

koridor-o, corridor, passage.
kork-o, cork (bark).
korn-o, horn.
korp-o, body, —**a**, corporeal.
korpus-o, corps (military).
kort-o, courtyard, court.
kortego, court (royal, etc.).
korv-o, raven.
kost-i, to cost.
kostum-o, costume.
kot-o, mud.
kotiz-i, to pay dues, pay one's share of an assessment.
kotlet-o, cutlet, chop.
koton-o, cotton.
kov-i, to brood (of birds).
kovert-o, envelope
kovr-i, to cover.
krab-o, crab.
krad-o, grating, grate, lattice.
krajon-o, pencil.
krak-i, to clack, crackle.
kran-o, faucet, tap.
kravat-o, cravat.
kre-i, to create.
kred-i, to believe (**265**).
krem-o, cream.
krepusk-o, twilight, half-light of dawn or evening.
kresk-i, to grow.
krestomati-o, chrestomathy, collection of selected passages.
kret-o, chalk.
krev-i (*intrans.*), to burst, crack open (suddenly and with noise).
kri-i, to cry out.
kribr-i, to sift (with a sieve).
krim-o, crime.
kring-o, ring-shaped biscuit.
kripl-a, crippled.
Krist-o, Christ.
kritik-i, to criticise.
kroĉ-i, to hook.
krom (*prep.*), beside, aside from, except, save, but.
kron-o, crown.
kruc-o, cross; —**umi**, to crucify.
kruĉ-o, pitcher, jug; **tekruĉo**, tea-pot.
kruel-a, cruel.
krur-o, leg.
krust-o, crust.

krut-a, steep.
kubut-o, elbow.
kudr-i, to sew.
kugl-o, bullet.
kuir-i, to cook.
kuk-o, cake; —**aĵo**, pastry.
kukum-o, cucumber.
kukurb-o, pumpkin.
kuler-o, spoon.
kulp-a, guilty.
kultur-i, to cultivate; terkulturi, to till the soil, farm.
kun (*prep.*), with (**70, 76, 120, 160, 159**).
kunikl-o, rabbit.
kupon-o, coupon.
kupr-o, copper (metal).
kur-i, to run.
kurac-i, to treat for illness, cure; —**ato**, a patient; —**isto**, a physician, medical man.
kuraĝ-o, courage.
kurb-o, curve.
kurioz-a, uncommon, curious.
kurs-o, course (of lessons).
kurten-o, curtain.
kusen-o, cushion.
kuŝ-i, to lie, recline (**239**).
kutim-o, custom, habit.
kuv-o, tub, large basin.
kuz-o, cousin.
kvadrat-o, square (equilateral rectangle).
kvalit-o, quality, texture.
kvankam (*conj.*), though, although, while (concessive).
kvant-o, quantity, amount.
kvar, (*adj.*), four (**136**).
kvartal-o, quarter (of a city).
kvazaŭ (*conj.*), as though, as if (**250**).
kverk-o, oak.
kviet-a, calm, quiet.
kvin, (*adj.*), five (**136**).
kvitanc-o, receipt (for payment).

L.

la (article), the (**II, 47, 201, 280, a**).
labor-i, to work, labor.
lac-a, tired, weary.
laĉ-o, string, lace (of shoe, etc.).
lad-o, tin plate (sheet iron covered with tin).

lag-o, lake.
lakt-o, milk.
laktuk-o, lettuce.
lam-a, lame.
lamp-o, lamp.
lan-o, wool.
lanc-o, lance, spear.
land-o, land, country.
lang-o, tongue (of the body).
lantern-o, lantern.
lanug-o, down (hairs, feathers).
lard-o, bacon.
larĝ-a, wide, broad.
larm-o, tear (of the eye).
las-i, (*trans.*), to leave, let, permit.
last-a, last (in a series).
latin-a, Latin.
laŭ (*prep.*), in accordance with, along, by (**191**).
laŭb-o, arbor, summer-house.
laŭd-i, to praise.
laŭt-a, loud.
lav-i, to wash.
lecion-o, lesson.
led-o, leather.
leg-i, to read.
legom-o, vegetable.
leĝ-o, law.
lek-i, to lick.
leon-o, lion.
lepor-o, hare.
lern-i, to learn.
lert-a, clever, skilful.
leter-o, letter (epistle).
lev-i, to raise, lift.
li (*pronoun*), he, him (**32, 37, 42**).
liber-a, free.
libr-o, book.
lig-i, to tie, bind, fasten; —**ilo**, bond; that which ties or fastens; —**aĵo**, knot; —**o**, league, alliance.
lign-o, wood.
lim-o, limit, boundary.
limonad-o, lemonade.
lingv-o, language.
lini-o, line; —**ilo**, ruler.
lip-o, lip; —**haroj**, moustache.
lit-o, bed (for sleeping).

liter-o, letter of the alphabet; laŭlitera, literal.
literatur-o, literature.
litr-o, liter (**284**).
liver-i, to deliver, supply, furnish.
log-i, to allure.
loĝ-i, to dwell, reside (**133**).
lok-o, place; —**a**, local.
lokomotiv-o, locomotive.
long-a, long.
lonicer-o, honeysuckle.
lorn-o, telescope, spyglass; —**eto**, opera-glasses.
lu-i, to hire, rent (engage and pay rent for).
lud-i, to play.
luks-o, luxury.
lul-i, to lull to sleep; —**ilo**, cradle.
lum-i, to shine (**275**).
lun-o, moon.
lunatik-o, lunatic.
lund-o, Monday.
lup-o, wolf.

M.

maĉ-i, to chew, masticate.
magazen-o, warehouse.
magi-o, magic.
magistr-o, master of arts (A.M.).
maiz-o, maize, Indian corn.
maj-o, May.
majest-a, majestic.
majones-a, mayonnaise.
majstr-o, master (of his art or profession).
makaroni-o, macaroni.
maksimum-o, maximum.
makul-o, spot, stain.
makzel-o, jaw; —**osto**, jawbone.
mal-, *prefix forming opposites* (**67**).
maleol-o, ankle.
malgraŭ (*prep.*), notwithstanding.
malic-a, malicious.
man-o, hand.
mandat-o, money-order.
manĝ-i, to eat.
manier-o, manner, way.
manik-o, sleeve.
mank-i (*intrans.*), to be lacking, wanting.
mantel-o, cloak, mantle.

manuskript-o, manuscript.
mar-o, sea.
marĉ-o, swamp, marsh.
mard-o, Tuesday.
Mari-o, Mary.
mark-o, mark.
marmelad-o, marmalade.
marmor-o, marble (stone),
marŝ-i, to walk.
mart-o, March.
martel-o, hammer.
mastr-o, master (of a house, etc.)
maŝin-o, machine.
maten-o, morning (**93**).
material-o, material.
matur-a, ripe, mature.
mebl-o, piece of furniture.
medicin-o, medicine (the science).
meĥanik-o, mechanics.
mejl-o, mile.
meleagr-o, turkey.
melk-i, to milk.
melodi-o, melody.
melon-o, melon.
mem (*pronoun*), self, selves (**219**).
membr-o, limb, member.
memor-i, to remember, keep in mind; rememori, to recall to memory.
mend-i, to order (of a store, etc.).
mensog-i, to lie, tell lies.
menton-o, chin.
menu-o, menu.
merit-i, to deserve, merit.
merkred-o, Wednesday.
merl-o, blackbird.
met-i, to put, place.
metal-o, metal.
meti-o, trade, handicraft.
metod-o, method, way.
metr-o, meter (**284**).
mez-o, middle.
mezur-i, to measure.
mi (*pronoun*), I, me (**32, 37**).
miel-o, honey.
mien-o, appearance, mien.
miks-i (trans.), to mix.
mil (*adj.*), thousand (**142**).

mild-a, mild.
milimetr-o, millimeter (**284**).
milion-o, million.
milit-i, to fight, wage war.
min-o, mine (of coal, silver, etc.).
minac-i, to threaten.
mineral-o, mineral.
minimum-o, minimum.
ministr-o, minister (political).
minut-o, minute.
miop-a, shortsighted.
mir-i, to wonder.
mister-o, mystery.
mizer-o, misery.
mod-o, mode, fashion.
model-o, model.
moder-a, moderate.
modest-a, modest.
mok-i, to mock.
mol-a, soft.
moment-o, moment; —a, momentary, instantaneous.
mon-o, money.
monaĥ-o, monk.
monarĥi-o, monarch.
monat-o, month.
mond-o, world.
mont-o, mountain.
montr-i (*trans.*), to show.
mor-o, conduct (in regard to right or wrong); —oj, morals.
moral-a, moral; —eco, morality.
mord-i, to bite.
morgaŭ (*adv.*), tomorrow (**171**).
mort-i, to die; —igi, to kill.
moŝt-o, *title of respect* (**258**).
mov-i (*trans.*), to move, put in motion.
muel-o, mill (for grinding).
muĝ-i, to roar, bellow.
mult-a, much (**81**).
mur-o, wall.
murmur-i, to murmur.
mus-o, mouse.
mustard-o, mustard.
muŝ-o, fly.
mut-a, dumb, mute.
muze-o, museum.
muzik-o, music.

N.

naci-o, nation.
naĝ-i, to swim.
naiv-a, artless, naive, ingenuous.
najbar-o, neighbor.
najl-o, nail (of metal).
nap-o, turnip.
nask-i, to produce, bring forth, give birth to.
natur-o, nature.
naŭ (*adj.*), nine (**136**).
naz-o, nose.
ne (*adv.*), no, not (27, 66, a, 171).
nebul-o, fog, mist.
neces-a, necessary.
negativ-o, negative (photographic).
neĝ-o, snow.
nek (*negative conj.*), neither, nor (**31**).
nenia, no kind of (**224**).
nenial (*adv.*), for no reason (**229**).
neniam (*adv.*), never (**226**).
nenie (*adv.*), nowhere (**225**).
neniel (*adv.*), in no way (**230**).
nenies (*pronoun, possessive*), nobody's (**221**).
nenio (*pronoun*), nothing (**233**).
neniom (*adv.*), none, not any (**231**).
neniu (*pronoun*), no one, nobody, no (**220**).
nep-o, grandson.
nepr-e, inevitably, certainly, unfailingly.
nerv-o, nerve.
nest-o, nest.
neŭtral-a, neutral, non-partisan.
nev-o, nephew.
ni (*pronoun*), we, us (**32, 37**).
nigr-a, black.
nivel-o, level.
-nj-, *suffix forming affectionate diminutives* (**283**).
nobel-o, nobleman.
nobl-a, noble (in character).
nokt-o, night.
nom-o, name; **—i**, to name, mention.
nombr-o, number (quantity).
nord-o, north.
norveg-o, Norwegian.
nostalgi-o, homesickness.
not-o, note.
nov-a, new, recent, novel; denove, anew, again.

novembr-o, November.
nu (*interjection*), well! (**273**).
nuanc-o, shade, tint, hue.
nub-o, cloud.
nud-a, bare, naked, nude.
nuks-o, nut.
nul-o, zero, naught.
numer-o, number, numeral (No.).
nun (*adv.*), now (**171**).
nur (*adv.*), merely, only.
nutr-i, to nourish, to feed.

O.

obe-i, to obey (**265**).
objekt-o, object, thing.
objektiv-o, lens, objective.
-obl-, *suffix forming multiples* (**186**).
oblikv-a, oblique, slanting.
observ-i, to observe, take note of.
obstin-a, obstinate.
ocean-o, ocean.
odor-i, to smell (good or bad).
ofend-i, to offend.
ofer-i, to sacrifice, offer.
ofic-o, office, employment; —**isto**, officer (of firm or organization); —**ejo**, office (the place).
oficial-a, official.
oficir-o, officer (military or naval).
oft-a, frequent.
ok (*adj.*), eight (**136**).
okaz-i, to happen, occur, take place.
okcident-o, west.
oktobr-o, October.
okul-o, eye.
okup-i, to occupy.
ol (*conj.*), than (**82, 97, 98**).
ole-o, oil.
oliv-o, olive.
ombr-o, shadow, shade.
ombrel-o, umbrella.
-on-, *suffix forming fractions* (**166**).
ond-o, wave.
oni (*pronoun*), one, they (**54**).
onkl-o, uncle.
-op-, *suffix forming collective numerals* (**261**).
oper-o, opera.

opini-i, to have the opinion, think.
oportun-a, handy, convenient, opportune.
or-o, gold.
oranĝ-o, orange (fruit).
ord-o, order (methodical or proper arrangement).
ordinar-a, ordinary; eksterordinara, extraordinary.
ordon-i, to order, bid, command.
orel-o, ear (of the body).
orf-o, orphan.
organ-o, organ (physical).
organiz-i, to organize.
orgen-o, organ, (musical instrument).
orient-o, east.
original-o, original.
orkestr-o, orchestra.
ornam-i, to ornament, adorn.
ort-a, right-angled.
osced-i, to gape, yawn.
ost-o, bone.
ostr-o, oyster.
ostracism-o, ostracism.
ov-o, egg.

P.

pac-o, peace.
pacienc-o, patience.
padel-i, to paddle.
paf-i, to shoot (with gun, etc.).
pag-i, to pay.
paĝ-o, page (of a book, etc.).
pajl-o, straw.
pak-i, to pack.
pal-a, pale.
palac-o, palace.
palis-o, stake; —aro, palisade.
palp-i, to feel (with the fingers, etc.); —ado, touch (the sense).
palpebr-o, eyelid.
pan-o, bread.
pantalon-o, trousers.
pantofl-o, slipper.
paper-o, paper (material).
papili-o, butterfly.
par-o, pair.
paradiz-o, paradise.
paragraf-o, paragraph.
paralel-a, parallel.

pardon-i, to forgive, pardon (**265**).
parenc-o, relative (person).
parfum-o, perfume.
park-o, park.
parker-e, by rote, by heart, from memory.
parol-i, to speak (**77**).
part-o, part, share.
particip-o, participle.
pas-i, (*intrans.*), to pass.
pasaĝer-o, passenger.
paser-o, sparrow.
pasi-o, passion.
pasiv-a, passive.
Pask-o, Easter.
pasteĉ-o, patty, small pie.
pastinak-o, parsnip.
pastr-o, pastor, clergyman, priest.
paŝ-i, to step.
paŝt-i (*trans.*), to pasture, feed; —**isto**, shepherd.
pat-o, pan, frying-pan.
patr-o, father.
paŭz-o, pause.
pavim-o, pavement.
pec-o, piece, morsel.
pejzaĝ-o, landscape.
pek-i, to sin.
pekl-i, to pickle (meat, etc.).
pel-i, to chase away, drive off.
pelt-o, coat or wrap of fur.
pen-i, to strive, try.
pend-i (*intrans.*), to hang.
penetr-i, to penetrate.
penik-o, paintbrush, hair pencil.
pens-i, to think.
pent-i, to repent.
pentr-i, to paint.
pep-i, to chirp, twitter.
per (*prep.*), by means of, with, by (**64**).
perd-i, to lose.
pere-i, to perish.
perfekt-a, perfect.
perfid-i, to betray; —**a**, perfidious, treacherous.
period-a, periodic.
perl-o, pearl.
permes-i, to permit, allow, let.
peron-o, platform (railway), stoop (entrance porch).

persekut-i, to persecute, prosecute.
persik-o, peach.
persist-i, to persist, persevere.
person-o, person.
peruk-o, wig.
pes-i (*trans.*), to ascertain the weight of; —**ilo**, scales, balance.
pet-i, to request, beg, ask.
petol-i, to be mischievous, saucy, roguish.
petrol-o, petroleum, kerosene.
petrosel-o, parsley.
pez-i (*intrans.*), to be heavy, weigh.
pi-a, pious.
pice-o, spruce (tree).
pied-o, foot; —**iranto**, pedestrian.
piedestal-o, pedestal.
pik-i, to prick, sting.
pilgrim-i, to go on a pilgrimage.
pilk-o, ball (to play with).
pin-o, pine (tree).
pinakotek-o, picture gallery.
pinĉ-i, to pinch.
pingl-o, pin.
pint-o, point, pinnacle, summit.
pionir-o, pioneer.
pip-o, pipe (for smoking).
pipr-o, pepper.
pir-o, pear.
pist-i, to crush, mash; —**aĵo**, purée.
pitoresk-a, picturesque.
piz-o, pea.
plac-o, public square, place (broad, short street or open space).
plaĉ-i, to please, to be pleasing (**265**).
plad-o, flat dish.
plafon-o, ceiling.
plan-o, plan, scheme.
pland-o, sole (of the foot).
planed-o, planet.
plank-o, floor.
plant-i, to plant.
plat-a, flat, plane.
plaŭd-i (*trans.*), to splash, dabble (a liquid).
plej (*adv.*), most (**74, 79, 81, 162**); malplej, least (**80**).
plekt-i, to weave, plait, braid.
plen-a, full; plenum-i, to fulfil.
plend-i, to complain.
plet-o, tray.

plezur-o, pleasure.
pli (*adv.*), more (**74, 79, 81**); malpli, less (**80**).
plor-i, to weep, cry.
plu (*adv.*), further, more, any more.
plug-i, to plow.
plum-o, pen, feather.
plumb-o, lead (metal); —**isto**, plumber.
pluv-o, rain.
pneŭmatik-o, pneumatic tire.
po (*prep.*), at the rate of (**175**).
poem-o, poem.
poet-o, poet.
poezi-o, poetry, poesy.
pokal-o, goblet, cup.
pol-o, Pole.
polic-o, police (force).
politik-o, politics.
polm-o, palm (of the hand).
polur-i, to polish, make smooth and glossy.
polus-o, pole (geographical).
polv-o, dust.
pom-o, apple.
pomp-o, pomp, splendor.
pont-o, bridge.
popol-o, a people, folk.
popular-a, popular.
por (*prep.*), for (**95, 98, 262**).
porcelan-o, porcelain, china.
porci-o, portion, share.
pord-o, door.
pork-o, swine, pig, hog.
port-i, to carry, bear.
portret-o, portrait.
posed-i, to possess, own.
post (*prep.*), after, behind (**89, 120**).
postul-i, to require, demand.
poŝ-o, pocket.
poŝt-o, post (mail); —**kesto**, mailbox; —**marko**, postage stamp; —**mandato**, postal money order.
pot-o, pot.
potenc-a, powerful, mighty.
pov-i, to be able, can (**72**).
pra-, *prefix indicating remoteness in line of descent* (**282**).
praktik-o, practice.
prav-a, right, in the right.
precip-a, principal, chief.

preciz-a, precise.
predik-i, to preach.
prefer-i, to prefer.
prefiks-o, prefix.
preĝ-i, to pray; —**ejo**, church.
prem-i, to press.
premi-o, premium, prize.
pren-i, to take.
prepar-i, to prepare.
pres-i, to print.
preskaŭ (*adv.*), almost.
pret-a, ready.
pretekst-i, to make pretext of, pretend, sham.
pretend-i, to make pretension to, lay claim to.
preter (*prep.*), beyond, past, by.
prez-o, price.
prezent-i, to present, offer.
prezid-i, to preside; —**anto**, presiding officer, president, chairman.
pri (*prep.*), concerning, about, of (160, 264, c).
princ-o, prince.
princip-o, principle.
printemp-o, spring (season).
pro (*prep.*), on account of, because of, for (**86**).
problem-o, problem.
procent-o, interest, percentage.
proces-o, lawsuit, legal process.
produkt-i, to produce.
profesi-o, profession, occupation, calling.
profesor-o, professor.
profil-o, profile.
profit-o, profit; —**i**, to profit (by).
profund-a, deep, profound.
progres-i, to progress.
projekt-o, project.
proklam-i, to proclaim.
prokrast-i, to delay, procrastinate.
proksim-a, near.
promen-i, to go walking, promenade.
promes-i, to promise.
propon-i, to propose, offer.
proporci-o, proportion.
propr-a, own (one's own); malpropra, other people's; —**igi al si**, to appropriate, make one's own.
prosper-i, to have success, prosper.
protekt-i, to protect.
protest-i, to protest.

protokol-o, minutes (of a meeting).
prov-i, to try, attempt, test.
proviz-i, to provide.
proz-o, prose; —aĵo, prose composition, piece of prose.
prudent-a, reasonable, sensible, rational.
prujn-o, hoar frost.
prun-o, plum.
prunt-o, loan; —i, (—e doni), to lend; —e preni, to borrow.
pruv-i, to prove, give proof of.
psalm-o, psalm.
publik-o, public (the); —igi, to publish.
puding-o, pudding.
pudr-i, to powder.
pugn-o, fist.
pulm-o, lung.
pulv-o, gunpowder.
pump-i, to pump.
pun-i, to punish.
punt-o, lace (point, etc.).
pup-o, doll.
pupitr-o, desk.
pur-a, clean, pure.
purpur-a, purple.
puŝ-i, to push; repuŝi, to repulse.
put-o, well (for water).

R.

rabarb-o, rhubarb.
rab-i, to pillage, plunder; —isto, robber.
rabat-i, to rebate, give a reduction, discount or rebate.
rad-o, wheel.
radi-o, ray (of light), spoke (of wheel), radius.
radik-o, root.
rafan-o, radish.
rafin-i, to refine; —ejo, refinery.
rajd-i, to ride (horse, etc.).
rajt-o, right (to something).
rakont-i, to relate, narrate (77).
ramp-i, to creep, crawl, clamber.
ran-o, frog.
rand-o, edge, border.
rang-o, rank, grade, dignity.
rapid-a, rapid, quick; —o, speed; —emo, haste.
raport-i, to report, give a report.
ras-o, race (tribe, people, nation).
rasp-i, to rasp, grate; —ilo, grater.

rat-o, rat.
raŭk-a, hoarse, raucous.
rav-i, to enchant.
raz-i, to shave.
re-, *prefix indicating repetition or return* (**223**).
real-a, real.
reciprok-a, reciprocal, mutual (**180**).
redakci-o, editorial department.
redakt-i, to edit.
redaktor-o, editor.
redingot-o, frock coat.
refut-i, to refute.
reg-i, to rule, govern, reign.
regal-i (*trans.*), to regale, treat (to food or drink).
region-o, region.
registr-i (*trans.*), to register, enroll.
regn-o, state, governed body; —**ano**, citizen, subject.
regul-o, rule, regulation.
reĝ-o, king.
reklam-i, to advertise.
rekomend-i, to recommend, register (a letter).
rekompenc-i, to recompense, reward.
rekt-a, straight, undeviating, direct.
rel-o, rail.
religi-o, religion.
rem-i, to row.
rembur-i, to upholster, stuff, pad.
renkont-i (*trans.*), to meet.
renvers-i (*trans.*), to upset.
reprezent-i, to represent.
respekt-i, to respect.
respond-i, to answer.
respublik-o, republic.
rest-i, to remain, stay.
restoraci-o, restaurant.
resum-i, to summarize, give in resumé.
ret-o, net, netting.
rev-i, to indulge in revery, dream, fancy.
revu-o, journal, review, magazine.
rezon-i, to reason (exert the power of reasoning).
rezult-i, to result.
ricev-i, to receive.
riĉ-a, rich.
rid-i, to laugh (**265**).
rifuz-i, to refuse.
rigard-i, to look.

rigl-i, to bolt (fasten).
rikolt-i, to harvest, reap.
rilat-i, to have relation (to) (**266**).
rimark-i, to notice, note.
rimed-o, means, way; vivrimedoj, means of livelihood.
rimen-o, thong, strap.
ring-o, ring.
rip-o, rib.
ripar-i, to mend, repair.
ripet-i, to repeat.
ripoz-i, to repose, rest.
riproĉ-i, to reproach.
river-o, river.
riz-o, rice.
rob-o, dress, robe.
Robert-o, Robert.
romp-i (*trans.*), to break.
rond-o, circle, ring, round.
ros-o, dew.
rost-i, to roast.
roz-o, rose (flower).
ruband-o, ribbon.
rubus-o, blackberry.
ruĝ-a, red.
ruin-o, ruin.
rul-i (*trans.*), to roll (ball, etc.).
rus-o, Russian.
rust-i, to rust.
rutin-o, routine.
ruz-a, crafty, cunning, sly.

S.

sabat-o, Saturday.
sabl-o, sand.
sag-o, arrow.
saĝ-a, wise.
sak-o, sack, bag.
sal-o, salt.
salajr-o, salary, wages.
salat-o, salad.
salon-o, parlor, drawing-room.
salt-i, to jump, leap.
salut-i, to salute, greet.
sam-a, same.
san-a, healthy, well.
sang-o, blood.

sankt-a, sacred, holy.
sap-o, soap.
sarden-o, sardine.
sat-a, sated; malsata, hungry.
saŭc-o, sauce, gravy, dressing.
sav-i, to save; rescue.
sci-i, to know (**117**).
scienc-o, science.
se (*conj.*), if (**240**).
sed (*conj.*), but.
seg-i, to saw.
seĝ-o, chair.
sek-a, dry.
sekret-o, secret.
sekretari-o, secretary.
sekund-o, second (of time).
sekv-i, to follow.
sel-o, saddle.
sem-o, seed; —i, to sow.
semajn-o, week.
sen (*prep.*), without (**248**).
senat-o, senate; —ano, senator.
senc-o, sense, meaning.
send-i, to send.
sent-i, to feel, perceive.
sep (*adj.*), seven (**136**).
septembr-o, September.
serĉ-i, to seek, hunt, look for.
serur-o, lock.
serv-i, to serve.
servic-o, course (of a meal).
ses (*adj.*), six (**136**).
sever-a, severe, stern.
sezon-o, season.
si (*pronoun, reflexive*), himself, herself, etc. (**40, 44, 274**).
sibl-i, to hiss, whistle (wind, etc.).
sid-i, to sit (**239**).
sigel-i, to seal.
sign-o, sign, trace, mark.
signif-i, to signify, mean.
silab-o, syllable.
silent-i, to be silent (**239**).
silk-o, silk.
simi-o, monkey.
simil-a, like, similar.
simpl-a, simple.

sinjor-o, gentleman, Mr. (**163**).
Sirakuz-o, Syracuse.
sitel-o, pail, bucket.
skatol-o, small box or case.
skiz-i, to sketch.
sklav-o, slave.
skot-o, Scot, Scotchman.
skrap-i, to scrape.
skrib-i, to write.
sku-i (*trans.*), to shake.
skulpt-i, to carve, sculpture.
societ-o, society.
soif-i, to be thirsty.
sojl-o, threshold.
Sokrat-o, Socrates.
sol-a, alone, sole, only.
soldat-o, soldier.
solen-a, formal, solemn.
somer-o, summer.
son-i (*intrans.*), to sound.
sonĝ-i, to dream (in sleep).
sonor-i (*intrans.*), to ring, sound; —**ilo**, bell.
sopir-i, to yearn, long, sigh.
sorb-i, to absorb; —**papero**, blotting-paper.
sorĉ-o, witchcraft; ensorĉi, to bewitch; —**isto**, sorcerer.
sort-o, destiny, fate, lot.
sovaĝ-a, wild, savage.
spac-o, space.
spec-o, kind, sort, species.
special-a, special.
specimen-o, specimen, sample.
spegul-o, mirror.
spert-a, experienced, expert.
spes-o, speso (international unit of money, 284).
spez-o, clearing (financial); elspezi, to disburse, expend, spend; enspezi, to take in, receive (funds).
spinac-o, spinach.
spir-i, to breathe; elspiri, to exhale.
spite (*prep.*), in spite of.
sprit-a, witty.
staci-o, station (railway, boat, etc.).
stamp-i, to mark officially, stamp.
standard-o, standard, flag.
stan-o, tin (metal).
stang-o, pole.
star-i, to stand (**239**).

stat-o, state (of being), condition.
stel-o, star.
stenografi-o, shorthand, stenography.
stil-o, style.
stimul-i, to stimulate.
stomak-o, stomach.
strang-a, strange, peculiar.
strat-o, street.
streĉ-i (*trans.*), to stretch.
strek-i, to make a streak, or line; substreki, to underline; surstreki, trastreki, to cross off, strike out.
stri-o, streak, stripe, band.
strik-o, strike (of labor).
stud-i, to study.
student-o, student (college, etc.).
stuf-i (*trans.*), to stew.
stump-o, stump (of tree, etc.).
sub (*prep.*), under, beneath (**121, 160**).
subit-a, sudden, abrupt.
substanc-o, substance.
sud-o, south.
sufer-i, to suffer, endure.
sufiĉ-i, to suffice; —**ega**, abundant.
sufiks-o, suffix.
sufok-i (*trans.*), to suffocate.
sugesti-i, to suggest.
suk-o, sap, juice (of plants, etc.); —**a**, succulent.
sukces-i, to succeed.
suker-o, sugar.
sulfur-o, sulphur.
sulk-o, furrow, wrinkle.
sum-o, sum, amount.
sun-o, sun.
sup-o, soup.
super (*prep.*), above, over (**159**); —**a**, superior.
superstiĉ-o, superstition.
supoz-i, to suppose.
supr-e (*adv.*), above; —**a**, upper, above; —**aĵo**, surface.
sur (*prep.*), on, upon (**160**).
surd-a, deaf.
surpriz-i, to surprise.
surtut-o, overcoat.
suspekt-i, to suspect.
sved-o, Swede.
sven-i, to faint, swoon.
sving-i (*trans.*), swing, brandish.

svis-o, Swiss.

Ŝ.

ŝaf-o, sheep; —aĵo, mutton; —ido, lamb; —idaĵo, lamb (meat); —viro, ram.
ŝajn-i, to seem, appear.
ŝal-o, shawl.
ŝanc-o, luck, chance; bonŝance, luckily.
ŝancel-i (*trans.*), to oscillate, vacillate, make tremble.
ŝanĝ-i (*trans.*), to change, alter.
ŝarĝ-i, to burden, load.
ŝat-i, to like, prize.
ŝaŭm-o, foam, froth.
ŝel-o, shell, peeling, bark.
ŝelk-o, suspender, supporter.
ŝerc-i, to joke, jest.
ŝi (*pronoun*), she, her (**32, 37, 42**).
ŝild-o, shield.
ŝink-o, ham.
ŝip-o, ship.
ŝir-i, to tear.
ŝirm-i, to shelter, shield; —ilo, screen.
ŝlim-o, slime.
ŝlos-i, to lock; —ilo, key.
ŝmir-i, to anoint, smear.
ŝnur-o, string.
ŝose-o, broad roadway, drive.
ŝov-i, to shove, push.
ŝovel-i, to shovel.
ŝpar-i, to spare, be economical of.
ŝpin-i, to spin.
ŝpruc-i, to gush, spout, spurt (of liquids).
ŝrank-o, cupboard, wardrobe.
ŝraŭb-o, screw.
ŝtal-o, steel.
ŝtat-o, state (political).
ŝtel-i, to steal (**252**).
ŝtip-o, log, block of wood.
ŝtof-o, cloth, stuff.
ŝton-o, stone.
ŝtop-i, to stop up, cork; —ilo, stopper.
ŝtrump-o, stocking.
ŝtup-o, step, round; —aro, stair-case.
ŝu-o, shoe; superŝuo, overshoe.
ŝuld-i, to owe, be indebted.
ŝultr-o, shoulder.
ŝut-o, chute; —i, to pour (as in a chute).

ŝvel-i, to swell, become swollen.
ŝvit-i, to perspire.

T.

tabak-o, tobacco.
tabel-o, table, index, tabulation.
tabl-o, table (furniture).
tabul-o, board, plank.
tag-o, day; —iĝo, dawn; —mezo, noon.
tajlor-o, tailor.
taks-i, to estimate, value, rate.
talent-o, talent.
tali-o, waist; beltalia, shapely, having a good figure.
tambur-o, drum.
tamen (*conj.*), nevertheless, however, yet, still.
tantiem-o, percentage of profit, royalty.
tapiŝ-o, carpet.
tarif-o, tariff, schedule of rates.
tas-o, cup; subtaso, saucer.
task-o, task.
taŭg-i, to be fit for, good for.
tavol-o, layer.
te-o, tea.
teatr-o, theatre; —aĵo, play.
ted-i, to be tedious.
teg-i, to cover, put a covering upon.
tegment-o, roof.
teks-i, to weave.
telefon-i, to telephone.
telegraf-i, to telegraph.
teler-o, plate; —meblo, sideboard.
tem-o, theme, subject.
temp-o, time.
tempi-o, temple (of the head).
templ-o, temple (building).
ten-i, to hold, keep.
tend-o, tent.
tenor-o, tenor (voice).
tent-i, to tempt.
teori-o, theory.
ter-o, earth, soil; enterigi, to inter.
teras-o, terrace.
teritori-o, territory.
termin-o, term, definition (word).
tern-i, to sneeze.
terpom-o, potato.

terur-o, terror.

tia, that kind of, such (**65**).

tial (*adv.*), therefore (**78, 83**).

tiam (*adv.*), then, at that time (**73**).

tibi-o, shin bone, tibia; — **karno**, calf (of the leg).

tie (*adv.*), there (**68**).

tiel (*adv.*), thus, so (**88, 156**).

tigr-o, tiger.

tikl-i, to tickle.

tili-o, linden.

tim-i, to fear, be afraid of.

timon-o, pole, tongue, shaft.

tint-i, to jingle, tinkle.

tio (*pronoun*), that (**233, 234**).

tiom (*adv.*), that much, so much (**104, 164**).

tir-i, to pull, draw.

tiran-o, tyrant.

titol-o, title.

tiu (*pronoun*), that one, that (**56**); tiu ĉi, this one, this (**60**).

tost-o, toast (sentiment).

tol-o, linen.

toler-i, to tolerate.

tomat-o, tomato.

tomb-o, tomb, grave.

ton-o, tone.

tond-i, to shear; — **ilo**, shears, scissors.

tondr-i, to thunder.

tord-i, to twist; — **a**, crooked, winding.

tra (*prep.*), through (**46, 160**).

trab-o, beam (wooden).

traduk-i, to translate.

traf-i, to reach, attain (that which was aimed at or sought); maltrafi, to miss.

trajt-o, feature.

trakt-i, to treat of (in essay, speech, etc.); — **ato**, treatise.

tram-o, tram; — **vojo**, tramway, street-car line; — **veturilo**, street-car.

tranĉ-i, to cut, sever.

trankvil-a, serene, tranquil, calm.

trans (*prep.*), across, the other side of (**160**).

tre (*adv.*), very, very much.

trem-i, to tremble.

tremp-i, to drench, dip.

tren-i, to drag, haul, draw; — **aĵo**, train (of a dress).

trezor-o, treasure.

tri (*adj.*), three (**136**).

trik-i, to knit.

trink-i, to drink.

tritik-o, wheat.
triumf-o, triumph.
tro (*adv.*), too, too much.
tromp-i, to deceive.
tron-o, throne.
tropik-o, tropic.
trot-i, to trot.
trotuar-o, sidewalk, pavement.
trov-i, to find.
tru-o, hole.
trud-i, to force upon, impose; altrudema, importunate.
trunk-o, trunk (of tree or body).
tualet-o, toilet.
tub-o, tube, pipe.
tuber-o, bulb, knot, tuber.
tuj (*adv.*), at once, immediately
tuk-o, piece of cloth.
tur-o, tower.
turk-o, Turk.
turment-i, to torment.
turn-i (*trans.*), to turn.
tus-i, to cough.
tuŝ-i, to touch; kortuŝi, to touch (the heart of).
tut-a, entire, whole, all.

U.

-uj-, *suffix indicating receptacle, that which bears or contains* (**181**).
-ul-, *suffix indicating person characterized by that in the root* (**132**).
ulm-o, elm.
-um-, indefinite suffix (**268**).
ung-o, nail (of finger); —ego, claw, talon.
univers-o, universe.
universitat-o, university.
unu (*adj.*), one (**136, 137, 180**); unuiĝo, union.
uragan-o, hurricane.
urb-o, city; ĉefurbo, capital.
urĝ-i, to be urgent or pressing.
urs-o, bear.
Uson-o, United States of America.
util-a, useful.
uz-i, to use; trouzi, to abuse.

V.

vad-i, to wade.
vafl-o, waffle.

vag-i, to wander, to roam; —**isto**, vagabond.

vagon-o, car, railway carriage.

vak-i, to be vacant.

vaks-o, wax.

val-o, valley.

valiz-o, valise, satchel, bag.

valor-i, to be worth.

vals-i, to waltz.

van-a, vain, fruitless.

vang-o, cheek.

vant-a, vain, conceited.

vapor-o, steam, vapor.

varb-i (*trans.*), to enlist, recruit.

varm-a, warm.

vast-a, vast, spacious, extensive.

vaz-o, vase, basin.

ve! (*interjection*), woe! ho ve! alas! (**273**).

veget-i, to vegetate, grow (as plants).

vegetar-a, vegetarian.

vejn-o, vein.

vek-i (*trans.*), to wake, awake.

vel-o, sail.

velk-i, to fade, wither, wilt.

velur-o, velvet.

ven-i, to come.

vend-i, to sell.

vendred-o, Friday.

venen-o, poison.

venĝ-i, to avenge.

venk-i, to conquer, vanquish.

vent-o, wind.

ver-o, truth.

verand-o, veranda, porch.

verd-a, green.

verk-i, to compose (music or literature).

verm-o, worm.

vermiĉel-o, vermicelli.

vers-o, verse.

verŝ-i, to pour (a liquid).

vertikal-a, vertical.

vesper-o, evening (**93**).

vest-i, to clothe, dress.

veŝt-o, vest, waistcoat.

vet-i, to wager, bet.

veter-o, weather.

vetur-i, to ride, go (in vehicle, boat, etc.).

vi (*pronoun*), you (**32, 37, 274**).
viand-o, meat.
vibr-i, to vibrate.
vic-o, turn, place in a series; laŭvice, in turn; siavice, in his (her, its, their) turn; vicprezidanto, vice-president.
vid-i, to see.
vidv-o, widower; —**ino**, widow.
vigl-a, alert, brisk.
vilaĝ-o, village.
vin-o, wine.
vinagr-o, vinegar.
vinber-o, grape; sekvinbero, raisin.
vintr-o, winter.
viol-o, violet.
violon-o, violin.
vip-i, to whip.
vir-o, man
virt-o, virtue.
viŝ-i, to wipe.
vitr-o, glass (material).
viv-i, to live (**133**).
vizaĝ-o, face, visage.
vizit-i, to visit.
voĉ-o, voice; —**doni**, to vote.
voj-o, road, way.
vojaĝ-i, to journey, travel, voyage.
vok-i, to call.
vokal-o, vowel.
vol-i, to be willing, will, wish.
volont-e, willingly.
volum-o, volume (book).
volumen-o, volume (of a body).
volv-i, to roll (something around something).
vort-o, word; —**aro**, dictionary.
vost-o, tail.
vual-o, veil.
vulgar-a, common, vulgar.
vulp-o, fox.
vund-i, to wound.

Z.

zenit-o, zenith.
zigzag-o, zigzag.
zingibr-o, ginger.
zink-o, zinc.
zon-o, girdle, belt, zone.

zoologi-o, zoology.
zorg-i, to care (for), be anxious (about).
zum-i, to hum, buzz.

ENGLISH-ESPERANTO VOCABULARY.

The following vocabulary includes all Esperanto roots used in the preceding lessons, all primary words of the language, and a large number of additional roots (to facilitate original composition). No attempt has been made, however, to include all of the roots of the language, or their various English meanings, for which an English-Esperanto Dictionary should be consulted.

References are to sections, unless the page (p.) is given. For other parts of speech than those indicated, see Word Formation, 116, 120, 159, 171, also the references under Prefixes and Suffixes in the Index. For formation of compound words other than those given, see 160, 167, 176, 184. The following abbreviations are used: adj. = adjective; adv. = adverb; conj. = conjunction; intrans. = intransitive; prep. = preposition; trans. = transitive; — = repetition of the English word.

A.

abandon, forlas-i.
abash, hontig-i.
(be) able, pov-i (**72**).
abominable, abomen-a.
about (*prep.*), ĉirkaŭ; (**concerning**) pri; (*adv.*), (approximately, proksimum-e.
above (*prep.*), super (**159**); (*adv.*), supr-e; ĉi supre.
abrupt, subit-a.
absorb, sorb-i.
abundant, sufiĉeg-a.
academy, akademi-o.
accelerate (*trans.*), akcel-i.
accent, akcent-o.
accept, akcept-i.
accident, akcident-o; (**chance**) okaz-o.
accompany, akompan-i.
(in) accordance with (*prep.*), laŭ (**191**).
account, kont-o; (**bill**) kalkul-o; (**story**) rakont-o.
(on) account of (*prep.*), pro (**86**).
accurate, akurat-a.
accusative, akuzativ-o.
accuse, akuz-i, kulpig-i.
accustomed, familiar-a, kutimit-a.
ache, dolor-o.
acid, acid-o.

(be) acquainted with, kon-i **(117)**; **become** —, konatiĝ-i. acquire, akir-i.
across (*prep.*), trans.
act, ag-i; **—on**, efik-i; **(behave)** kondut-i; **(of play)** akt-o.
active, agema; **(grammatical)**, aktiv-a.
actor, aktor-o.
actual, efektiv-a, ver-a.
acute, akr-a.
add, aldon-i **(160)**.
address (on letters, etc.) adres-o; **(lecture)** parolad-o.
adequate, sufiĉ-a.
adjacent, apud-a **(159)**.
adjective, adjektiv-o.
administer (manage), administr-i.
admire, admir-i.
admit, konfes-i; **(let in)** allas-i.
admonish, admon-i.
adore, ador-i.
adorn, ornam-i.
adverb, adverb-o.
advantage, util-o, profit-o.
advertise, reklam-i.
advise, konsil-i.
affable, afabl-a.
affair, afer-o; **regrettable** —, domaĝ-o.
affirmative, jes-a **(171)**.
(be) afraid, tim-i.
Africa, Afrik-o.
after (*prep.*), post **(89)**.
afternoon, posttagmez-o.
again, denov-e, re-e **(223)**.
against (*prep.*), kontraŭ.
age, aĝ-o; **of** —, plenaĝ-a; **old** —, maljunec-o.
(give an) agency, komisi-i.
agent, agent-o.
agitate, agit-i.
agony, agoni-o.
agree, konsent-i; **(contract)** kontrakt-i.
agreeable, agrabl-a.
aid, help-i.
aim at, cel-i.
air, aer-o; **to** —, aerum-i; **(music)** ari-o.
alas!, ho ve **(273)**.
alcohol, alkohol-o.
alcove, alkov-o.
alert, vigl-a.
Alexander, Aleksandr-o.

Alexandria, Aleksandri-o.
Alfred, Alfred-o.
algebra, algebr-o.
alive, viv-a.
all (*pronoun and adj.*), ĉiuj (**173**); (*indefinite pronoun*) ĉio (**233**); (*adv. of quantity*) ĉiom (**194**); (**whole, entire**) tut-a.
alliance, lig-o.
allow, permes-i.
allude, alud-i.
allure, log-i.
almanac, almanak-o.
almost (*adv.*), preskaŭ.
alms, almoz-o.
alone, sol-a.
along (*prep.*), laŭ (**191**); — **with**, kune kun.
aloud, laŭt-e.
alphabet, alfabet-o.
already (*adv.*), jam.
also (*adv.*), ankaŭ.
altar, altar-o.
alter (*trans.*), ŝanĝ-i, aliig-i.
although (*conj.*), kvankam.
always (*adv.*), ĉiam (**187**).
America, Amerik-o.
amiable, afabl-a, amind-a.
amid, meze de, inter (**85**).
among (*prep.*), inter (**85**).
amount, sum-o, kvant-o; **a certain** —, iom (**217**).
amphibious, amfibi-a.
amphitheatre, amfiteatr-o.
amuse, amuz-i.
analyse, analiz-i.
ancestor, prapatr-o (**282**).
anchor, ankr-o.
ancient, antikv-a.
and (*conj.*), kaj (**26**).
anecdote, anekdot-o.
anew, denov-e.
angel, anĝel-o.
angle, angul-o.
angry, koler-a.
animal, best-o.
ankle, maleol-o.
announce, anonc-i.
annoy, ĉagren-i.
anoint, ŝmir-i.

answer, respond-i.
ant, formik-o.
antelope, antilop-o.
antipathy, antipati-o.
antique, antikv-a.
anvil, ambos-o.
anxious, maltrankvil-a.
any (*pronoun and adj.*), iu (**203**); (*adv. of quantity*) iom (**217**); —kind, —time, —thing, etc., see table, 235.
any more (*adv.*), plu.
apartment, apartament-o.
apathy, apati-o.
apologise, pardonon pet-i.
apology (**defence**), apologi-o.
apparatus, aparat-o.
appear (**come in sight**), aper-i; (**seem**) ŝajn-i.
appearance (**aspect**), aspekt-o, mien-o, vidiĝ-o.
appetite, apetit-o.
applaud, aplaŭd-i.
apple, pom-o.
apply (**put on**), almet-i; — to (**for information, etc.**), sin turni al.
approach, alproksimiĝ-i al.
appropriate, proprigi al si; (**suitable**), konven-a, dec-a.
approve, aprob-i.
approximate, proksimum-a.
apricot, abrikot-o.
April, april-o.
apron, antaŭtuk-o.
aquarium, akvari-o.
Arab, arab-o; **street** —, bub-o.
arbitrate, arbitraci-i.
arbor, laŭb-o.
arc, ark-o.
arcade, arkad-o.
archer, pafarkist-o.
Archimedes, Arĥimed-o.
architecture, arĥitektur-o.
arena, aren-o.
argue, argument-i.
Aristeides, Aristejd-o.
aristocrat, aristokrat-o.
Aristotle, Aristotel-o.
arithmetic, aritmetik-o.
arm (**of the body**), brak-o; (**weapon**) armil-o.
army, arme-o.
aroma, arom-o.

around (*prep.*), ĉirkaŭ (**89, 160**).
arouse, incit-i, vek-i.
arrange, aranĝ-i.
arrest, arest-i.
arrive, alven-i.
arrogant, arogant-a.
arrow, sag-o.
art, art-o.
Arthur, Artur-o.
article (**grammatical, literary**) artikol-o.
artificial, artefarit-a.
artless, naiv-a.
as (*adv.*) kiel; as ... as ... tiel ... kiel ... (**156**); — **if**, — **though**, kvazaŭ (**250**); — **far as**, ĝis (prep., **46**); — **much ... as ...**, tiom ... kiom (**164**).
ascertain, certiĝ-i; — **the truth of**, konstat-i.
(be) ashamed, hont-i.
ashes, cindr-o.
Asia, Azi-o.
aside from (*prep.*), krom.
ask (**inquire**), demand-i; (**request**), pet-i.
asparagus, asparag-o.
aspect, aspekt-o, mien-o.
ass, azen-o.
assemble, kunven-i, kunvok-i.
assist, help-i.
association (**organization**), asoci-o.
assurance, aplomb-o, certigo.
at (*prep.*), ĉe (**125, 160**), je (**260**); — **the rate of**, po (**175**).
athlete, atlet-o.
atmosphere, atmosfer-o.
attack, atak-i.
attain, ating-i, traf-i.
attempt, prov-i.
attentive, atent-a.
attest, atest-i.
attribute, atribut-o.
August, aŭgust-o.
Australia, Aŭstrali-o.
author, aŭtor-o, verkist-o.
automatic, aŭtomat-a.
autumn, aŭtun-o.
avaricious, avar-a.
avenge, venĝ-i.
avenue, ale-o, bulvard-o.
avoid, evit-i.
awake (*trans.*), vek-i.

away (*adv.*), for (**71**); (**distant**), malproksim-e (**170**).
axe, hakil-o.
axis (**axle**), aks-o.

B.

babble, babil-i.
baby, infanet-o.
bachelor, fraŭl-o; — **of arts (A.B.)**, abiturient-o.
back (**of the body**), dors-o; to the rear (*adv.*), malantaŭen (**121**).
bacon, lard-o.
bag, sak-o, valiz-o.
bagatelle, bagatel-o.
bake (*trans.*), bak-i.
balance (*trans.*), balanc-i; (**scales**), pesil-o.
ball (**to play with**), pilk-o; (**dance**), bal-o; (**globe**), glob-o.
banana, banan-o.
band (**stripe**), stri-o; (**music**), orkestr-o; (**group**), ar-o (**126**).
bandage, bandaĝ-i.
banish, ekzil-i.
bank (**financial**), bank-o; (**shore**), bord-o.
(become) bankrupt, bankrot-i
banner, flag-o, standard-o.
banquet, festen-o.
bar, bar-i.
barbarian, barbar-o.
bare, nud-a.
bark (**of trees**), ŝel-o; (**of dogs**), boj-i.
barrel, barel-o; — **organ**, gurd-o.
barren, senfrukt-a.
barrister, advokat-o.
barytone, bariton-o.
base (**foundation**), fundament-o, baz-o; (**ignoble**), malnobl-a.
basin, vaz-o, kuv-o.
basket, korb-o.
bass (**voice**), bas-o.
bathe (*trans.*), ban-i.
battle, batal-i.
be, est-i (**109**).
beak, bek-o.
beam (**wooden**), trab-o; (**light**), radi-o.
bean (**leguminous fruit**), fab-o; (**garden bean**), fazeol-o.
bear (**animal**), urs-o; (**carry**), port-i; (**endure**), elport-i, sufer-i; (**produce, give birth to**), nask-i.
beard, barb-o.
beast, best-o.
beat, bat-i; (**surpass**), super-i, venk-i.

beautiful, bel-a.
because (*conj.*), ĉar (**83**), tial ke (**83**); — **of** (*prep.*), pro (**86**).
become, iĝ-i, fariĝ-i (**232**); (**be suitable**), konven-i, dec-i.
bed, lit-o.
bee, abel-o.
beef, bovaĵ-o (**227**, c).
beefsteak, bifstek-o.
beet, bet-o.
before (*prep.*), antaŭ (**89, 90, 120, 159, 160**); (*conj.*), antaŭ ol (**97, 98**); (*adv.*), antaŭe, ĵus antaŭe.
beg (request), pet-i; (ask alms), almozon pet-i.
beggar, almozul-o.
begin (*trans.*), komenc-i (*see also prefix* ek-, **206**).
behave, kondut-i.
behind (*prep.*), post.
behold, rigard-i, vid-i; (*adv.*), jen (**228**).
Belgian, belg-o.
believe, kred-i (**265**).
bell, sonoril-o.
belong, aparten-i.
below (*prep.*), sub; (*adv.*), sub-e, malsupr-e.
belt, zon-o.
bench, benk-o.
bend (*trans.*), klin-i, fleks-i.
benevolence, bonfar-o.
berry, ber-o.
beside (*prep.*), krom; (near), apud; (**at the side of**), flanke de.
bet, vet-i.
betray, perfid-i.
betrothed (**man**), fianĉ-o.
between (*prep.*), inter (**85, 89**).
bewitch, ensorĉ-i.
beyond (*prep.*), preter.
bicycle, bicikl-o.
bid (**order**), ordon-i; — **farewell**, adiaŭ-i.
big, grand-a.
bill (**of bird**), bek-o; **bank** —, bankbilet-o; **hand—**, afiŝ-o; (**reckoning**), kalkul-o.
bind (**fasten**), lig-i; (**wounds**), bandaĝ-i.
bird, bird-o.
biscuit, biskvit-o; (**ring-shaped**), kring-o.
bit (**piece**), pec-o; (*adv.*), iom (**217**).
bite, mord-i.
black, nigr-a; **to** — (**shoes, etc.**), cir-i.
blackberry, rubus-o.
blackbird, merl-o.

blacking, cir-o.
blade (of knife, etc.), kling-o.
bleat, blek-i.
bless, ben-i.
blind, blind-a.
block (of wood), stip-o.
blood, sang-o.
bloom, flor-i **(116).**
blot (spot), makul-o.
blotter, sorbil-o, sorbpaper-o.
blouse, bluz-o, kitel-o.
blow, blov-i; **(stroke),** bat-o.
blue, blu-a; —**ish,** dubeblu-a.
blush, ruĝiĝ-i.
board (plank), tabul-o; **(food),** nutrad-o.
boast, fanfaron-i.
boat, boat-o, ŝipet-o.
body, korp-o.
boil (*intrans.*), bol-i **(275).**
bolt (fasten), rigl-i.
bonbon, bombon-o.
bond (fastening), ligil-o.
bone, ost-o.
book, libr-o; **note**—, **copy**—, kajer-o.
boot, bot-o.
border (edge), rand-o.
bore (holes), bor-i; **(weary),** enuig-i.
(be) born, naskiĝ-i.
borrow, pruntepren-i.
Boston, Boston-o.
both (*pronoun and adj.*), ambaŭ **(238);** (*adv.*), kaj **(26).**
bottle, botel-o.
bottom, fund-o, malsupr-o.
bough, branĉ-o.
boulevard, bulvard-o.
boundary, lim-o.
bouquet, buked-o.
bow (of ribbon), bant-o; **(for shooting),** pafark-o.
bow (bend), kliniĝ-i, salut-i.
box, kest-o; **small** —, skatol-o.
boy, knab-o.
bracket (shelf), bret-o.
brag, fanfaron-i.
braid, plekt-i.
brain, cerb-o.
branch (of tree), branĉ-o; **(of work or study),** fak-o.

brandish, sving-i.
brandy, brand-o.
brave, brav-o.
bread, pan-o.
break (*trans*)., romp-i; — **to pieces**, frakas-i.
breakfast, matenmanĝ-o.
breathe, spir-i.
brick, brik-o.
bridge, pont-o.
bridle, brid-o.
bright (**clear**), hel-a.
bring, alport-i; — **forth** (**produce**), nask-i; — **up** (**educate**), eduk-i.
brisk, vigl-a.
Briton, Brit-o.
broad, larĝ-a.
brochure, broŝur-o.
bronze, bronz-o.
brood (**birds**), kov-i.
brother, frat-o.
brown, brun-a.
brownie, kobold-o.
bruise, kontuz-i.
brush, bros-i.
brute, brut-o.
bucket, sitel-o.
buckle, buk-o.
bud, burĝon-o.
build, konstru-i.
bulb, tuber-o, bulb-o.
Bulgarian, Bulgar-o.
bull, bovvir-o.
bullet, kugl-o.
bunch, fask-o.
bundle, fask-o, pakaĵ-o.
bungle, fuŝ-i.
burden, ŝarĝ-i.
burn (*intrans.*), brul-i (**275**).
burst (*intrans.*), krev-i.
bury, enterig-i.
but (*conj.*), sed; (*prep.*), krom.
butcher, buĉ-i.
butter, buter-o.
butterfly, papili-o.
button, buton-o; **to —**, butonum-i.
buy, aĉet-i.
buzz, zum-i.

by (*prep.*), per (**64**); de (**169, 170**); (**past**), preter; (**according to**), laŭ (**191**).

C.

cab, fiakr-o.
cabbage, brasik-o.
cage, kaĝ-o.
cake, kuk-o.
calculate, kalkul-i.
caldron, kaldron-o.
calendar, kalendar-o.
calf, bovid-o; (**of the leg**), tibikarn-o.
call, vok-i; (**visit**), vizit-i.
calling (**profession**), profesi-o.
calm, kviet-a, trankvil-a.
camel, kamel-o.
camera, kamer-o.
can (be able), pov-i (**72**); (**preserve fruit, etc.**), konfit-i.
candle, kandel-o.
candy, kand-o.
canoe, kanot-o.
cap, ĉap-o.
capable, kapabl-a.
capital (**money**), kapital-o; (**excellent**), boneg-a; (**city**), ĉefurb-o.
capitol, kapitol-o.
car, vagon-o.
card, kart-o; **visiting** —, vizitkart-o.
care (**for**), zorg-i (pri).
caress, dorlot-i, kares-i.
carpet, tapiŝ-o.
carriage, kaleŝ-o, veturil-o.
carrot, karot-o.
carry, port-i.
carve, skulpt-i.
case (**small box**), skatol-o; (**chest**), kest-o; (**legal**), proces-o; (**holder**), uj-o (**181**), ing-o (**237**); (**occasion**), okaz-o; (**grammatical**), kaz-o.
cashier, kasist-o.
cascade, kaskad-o.
cast, ĵet-i.
castle, kastel-o.
cat, kat-o.
catch, kapt-i.
cattle, brut-o, brutar-o.
cauliflower, florbrasik-o.
cause, ig-i (**214**); (**produce a result**), kaŭz-i; (**motive**), kial-o; tial-o; (**espoused or advocated**), afer-o; (**legal**), proces-o.
caution, avert-i.

cavity, kav-o.
cease (*intrans.*), ĉes-i.
ceiling, plafon-o.
celebrate, fest-i, solenig-i; —**ed**, fama.
celery, celeri-o.
cellar, kel-o.
cent, cend-o.
center, centr-o.
centigram, centigram-o (**284**).
centiliter, centilitr-o (**284**).
centimeter, centimetr-o (**284**).
certain, cert-a; **a** — (**one**), iu (*pronoun and adj.*, 203); — **amount, etc.**, *see table*, 235.
certainly, nepr-e, cert-e, ja (**215**).
certify, atest-i, certig-i, konstat-i.
chain, ĉen-o; (**fetter**), katen-o; (**of mountains**), montar-o.
chair, seĝ-o.
(be) chairman, prezid-i.
chalk, kret-o.
chance, ŝanc-o; (**hazard**), hazard-o; (**opportunity**), okazo.
change (*trans.*), ŝanĝ-i; (**coins**), moner-oj.
chapel, kapel-o.
chapter, ĉapitr-o.
character, karakter-o.
charge (**commission**), komisi-o; (**burden**), ŝarĝ-o; (**price, cost**), prez-o, kost-o.
charm, ĉarm-i.
chase (**game, etc.**), ĉas-i; (**drive off**), forpel-i.
chatter, babil-i.
check (**on bank**), ĉek-o.
cheek, vang-o.
cheese, fromaĝ-o.
chemise, ĉemiz-o.
chemistry, ĥemi-o.
chemist's shop, apotek-o.
cheque, ĉek-o.
cherry, ĉeriz-o.
chest (**box**), kest-o; (**with a lid**), kofr-o.
chestnut, kaŝtan-o.
chew, maĉ-i.
chief, ĉef-a, precip-a; (**leader**), estr-o (**253**).
child, infan-o, id-o (**207**).
chimney, kamen-o.
chin, menton-o.
china (**porcelain**), porcelan-o; (**country**), Ĥinuj-o.
Chinaman, ĥin-o.
chirp, pep-i.

chocolate, ĉokolad-o.
choir, ĥor-o.
choose, elekt-i.
chop, hak-i; (**cutlet**), kotlet-o.
chrestomathy, krestomati-o.
Christ, Krist-o.
church (**building**), preĝej-o.
chute, ŝut-o.
cigar, cigar-o.
cigarette, cigared-o.
cinnamon, cinam-o.
cipher, cifer-o.
circle, cirkl-o, rond-o.
circular (**letter, etc.**), cirkuler-o.
circumstance, okaz-o, detal-o, cirkonstanc-o.
citizen, regnan-o, urban-o.
city, urb-o.
civilise, civiliz-i.
clack, krak-i.
claim, pretend-i.
clamber, ramp-i.
clap (*trans.*), klak-i.
class, klas-o.
clatter, (*trans.*), klak-i.
claw, ungeg-o.
clay, argil-o.
clean, pur-a.
clear (**bright**), hela; (**distinct**), klar-a.
clearing (**financial**), spez-o.
clergyman, pastr-o.
clerk, komiz-o.
clever, lert-a.
climate, klimat-o.
climb up, grimp-i, supren ramp-i.
cloak, mantel-o.
clock, horloĝ-o.
close (*trans.*), ferm-i; (**dense**), dens-a; — **to** (*prep.*), apud; proksim-e de (**170**).
cloth (**in general**), ŝtof-o; (**woollen, etc.**), drap-o; (**piece of**), tuk-o; **table—**, tablotuk-o.
clothe, vest-i.
cloud, nub-o.
club (**organization**), klub-o; (**weapon**), bastoneg-o.
coal, karb-o.
coat, vest-o; (**short**), jak-o; (**frock**), redingot-o; **over—**, surtut-o.
cock (**fowl**), kok-o.
coffee, kaf-o.

collect (*trans.*), kolekt-i.
college, kolegi-o.
colonel, kolonel-o.
color, kolor-o.
column, kolon-o.
comb, komb-i.
come, ven-i.
comedy, komedi-o.
comfort (**console**), konsol-i; (**freedom from pain, etc.**), komfort-o.
command, ordon-i; (**military and naval**), komand-i.
commerce, komerc-o.
commission (**entrusted**), komisi-o; (**percentage of profit**), tantiem-o, komisi-pag-o.
committee, komitat-o.
common (**general**), ĝeneral-a; (**mutual**), komun-a; (**vulgar**), vulgar-a.
communicate, komunik-i.
company (**commercial**), kompanio; (**guests**), gastar-o; (**presence**), ĉeest-o.
compare (*trans.*), kompar-i (**266**).
compassion, kompat-o.
compete, konkur-i.
competition, konkurad-o; (**for prizes**), konkurs-o; (**in business**), konkurenc-o.
complain, plend-i.
complicate, komplik-i.
compose (**music or literature**), verk-i.
compositor (**of type**), kompostist-o.
conceal, kaŝ-i (**252**).
concern, koncern-i (**266**); (**anxiety**), maltrankvilec-o.
concerning (*prep.*), pri. (**264, c**).
concert (**musical**), koncert-o.
condemn, kondamn-i.
condition, cirkonstanc-o; (**stipulation**), kondiĉ-o; (**state**), stat-o.
conduct (**lead**), konduk-i; — **oneself** (**behave**), kondut-i.
conduct (**behavior**), kondut-o; (**in regard to right or wrong**), mor-o.
conductor (**of car, etc.**), konduktor-o.
confess, konfes-i.
confide, konfid-i.
conform, konform-i (**266**).
confound (**confuse**), konfuz-i.
congratulate, gratul-i.
congress, kongres-o.
conquer, venk-i.
conscience, konscienc-o.
(be) conscious, konsci-i.
consent, konsent-i.
consequently, sekv-e, do; tial (**78**).

(be) conservative, konservativ-a.
consist, konsist-i.
console, konsol-i.
consonant (letter), konsonant-o.
conspire, konspir-i.
constant, konstant-a.
constitution, konstituci-o.
consul, konsul-o.
consult, konsult-i, pet-i konsilon de.
contaminate, infekt-i.
content, kontent-a.
continent (land), kontinent-o.
continue, daŭr-i, daŭrig-i.
contour, kontur-o.
contract (commercial and legal), kontrakt-i.
contralto, kontralt-o.
contrary, mal-o **(67)**; kontraŭstarem-a.
control, kontrol-i; **(govern)**, reg-i.
convenient, konven-a, oportun-a.
convince, konvink-i.
cook, kuir-i.
copper, kupr-o.
copy, kopi-i; **(of a book, etc.)**, ekzempler-o.
coquettish, koket-a.
cork, ŝtop-i; **(bark of cork tree)**, kork-o.
corner, angul-o.
corporal, corporeal, korp-a.
corps (military), korpus-o.
corpse, kadavr-o.
correct, korekt-i; **(right)**, prav-a.
correspond, korespond-i.
corridor, koridor-o.
cost, kost-i.
costume, kostum-o.
cotton, koton-o.
cough, tus-i.
counsel, konsil-i.
count, kalkul-i, sum-i, nombr-i; **(person)**, graf-o.
county, grafland-o.
country, land-o; **(as opposed to city)**, kampar-o.
coupon, kupon-o.
(be) courageous, kuraĝ-i.
course (of lessons), kurs-o; **(of a meal)**, servic-o; **of —**, kompreneble; **in the — of**, en la daŭro de.
court, kort-o, korteg-o, juĝej-o.
courteous, ĝentil-a.

courtesy, ĝentilec-o; (**kindness**), komplez-o.
cousin, kuz-o.
cover, kovr-i; (**put covering upon**), teg-i.
crab, krab-o.
crack (**split**) (*trans.*), fend-i; (**crackle**), krak-i; (**burst open**) (*intrans.*), krev-i.
cradle, lulil-o.
crafty, ruz-a.
cravat, kravat-o.
crawl, ramp-i.
crazy, frenez-a.
cream, krem-o.
create, kre-i.
creep, ramp-i; — **up**, grimp-i.
crime, krim-o.
crippled, kripl-a.
criticise, kritik-i.
crooked, tord-a, malrekt-a, kurb-a.
cross, kruc-o; (**angry**), koler-a; — **off**, trastrek-i.
crowd, amas-o, anar-o (**145, 126**).
crown, kron-o.
crucify, krucum-i.
cruel, kruel-a.
crush, pist-i, premeg-i.
crust, krust-o.
cry (**weep**), plor-i; (**shout**), kri-i; (**of animals**), blek-i.
cucumber, kukum-o.
cultivate, kultur-i; — **the soil**, terkultur-i.
cunning, ruz-a.
cup, tas-o; (**goblet**), pokal-o.
cupboard, ŝrank-o.
curious (**odd**), kurioz-a; (**inquisitive**), scivol-a.
curl (**of hair**), bukl-o.
curtain, kurten-o.
curve, kurb-o.
cushion, kusen-o.
custom, kutim-o; (**tax**), impost-o.
cut, tranĉ-i; (**of a garment**), fason-o.
cutlet, kotlet-o.
cylinder, cilindr-o.
Cyrus, Cirus-o.

D.

dabble (**a liquid**), plaŭd-i.
dainty, delikat-a.
damage, difekt-i.
Damocles, Damokl-o.

Dane, dan-o.
danger, danĝer-o.
dance, danc-i.
date (fruit), daktil-o; **(time)**, dat-o.
dawn, tagiĝ-o.
day, tag-o.
deaf, surd-a.
dear (prized), kar-a; **(expensive)**, multekost-a.
debase (adulterate), fals-i; **(make bad)**, malbonig-i.
decay (mould), ŝim-o; **(in health)**, kaduk-i.
deceive, tromp-i.
December, decembr-o.
decide, decid-i.
decigram, decigram-o **(284)**.
deciliter, decilitr-o **(284)**.
decimeter, decimetr-o **(284)**.
deck (of ship), ferdek-o; **(adorn)**, ornam-i.
declaim, deklam-i.
deep, profund-a.
deer, cerv-o.
defend, defend-i.
define, defin-i, priskrib-i.
degree, grad-o.
dekagram, dekagram-o **(284)**.
dekaliter, dekalitr-o **(284)**.
dekameter, dekametr-o **(284)**.
delay, prokrast-i.
delegate, deleg-i.
delicate, delikat-a.
delightful, ĉarm-a, plaĉeg-a.
deliver (supply), liver-i; **(set free)**, liberig-i.
delusion, iluzi-o.
demand, postul-i.
dense, dens-a.
deny, ne-i **(171)**.
department (of work, etc.), fak-o.
desert, dezert-o; **(just reward)**, merit-o.
deserve, merit-i.
desire, dezir-i.
desk, pupitr-o, skribtabl-o.
dessert, desert-o.
destine, destin-i; difin-i.
destiny, destin-o; **(lot)**, sort-o.
destroy, detru-i, neniig-i.
detail, detal-o.
dew, ros-o.

diamond, diamant-o.
dictionary, vortar-o.
dictate (letters), dikt-i.
die, mort-i.
different, divers-a, malsam-a, diferenc-a.
differentiate, diferencig-i.
dig, fos-i.
dignity (rank), rang-o.
diligent, diligent-a.
dimension, dimensio; **(size)**, ampleks-o.
Diogenes, Diogen-o.
dip (in liquid), tremp-i.
diploma, diplom-o; **holder of** —, diplomit-o.
diplomat, diplomat-o.
direct (guide), direkt-i; **(undeviating)**, rekt-a.
disburse, elspez-i, elpag-i.
discount, rabat-i.
discuss, diskut-i, priparol-i.
disdain, malŝat-i, malestim-i.
dish (flat), plad-o.
dispatch (letter), depeŝ-o.
distance, distanc-o.
distinct, klar-a.
distinguish, disting-i.
distract (the attention), distr-i; **(confuse)**, konfuz-i.
disturb, ĝen-i, maltrankvilig-i.
diverse, divers-a.
divide (*trans.*), divid-i.
do, far-i; **(suffice)**, sufiĉ-i.
doctor, doktor-o; **(medical)**, kuracist-o.
dog, hund-o.
doll, pup-o.
dollar, dolar-o.
donkey, azen-o.
door, pord-o; —**handle,** ans-o.
doubt, dub-i.
down (hair or feathers), lanug-o; **(downward)** (*adv.*), malsupren.
dove, kolomb-o.
drag (*trans.*), tren-i.
draw (pull), tir-i; **(sketch)**, skiz-i.
drawer, tirkest-o.
drawing-room, salon-o.
dream (in sleep), sonĝ-i; **(fancy)**, rev-i.
drench, tremp-i.
dress, vest-i (sin); **(frock)**, rob-o; —**suit**, frak-o.
dressing (sauce), saŭc-o.

drink, trink-i.
drip, gut-i.
drive (off), pel-i; **(vehicle)**, veturig-i; **(roadway)**, ŝose-o.
drown (*intrans.*), dron-i.
drug, drog-o; —**store**, apotek-o.
drum, tambur-o.
dry, sek-a.
duck, anas-o.
dues, kotizaĵ-o; **pay** —, kotiz-i.
dumb, mut-a; — **animal**, brut-o.
during (*prep.*), dum (**96**); en la daŭro de-.
dusk, krepusk-o.
dust, polv-o; **remove the** —, senpolvig-i.
duty, dev-o; **be on** —, deĵor-i.
dwell, loĝ-i.

E.

each (*adj. and pronoun*), ĉiu (**173**).
eager, avid-a.
eagle, agl-o.
ear (of the body), orel-o.
early, fru-a.
earth, ter-o; **(the planet)**, terglob-o.
east, orient-o.
Easter, Pask-o.
easy, facil-a.
eat, manĝ-i.
echo, eĥ-o.
economical, ŝparem-a.
edge, rand-o; **(of rivers, etc.)**, bord-o.
edit, redakt-i.
editor, redaktor-o.
editorial body, redakci-o.
educate, **(rear)**, eduk-i; **(teach)**, instru-i.
effect, efekt-o.
effective, efektiv-a.
(be) efficacious, efik-i.
egg, ov-o.
Egypt, Egipt-o.
eight (*adj.*), ok (**136**).
either (*pronoun and adj.*), iu (**203**); ĉiu (**173**); unu aŭ la alia; (*adv.*), aŭ; **on** —
side (*adv.*), ambaŭflanke (**238**).
elbow, kubut-o.
electric, elektr-a.
elk, alk-o.
elm, ulm-o.

eloquent, elokvent-a.
embroider, brod-i.
eminent, eminent-a.
empire, imperi-o.
employ (**hire**), dung-i; — **oneself**, sin okupi; (**use**), uz-i.
employee, komiz-o, dungit-o, oficist-o.
employment, ofic-o, okupad-o.
enchant, ensorĉ-i, rav-i.
encore (*adv.*), bis.
end (*trans.*), fin-i.
endow, dot-i.
endure, sufer-i, elport-i.
engineer, inĝenier-o.
Englishman, angl-o.
enjoy, ĝu-i; — **oneself**, sin amuz-i.
enlightened, kler-a.
enlist (*trans.*), varb-i.
enroll (*trans.*), registr-i, varb-i.
enthusiasm, entuziasm-o.
entire, tut-a.
entrust, komisii, alkonfid-i.
envelope (**of letter**), kovert-o.
envy, envi-i.
(**be an**) **epicure**, frand-i.
epoch, epok-o.
equal, egal-a.
err, erar-i.
establish, establ-i, fond-i; (**prove, etc.**), konstat-i.
estate, bien-o.
esteem, estim-i.
estimate, taks-i.
eternal, etern-a, ĉiam-a.
Europe, Eŭrop-o.
evangel, evangeli-o.
even (**level**), eben-a; — **number**, parnombro; (**actually**) (*adv.*), eĉ.
evening, vesper-o (**93**); — **dress** (**of man**), frak-o.
ever (*adv.*), iam (**212**); (*indefinite adv.*), ajn (**236**); (**always**), ĉiam (**187**).
every (**one**), (*pronoun and adv.*), ĉiu (**173**); —**thing**, — **way**, etc., *see table*, 235.
evolution, evoluci-o.
exact, akurat-a, ĝust-a; (**demand**), postul-i.
examine, ekzamen-i; — **and check**, kontrol-i.
example, ekzempl-o; (**model**), model-o.
Excellency (*title*), moŝt-o (**258**).
except, escept-i (**266**); (*prep.*), krom.
excite, ekscit-i.
exercise (*trans.*), ekzerc-i.

exhale, elspir-i.
exhort, admon-i.
exile, ekzil-i.
exist, ekzist-i.
expect, atend-i.
expend (money), elspez-i; (energy, etc.), uz-i, eluz-i.
experienced, spert-a.
experiment, eksperiment-i.
expert, spert-a, lert-a.
explode (*intrans.*), eksplod-i (275).
explore, esplor-i.
express, esprim-i; (train), rapida vagonaro.
extend (*trans.*), etend-i, pligrandig-i, plilongig-i.
extensive, vast-a, vastampleks-a.
extent (size), ampleks-o.
extinguish, esting-i.
extraordinary, eksterordinar-a.
eye, okul-o; —brow, brov-o; —lid, palpebr-o.

F.

fable, fabel-o.
face, vizaĝ-o.
fact, fakt-o; in —, fakt-e, efektiv-e, ja (215).
fade, velk-i.
fair (just), just-a; (beautiful), bel-a.
fairy, fe-o, fein-o.
faint, sven-i.
faithful, fidel-a.
fall, fal-i; (autumn), aŭtun-o.
false, fals-a; (treacherous), perfid-a.
fame, fam-o.
familiar, familiar-a, kutim-a.
family, famili-o.
fancy, imag-i, rev-i.
far, malproksim-e; as — as (*prep.*), ĝis (46).
farm (as a tenant), farm-i; (till the soil), terkultur-i.
farewell (*adv. and interjection*), adiaŭ (171, 273).
fashion, fason-o, mod-o.
fasten, lig-i.
fat, gras-o; (corpulent), dik-a.
fatal, fatal-a.
fate, sort-o, fatal-o, destin-o.
father, patr-o.
faucet, kran-o.
favor, favor-i; a —, komplezo.
favorable, favor-a.

fay, fe-o, fein-o.
fear, tim-i.
feather, plum-o.
feature, trajt-o.
feed, nutr-i; — **flocks**, paŝt-i.
feel, sent-i; (**with fingers, etc.**), palp-i.
female, in-o (**59**).
fervor, fervor-o.
fetter (**chain, etc.**), katen-o.
fever, febr-o.
fiancé, fianĉ-o.
fie (*interjection*), fi (**273**).
field, kamp-o.
fight, batal-i, milit-i.
fill, plenig-i.
find, trov-i.
fine, bel-a, delikat-a; (**of money**), monpun-o.
finger, fingr-o; **index** —, montra fingro; **little** —, malgranda fingro; **middle** —, longa fingro; **ring** —, ringa fingro.
finish (*trans.*), fin-i.
fir, abi-o.
fire, fajr-o; **set** — **to**, ekbrulig-i.
firm, firm-a.
fish, fiŝ-o; (**catch fish**), fiŝkapt-i.
fist, pugn-o.
fit, almezur-i; (**be**) —, taŭg-i.
(**be**) **fitting**, konven-i; (**decent**), dec-i.
five (*adj.*), kvin (**136**).
flag, flag-o; standard-o.
flat, glat-a, eben-a; plat-a.
flesh, karn-o.
flex (*trans.*), fleks-i.
floor, plank-o.
flour, farun-o.
flow, flu-i.
flower, flor-o (**116**).
fluid, fluid-a.
fly, flug-i; (**insect**), muŝ-o.
foam, ŝaŭm-o.
focus, fokus-o.
fog, nebul-o.
fold, fald-i.
folk, popol-o.
follow, sekv-i, postven-i, postir-i.
(**be**) **fond of sweets**, frand-i.
fondle, dorlot-i.

foot (of the body), pied-o; **(measure)**, fut-o.
for (*prep.*), por (**95, 98, 262**); pro (**86**); (*conj.*), ĉar (**83**).
force, fort-o; (compel), devig-i; — **(upon)**, altrud-i (al).
fore-, pra- (**282**).
forehead, frunt-o.
foreign, fremd-a.
forge (falsify), fals-i.
forget, forges-i.
forgive, pardon-i.
fork, fork-o.
form, form-i, alform-i, model-i.
formal, solen-a.
found, fond-i.
foundation, fundament-o.
four (*adj.*), kvar (**136**).
fount, font-o.
fountain, fontan-o.
fox, vulp-o.
fragrance, arom-o, bonodor-o.
frame (of picture), kadr-o.
frank, afrank-i.
Frederick, Frederik-o.
free, liber-a.
Frenchman, franc-o.
frequent, oft-a; **(visit often)**, vizitad-i.
fresh, freŝ-a, nov-a.
Friday, vendred-o.
friend, amik-o.
fringe, franĝ-o.
frivolous, malserioz-a.
frock coat, redingot-o.
frog, ran-o.
from (*prep.*), de (**89, 170**); el; **(cause)**, pro (**86**).
frost, frost-o; **(hoar)**, prujn-o.
froth, ŝaŭm-o.
fruit, frukt-o.
fruitless (vain), van-a.
fry (*trans.*), frit-i.
function (of machinery, etc.), funkci-i.
funereal, funebr-a.
fulfil, plenum-i.
full, plen-a.
fur, fel-o; **(coat or wrap)**, pelt-o.
furious, furioz-a.
furnish (supply), liver-i; **(provide)**, proviz-i; **(a house)**, mebl-i.
furniture (piece of), mebl-o.

furrow, sulk-o.
further (*adv.*), plu.
fuse (*trans.*), fand-i.
futile, van-a.
future, estontec-o; (**grammatical**), estont-o; (*adj.*), estont-a.

G.

gain, gajn-i, obten-i.
gallery, galeri-o; (**for pictures**), pinakotek-o.
gallop, galop-i.
gamin, bub-o.
gape (**yawn**), osced-i.
garden, ĝarden-o.
garland, girland-o.
gas, gas-o.
gather (*trans.*), kolekt-i.
gay, gaj-a.
gaze, fikse rigard-i.
gazette, gazet-o.
general, ĝeneral-a, komun-a; (**military**), general-o.
gentleman, sinjor-o.
geometry, geometri-o.
German, german-o.
Gertrude, Gertrud-o.
ghost, fantom-o.
gift, donac-o.
ginger, zingibr-o.
girdle, zon-o.
give, don-i; (**as a gift**), donac-i; — **information**, inform-i; — **notice**, aviz-i; — **witness**, atest-i; — **birth to**, nask-i.
(be) glad, ĝoj-i (**116**).
glass (**material**), vitr-o; (**tumbler**), glas-o.
glide, glit-i.
globe, glob-o.
glory, glor-o.
glossy (**polished**), polurit-a.
glove, gant-o.
glue, glu-i.
gnash, grinc-i.
go, ir-i; (**in vehicle, boat, etc.**), vetur-i; — **on a pilgrimage**, pilgrim-i.
goal, cel-o.
goblet, pokal-o.
God, Di-o.
good, bon-a; **be — for**, taŭg-i por.
good-bye (*adv. and interjection*), adiaŭ (**171, 273**).
goose, anser-o.

gospel, evangeli-o.
govern, reg-i.
graceful, graci-a.
grade, grad-o; (**rank**), rang-o.
grain (**wheat, etc.**), gren-o; (**unit**) er-o (**276**).
gram, gram-o (**284**).
grammar, gramatik-o.
grandfather, av-o.
grandson, nep-o.
grape, vinber-o.
grass, herb-o.
grasshopper, akrid-o.
grate, rasp-i; grater, raspil-o.
grating (**bar or lattice**), krad-o.
grave, tomb-o; (**serious**), grav-a.
gravitate, gravit-i.
gravy, saŭc-o.
gray, griz-a.
grieve (*trans.*), ĉagren-i, malĝojig-i; (*intrans.*) malĝoj-i.
grind, grinc-i.
great, grand-a; (**remote in ancestry**), pra- (**282**).
Greek, grek-o.
green, verd-a; —**ish**, dubeverd-a.
greet, salut-i.
groan, ĝem-i.
group, grup-o, ar-o (**126**).
ground, ter-o; — **floor**, teretaĝ-o.
grow, kresk-i, veget-i.
guard, gard-i.
guess, diven-i.
guest, gast-o.
guide, gvid-i, direkt-i.
guilty, kulp-a.
gunpowder, pulv-o.
gush (**of liquids**), ŝpruc-i.

H.

habit, kutim-o.
hack, hak-i; (**carriage**), fiakr-o.
hail (**frozen rain**), hajl-o.
(**a**) **hair**, har-o; — **pencil**, penik-o.
half, duon-o (**166, 277**).
halt (*intrans.*), halt-i.
ham, ŝink-o.
hammer, martel-o.
hand, man-o; (**of clock**), montril-o.

handbill, afiŝ-o.
handicraft, meti-o.
handsome, bel-a.
hang (*intrans.*), pend-i.
handy, oportun-a.
happen, okaz-i.
happy, feliĉ-a.
harbor, haven-o.
hardly (*adv.*), apenaŭ.
hare, lepor-o.
haricot (**bean**), fazeol-o.
harness, jung-i.
harvest, rikolt-i.
hasten (*trans.*), akcel-i; (*intrans.*) rapid-i.
hat, ĉapel-o.
haughty, fier-a.
haul, tren-i.
have, hav-i; — **to**, dev-i.
hay, fojn-o.
hazard, hazard-o.
hazel-nut, avel-o.
he (*pronoun*), li (**32, 37, 42**).
head, kap-o; (*adj.*), ĉef-a.
health, san-o; **state of (good or bad)** —, fart-o.
hear, aŭd-i.
heart, kor-o; **by** —, (**by rote**), parker-e.
heat (*trans.*), hejt-i, varmig-i.
heaven, ĉiel-o; heavenly body, astr-o.
heavy, pez-a.
Hebrew, hebre-o.
heel (**of foot**), kalkan-o; (**of shoe**), kalkanum-o.
hektare, hektar-o (**284**).
hektogram, hektogram-o (**284**).
hektoliter, hektolitr-o (**284**).
hektometer, hektometr-o (**284**).
help, help-i (**265**).
hen, kokin-o.
herb, herb-o.
hero, hero-o.
hesitate, hezit-i.
hide, kaŝ-i (**252**); (**skin of animals**), fel-o.
Hiero, Hieron-o.
high, alt-a.
hinge, ĉarnir-o.
hip, koks-o.
hire (**persons**), dung-i; (**houses, etc.**), lu-i.

hiss, sibl-i.
history, histori-o.
ho (*interjection*), ho (**273**).
hoar (frost), prujn-o.
hoarse, raŭk-a.
hog, pork-o.
hold, ten-i.
holder (**handle**), tenil-o, ans-o; (**receptacle**), uj-o (**181**); ing-o (**237**).
hole, tru-o; (**cavity**), kav-o.
Holland, Holand-o.
holy, sankt-a.
home, hejm-o; **at —**, ĉehejme.
homesickness, nostalgi-o.
honest, honest-a.
honey, miel-o.
honeysuckle, lonicer-o.
honor, honor-i; (*as term of address*), moŝt-o (**258**).
hook, kroĉ-i.
hope, esper-i.
horizon, horizont-o.
horizontal, horizontal-a.
horn, korn-o.
horse, ĉeval-o.
horse-radish, armoraci-o.
hose, ŝtrump-oj; **— supporter**, ŝelk-o.
hotel, hotel-o.
hour, hor-o (**185**).
house, dom-o; **at the — of** (*prep.*), ĉe (**125, 160**).
how (*adv.*), kiel (**134**); kiamanier-e; **— much**, kiom (**140, 185**).
however (*conj.*), tamen; (*adv.*), ajn (**236**).
hue, nuanc-o.
hum, zum-i.
human being, hom-o.
humble, humil-a.
humor, humor-o.
hundred (*adj.*), cent (**142**).
hungry, malsat-a.
hunt, serĉ-i; (**game or wild animals**), ĉas-i.
hurdy-gurdy, gurd-o.
hurl, ĵet-i.
hurrah (*interjection*), hura (**273**).
hurricane, uragan-o.
hurry, rapid-i.
husband, edz-o.
hypocrite, hipokrit-o.

I.

I (*pronoun*), mi (**32, 37, 274**).
ice, glaci-o; (**food**), glaciaĵ-o.
idea, ide-o.
ideal, ideal-o.
identical, ident-a.
idiom, idiom-o.
idiot, idiot-o.
if (*conj.*), se (**240**); **as —**, kvazaŭ (**250**); (**whether**), ĉu.
ignore, ignor-i.
illusion, iluzi-o.
illustrate, ilustr-i.
image, bild-o.
imagine, imag-i.
imitate, imit-i.
immediate, tuj-a (**171**).
implicate, implik-i.
important, grav-a, serioz-a.
importunate, altrudem-a.
impose, trud-i.
impost, impost-o.
impress, impres-i.
impulse, impuls-o.
in (*prep.*), en (**46, 89, 160**); **— the presence of**, ĉe (**125, 160**).
inch, col-o.
incite, incit-i.
incline (*trans.*), klin-i.
incommode, ĝen-i.
(be) indebted, ŝuld-i.
indeed (*adv.*), ja (**215**); do; efektiv-e.
index, tabel-o.
Indian (**American**), indian-o, ruĝhaŭtul-o; **— corn**, maiz-o.
indifferent, indiferent-a.
industry (**trade**), industri-o.
inebriate, ebri-a.
inevitable, nepr-a, neevitebl-a.
infect, infekt-i.
influence, influ-i.
inform, inform-i, sciig-i.
ingenuous, naiv-a.
inhabitant, loĝant-o, an-o (**145**).
inhale, enspir-i.
ink, ink-o.
inquire, demand-i.
insect, insekt-o.
inside (*adv.*), intern-e; (*prep.*), en.

insist, insist-i.
inspect, inspekt-i, ekzamen-i, rigard-i, kontrol-i.
inspire, inspir-i.
instantaneous, moment-a.
instead of (*prep.*), anstataŭ (**98, 159**).
instruct, instru-i; (**order**), ordon-i.
insult, insult-i.
insure (**with a company**), asekur-i; (**make certain**), certig-i.
intelligent, inteligent-a.
intend, intenc-i.
interest, interes-i; (**of money**), procent-o.
(be) intermittent, intermit-i.
internal, intern-a.
interpret, interpret-i.
intimate, intim-a.
intoxicated, ebri-a.
investigate, esplor-i, ekzamen-i, elserĉ-i.
invite, invit-i.
iron (**metal**), fer-o; (**linen**), glad-i.
island, insul-o.
it (*pronoun*), ĝi (**32, 37, 42, 274**); *see also* 50, 51.
Italian, ital-o.

J.

jacket, jak-o.
jail, karcer-o.
jam, kompot-o, fruktaĵ-o.
January, januar-o.
jaw (**orifice, opening**), faŭk-o; (**of the skull**), makzel-o; —**bone**, makzelost-o.
jealous, ĵaluz-a.
jest, ŝerc-i.
Jesus, Jesu-o.
Jew, hebre-o.
jewel, juvel-o.
jingle (*intrans.*), tint-i.
John, Johan-o.
joint, artik-o.
joke, ŝerc-i.
journal, ĵurnal-o, revu-o.
journey, vojaĝ-i.
judge, juĝ-i.
jug, kruĉ-o.
juggle, ĵongl-i.
July, juli-o.
jump, salt-i.
June, juni-o.

jurist, jurist-o.
just (**upright**), just-a; (**exact**), ĝust-a; (*adv.*), ĝust-e, ĵus.

K.

keep, ten-i, gard-i; (**preserve**), konserv-i; — **in mind**, memor-i.
kerosene, petrol-o.
key, ŝlosil-o; (**of piano, etc.**), klav-o.
kill, mortig-i.
kilogram, kilogram-o (**284**).
kiloliter, kilolitr-o (**284**).
kilometer, kilometr-o (**284**).
kind (**species**), spec-o; (**good**), bon-a, bonkor-a; **that** —, **what** —, etc., *see table*, 235.
kindness, komplez-o, bonkorec-o.
king, reĝ-o; —**dom**, reĝolando.
kiss, kis-i.
knave, fripon-o.
knee, genu-o.
kneel, genufleks-i.
knit, trik-i.
knock, frap-i.
knot, tuber-o; (**tied**), ligaĵ-o; (**of ribbon**), bant-o.
know, sci-i; (**be acquainted with**), kon-i (**117**).
kobold, kobold-o.

L.

labor, labor-i; — **for the success or completion of something**, klopod-i.
lace, punt-o; (**of a shoe**), laĉ-o.
(be) lacking (*intrans.*) mank-i.
lake, lag-o.
lamb, ŝafid-o; (**meat**), ŝafidaĵ-o.
lame, lam-a.
lamp, lamp-o.
lance, lanc-o.
land, land-o; (**estate**), bien-o; (**soil**), ter-o.
landscape, pejzaĝ-o.
language, lingv-o.
lantern, lantern-o.
large, grand-a.
lark (**bird**), alaŭd-o.
last (*intrans.*), daŭr-i; (**in a series**), last-a; (**previous**) pasint-a, antaŭ-a.
latch, ans-o.
late, malfru-a.
Latin, latin-a.
latter, ĉi-tiu (**61, 62**).

lattice, krad-o.
laugh, rid-i (**265**).
law, leĝ-o; —**suit**, proces-o; (**rule**), regul-o.
lawyer, advokat-o, leĝist-o.
lay, meti, kuŝig-i; — **aside**, demet-i; — **claim**, pretend-i.
layer, tavol-o.
lead, konduk-i.
lead (**metal**), plumb-o.
leaf, foli-o.
league (**alliance**), lig-o.
lean (*trans.*), apog-i, klin-i; (**not fat**), malgras-a.
leap, salt-i; —**year**, superjar-o.
learn, lern-i; (**news, etc.**), sciiĝ-i.
learned, kler-a.
least (*adv.*), malplej (**80**), malpli multe (**81**); **at** —, almenaŭ.
leather, led-o.
leave (*trans.*), las-i; — **off** (*intrans.*), ĉes-i.
leg, krur-o.
legal, leĝ-a; — **process**, proces-o.
lemon, citron-o.
lemonade, citronaĵ-o, limonad-o.
lend, prunt-i, pruntedon-i.
lens, objektiv-o.
lengthen (*trans.*), etend-i, plilongig-i.
less (*adv.*), malpli (**80**); malpli multe (**81**).
lesson, lecion-o.
let (*trans.*), las-i; (**rent**), luig-i; (**permit**), permes-i.
letter (**epistle**), leter-o; (**of the alphabet**), liter-o.
lettuce, laktuk-o.
level, nivel-o; (**flat**), eben-a.
library, bibliotek-o; (**collection of books**), librar-o.
lick, lek-i.
lie (**recline**), kuŝ-i (**239**); (**tell falsehoods**), mensog-i.
lift, lev-i.
light, lum-a, hel-a; (**not heavy**), malpez-a.
lightning, fulm-o.
like, ŝat-i; (**similar**), simil-a; see also 250.
limb, membro; (**of a tree**), branĉ-o.
limit, lim-i.
linden, tili-o.
line, lini-o, vic-o, strek-o.
linen, tol-o.
lion, leon-o.
lip, lip-o.
liquid, fluid-a.
listen, aŭskult-i.

liter, litr-o (**284**).
literal, laŭliter-a.
literature, literatur-o.
little, malgrand-a; (*with slightly affectionate sense*), et-a (**198**); (*adv.*), malmulte, iom (**217**); — **by** —, iom post iom.
live, viv-i; (**dwell**), loĝ-i (**133**).
load, ŝarĝ-i.
loan, prunt-i, pruntedon-i.
local, lok-a.
lock, ŝlos-i; (**fastening**), serur-o.
locomotive, lokomotiv-o.
lodge, loĝ-i.
log, ŝtip-o.
long, long-a; — **for**, sopir-i je.
look, rigard-i; — **for**, serĉ-i.
lose, perd-i; (**fail to profit**), malgajn-i; — **time**, malfru-i.
lot (**fate**), sort-o.
loud, laŭt-a.
love, am-i; **make** —, amindum-i.
loyal, fidel-a, lojal-a.
luck, ŝanc-o; lucky, bonŝanc-a.
lull, kvietig-i; (**to sleep**), lul-i.
lunatic, lunatik-o.
lung, pulm-o.
luxury, luks-o.

M.

macaroni, makaroni-o.
machine, maŝin-o.
mad, frenez-a.
magazine, gazet-o, ĵurnal-o, revu-o.
magic, magi-o.
mail, poŝt-o, enpoŝtig-i; — **box**, poŝtkest-o.
maize, maiz-o.
majestic, majest-a.
majesty (*term of address*), moŝt-o (**258**).
make, far-i (see also 214); — **mistakes**, erar-i; — **love**, amindum-i.
malicious, malic-a.
man, vir-o.
manage, administr-i, direkt-i; (**a household**), mastrum-i.
manner, manier-o; (**right or wrong**), mor-o; **in that** —, **in every** —, etc., *see table*, 235.
mantle, mantel-o.
manufacture, fabrik-i.
manuscript, manuskript-o.
maple, acer-o.

marble (stone), marmor-o.
march, marŝad-i.
March, mart-o.
mark, mark-o, sign-o; (**official**), stamp-o.
marmalade, marmelad-o.
marry (**become married**), edziĝ-i.
master, mastr-o; (**of his profession or art**), majstr-o; — **of Arts (A.M.)**, magistr-o.
match (**for fire**), alumet-o.
material, material-o; (**cloth**), ŝtof-o.
matter, afer-o.
mature, matur-a.
maximum, maksimum-o.
May, maj-o; (**auxiliary verb**), *see* 269, 270.
mayonnaise, majones-a.
mean, signif-i, intenc-i, malnobl-a.
meaning, senc-o.
means, rimed-o; **by — of** (*prep.*), per (**64**).
measure (*trans.*), mezur-i.
meat, viand-o.
mechanics, meĥanik-o.
medical, medicin-a, kuracist-a.
medicine (**drug, etc.**), kuracil-o; (**science**), medicin-o, kuracart-o.
meet (*trans.*), renkont-i, traf-i; (**assemble**), kunven-i.
melody, melodi-o.
melon, melon-o.
melt, fluidig-i, fluidiĝ-i, degel-i.
member, membr-o, an-o (**145**).
memory, memor-o; **by —**, parker-e, memor-e.
mend, ripar-i; (**patch**), flik-i.
mention, nom-i; cit-i.
menu, menu-o.
merely (*adv.*), nur.
merit, merit-i.
merry, gaj-a; **make —**, festen-i.
merry-go-round, karusel-o.
metal, metal-o.
meter, metr-o (**284**).
method, metod-o.
middle, mez-o, centr-o.
mien, mien-o.
mild, mild-a.
mile, mejl-o.
milk, lakt-o; (**draw the milk of**), melk-i.
mill, muel-o.
millimeter, milimetr-o (**284**).

million, milion-o.
mine (coal, etc), min-o; (*possessive adj.*), mi-a (**43**).
mineral, mineral-o.
minimum, minimum-o.
minister (political), ministr-o; (**clergyman**), pastr-o.
minute (time), minut-o; (*adj.*), detal-a, malgrand-a.
minutes (of a meeting), protokol-o.
mirror, spegul-o.
miserly, avar-a.
misery, mizer-o.
miss (fail to reach), maltraf-i; (**be missing**), mank-i; (**notice the absence of**),
senti la foreston de; (**young lady**), fraŭlin-o (**163**).
mist, nebul-o.
mistake, erar-o.
Mister, Sinjor-o (**163, 286**).
mix (*trans.*), miks-i.
mock, mok-i.
mode, fason-o, mod-o.
model, model-o.
moderate, moder-a.
modest, modest-a.
moment, moment-o; **a — ago**, (*adv.*), ĵus.
monarch, monarĥ-o.
Monday, lund-o.
money, mon-o; **— box**, kas-o; **— order**, mandat-o.
monk, monaĥ-o.
monkey, simi-o.
month, monat-o.
moon, lun-o.
moral, moral-a, bonmor-a; morals, moroj.
more (*adv.*), pli (**74, 79**); (**quantity**), pli multe (**81**); (**further**), plu; **the —**, ju pli,
des pli (**84**).
morning, maten-o (**93**).
morsel, pec-o.
most (*adv.*), plej (**74, 79**); (**quantity**), plej multe (**81**).
mould, ŝim-o.
mountain, mont-o.
mourning, funebr-o.
mouse, mus-o.
moustache, lipharoj.
mouth, buŝ-o; (**of river**), enflu-o, elflu-o.
move (*trans.*), mov-i; (**change residence**) transloĝ-i.
much, mult-a (**81**); (**very**), tre.
mud, kot-o.
murmur, murmur-i.
museum, muze-o.

mushroom, fung-o.
music, muzik-o.
must, dev-i (**247**).
mute, mut-a.
mutton, ŝafaĵ-o.
mutual, reciprok-a (**180**), komun-a.
myopic, miop-a.
mystery, mister-o.

N.

nail (**metal**), najl-o; (**of the finger or toe**), ung-o.
naive, naiv-a.
naked, nud-a.
name, nom-o.
narrate, rakont-i.
nation, naci-o.
nature, natur-o.
naught, nul-o; (**none**), neniom (**231**).
near, proksim-a (**170**); (*prep.*), apud (**120, 159**).
necessary, neces-a.
neck, kol-o.
need, bezon-i.
needle, kudril-o.
negative, ne-a (**171**); (**photographic**), negativ-o.
neighbor, najbar-o.
neither (*conj.*), nek (**31**); (*pronoun and adj.*), neniu (**220**).
nephew, nev-o.
nerve, nerv-o.
nest, nest-o.
net, ret-o.
neutral, neŭtral-a.
never (*adv.*), neniam (**226**).
nevertheless (*conj.*), tamen.
new, nov-a, freŝ-a; news, novaĵ-o.
newspaper, ĵurnal-o, tagĵurnal-o.
nice, delikat-a.
night, nokt-o.
nine (*adj.*), naŭ (**136**).
nitrogen, azot-o.
no (*adv.*), ne (**27, 66, a**); (*adj.*), neniu (**220**); — one, —where, etc., see *table*, 235.
noble, nobl-a,
nobleman, nobel-o.
nobody (*pronoun*), neniu (**220**).
nod (**the head**), balanc-i (**la kapon**).
noise, bru-o.
none (*adj. and pronoun*), neniu (**220**); (*adv.*), neniom (**231**).

non-partisan, neŭtral-a.
noon, tagmez-o.
nor (*conj.*), nek (**31**).
north, nord-o.
Norwegian, norveg-o.
not (*adv.*), ne (**27, 66, a**).
note, not-o, bilet-o; —**book**, kajer-o; (**notice**), rimark-i, not-i.
nothing, nenio (**233**).
notice, rimark-i; not-i; **give** —, aviz-i.
notwithstanding (*prep.*), malgraŭ; (**conj.**), tamen.
nourish, nutr-i.
novel, nov-a; (**book**), roman-o.
November, novembr-o.
now (*adv.*), nun.
nude, nud-a.
nullify, nulig-i, neniig-i.
number (quantity), nombr-o; (**numeral**), numer-o.
nut, nuks-o.

<h1 style="text-align:center">O.</h1>

oak, kverk-o.
(make) oath, ĵur-i.
oats, aven-o.
obey, obe-i (**265**).
object, objekt-o; (**aim**), cel-o; (**oppose**), kontraŭparol-i, kontraŭstar-i, protest-i.
objective, objektiv-o.
obligation (financial), ŝuld-o; (**moral**), dev-o.
oblige (compel), devig-i; (**render service**), far-i komplezon, serv-i.
oblique, oblikv-a.
observe, observ-i, rimark-i, not-i.
obstinate, obstin-a.
obstruct, bar-i.
occasion, foj-o (**127**); okaz-o.
occupation, profesi-o, okup-o, meti-o.
occupy, okup-i.
occur, okaz-i.
ocean, ocean-o.
October, oktobr-o.
odor, odor-o.
of (*prep.*), de (**49, 100, 160, 170**); da (**99, 101, 103**); el; (**concerning**), pri (160, 264, c).
offend, ofend-i.
offer, propon-i, prezent-i, ofer-i.
office, ofic-o; (**place**), oficej-o.
officer (of organization or firm), oficist-o; (**military or naval**), oficir-o.

official, oficial-a.
often (*adv.*), oft-e, multfoj-e.
oh (*interjection*), ho (**273**).
oil, ole-o.
olive, oliv-o.
on (*prep.*), sur; — **account of**, pro (**86**).
once (*adv.*), unufoj-e; — **on a time**, iam (**212**); **at** —, tuj; — **more**, bis.
one (*adj.*), unu (**136, 137, 180**); (*pronoun*), oni (**54**). See 235.
onion, bulb-o.
only, sol-a; (**mere**), nur-a.
opera, oper-o; — **glasses**, lornet-o.
opinion, opini-o.
opportune, oportun-a.
opposed to (*prep.*), kontraŭ.
opposite (**converse**), mal-o (**67**); (*prep.*), kontraŭ.
or (*conj.*), aŭ.
orange (fruit), oranĝ-o.
orchestra, orkestr-o.
order, ordon-i; (**of store, etc.**), mend-i; (**methodical or proper arrangement**), ord-o; **money** —, mandat-o.
ordinary, ordinar-a.
organ (**physical**), organ-o; (**musical**), orgen-o.
organize, organiz-i.
original, original-o.
ornament, ornam-i.
orphan, orf-o.
oscillate (*intrans.*), balanciĝ-i.
ostracism, ostracism-o.
other, ali-a; (**remaining**), ceter-a; — **people's**, malpropr-a; —**wise**, ali-e.
out of, el.
outline, kontur-o; (**profile**), profil-o; (**sketch**), skiz-o.
outside (*prep.*), ekster (**120, 121**).
over (*prep.*), super; (**across**), trans; (**concerning**), pri; —**coat**, surtut-o; —**shoe**, supersu-o; (*adv.*), (**too**), tro.
owe, ŝuld-i.
own, posed-i, propr-a.
ox, bov-o.
oyster, ostr-o.

P.

pack, pak-i.
pad, rembur-i.
paddle, padel-i.
page (**of book, etc.**), paĝ-o.
pail, sitel-o.
pain, dolor-o; (**effort**), pen-o; **take pains**, pen-i.

paint, pentr-i; (**material**), kolorigil-o; —**brush**, penik-o.
pair, par-o.
palace, palac-o.
pale, pal-a.
palisade, palisar-o.
palm (**of the hand**), polm-o.
pamphlet, broŝur-o.
pan, pat-o.
paper (**material**), paper-o; **news**—, ĵurnal-o.
paradise, paradiz-o.
paragraph, paragraf-o.
pardon, pardon-i (**265**).
parallel, paralel-a.
park, park-o.
parlor, salon-o.
parsley, petrosel-o.
parsnip, pastinak-o.
part, part-o; of a work or book, kajer-o; separate (*trans.*), disir-i, apartig-i, disdivid-i.
participle, particip-o.
pass (*intrans.*), pas-i.
passage, koridor-o.
passenger, pasaĝer-o.
passion, pasi-o.
passive, pasiv-a.
past (*prep.*), preter; (**time**), estintec-o; (**grammatical**), estint-o; (**bygone**), estint-a.
paste (**glue**), glu-i.
pasteboard, karton-o.
pastor, pastr-o.
pastry, kukaĵ-o.
pasture (*trans.*), paŝt-i.
patch, flik-i.
path, vojet-o.
patience, pacienc-o.
patient (**ill person**), kuracat-o.
patty, pasteĉ-o.
pause, paŭz-i.
pavement, pavim-o; (**sidewalk**), trotuar-o.
pay, pag-i; — dues, kotiz-i.
pea, piz-o.
peace, pac-o.
peach, persik-o.
pear, pir-o.
pearl, perl-o.
peculiar, strang-a, kurioz-a.

peddle, kolport-i.
pedestal, piedestal-o.
pedestrian, piedirant-o.
peeling, ŝel-o.
pen, plum-o; (**enclosure**), ej-o (**III**).
pencil, krajon-o; **hair—**, penik-o.
penetrate, penetr-i.
people, popol-o; (*indefinite pronoun*), oni (**54**).
pepper, pipr-o.
perceive, sent-i; (**see**), vid-i.
percentage, procent-o; (**of profit**), tantiem-o.
perfect, perfekt-a.
perfidious, perfid-a.
perform (act), ag-i; (**fulfil**), plenum-i; (**do**), far-i.
perfume, parfum-o; (**odor**), bonodor-o.
period, period-o; (**of time**), epok-o; (**punctuation**), punkt-o.
perish, pere-i.
permit, permes-i.
persecute, persekut-i; (**worry**), turment-i, ĝen-i.
persevere, persist-i.
person, person-o.
perspire, ŝvit-i.
persuade, konvink-i.
pet, dorlot-i.
petroleum, petrol-o.
phantom, fantom-o.
Pharaoh, faraon-o.
pharmacy, farmaci-o; (**shop**), apotek-o.
philosopher, filozof-o.
photograph, fotograf-i.
phrase, fraz-o.
physician, kuracist-o.
physics, fizik-o.
pick (**choose**), elekt-i; (**gather**), kolekt-i.
pickle, pekl-i.
picture, bild-o; (**portrait**), portret-o; **— gallery**, pinakotek-o.
picturesque, pitoresk-a, pentrind-a.
pie, kukaĵ-o; (**patty**), pasteĉ-o.
piece, pec-o.
pig, pork-o.
pigeon, kolomb-o.
(be a) pilgrim, pilgrim-i.
pillage, rab-i.
pillar, kolon-o.
pin, pingl-o.
pinch, pinĉ-i.

pine (tree), pin-o; — **for**, sopir-i je.
pineapple, ananas-o.
pinnacle, pint-o.
pioneer, pionir-o.
pious, pi-a.
pipe, tub-o; (**for smoking**), pip-o.
pitcher, kruĉ-o.
pity, kompat-i; (**regrettable affair**), domaĝ-o.
placard, afiŝ-o.
place, lok-o; (**for something**), -ej-o (**111**); (**broad, short street or open space**), plac-o; (**put**), met-i.
plait, plekt-i.
plan, plan-o, projekt-o, skiz-o.
plane, plat-a.
planet, planed-o.
plank, tabul-o.
plant, plant-i; (**vegetable growth**), kreskaĵ-o, vegetaĵ-o.
plate, plat-o; (**dish**) teler-o.
platform (railway), peron-o.
play, lud-i; (**music**), muzik-i; (**theatrical**), teatraĵ-o.
player (theatrical), aktor-o.
pleasant, agrabl-a, dolĉ-a, afabl-a.
please, plaĉ-i (**265**); kontentig-i, far-i plezuron al; (**in requests**), bonvolu, mi petas.
pleasure, plezur-o; **take — in**, ĝu-i.
plot, konspir-i.
plow, plug-i.
plum, prun-o.
plumber, plumbist-o.
plunder, rab-i.
plural, multenombr-o.
pneumatic, pneumatik-a.
pocket, poŝ-o.
poem, poem-o.
poet, poet-o.
poetry, poezi-o.
point, punkt-o; (**sharp**), pint-o; — **out**, montr-i.
poise (*trans.*), balanc-i; (of manner), aplomb-o.
poison, venen-o.
pole, stang-o; (**shaft of vehicle**), timon-o; (**geographical**), polus-o.
Pole, pol-o.
police, polic-o.
polite, ĝentil-a.
politics, politik-o.
polish, polur-i; polished, polurit-a, glat-a.
pomp, pomp-o.

popular, popular-o, popol-a.
porcelain, porcelan-o.
porch, verand-o; (**stoop**), peron-o; (**balcony**), balkon-o.
pork, porkaĵ-o.
port, haven-o.
portion, porci-o, part-o.
portrait, portret-o.
possess, posed-i.
possible, ebl-a (**161, 162**); kredebl-a (**270**).
post (pole), stang-o; (**mail**), poŝt-o; —**card**, poŝtkart-o; —**paid**, afrankit-e.
postage (cost), poŝtelspezo; — **stamp**, poŝtmark-o.
poster, afiŝ-o.
pot, pot-o.
potato, terpom-o; **sweet** —, batat-o.
pound, pist-i; (**measure**), funt-o.
pour (liquids), verŝ-i; (**as in a chute**), ŝut-i.
powder, pudr-o.
power, pov-o, potenc-o.
practice, praktik-i.
praise, laŭd-i.
pray, preĝ-i.
preach, predik-i.
precise, preciz-a, ĝust-a.
predestined, fatal-a.
prefer, prefer-i.
prefix, prefiks-o.
premium, premi-o.
prepare, prepar-i.
prepay, afrank-i.
presence, ĉeest-o, apudest-o; **in the — of** (*prep.*), ĉe (**125**), antaŭ.
present (gift), donac-o; (**time**), estantec-o, estant-a, nun-a (**171**); (**in attendance**), ĉeestant-a.
present, prezent-i, donac-i, don-i.
preserve (keep), ten-i; (**keep safe**), konserv-i; (**food**), kompot-o, konfitaĵ-o.
preside, prezid-i.
president, prezidant-o.
press, prem-i; (**print**), pres-i; (**wardrobe**), ŝrank-o; (**be urgent**), urĝ-i.
pretend (make pretext of), pretekst-i; (**feign**), ŝajnig-i; (**lay claim**), pretend-i.
price, prez-o, kost-o.
prick, pik-i.
priest, pastr-o.
prince, princ-o, reĝid-o.
principal, precip-a, ĉef-a.
print, pres-i.
prize, ŝat-i; (**premium**), premi-o.
prized, kar-a, altetaksat-a, ŝatat-a.

problem, problem-o.
process, metod-o; (**legal**), proces-o.
proclaim, proklam-i.
procrastinate, prokrast-i.
produce, produkt-i; — **a result**, efik-i; (**give birth to**), nask-i.
profession, profesi-o.
professor, profesor-o.
profile, profil-o.
profit, profit-i; (**percentage**), tantiem-o.
profound, profund-a.
progress, progres-i.
project, projekt-o.
promenade, promen-i.
promise, promes-i.
propensity, inklin-o, em-o (**192**).
(be) proper, dec-i.
property, propraĵ-o, posedaĵ-o; (**land**), bien-o; (**characteristic**), ec-o (**202**).
proportional, proporci-a.
propose, propon-i, sugesti-i.
prose, prozo; **piece of —**, prozaĵo.
prosecute, persekut-i.
prosper, prosper-i.
protect, protekt-i, gard-i.
protest, protest-i.
proud, fier-a
prove, pruv-i; (**test**), prov-i.
provoke, incit-i, ekscit-i, kaŭz-i, nask-i, kolerig-i.
psalm, psalm-o.
public, publik-o.
publish, publikig-i, eldon-i.
pudding, puding-o.
pull, tir-i.
pump, pump-i.
pumpkin, kukurb-o.
punish, pun-i.
pure, pur-a.
puree, pistaĵ-o.
purple, purpur-a.
purpose, cel-i, intenc-i.
push, puŝ-i; (**shove**), ŝov-i.
put, met-i; — **off**, prokrast-i.

Q.

quality, ec-o (**202**); (**texture, etc.**), kvalito.
quantity, kvant-o; **any —, a certain —**, iom (**217**); *see table*, 235.
quarter (of a city), kvartal-o; (**fourth**), kvaron-o; **—ly**, trimonat-a.

question, demand-o; (**problem**), problem-o; (**doubt**), dub-o.
quick, rapid-a; (**lively**), viv-a.
quiet, kviet-a, trankvil-a, silent-a.
quince, cidoni-o.
quite (*adv.*), tut-e.
quote, cit-i.

R.

rabbit, kunikl-o.
race (**people**), ras-o.
radish, rafan-o; **horse—**, armoraci-o.
radius, radi-o.
rag, ĉifon-o.
raging, furioz-a.
rail, rel-o; **—way**, fervoj-o; **—way carriage**, vagon-o; **—way station**, staci-dom-o.
rain, pluv-o; **—bow**, ĉielark-o.
raise, lev-i.
raisin, sekvinber-o.
rank, rang-o; (**grade**), grad-o.
rap, frapet-i.
rapid, rapid-a.
rascal, fripon-o, kanajl-o.
rasp, rasp-i.
raspberry, framb-o.
rat, rat-o.
rate, taks-i; (**schedule of prices**), tarif-o, prezar-o; (**percentage**), procent-o; **at the — of** (*prep.*), po (**175**).
rational, prudent-a, racional-a.
raucous, raŭk-a.
raven, korv-o.
ravishing, rav-a.
raw, nekuirit-a.
ray (**of light**), radi-o.
reach, ating-i; (**a goal**), traf-i.
read, leg-i.
ready, pret-a.
real, efektiv-a, real-a; ver-a.
reap, rikolt-i.
reason (**exert the power of reasoning**), rezon-i; (**cause**), kaŭz-o; (**motive**), kial-o; **for what —, for any —,** etc., *see table*, 235.
reasonable, prudent-a.
rebate, rabat-i.
recall, revok-i; (**to memory**), rememor-i; (**to another's memory**), rememo-rig-i.
receive, ricev-i; (**accept**), akcept-i; (**money**), enspez-i.

receipt (for payment), kvitanc-o.
reckon, kalkul-i.
recent, nov-a, antaŭnelong-a (**90**).
receptacle, uj-o (**237**); (**for one object**), ing-o (**181**).
recess (alcove), alkov-o; (**vacation**), libertemp-o.
reciprocal, reciprok-a (**180**).
recite, deklam-i.
recline, kuŝ-i (**239**).
recommend, rekomend-i.
recompense, rekompenŝ-i.
recover (find), retrov-i; (**get well**), resaniĝ-i.
red, ruĝ-a; reddish, duberuĝ-a.
reduction (of price), rabat-o.
refine, rafin-i.
refuse, rifuz-i, malpermes-i.
refute, refut-i.
regale, regal-i.
region, region-o.
register (*trans.*), registr-i; (**letters**), rekomend-i.
regret, bedaŭr-i; (**be penitent for**), pent-i.
regrettable, bedaŭrind-a; — **affair (pity)**, domaĝ-o.
regulation, regul-o, leĝ-o.
reign, reg-i.
rejoice, ĝoj-i (**116**).
relate, rilat-i (**266**); (**tell**), rakont-i.
relative (person), parenc-o.
religion, religi-o.
rely, konfid-i; fid-i.
remain, rest-i; remaining (**other**), ceter-a.
remember, memor-i; (**recall to memory**), rememor-i.
render, far-i, ig-i (**214**); (**an account**), don-i, prezent-i, liver-i.
renown, fam-o, glor-o.
rent, lu-i; (**let**), luig-i; (**farm out**), farm-i; (**price**), luprez-o.
repair, ripar-i; (**patch**), flik-i.
repeat, ripet-i.
repent, pent-i.
report, raport-i.
repose, ripoz-i.
represent, reprezent-i.
reproach, riproĉ-i.
republic, respublik-o.
repulse, repuŝ-i, repel-i.
request, pet-i.
require, postul-i; (**need**), bezon-i.
rescue, sav-i.
reside, loĝ-i.

respect, respekt-i.
rest (repose), ripoz-i; **(remain)**, rest-i; **(— upon)**, apog-i sur.
restaurant, restoraci-o.
result, rezult-i.
resume, resum-o.
return (go back), reir-i; **(come back)**, reven-i; **(give back)**, redon-i.
revery, rev-o.
review (magazine), revu-o.
reward, rekompenc-i.
rhubarb, rabarb-o.
rib, rip-o.
ribbon, ruband-o.
rice, riz-o.
rich, riĉ-a.
ride, rajd-i; **(in vehicle, boat, etc.)**, vetur-i.
ridicule, mok-i; worthy of — **(ridiculous)**, ridind-a.
right, prav-a; **(to something)**, rajt-o; **(not left)**, dekstr-a.
right-angled, ort-a.
ring (*intrans.*), sonor-i; **(circlet)**, ring-o.
ringlet (of hair), bukl-o.
ripe, matur-a.
river, river-o.
road, voj-o; **(broad roadway)**, ŝose-o.
roam, vag-i.
roar, muĝ-i.
roast, rost-i.
rob, rab-i, ŝtel-i.
robber, rabist-o.
robe, rob-o.
Robert, Robert-o.
roguish, petol-a; **(rascally)**, fripon-a.
roll (*trans.*), rul-i; **(something around something else)**, volv-i; **(bread)**, bulk-o; **(list)**, list-o, registr-o.
roof, tegment-o.
room, ĉambr-o; **(space)**, spac-o.
root, radik-o.
rose, roz-o.
(by) rote, parker-e.
round, rond-o; **(of ladder)**, ŝtupet-o; **(roundabout)** (*prep.*) ĉirkaŭ (**89, 120, 159, 160**).
routine, rutin-o.
row (boats), rem-i.
royalty, reĝec-o; **(share of profit)** tantiem-o.
rub, frot-i.
ruin, ruin-o.
rule, reg-i; **(draw lines)**, lini-i; **(regulation)**, regul-o.

rumor, fam-o; rumored, laŭdir-a.
run, kur-i; **(of fluids)**, flu-i.
Russian, rus-o.
rust, rust-i.

S.

sack, sak-o; **(plunder)**, rab-i.
sacred, sankt-a.
sacrifice, ofer-i, oferdon-i.
saddle, sel-o.
safe, sendanĝer-a, senrisk-a; **(chest)**, monkest-o.
sail, vel-o.
salad, salat-o.
salary, salajr-o.
salt, sal-o.
salute, salut-i.
same, sam-a.
sample, specimen-o.
sand, sabl-o.
sap, suk-o.
sardine, sarden-o.
satchel, valiz-o.
sated, sat-a.
satin, atlas-o.
satisfied, kontent-a; **(of hunger)**, sat-a.
Saturday, sabat-o.
sausage, kolbas-o.
sauce, saŭc-o.
saucer, subtas-o, teleret-o.
saucy, petol-a, malĝentil-a, insultem-a.
savage, sovaĝ-a.
save, sav-i; **(keep)**, konserv-i; **(economize)**, ŝpar-i; (*prep.*), krom, escepte de.
saw, seg-i.
say, dir-i (**77**).
scales (for weighing), pesil-o.
scarcely (*adv.*), apenaŭ.
scent (*trans.*), flar-i.
schedule (of rates), tarif-o.
science, scienc-o.
scissors, tondil-o.
Scot (Scotchman), skot-o.
scoundrel, kanajl-o, fripon-o.
scrape, skrap-i.
screen, ŝirm-i.
screw, ŝraŭb-o; —**driver**, ŝraŭbturnil-o.
sculpture, skulpt-i.

sea, mar-o.
seal, sigel-i.
season (**of the year**), sezon-o.
second (**of time**), sekund-o; (**in order**), dua; **a — time** (*adv.*), duafoje, bis.
secret, sekret-o.
secretary, sekretari-o.
section, sekci-o, part-o, er-o (**276**).
see, vid-i; **— to**, zorg-i pri.
seed, sem-o.
seek, serĉ-i; **— advice of**, konsult-i.
seem, ŝajn-i; **—ing**, ŝajn-a, kvazaŭ-a.
seize, kapt-i.
select, elekt-i.
self (*reflexive*), *see* 39, 40, 44; (*intensive*), mem (**219**).
self-command, aplomb-o.
sell, vend-i.
senate, senat-o.
send, send-i.
sense, prudent-o, saĝ-o; (**meaning**), senc-o; (**feeling**), sent-o.
sentence, fraz-o; (**legal**), juĝ-o, kondamn-o.
separate (*intrans.*), disiĝ-i, disir-i; (**distinct**), apart-a.
September, septembr-o.
serene, trankvil-a.
series, seri-o, vic-o.
serious, serioz-a, grav-a.
serve, serv-i; (**be good for**), taŭg-i por.
set, met-i; (**of the sun**), subir-i; (**type**), kompost-i; **— free**, liberig-i; **— out**
(**start**), forir-i, ekir-i.
seven (*adj.*), sep (**136**).
several, kelk-aj, kelk-e.
severe, sever-a.
sew, kudr-i.
shade (**shadow**), ombr-o; (**tint**) nuanc-o; (**screen**), ŝirmil-o.
shaft (**of vehicle**), timon-o.
shake (*trans.*), sku-i; (**oscillate**), ŝancel-i; **— hands**, manprem-i.
sham, pretekst-i.
shape, form-o; **—ly**, beltali-a.
share, partopren-i, divid-i, part-o, porci-o.
sharp, akr-a; (**pointed**), pint-a.
shatter, frakas-i.
shave, raz-i.
shawl, ŝal-o.
she (*pronoun*), ŝi (**32, 37, 42**).
shear, tond-i.
sheep, ŝaf-o.
shelf, bret-o.

shell, ŝel-o; **(of mollusk)**, konk-o; **to remove the —**, senŝelig-i.
shelter, ŝirm-i.
shepherd, paŝtist-o.
shield, ŝild-o; **(protect)**, ŝirm-i.
shin-bone, tibi-o.
shine, bril-i, lum-i.
ship, ŝip-o.
shirt, ĉemiz-o.
shoe, ŝu-o.
shoot (with gun, etc.), paf-i.
shop, butik-o.
shore, bord-o, marbord-o.
short, mallong-a; **—sighted**, miop-a; **—hand**, stenografi-o.
shoulder, ŝultr-o.
shove, ŝov-i.
shovel, ŝovel-i.
show (*trans.*), montr-i.
shrill, akr-a, akrason-a.
shun, evit-i.
shut (trans.), ferm-i.
side, flank-o; **—board**, telermebl-o; **—walk**, trotuar-o; **—wise**, oblikv-a.
sift, kribr-i.
sigh, sopir-i.
sign, sign-o; **— the name**, subskrib-i.
signify, signif-i.
silent, silent-a **(239)**.
silk, silk-o.
silver, arĝent-o.
similar, simil-a.
simple, simpl-a.
sin, pek-i.
since (*conj.*), ĉar, tial ke **(83)**; (*prep.*), de, depost **(89)**; (*adv.*), de tiam.
sing, kant-i.
single, sol-a, unuop-a; **— man (unmarried man)**, fraŭl-o.
sit, sid-i **(239)**.
six (*adj.*), ses **(136)**.
sketch, skiz-i.
skill, lertec-o; **trial of —**, konkurs-o.
skin (human), haŭt-o; **(of animals)**, fel-o.
skirt, jup-o.
sky, ĉiel-o.
slanting, oblikv-a, klin-a.
slate (stone), ardez-o.
slaughter, buĉ-i.
slave, sklav-o.
sleep, dorm-i; **lull to —**, lul-i.

sleeve, manik-o.
slide, glit-i.
slime, ŝlim-o.
slipper, pantofl-o.
sly, ruz-a.
smear, ŝmir-i.
smell (*trans.*), flar-i; (*intrans.*), odor-i.
smile, ridet-i.
smoke, fum-i.
smooth, glat-a; (**polished**), polurit-a.
sneeze, tern-i.
snow, neĝ-i.
so (*conj.*), do; (*adv.*), (**thus**), tiel (**88, 156**); (**therefore**), tial (**78**); — **much**, tiom (**104, 164**).
society, societ-o.
Socrates, Sokrat-o.
sofa, kanap-o.
soft, mol-a.
soil, ter-o; soiled, malpur-a.
soldier, soldat-o; (**professional**), militist-o.
sole, sol-a; (**of foot**), pland-o; (**of shoe**), ledpland-o.
solemn, solen-a.
some, kelk-a, kelk-e, iom (**217**); —**one**, —**how**, etc., *see table*, 235.
son, fil-o.
soon (*adv.*), baldaŭ.
sorcerer, sorĉist-o.
sort, spec-o, klas-o; (**put in order**), ordig-i, enfakig-i.
soul, anim-o.
sound (*intrans.*), son-i; (**of bells**), sonor-i; (**in good condition**), bonstat-a.
soup, sup-o.
sour, acid-a, maldolĉ-a.
south, sud-o.
sow, sem-i.
space, spac-o.
spacious, vast-a, grandspac-a, grandampleks-a.
Spaniard, hispan-o.
spare (save), ŝpar-i; (**pardon**), pardon-i.
sparrow, paser-o.
speak, parol-i (**77**).
spear, lanc-o.
special, special-a, apart-a.
specialty, fak-o.
species, spec-o.
specimen, specimen-o, model-o.
spectre, fantom-o.
speed, rapid-o, rapidec-o.

spell, silab-i; (**witchcraft**), sorĉaĵ-o.
spend (**money**), elspez-i; (**time**), pasig-i.
speso, spes-o (**285**).
spider, arane-o.
spin, ŝpin-i.
spinach, spinac-o.
spite, malic-o; **in — of**, (*prep.*), malgraŭ, spite.
splash (*trans.*), plaŭd-i.
splendor, pomp-o, bril-o, belegec-o.
split (*trans.*), fend-i.
spoil (*trans.*), difekt-i.
spoke (**of wheel**), radi-o.
spoon, kuler-o.
spot, makul-i.
spout (**liquids**), ŝpruc-i.
spring (**season**), printemp-o; (**of water**), font-o.
sprite, kobold-o, fe-o.
spruce (**tree**), pice-o.
spurt (**of liquids**), ŝpruc-i.
spy, spion-o; (**catch sight of**), ekvid-i; **—glass**, lorn-o.
square, kvadrat-o; (**public**), plac-o.
stain, makul-i.
stair (**staircase**), ŝtupar-o.
stag, cerv-o.
stake (**of palisade**), palis-o.
stamp (**officially**), stamp-i; (**with foot**), piedfrap-i; **postage —**, poŝtmark-o.
stand, star-i (**239**); (**endure**), sufer-i, elport-i.
standard (**model**), model-o; (**flag**), standard-o.
star, stel-o; (**any heavenly body**), astr-o.
starch, amel-o.
state (**condition**), stat-o; (**political**), ŝtat-o; (**governed body**), regn-o.
station (**state**), stat-o; (**railway, etc.**), staci-o, stacidom-o.
stay, rest-i.
steady, firm-a, konstant-a, nemovebl-a.
steal, ŝtel-i, rab-i (**252**).
steam, vapor-o.
steel, ŝtal-o.
steep, krut-a.
step, paŝ-i; (**of stairs**), ŝtup-o.
stern, sever-a.
stew (*trans.*), stuf-i.
stick, baston-o; (**adhere**), algluiĝ-i.
still (**silent**), silent-a; (*adv.*), ankoraŭ; jam; (*conj.*), tamen.
stimulate, stimul-i, incit-i.
sting, pik-i.
stipulate, kondiĉ-o.

stocking, ŝtrump-o.
stomach, stomak-o.
stone, ŝton-o.
stoop, kliniĝ-i; (**entrance porch**), peron-o.
stop (*intrans.*), halt-i; (**leave off**), ĉes-i; — **up**, ŝtop-i.
stopper, ŝtopil-o.
store (**shop**), butik-o; (**warehouse**), magazen-o, konservej-o, tenej-o.
story (**tale**), fabel-o, rakont-o; (**of house**), etaĝ-o.
stove, forn-o.
straight, rekt-a.
strange, strang-a, kurioz-a; (**foreign**), fremd-a.
strap, rimen-o.
straw, pajl-o.
strawberry, frag-o.
streak, stri-o; **make a —**, strek-i.
street, strat-o; — **arab**, bub-o.
street-car, tramveturil-o; — **line**, tramvoj-o.
stress, akcent-o; (**force**), fort-o.
stretch (*trans.*), etend-i; (**forcibly**), streĉ-i.
string, ŝnur-o; (**shoelace**), laĉ-o; — **bean**, fazeol-o.
strike, frap-i, bat-i; (**of laborers**), strik-o; — **out**, trastrek-i.
strip (**of paper, cloth, etc.**), banderol-o; — **off**, senig-i.
stripe, stri-o.
strive, pen-i.
strong, fort-a.
struggle, barakt-i.
student, student-o; (**person studying**), studant-o.
study, stud-i.
stuff, ŝtof-o; (**furniture, etc.**), rembur-i.
stump, stump-o.
style, stil-o, mod-o, fason-o.
subject (**theme**), tem-o; (**grammatical**), subjekt-o; (**ruled**), regat-o.
subscribe, subskrib-i; (**to magazine, etc.**), abon-i.
substance, substanc-o.
succeed, sukces-i; (**fare well**), prosper-i; (**follow**), sekv-i, postven-i.
succulent, suk-a, sukplen-a.
such, tia (**65**); (*adv.*), tiel (**88**).
sudden, subit-a, neatendit-a.
suffer, sufer-i, toler-i; (**permit**), permes-i.
suffice, sufiĉ-i.
suffix, sufiks-o.
suffocate (*trans.*), sufok-i.
sugar, suker-o.
suggest, sugesti-i, propon-i.
suit (**of clothes**), vest-oj, komplet-o; (**at law**), proces-o.
suitable, konven-a, konform-a, taŭg-a, dec-a.

suite (of rooms), apartament-o.
sulphur, sulfur-o.
sum, sum-o; (**total**), tut-o.
summarize, resum-i.
summer, somer-o; —**house**, laŭb-o.
summit, pint-o, supr-o.
sun, sun-o.
Sunday, dimanĉ-o.
superior, super-a; (**person**), superul-o.
superstition, superstiĉ-o.
supply, liver-i, proviz-i.
suppose, supoz-i; opini-i.
sure, cert-a.
surface, supraĵ-o.
surprise, surpriz-i.
suspect, suspekt-i.
suspend, pendig-i.
suspenders, ŝelk-o.
swallow, glut-i; (**bird**), hirund-o.
swamp, marĉ-o.
swan, cign-o.
swear, ĵur-i.
Swede, sved-o.
sweep (floors, etc.), bala-i.
sweet, dolĉ-a; —**potato**, batat-o.
sweetmeat, bombon-o, sukeraĵ-o, konfitaĵ-o; **be fond of** —, frand-i.
swim, naĝ-i.
swine, pork-o.
swing (*trans.*), sving-i; (**balance**), balanc-i (**279**).
Swiss, svis-o.
swoon, sven-i.
sword, glav-o.
syllable, silab-o.
Syracuse, Sirakuz-o.

T.

table (furniture), tabl-o; (**tabulation**), tabel-o.
tail, vost-o.
tailor, tajlor-o.
take, pren-i; (**magazines, etc.**), abon-i; — **in (money)**, enspez-i; — **place**, okaz-i; — **note of**, observ-i, rimark-i; — **oath**, ĵur-i; — **steps toward accomplishing**, klopod-i; — **pleasure in**, ĝu-i; — **the attention of**, distr-i.
tale, fabel-o.
talent, talent-o.
tall, alt-a, altkresk-a, grand-a.
talon, ungeg-o.

tap (rap), frapet-i; (**faucet**), kran-o.
tariff, tarif-o.
task, task-o.
taste, gust-o, gustum-i.
tax, impost-o.
tea, te-o; — **caddy**, teuj-o (**181**); —**pot**, tekruĉ-o.
teach, instru-i.
tear, ŝir-i; (**of the eye**), larm-o.
tease, turmentet-i, ĉagren-i.
tedious, ted-a, enuig-a, lacig-a.
telegraph, telegraf-i.
telephone, telefon-i.
telescope, teleskop-o.
tell, dir-i, rakont-i (**77**); — **lies**, mensog-i.
temper, humor-o; **lose the —**, koler-i.
temple (**of the head**), tempi-o; (**building**), templ-o.
tempt, tent-i.
ten (*adj.*), dek (**136**).
tender, delikat-a, mol-a, kares-a.
tenor (**voice**), tenor-o; (**course**), daŭr-o.
tent, tend-o.
term (**word**), termin-o; (**condition**), kondiĉ-o; (**time**), templim-o.
terrace, teras-o.
territory, teritori-o.
terror, terur-o.
test, prov-i, ekzamen-i.
texture, kvalit-o; (**thing woven**), teksaĵ-o.
than (*conj.*), ol (**82, 97, 98**).
thank, dank-i (**265**).
that (*conj.*), ke (**53, 83, 105, 259, 262**); (*pronoun*), tiu (**56**); tio (**233, 234**); —
kind, tia (**65**); (*adv.*), tiel (**88, 156**); — **way**, tiamanier-e, tiel (**88**); — **much**, tiel
mult-e, tiom (**104, 164**); (**when**) (*adv.*), kiam (**155**).
thaw (*intrans.*), degel-i.
the (*article*), la (**11, 47, 201, 280, a**); (*adv.*), ju, des (**84**).
theatre, teatr-o.
theme, tem-o.
then (*conj.*), do; (*adv.*), tiam (**73**); (**afterwards**), post-e.
theory, teori-o.
there (*adv.*), tie (**68**); (*adv. calling attention*), jen (**228**); *see also* 51.
therefore (*adv.*), tial (**78**); pro tio, sekv-e.
they (*pronoun*), ili (**32, 37, 42**); (*indefinite*), oni (**54**).
thick, dik-a, dens-a.
thigh, femur-o.
thing, afer-o, objekt-o, aĵ-o (**227**); **any—, what —**, etc., *see table*, 235.
think, pens-i; (**have the opinion**), opini-i.
(**be**) **thirsty**, soif-i.

this (*pronoun*), tio ĉi (**233, 234**); (*pronoun and adj.*), tiu ĉi (**60**); **all —**, ĉio ĉi. *See table*, 235.

thong, rimen-o.

thorn, dorn-o.

thou (*pronoun*), ci (**40**).

though (*conj.*), kvankam; **as —**, kvazaŭ (**250**).

thousand (*adj.*), mil (**142**).

thread, faden-o; **— a needle**, enkudrilig-i fadenon.

threaten, minac-i.

three (*adj.*), tri (**136**).

threshold, sojl-o.

thrifty, ŝparem-a.

throat, gorĝ-o.

throne, tron-o.

throng, amas-o, ar-o (**126**).

through (*prep.*), tra (**46, 160**); (**by means of**), per (**64**); (**because of**), pro (**86**), de (**170**).

throw, ĵet-i.

thumb, dika fingr-o.

thunder, tondr-i.

Thursday, ĵaŭd-o.

thus (*adv.*), tiel (**88, 156**), tiamanier-e.

ticket, bilet-o; **— window**, giĉet-o.

tickle, tikl-i.

tie, lig-i; (**shoes, etc.**), laĉ-i.

tiger, tigr-o.

tile, kahel-o; (**brick**), brik-o.

till (**money box**), kas-o; (*prep.*), ĝis (**46, 89**); **— the soil**, terkultur-i.

time (**in general**), temp-o; (**occasion**), foj-o (**127**); (**epoch**), epok-o; (**of day**), hor-o.

tin (**metal**), stan-o; **— plate (sheet iron covered with tin)**, lad-o.

tinkle, tint-i.

tint, nuanc-o, kolor-o.

tire (*trans.*), lacig-i, enuig-i; (**pneumatic**), pneŭmatik-o.

to (*prep.*), al (**46, 160, 251, 252**); ĝis (**46, 89**).

toad, buf-o.

toast (**bread**), panrostaĵ-o; (**sentiment**), tost-o.

tobacco, tabak-o.

today (*adv.*), hodiaŭ (**93, 171**).

toe, piedfingr-o.

toilet, tualet-o.

tolerate, toler-i, sufer-i.

tomato, tomat-o.

tomb, tomb-o.

tomorrow (*adv.*), morgaŭ (**93, 171**).

tone, ton-o.

tongue (of the body), lang-o; **(of vehicle)**, timon-o; **(language)**, lingv-o.
too (*adv.*), tro; **(too much)**, tro multe, tro.
tool, il-o **(63)**.
tooth, dent-o.
top, supr-o.
torment, turment-i.
total, tut-o.
touch, tuŝ-i; **(feel with the fingers, etc.)**, palp-i; **sense of** —, palpad-o; — **the heart of**, kortuŝ-i.
toward (*prep.*), al **(46, 160, 251, 252)**.
tower, tur-o; — **above**, superstar-i.
trace, sign-o, postsign-o.
trade (occupation), meti-o; **(commerce)**, komerc-o; **(exchange)**, interŝanĝ-i.
train (of cars), vagonar-o; **(of dress)**, trenaĵ-o.
tram, tram-o; —**way**, tramvoj-o; — **car**, tramveturil-o.
tranquil, trankvil-a; kviet-a.
translate, traduk-i.
travel, vojaĝ-i; **(by vehicle)**, vetur-i.
tray, plet-o.
treacherous, perfid-a.
treasure, trezor-o.
treasurer, kasist-o.
treasury, kas-o.
treat (in speech or writing), trakt-i; **(for illness)**, kurac-i; **(act towards)**, kondut-i kontraŭ; **(regale)**, regal-i.
treatise, traktat-o.
tree, arb-o.
tremble, trem-i; **(vacillate)**, ŝanceliĝ-i.
trial, juĝa aŭskultado, esplorad-o; **(of skill)**, konkurs-o; **(affliction)**, malĝoj-o, sufer-o; **(test)**, prov-o, ekzamen-o; **(attempt)**, prov-o.
trifle, bagatel-o.
triumph, triumf-o.
tropic, tropik-o.
trot, trot-i.
trousers, pantalon-o.
trunk (chest with lid), kofr-o; **(of tree)**, trunk-o.
trust, fid-i, konfid-i; **(financial)**, trust-o.
truth, ver-o.
try (legally), juĝ-i; **(strive)**, pen-i; **(attempt, test)**, prov-i.
tub, kuv-o.
tube, tub-o.
tuber, tuber-o.
Tuesday, mard-o.
tumbler (for drinking), glas-o; **(juggler)**, ĵonglist-o.
tune, ari-o, melodi-o.
Turk, turk-o.

turkey, meleagr-o.
turn (*trans.*), turn-i; (**in a series**), vic-o.
turnip, nap-o.
turnstile, giĉet-o.
twilight, krepusk-o.
twist (*trans.*), tord-i.
twitter, pep-i.
two (*adj.*), du (**136**).
tyrant, tiran-o.

U.

umbrella, ombrel-o.
uncle, onkl-o.
unanimous, unuvoĉ-a, unuanim-a.
uncommon, kurioz-a, nekomun-a.
unconcerned, indiferent-a; nezorgem-a.
under (*prep.*), sub (**121, 160**).
underline, substrek-i.
understand, kompren-i.
undertake, entrepren-i; — **initiative work**, klopod-i.
undeviating, rekt-a.
unfailing (*adv.*), nepr-e, cert-e.
unimportant, indiferent-a, negrav-a.
union, unuig-o, unuiĝ-o, kunig-o, kuniĝ-o.
universe, univers-o.
university, universitat-o.
until (*prep.*), ĝis (**89**)
up (*adv.*), supre, supren (**121**); — **to**, ĝis (**46**).
upholster, rembur-i.
upper, supr-a.
upon (*prep.*), sur (**160**).
upright, just-a; (**vertical**), vertikal-a.
urge, urĝ-i, insiste pet-i.
upset (*trans.*), renvers-i.
utmost, ekstrem-a, ebl-o (**161**, *see also* **162**).

V.

(be) vacant, vak-i, esti neokupata.
vacillate, ŝanceliĝ-i.
vagabond, vagist-o.
vain (**futile**), van-a; senutil-a, senfrukt-a; (**proud**), vant-a, fier-a; in —, vane.
valise, valiz-o.
valley, val-o.
value (**appraise**), taks-i; (**like**), ŝat-i; **have the — of**, valor-i.
vanquish, venk-i.

vapor, vapor-o.
varied, divers-a, malsimil-a.
vase, vaz-o.
vast, vast-a, grand-a.
vaunt, fanfaron-i, vantparol-i.
veal, bovidaĵ-o (207, c).
vegetable (edible), legom-o; **(plant growth)**, vegetaĵ-o, kreskaĵ-o (227, a).
vegetarian, vegetar-a.
vegetate, veget-i.
veil, vual-o.
vein, vejn-o.
velvet, velur-o.
veranda, verand-o.
verify, konstat-i, kontrol-i.
vermicelli, vermiĉel-o.
verse, vers-o; **(poesy)**, poezi-o.
vertical, vertikal-a.
very (very much) (*adv.*), tre, tre multe; (*adj.*), sam-a, ident-a, (*intensive*) mem (**219**).
vex, ĉagren-i.
vibrate (*intrans.*), vibr-i.
vice (wickedness), malvirt-o; (*prefix*), vic-.
vie, konkur-i.
village, vilaĝ-o.
vindication, apologi-o.
vinegar, vinagr-o.
violet, viol-o.
violin, violon-o.
virtue, virt-o.
visage, vizaĝ-o.
visit, vizit-i.
vivid, hel-a.
voice, voĉ-o.
volume (book), volum-o; **(of a body)**, volumen-o.
vote, voĉdon-i, balot-i.
vowel, vokal-o.
voyage, vojaĝ-i.

W.

wade, vad-i.
waffle, vafl-o.
wager, vet-i.
wages, salajr-o.
wait (wait for), atend-i; — **on**, serv-i.
waiter (in restaurant, etc.), kelner-o.
waist, tali-o; —**coat**, veŝt-o

wake (*trans.*), vek-i.
walk, marŝ-i; (**for pleasure**), promen-i; (**of park, etc.**), ale-o; **side—**, trotuar-o.
wall, mur-o.
waltz, vals-i.
wander, vag-i.
want (**need**), bezon-i; (**desire**), dezir-i, vol-i; (**be lacking**), mank-i; (**extremity**), mizereg-o.
war, milit-i.
wardrobe (**garments**), vestar-o; (**furniture**), ŝrank-o, vestoŝrank-o.
warehouse, magazen-o.
warm, varm-a; **make —**, varmig-i, hejt-i.
warn, avert-i; (**give notice**), aviz-i, antaŭsciig-i.
wash, lav-i.
waste (**prodigality**), malŝpar-o; (**refuse**), forĵetaĵ-o; (**desert**), dezert-o.
watch (**look at**), rigardad-i; (**timepiece**), poŝhorloĝ-o; **— over**, gard-i.
water, akv-o; **— color**, akvarel-o; **—fall**, kaskad-o.
wave, ond-o; (**flutter, brandish**), flirt-i, sving-i.
wax, vaks-o.
way (**manner**), manier-o; (**custom**), kutim-o; (**method**), metod-o; (**means**), rimed-o; (**road**), voj-o; **— in**, enirejo; **this —, any—, etc.**, *see table*, 235.
we (*pronoun*), ni (**32, 37**).
wear, port-i; **— out**, eluz-i.
(be) wearied, enu-i.
weather, veter-o; **—cock**, ventoflag-o.
weave, teks-i; (**plait**), plekt-i.
Wednesday, merkred-o.
week, semajn-o.
weep, plor-i.
weigh (*trans.*), pes-i; (*intrans.*), (**be heavy**), pez-i; (**meditate upon**), pripens-i (**264, c**).
welcome, bonven-i; bone akcept-i; **you are —**, (**"no thanks needed"**), estas nenio, volonte farite.
well (**healthy**), san-a; (**for water**), put-o; (*adv.*), bon-e; (*interjection*), nu (**273**), bon-e; **— informed**, kler-a; **— nigh** (*adv.*), preskaŭ.
west, okcident-o.
wet, malsekig-i, tremp-i.
whale, balen-o.
what (*pronoun*), kio (**233, 234**); (*pronominal adj.*), kiu (**106, 146**); **— kind, — way, — time, etc.**, *see table*, 235.
wheat, tritik-o.
wheel, rad-o.
when (*adv.*), kiam (**125, 155**); (**while**), dum (**96**).
where (*adv.*), kie (**118, 151**); **—fore**, kial (**129**), tial (**78**).
whether (*conj.*), ĉu (**30, 66, a**).
which (*pronoun*), kio (**233, 234**); (*pronoun and adj.*), kiu (**106, 146**); **— way, — kind, etc.** *see table*, 235.

while (*prep.*), dum (**120, 159**); (*conj.*), dum (**96**); (concessive), kvankam; a —, iom da tempo.

whip, vip-i.

whistle, fajf-i; (**hiss**), sibl-i.

white, blank-a; whitish, dubeblank-a.

who (*pronoun*), kiu (**106, 143**); whose, kies (**107, 147**).

whole (**entire**), tut-a.

why (*adv.*), kial (**129**), pro kio.

wicket, giĉet-o.

wide, larĝ-a; **make —**, plilarĝig-i, etend-i.

widow, vidvin-o; widower, vidv-o.

wig, peruk-o.

wild, sovaĝ-a.

(be) willing, vol-i.

willingly, volont-e.

wilt, velk-i.

wind, vent-o, survolv-i; (**twist**), tord-i; (**a watch**), streĉ-i.

winding, tord-a.

window, fenestr-o; **ticket —**, giĉet-o.

wine, vin-o.

winter, vintr-o.

wipe, viŝ-i.

wise, saĝ-a.

wish, vol-i, dezir-i.

witch, sorĉistin-o; **—craft**, sorĉ-o.

with (*prep.*), kun (**70, 76, 120, 159, 160**); (**by means of**), per (**64**); (*agent of the passive*), de (**169**); je (**260**); **— regard to**, rilate (**266**); **—draw**, elir-i, forir-i; (**= having**), havante (**222**).

wither, velk-i.

without (*prep.*), sen (**248**).

(give) witness, atest-i.

witty, sprit-a.

woe, malĝoj-o; (*interjection*), ve (**273**).

wolf, lup-o.

wonder, mir-i.

woo, amindum-i.

wood, lign-o.

wool, lan-o.

word, vort-o; (**spoken**), parol-o.

work, labor-i; (**of machinery**), funkci-i; (**literary composition**), verk-o.

world, mond-o.

worm, verm-o.

worship, ador-i; (**divine service**), Diserv-o.

(be) worth, valor-i.

worthy, ind-a (**154**).

wound, vund-i.

wreath, girland-o.
wrestle, barakt-i.
wretch, fripon-o, kanajl-o; —**ed**, mizer-a, aĉ-a (**272**).
wrinkle, sulket-o, faldet-o.
write, skrib-i; (**books, articles, music**), verk-i.
wrong, malprav-a, erar-a, maljust-a.

Y.

yawn, osced-i; (**open**), fendiĝ-i.
year, jar-o.
yearn, sopir-i; dezireg-i.
yellow, flav-a; —**ish**, dubeflav-a.
yes (*adv.*), jes (**171**).
yesterday (*adv.*), hieraŭ (**93, 171**); **day before** —, antaŭ-hieraŭ.
yet (*adv.*), ankoraŭ; jam; (*conj.*), tamen.
yoke, jug-o.
you (*pronoun*), vi (**32, 37, 39**); *see also* oni (**54**).
young, jun-a; (**offspring**), id-o (**207**).

Z.

zeal, fervor-o.
zenith, zenit-o.
zero, nul-o.
zigzag, zigzag-o.
zinc, zink-o.
zone, zon-o.
zoology, zoologi-o.

INDEX.

The references are to sections, unless the page (p.) is given. The following abbreviations are used: ace. = accusative; adj. = adjective; adv. = adverb; expr. = expressed; ftn. = footnote; inf. = infinitive; intrans. = intransitive; prep. = preposition; trans. = transitive. For Esperanto words whose use or meaning is specially explained, references are given in the Vocabulary.

A.

Abbreviations, 286; of ordinals, p. 107, ftn. **Abstract nouns**, 202. **Accent**, 8; of elided word, 280, b. **Accompaniment**, 70; distinguished from instrumentality and opposition, p. 49, ftn. **Accordance**, expr. by *laŭ*, 191. **Active voice**, participles of, 108, 119, 152; tenses of, see Tenses; synopsis of, 267. **Accusative**, ending, 23; of adj., 24; of pronoun, 37; of adv., 69, 121; of direction, 46, 108; of measure, 139; of time, 91; distinguished from temporal adv., 94; with temporal adv., 93; when avoided, 92; after adv., 266; with intrans. verb, 264; with nouns expressing motion, 263; in composition, p. 132, ftn.; instead of prepositional phrase, 265, 266; not used after prep., 36, (*al, ĝis, tra*) 46, (*preter*) p. 139, ftn.; not used with article, 25; not used with predicates, 25, 210; "cognate," see acc. with intrans. verbs, 264, a. **Adjectives**, defined, 12; ending of, 12; formation of, 116, (from adv.) 171, (from prep.) 159; attributive, 13; acc. of, 24; plural of, 17; agreement, (with nouns) 17, 21, 24, (with pronouns) 33, (with words connected by *nek*) 31; comparison of, 74; possessive, 43, (pronominal use of) 45; predicate, 19, (after trans, verbs) 210; use of, distinguished from adv. with *da*, 103; demonstrative, 65; distributive, 177; indefinite, 208; interrogative, 112; negative, 224; reflexive possessive, 44; relative, 150; causative verbs from roots of, 214, a; intrans. verbs from roots of, 232, c; cardinal, 136; ordinal, 149. **Adverbs**, defined, 66; primary, 66; derived, 79; (from prep.) 120; demonstrative, (*tie*) 68, (*tiam*) 73, (*tial*) 78, (*tiel*) 88, (*tiom*) 104; interrogative, (*kie*) 118, (*kiam*) 123, (*kial*) 129, (*kiel*) 134, (*kiom*) 140, (*ĉu*) 30, p. 38, ftn.; relative, (*kie*) 151, (*kiam*) 155, (*kiel*) 156, p. 170, ftn., (*kiom*) 164; distributive, (*ĉie*) 182, (*ĉiam*) iS7, (*ĉial*) 188, (*ĉiel*) 193, (*ĉiom*) 194; indefinite, (*ie*) 209, (*iam*) 212, (*ial*) 213, (*iel*) 216, (*iom*) 217; negative, (*nenie*) 225, (*neniam*) 226, (*nenial*) 229, (*neniel*) 230, (*neniom*) 231, (*ne*) 27, 66, a; generalizing, (*ajn*) 236; numeral, 158; position of, 66, a; expressing direction of motion, 69, 121; with expressions of time, 93; distinguishing from acc. of time, 94; with acc., 266; with prep., 87; calling attention, (*jen*) 228; causative verbs from, 214, c; intrans. verbs from, 232, d; as interjections, p. 216, ftn.; derivation of words from primary, 171. **Adverbial clauses**, p. 168, ftn.; participle, 222, (translating "without") p. 193, ftn. **Adversative conjunctions**, p. 32, ftn. **Advice**, expression of, 257, 259. **Affectionate diminutives**, 283 (also 198, and ftn., p. 221). **Affirmation**, 66. **Affixes**,

Q.

ENDNOTES

[*] There is another pronoun **ci**, *thou*, for the second person singular, used in solemn style, as in the Bible, in poetry, and also for intimate or familiar address when desired, like German *du*, French *tu*, etc.

[†] The adverb **ankoraŭ** expresses the ideas "until and during the present time", "in the future as now and before", "in constant or uniform succession", "in an increasing or additional degree", given sometimes by English *yet*, sometimes by *still*:

Mi estas ankoraŭ sidanta ĉi tie, *I am still sitting here.*
Li ankoraŭ ne venis, *still he has not come (he has not come yet).*
Li ankoraŭ restos tie, *he will still stay there.*
Ankoraŭ ili venas, *still they come.*
Li estos ankoraŭ pli ruza, *he will be still (yet) more crafty.*

[‡] The adverb **ĵus** indicates the elapsing of the least possible time since the act or condition indicated, or between the two acts or conditions indicated.

Ni ĵus venis, *we just came (we came but a moment ago).*
Mi havas la saman opinion kian vi ĵus diris, *I have the same opinion as you just gave (said).*
Mi vidis lin ĵus kiam li estis forironta, *I saw him just when he was about to depart.*
Ĵus kiam vi venis li foriris, *just as you came he went away.*

[§] Like English "out" the preposition **el** often develops in composition a secondary sense of "thoroughly" or "completely" (*cf.* "I am tired out"):

eltrovi, *to find out, to discover.*
elpensi, *to think out, to invent.*
ellabori, *to work out, to elaborate.*
ellerni, *to learn thoroughly, to master.*
eluzi, *to use completely, to wear out* (transitive).

[¶] The adverb **jam** indicates a change from some preceding action or state to the different one expressed in the sentence, clause or phrase containing **jam**. It may often be translated "yet," "now," etc.

Mi jam vidis lin, *I already saw (have already seen) him.*
Ĉu vi jam trovis ĝin? Ne, mi ankoraŭ ne trovis ĝin. *Have you yet (have you already) found it? No, I have not yet (still not) found it.*
Li jam ne vivas, *he no longer lives (he already is-not-alive).*
Jam ne neĝas, *it is not snowing now (already not snowing).*

[**]   The words **antikva, maljuna, malnova**, all of which may at times be translated "old," must not be confused in use:

Mi havas malnovan ĉapelon, *I have an old hat (a hat which is not new).*
Li estas maljuna sinjoro, *he is an old (aged) gentleman.*
Li estas malnova amiko mia, *he is an old friend of mine (a friend of long standing).*
La ĥinoj estis kleraj eĉ en la antikva tempo, *the Chinese were learned even in the olden time (in ancient time).*
La antikvaj kleruloj jam sciis tre multe, *the ancient learned (enlightened) men already knew a great deal.*
La maljuna sinjoro en la malnovaj vestoj estas antikvisto, *the old gentleman with the old clothes is an antiquary.*

[††]   The preposition **preter** indicates the movement of something alongside of and passing beyond something else. Since it does not express motion *toward* its complement, it cannot be followed by the accusative.

[‡‡]   *Cf.* the difference between **viro**, *man* (in contrast to **virino**, *woman*), and **homo**, *man in the generic sense*, including both men and women.

[§§]   *Cf.* the difference in meaning and use between **esti indiferenta**, *to be indifferent*, and **ne esti zorga**, *not to be careful*, both of which may be translated "not to care for":

Li estas indiferenta al la libro, *he does not care about (is indifferent to) the book.*
Li ne zorgas pri la libro, *he does not care for (take care of) the book.*
Estas indiferente al mi ĉu li venos, aŭ ne, *I do not care whether he is coming or not.*

[¶¶]   The adverb **plu** gives an idea of *continuance* to the word which it modifies. When used with **ne**, the two together give an idea of cessation concerning a previous continuous act or state:

Ambaŭ parolos plu morgaŭ, *both will talk further tomorrow.*
Mi ne plu haltos, *I shall not stop (any) more.*
Li ne plu ŝajnis muta, *he no longer seemed mute.*

[***]   Care must be taken to distinguish **ĝusta**, *exact*, **ĝuste**, *exactly*, *just*, from **justa**, *upright, just*, **juste**, *justly*, and also from the adverb **ĵus** *just*.

[†††]   The interjection **fi** is sometimes used as a disparaging prefix, like **-aĉ-** (272), as **fibirdo**, *ugly bird*, **fiĉevalo**, *a sorry nag*.

[‡‡‡]   **Ĉef-** is often used in descriptive compounds (167, b), as **ĉefkuiristo**, *chief (head) cook, chef*, **ĉefurbo**, *chief city, capital*, **ĉefanĝelo**, *archangel*.

[§§§]   *Cf.* the difference between **provi**, *to try* in the sense of testing, making an essay or endeavor, **peni**, *to try* in the sense of taking pains or making an effort, and **juĝi**, *to try* in a judicial sense.

Lector House believes that a society develops through a two-fold approach of continuous learning and adaptation, which is derived from the study of classic literary works spread across the historic timeline of literature records. Therefore, we aim at reviving, repairing and redeveloping all those inaccessible or damaged but historically as well as culturally important literature across subjects so that the future generations may have an opportunity to study and learn from past works to embark upon a journey of creating a better future.

This book is a result of an effort made by Lector House towards making a contribution to the preservation and repair of original ancient works which might hold historical significance to the approach of continuous learning across subjects.

HAPPY READING & LEARNING!

LECTOR HOUSE LLP
E-MAIL: lectorpublishing@gmail.com

9 789353 420161

Lightning Source UK Ltd.
Milton Keynes UK
UKHW010654150221
378806UK00005B/582